Aetius
Attila's Nemesis

Aetius
Attila's Nemesis

Ian Hughes

Pen & Sword
MILITARY

First published in Great Britain in 2012 by
Pen & Sword Military
an imprint of
Pen & Sword Books Ltd
47 Church Street
Barnsley
South Yorkshire
S70 2AS

ISBN: 978-1-84884-279-3

A CIP catalogue record for this book is
available from the British Library.

Typeset in 10.5/12.5pt Ehrhardt by
Concept, Huddersfield, West Yorkshire

Printed and bound by
CPI Group (UK) Ltd, Croydon, CRO 4YY

Pen & Sword Books Ltd incorporates the Imprints of Pen & Sword
Aviation, Pen & Sword Family History, Pen & Sword Maritime, Pen & Sword
Military, Pen & Sword Discovery, Wharncliffe Local History, Wharncliffe True
Crime, Wharncliffe Transport, Pen & Sword Select, Pen & Sword Military Classics,
Leo Cooper, The Praetorian Press, Remember When, Seaforth Publishing and
Frontline Publishing.

For a complete list of Pen & Sword titles please contact
PEN & SWORD BOOKS LIMITED
47 Church Street, Barnsley, South Yorkshire, S70 2AS, England
E-mail: enquiries@pen-and-sword.co.uk
Website: www.pen-and-sword.co.uk

Contents

List of Plates

List of Maps

Acknowledgements

As is usual, my gratitude must go to Philip Sidnell for keeping faith with an unknown author. I hope that this third book continues to repay that confidence.

I would like to thank Adrian Goldsworthy for agreeing to read through early drafts of the entire book. For reading excerpted chapters I would like to thank Philip Matyszak. Finally, I would like to express my extreme gratitude to Perry Gray for not only reading the whole manuscript but for taking the time to discuss significant points throughout the process. The comments, criticisms and corrections of the above have been a valuable asset in the writing process. However, it should not be taken for granted that they agree with all that is written here, and for any mistakes that remain I am solely responsible.

For helping me to secure otherwise impossible-to-acquire books, I would once again like to thank the staff at Thurnscoe Branch Library, Barnsley, and especially Andrea World of the Inter-Library Loans Department of Barnsley Libraries.

I would very much like to thank the following people for kindly allowing me to use their photographs in the plates: Beast Coins (www.beastcoins.com), CNG coins (www.cngcoins.com), Giovanni Dall'Orto of Wikimedia, Sean Pruitt, Didier Rykner, Nigel Rodgers, and 'Antiquité Tardive' of Flickr. Their generosity is very much appreciated.

For their patience and for permission to use photographs from their extensive and valuable libraries I would like to thank Dr Manfred Clauss of ILS, and Dr Andreas Faßbender and Dr Manfred G. Schmidt of CIL.

My gratitude also goes to Raffaele D'Amato, Roy Boss and Graham Sumner for their correspondence regarding depictions of Aetius in ancient monuments and diptychs, although they may not agree with the conclusions I have drawn.

As with my first two books, this book would not have been the same without the contributions of the members of both www.romanarmytalk.com/rat/ and www.unrv.com.forum. They have yet again been exceptionally patient, especially with regards to questions about the availability of photographs.

My utmost gratitude goes to the individuals and institutions who have made available the ever-growing corpus of source material on the internet. I will, however, refrain from mentioning individuals by name, since a look at the bibliography will show that it would need a separate book to list all of the people involved and to single individuals out for special praise would be unfair.

To all of these people, once again, my heartfelt thanks.

However, most of all I would like to thank Joanna for her endurance in reading through a third book about 'some bloke from ancient Rome'. For her seemingly endless patience and understanding I remain forever in her debt.

Finally, to my son Owen – again, I would like to apologize for all of the times when you have wanted to play and been told, 'Not now, Daddy is working.' Unfortunately, this will continue, as I have now signed a deal for another book. Sorry!

Foreword

Historians of the fourth and fifth centuries have a particularly difficult life. Those used to the relative certainties of the late republic and early empire can only look on with admiration at those brave souls who plunge into the mess that is late antiquity.

'Mess' is not putting it too strongly. Firstly, the Roman Empire itself was in a mess, and particularly so the western empire. A series of barbarian invasions not only tore through the countryside, but also through the social and economic fabric of the affected provinces. The empire was bankrupt, the peasantry surly and mutinous (and often likely to side with the invaders) and the soldiers too few and of dubious loyalty.

Secondly, the evidence is in a mess. Barbarian invasions and civil wars tend to be confusing events even at the time, let alone 1,500 years later, when the historian has to make sense of the fragmentary writings of people who themselves had little idea of what was actually going on. Furthermore, the motives of the main protagonists are often obscure. And that is even if we assume that the actions of the protagonists are accurately reported and dated – an assumption any chronicler of late antiquity is likely to greet with sardonic laughter. Documents are scanty and tend to refer even to major events in oblique terms. Entire battles have gone missing. To give but one example, early in the period Britain drifted out of imperial control. One might think this would be significant enough to warrant a detailed description in the primary sources, and perhaps even an analysis of the causes. In reality, the historian of late antiquity settles gratefully for any passing mention.

Thirdly, and most importantly, almost everyone writing in this period had an agenda in which the accurate reporting of events was either irrelevant at best, or at worst something to be avoided at all costs. The sources for this period seldom say what they mean, or mean what they say. Sometimes the motive is political, as when a writer is attempting to praise one emperor at the cost of a rival, or trying to obfuscate his own involvement with that rival. At other times the issue is religious. The fourth and early fifth centuries saw the triumph of Christianity over paganism and much, in fact most, of what we know of the history in that period is seen through the lens of that process.

One consequence of such ideological involvement is that battles are seen as tests of the religious convictions of the generals involved. Writers such as Jerome are apparently convinced that a prayer at the right moment affected events more powerfully than a well-deployed legion. And since Jerome seldom takes interest in the actual deployment of the armies, there is no telling whether he was right. What we do know is that his reports, like those of his contemporaries, must be filtered for bias, poetic exaggeration, hyperbole and plain ignorance.

Furthermore, the religious struggle of the period was a complex affair in which the pagans were sometimes mere interested spectators to vicious in-fighting between catholic Christians, Arians, Monophysites, Donatists and others. It would be fair to say that most historians of the period would gladly sacrifice, say, the minutiae of the struggle against the Pelagian heresy for a proper description of a secular event or two – for example, the invasion of Italy by Radagaisus.

To repeat: from a historian's perspective, the period is a mess. Yet it is a critically important mess. The huge structure of the Roman Empire in the west was changing dramatically and the edifice of imperial control was rushing toward final collapse. We cannot draw a veil over this critical period in world history simply because it is too untidy. It is momentously important. Out of this chaos, medieval Europe was born, and the outcome of the ideological battles fought in those days continues to shape our lives. How can one not study such events?

Yet, if the preceding part of this foreword has not already warned the casual reader that this is a topic to be approached with extreme caution, it has often been said that there is nothing like an absence of facts for a good argument, and modern studies of late antiquity are almost as riddled with opposing viewpoints and arcane argument as the shibboleths they analyze. 'Pagan' and 'barbarian' are loaded terms that the historian must use with care, and even to talk of the 'fall' of the Roman Empire in the west identifies one as belonging to a particular school of historical thought.

Under these circumstances one reaches gratefully for the work of a writer such as Ian Hughes, whose intent is simply to explain, and explain as clearly as possible, who did what during those dramatic and desperate years. If one is looking for a guide through the morass of events at the end of the western Roman Empire, then perhaps it can be found in the lives of the men who struggled to hold things together as the world they knew went through wrenching changes. Biography is almost by definition narrative, and a narrative that has a single clear focus.

As his groundbreaking biography of Stilicho (Pen & Sword, 2010) has shown, Ian Hughes has the expertise to understand the complexities of the period and the confidence to present and argue his point of view even against established orthodoxies. Even better, he does so with a clarity and enthusiasm that makes him as accessible to the general reader as to the specialist scholar.

The end of the Roman Empire is one of the pivotal events in European history. Yet this is not the only reason for reading this book, or even the best one. The simple fact is that the life of Aetius was both important and fascinating. He is worth reading about for his own sake.

Philip Matyszak
February 2011

Introduction

Aetius was born sometime around the year AD 391. At the time of his birth all must have seemed well. The two halves of the Roman Empire were still strong and able to defend themselves. Yet within a few years the first signs of weakness were apparent. When Theodosius 'the Great' re-united the two halves of the empire after a civil war in 394 the losses inflicted by his troops on the western army severely weakened the west. Further, thanks to internal and external pressures on the empire, even a strong emperor such as Theodosius was forced to accept that it was too large to be ruled by one individual. He immediately arranged for his younger son, Honorius, to rule in the west. Theodosius died shortly after his victory, in January 395.

By the time of Aetius' death the West was almost unrecognizable. Britain had seceded from the Empire, large parts of Gaul and Spain were in the hands of barbarian leaders and the Vandals had conquered 'Africa'. In 444 the Western Emperor Valentinian III was forced to accept that his empire was bankrupt.

Aetius was in control of the West during this tumultuous time, and with so much going wrong it is surprising that he is still perceived as the 'the man who was universally celebrated as the terror of the Barbarians and the support of the republic'.[1] This book aims to tell his story, chronicling the steady decline of the West and the strategies Aetius used to halt that decline.

The fact that there have been few attempts to tell Aetius' story in detail is a little surprising, as the period when he rose to power is both pivotal and fascinating. This reluctance, though, is due to the (perceived) nature of the sources. In most cases these are vague, contradictory and usually extremely brief, consisting largely of single-line entries in the surviving chronicles.

Alongside the poor quality of the sources are disagreements amongst historians concerning such fundamentals as a chronology for Aetius' lifetime. This uncertainty has created reluctance on the part of many historians to make definitive judgements, which are open to instant criticism. This is understandable: certainty is impossible and negative comments virtually certain.

The difficulties with the sources have one major repercussion on the present work. This book is not a biography in the modern sense. If the fragmentary nature of the sources and the lack of detailed information make it impossible to outline a clear passage of events, it is obvious that any attempt to reach conclusions concerning Aetius' military ability or his personal thoughts and beliefs is due to failure. Instead, the book will venture to fill as many gaps as possible, create a chronology that incorporates all of the evidence, and attempt to peel away the years to study Aetius

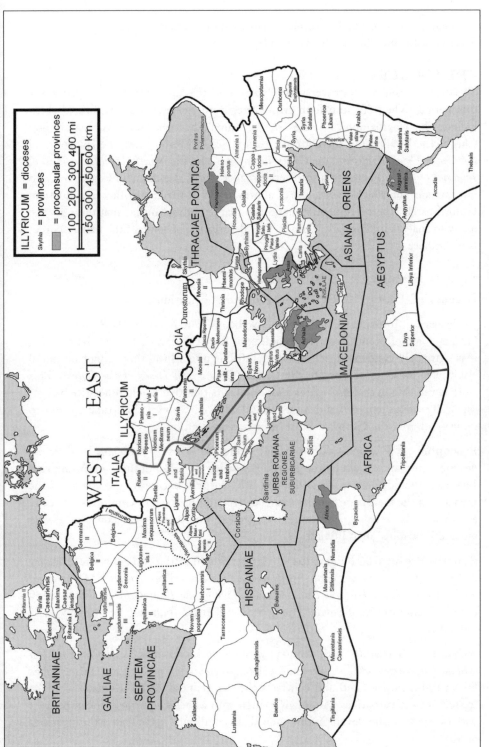

Map 1. The empire at the time of Theodosius I

as a man, in so far as this is possible. Scholars of this period will find much that they disagree with, but this cannot be avoided.

THE SOURCES

The main causes of controversy revolve around the surviving sources that cover this period. They fall into four broad categories: Ecclesiastical Histories (which include the Hagiographies – lives of the saints), Secular Histories, Letters and Chronicles. In addition, there are the panegyrics of Merobaudes, the law codes of the *Codex Theodosianus* and the *Codex Justinianus*, and the *Notitia Dignitatum* (*List of Imperial Offices*). There are also several smaller works that sometimes give relevant information, for which see the list of abbreviations at the end of this Introduction. Unfortunately, their fragmentary nature and large number means that there are too many to analyze individually. Only a brief description of some of the major sources is given here.

Secular Histories

Gregory of Tours   See Renatus Profuturus Frigeridus

Jordanes   Jordanes (fl. 550s) wrote two books. The *Romana* (*On Rome*) is a very brief epitome of events from the founding of Rome until 552. Due to the fact that it is extremely condensed, it can be useful, but offers little that cannot be found elsewhere. Jordanes also wrote the *Getica* (*Origins and Deeds of the Goths*). This work is valuable in that it contains a lot of information that would otherwise be lost, especially those sections that demonstrate a Gothic viewpoint. Unfortunately, due to its bias towards the Goths, it must be used with caution.[2]

Procopius   Procopius (c.500–c.554) wrote the *Wars of Justinian*. In these he describes the wars fought by the general Belisarius on behalf of the eastern Emperor Justinian. Included are many asides and brief entries concerning the history of the west and of the Germanic peoples who had overrun the western empire. It is usually assumed to be reliable, but caution is needed where the work concerns events outside Procopius' own lifetime.

Renatus Profuturus Frigeridus   Frigeridus (fl. fifth century) wrote a history that only survives in fragments. Fortunately, he was used as a source by Gregory of Tours for his book *Historia Francorum* (*History of the Franks*), from which many items of value can be gleaned. The accuracy of these fragments is in many cases unknown.

Salvian   Salvian (fl. fifth century) wrote a work known as *De gubernatione Dei* (*On the Government of God*, also known as *De praesenti judicio*), in which he describes life in fifth-century Gaul and contrasts the 'wickedness' of the Romans with the 'virtues' of the barbarians. Although written with a specific purpose, it can be used with care to furnish relevant information about conditions in Gaul after the invasions of 406.

Victor of Vita   Victor of Vita (b. c.430) wrote the *Historia persecutionis Africanae Provinciae, temporibus Geiserici et Hunirici regum Wandalorum* (*History of the Vandal Persecution in the time of Gaiseric and Huneric, Kings of the Vandals*, usually abbreviated to *History of the Vandal Persecution*) during the persecution of Catholics by Huneric. It depicts the horrors of the era, but was updated after the worst was over, following which it reflects 'happier times'.[3] Victor's hatred of the Vandals can lead him to exaggerate their more disagreeable actions, so the work needs to be used with caution.

Zosimus   Zosimus (c.500) wrote the *Historia Nova* (*New History*), which covers the period from the mid third century to 410. He appears to have used two main sources for his information: Eunapius for events to 404 and Olympiodorus for the years c.407–410. Zosimus was a pagan, writing in Constantinople, who was determined to show that Christianity was the reason for the disasters suffered by the empire. He closely follows Eunapius and Olympiodorus and is not critical of his sources, so although his work is useful one must use it with a great amount of caution.

Ecclesiastical Histories and Associated Works

Augustine   Augustine (354–430) wrote many works, including *De civitate dei* (*The City of God*), which was written after the Gothic sack of Rome in 410. It includes information that is useful in reconstructing events concerning the early years of Aetius' life, but the moralizing Christian nature of the work needs to be taken into account.

Hagiographies   Several of the 'lives of the saints', for example Possidius' *Life of Saint Augustine* and Constantius' *Life of Saint Germanus of Auxerre*, contain information concerning the era during which Aetius was in control in the west. However, the fact that these works are aimed almost exclusively at promoting the sanctity of the individual being described means that they are not subjective and so extreme caution is needed in these cases.

Socrates Scholasticus   Socrates (b. c.380) wrote the *Historia Ecclesiastica* (*Church History*), which covers the years 305–439. It was written during the reign of Emperor Theodosius II (408–450) solely as a history of the church. However, it does contain much information about secular events, but mainly only where they impinge on church history. However, these items are otherwise unrecorded, so they can offer unique insights.

Theodoret   Theodoret (c.393–c.457) wrote many works on Christian doctrine, but more importantly a *Historia Ecclesiastica* (*Church History*), which begins in 325 and ends in 429. He used several sources, including, amongst others, Sozomen, Rufinus, Eusebius and Socrates. Possibly due to the mixed nature of his sources, the work is chronologically confused, and must be used with caution.

Letters

Many letters written at this time survive. Although most are obviously of a personal nature, some include information on secular events and on some of the leading men of the time, including Aetius. These can be valuable in filling in details, but their accuracy in most areas remains unknown.

Augustine   Augustine, apart from his religious treatises, was a prolific writer of letters, many of which are still extant. They give an impression of what life was like in early fifth-century Africa as well as occasionally giving useful information concerning secular events.

Sidonius Apollinaris   Sidonius Apollinaris (c.430–489) is the most important source for conditions in Gaul during the last years of the west. His many letters illuminate relations between Goths and the Roman elite as well as demonstrating the changing attitudes of the aristocracy towards their 'barbarian' overlords. However, at all times the biases of a Roman aristocrat need to be borne in mind, along with the position of the recipient of the letter: a letter to a fellow aristocrat may contain disparaging remarks about the Goths, whereas a letter to a Goth would certainly not contain these.

Chronicles[4]

The chronicle was the form of history that 'so well suited the taste of the new Christian culture that it became the most popular historical genre of the Middle Ages'.[5] The positive aspect of this popularity is that several chronicles have survived. The negative aspect is that they displaced conventional history as the means of transmitting information about the past, and so no complete histories written during the fifth century survive.

There is a further feature that causes difficulty when analyzing the chronicles, especially the fragmentary ones. Several collections of these sources were made prior to the twentieth century. Each of these collections could give the sources different titles. For example, the works referenced as the *Anonymus Cuspiniani* in secondary sources from the early twentieth century and before are now referred to as the *Fasti Vindobonenses Priori*, following Mommsen's description in the *Chronica Minora*, Vol. 1 (see Bibliography). Therefore readers should be aware that references in this book are likely to differ from these earlier works.

The *Chronica Gallica of 452* is a continuation of the Chronicle of Jerome covering the years 379 to 452. The *Chronica Gallica of 511* also begins in 379 and continues to 511. Due to the similarity between the two, it is possible to see the chronicle of 511 as a continuation of the chronicle of 452. Both of these works contain useful information but need to be used with care, since the dates given may not in fact be accurate. The Gallic Chronicle of 452 only becomes accurate after 447, and here the events in Gaul are the most accurately dated. Prior to 447 the chronology is extremely confused.[6] The Gallic Chronicle of 452 has some entries undated. In these the reference is simply to the modern 'number' given to the entry.

For example, the invasion of Italy by Radagaisus is undated and is therefore referenced simply as 'no. 50'.

The ***Chronicon Paschale*** (*Easter Chronicle*, so-called because of the author's use of Easter as the focus of his dating system) is an anonymous chronicle dating from the early seventh century, compiled in Constantinople.[7] Although it is a later document, and some of the dates and facts are wrong, the *Chronicon Paschale* is useful in confirming other sources and adding detail to events. However, it must be used with caution thanks to the temporal distance between its compilation and the early–mid fifth century.

Hydatius   Hydatius (c.400–c.469) wrote a continuation of the Chronicles of Eusebius and Jerome, beginning with the accession of Theodosius in 379 and finishing in 468, so he appears to have finished writing in 469. His work has serious errors in dating that are still confusing. These are probably caused by the fact that much of his information was late arriving in Spain, being taken there by embassies and merchants whose dating was insecure.[8] For events in Spain, especially concerning the Vandals, his work is good and relatively accurate.[9] Although potentially valuable, the errors mean that Hydatius must be used with caution, with dates especially being confirmed by other sources whenever possible.

John Malalas   John Malalas (fl. sixth century) wrote a chronicle intended to be used by both churchmen and laymen. Unfortunately, the work covers 'history' from the biblical period to the reign of Justinian in one book, so much is glossed over or omitted. As a result, the work is useful in places, but this is rare.

Marcellinus Comes   Marcellinus (fl. sixth century) wrote a chronicle that covers the period from 379 to 534 (an unknown writer continued the chronicle down to 566). It is mainly concerned with the eastern empire, but includes some information concerning the west, drawn mainly from Orosius. Where possible this information needs to be confirmed by independent sources to ensure the accuracy of dates and the reliability of information contained.

Prosper Tiro   Also known as Prosper of Aquitaine, c.390–c.455, he wrote a continuation of Jerome's Chronicle. Prosper's Chronicle finishes in 455. The early sections contain many errors, but between the years 433 and 455, when Prosper was personally involved in events, he is accepted as being the most reliable of the chroniclers, giving 'careful and accurate' dating.[10] Prosper was not a clergyman, but his close association with the clergy and especially his contacts with Pope Leo I and Saint Augustine resulted in his viewpoint being heavily biased towards the church. Prosper doesn't approve of Aetius. Possibly thanks to Augustine's friendship with Boniface, Boniface is the only western general Prosper praises. This bias needs to be taken into account when reading the chronicle.[11]

Difficulties with the Chronicles   The modern concept of a chronicle is that events are accurately dated and each single occurrence is allocated a separate entry in its relevant date. This preconception has badly affected perceptions of the chronicles, leading to accusations of inaccuracy and a poor grasp of time. In fact, some of these observations are unfair to the chroniclers. Even in the modern era, where access to periodicals, newspapers and the internet is common, one of the most common radio competitions is 'Guess the Year'. It is clear that without modern methods of establishing specific dates, such as newspaper archives, human error in reporting events is to be expected.

Furthermore, ancient chroniclers were not writing with modern expectations in mind. As long as events were in roughly the correct order the chronicle would fulfil its purpose. Therefore it is a common occurrence for the chronicler to include later events at a convenient place earlier in his account.

Instances of the chroniclers predicting events are common. For example, in Hydatius' entry for 430 he notes the defeat of a Gothic force by Aetius before extolling Aetius' ability by noting that 'Juthungi as well as Nori were vanquished by him in the same way.' At first sight, these campaigns must therefore have taken place in 430. However, Hydatius' entry for 431 includes the sentence 'Aetius, general of both services, subdued the Nori, who were in rebellion.' On reflection, the second campaign must date to the latter entry.

A more extreme example is in the *Chronicon Paschale* in the entry dated to 437, where the chronicler describes the marriage of Valentinian III and Eudoxia: 'And he celebrated his nuptial, taking Eudoxia, the daughter of Theodosius and Eudocia Augusti, in the month Hyperberetaeus, on day four before Kalends of November, and by her he had two daughters, Eudocia and Placidia.' The entry highlights the fact that the chroniclers were including later events at convenient places within the earlier entries, unless Eudoxia experienced two extremely fast gestation periods.

A further problem with the chroniclers is that they use different methods for calculating dates. For example, Prosper and Hydatius use a different method of calculating Christ's passion, Prosper dating this to the fifteenth year of Tiberius, Hydatius to the start of Tiberius' fifteenth regnal year. This discrepancy helps to explain the differences in dates between the two chronicles.[12] The consular date used by Prosper, plus his closer proximity to events, results in his dating system being preferred on the majority of occasions.

Panegyrics

When reading panegyrics one piece of advice is worth remembering: 'the aim of the panegyrist is not to tell the truth, but to glorify his subject, exaggerating the good and suppressing or distorting the bad, the inappropriate, or the inconvenient'.[13] With this in mind, it is possible to look at the two writers of panegyrics to have survived from this period in the fifth century.

Flavius Merobaudes[14]   Merobaudes was probably of Frankish origin, having an ancestor who was either a Romanized Frank or Frankish noble who took service with the empire – possibly the Merobaudes who lived during the reigns of Valentinian I (364–375) and Gratian (375–383).[15]

Perhaps originally from Gaul, he appears to have moved to Spain, where he married the daughter of Astyrius, a member of the old Spanish aristocracy. In the early fifth century the majority of the aristocracy withdrew from public life, but Merobaudes followed the example of his father-in-law and entered into an imperial career.[16] Famed for his talents as a rhetorician and writer, he also gained a positive reputation as a military commander.[17] Obtaining the position of either *comes rei militaris* ('count' of the military) or *dux* (duke), his military and literary abilities resulted in entry to the Senate and then a rapid rise through its ranks. On 30 July 435 he was honoured by having a statue erected to him in the Forum of Trajan in Rome.

After these successes Merobaudes appears to have focused mainly on his literary works. He may have delivered a panegyric to Aetius, as well as an ode honouring the wedding of Valentinian III and Eudoxia, daughter of Theodosius II, both in 437. Unfortunately, both have been lost. The latter may have been in emulation of Claudian (d. 404), the panegyrist of Stilicho (395–408). It is possible that Aetius and Merobaudes enjoyed a similar relationship to the earlier pair, although the fragmentary nature of the evidence means that this hypothesis must remain conjecture.[18] The ode celebrating Valentinian's wedding in Constantinople may also have been at least partly responsible for Merobaudes receiving the title of *patricius* from Theodosius, the eastern emperor.[19]

In 438 Merobaudes appears to have written verses celebrating the birth of Eudocia, Valentinian and Eudoxia's first child, and probably in the winter of 441–442 he wrote a *genethliakon* ('birthday poem', 'ode composed for a person's birthday', now known as *Carmen IV*) on the first birthday of Gaudentius, Aetius' son.

Also in the early 440s, although the exact date is unknown, Merobaudes wrote an *ekphrasis* (an attempt to describe physical works of art in literary form and which is now known as *Carmen III*) for his friend Anicius Acilius Glabrio Faustus. Probably in 443 he wrote two poems to celebrate the baptism of Placidia, daughter of Valentinian and Eudoxia, which may be *Carmen I* and *Carmen II*, both of which are ekphrastic poems, although it should be noted that their actual purpose and content remains the matter of debate.[20] All of these works are useful sources of information in their own right, but obviously they need to be used with care.

Shortly after writing these two poems Merobaudes was appointed *magister utriusque militiae* and sent to Spain, where he succeeded his father-in-law Astyrius in command. After his recall in 444 Merobaudes composed another panegyric to Aetius, which he delivered in Rome to the Senate and which is now known as *Panegyric I*.[21] Shortly after this he composed yet another panegyric, now known as *Panegyric II*, which he delivered on 1 January 446.

Unfortunately, little is known of Merobaudes' later career, and it is believed that he died before 460. He was obviously a man of influence and power and of considerable literary and military ability. Like Claudian before him, it would appear that Merobaudes took a full part in the regime set up by the ruling *magister militum*, in this case Aetius. There is little doubt that Merobaudes' efforts on Aetius' part helped to maintain the latter's popularity and esteem.

Sidonius Apollinaris   In addition to his letters, Sidonius Apollinaris wrote panegyrics on three individuals who became emperor after Aetius' death, namely Avitus, Majorian and Anthemius. Within these panegyrics are events from the earlier lives of the three emperors, including some information concerning events during Aetius' lifetime. However, it should be remembered that their aim was to praise their recipients, not to serve the interests of the historian in the life and deeds of Aetius, so they need to be read with care.

Other Sources

Notitia Dignitatum   The *Notitia Dignitatum* is an extremely important document. It purports to list the bureaucratic and military organization of both the eastern and western empires. Thousands of offices are listed. Dated to c.420 for the west and c.395 for the east, it is potentially a mine of statistical and legal information. Unfortunately, there are many problems. Probably originating with the Emperor Theodosius in the east, it may in theory have been intended as a full list of offices. The eastern section of the *Notitia* appears to date from the early 400s. As a result, it is usually believed that the surviving document is a copy preserved in the west of the eastern *Notitia* dating from the reign of Arcadius (395–408). Unfortunately, it was not kept strictly up to date and there are many omissions and duplications. Moreover, due to the fragmentation of the Empire during and immediately after Stilicho's death in 408, it is uncertain whether many of the army units listed existed in reality or only on paper. As a consequence, information taken from the *Notitia* should be accepted as possible rather than certain.

There appear to have been later attempts to update the western portion of the document and evidence suggests that these were last compiled at some date in the 420s, possibly under the orders of Constantius III (*magister militum* in the west from 411 and Emperor from February to September 421).

Unfortunately, there are internal problems with the *Notitia*, which suggests that it does not reflect reality. For example, although the provinces of Britain had drifted out of the imperial orbit in the early 410s, the leaders and troops associated with the island are still included in the *Notitia*. The same is true of the provinces of Belgica and Germania. The fact that these are 'unquestionably anachronistic' suggests that the document includes material reflecting what had once been available to the empire rather than the current military status.[22] Yet the document may also have been a statement of intent. If it was compiled under the orders of Constantius III in 421, it may have been his intention as emperor to restore the glory of the west and incorporate the lost provinces back into the empire.

As well as being useful in outlining what the Roman bureaucracy believed should have been the case, it is also possible to analyze the document in the hope of gleaning material concerning the condition and deployment of the army. This is covered in more depth in Chapter 6.

What is often forgotten, or at least ignored, is the fact that the *Notita* was not updated after some time around 420. Due to the complicated nature of events from

423 onwards it is quite possible that by the time Aetius achieved sole dominance in the mid 430s events had rendered the *Notitia* completely obsolete. As a result, it must be used with extreme caution when discussing the later army in existence during the dominance of Aetius.

Codex Theodosianus   The *Codex Theodosianus* is a collection made during the reign of Theodosius II in the east of all of the laws issued since the reign of Constantine I (306–337). Added to this body of laws were the new laws (*novellae*) passed by Theodosius II (*Nov. Th.*) and Valentinian (*Nov. Val.*) after 439. These were also collected and kept with the Codex and now form part of the main text.

The 'Code' and the 'Novels' are a valuable source of material for the period. It is possible to analyze the laws to establish their context and so determine the reasons for their passing. Furthermore, the laws are accompanied by the name(s) of the emperor(s) that passed them, in most cases by the precise date on which they were passed, and by the name of the city in which the emperor passed the law. This allows us to trace some of the movements of the emperor, and also enables us to link specific laws with specific events in the lifetime of Aetius. One example is the law allowing citizens to bear arms (*Nov. Val.* 9.1, dated 24 June 440) being related to the conquest of Africa by the Vandals in October 439. Therefore close analysis of the *Codex* can open a window into aspects of Aetius' life and policies that would otherwise be blank.

It is also interesting to note that one of the laws dismisses laws that were destined to be 'valid for the cases of their own time only'.[23] This highlights the fact that, like modern law, some laws passed by emperors were meant to deal with specific emergencies and events. After these had passed, the laws were naturally allowed to lapse. Modern examples include the laws passed to deal with the emergency that was the Second World War. Once this war was over, these laws were repealed and 'normality' resumed.

CONCLUSION

The information that is available in the sources should not detract us from the knowledge that they were all written with a purpose. Even when this bias is openly declared it can easily be overlooked or forgotten. If this is the case with the major sources as listed above, it is even more the case with the multitude of minor sources not listed. The less-important sources that are used are of varying accuracy and utility and where necessary an analysis of these will be dealt with in the body of the text. However, if the source only gives us one or two snippets of information, then it is possible that it will not be analyzed.

One problem with all of the sources needs to be highlighted. This is where they inform the reader of political intrigue. The difficulty lies with the fact that the sources claim to know details of the kind that are always most suspicious: 'tales of secret intrigues and treasons which could not be known to the world at large'.[24] Whenever this kind of information is encountered a full analysis will be attempted to decide whether there is the possibility of the author knowing the full details of events.

SPELLING AND TERMINOLOGY

Wherever possible, the simplest definitions and spellings have been used throughout the book. There are many examples in the ancient sources of variations in the spelling of individuals' names, such as Gaiseric being spelt 'Zinzirich'.[25] Also, in most modern works Roman spellings are usually 'modernized' by removing the common 'us' endings and substituting a modern variant, for example 'Bonifatius' becoming 'Boniface'. Wherever possible the most widely used variant has been employed in the hope of avoiding confusion.

When describing both the tribes along the Rhine and those who successfully invaded the Empire, at times 'barbarian' rather than 'German' has been used. Although the word 'barbarian' is now out of fashion, largely due to its negative aspects regarding comparative civilization levels with the Romans, it has been used, as it is an otherwise neutral term, whereas the use of the word 'German' often implies 'community and ethnicity on the basis of shared language', which is actually misleading.[26]

In most cases 'Goth(s)' has been used rather than 'Visigoth(s)'. Contemporary sources describe both the Visigoths and the Ostrogoths simply as Goths.[27] During Aetius' lifetime there was only one Gothic threat, and that was the Goths in the west. The Ostrogoths were peripheral, living in the faraway regions of eastern Europe. It was only after their invasion of Italy under Theoderic in 493 that the west was forced to divide the terminology. Only where there may be confusion between the two 'tribes', such as Attila's invasion of Gaul in 451, will the terms Visigoth and Ostrogoth be used.

ABBREVIATIONS

In order to make the references more manageable, the following abbreviations have been used for ancient sources:

Additamenta Ad Chronicon Prosperi Hauniensis Addit.	*Ad Prosp. Haun.*
Agathias	Agath.
Ammianus Marcellinus	Amm. Marc.
Annales Ravennae	*Ann. Rav.*
Augustine	Aug.
Aurelius Victor	Aur. Vict.
Cambridge Ancient History	CAH
Callisthenes	Call.
Cassiodorus, *Chronicle*	Cass. *Chron.*
Chronica Gallica of 452	*Chron. Gall. 452*
Chronica Gallica of 511	*Chron. Gall. 511*
Chronica Minora (Mommsen)	*Chron. Min.*
Chronicon Paschale	*Chron. Pasch.*
Claudian Claudianus (Claudian)	Claud.
Codex Justinianus	*Cod. Just.*
Codex Theodosianus	*Cod. Th.*

Collectio Avellana	*Collect. Avell.*
Constantius of Lyon	Const.
Eunapius of Sardis	Eun.
Eutropius	Eut.
Evagrius	Evag.
Fasti vindobonenses posteriores	*Fast. Vind. Post.*
Fasti vindobonenses priores	*Fast. Vind. Prior*
Gaudentius	Gaud.
Gildas	Gild.
Gregory of Tours	Greg. Tur.
Hydatius	Hyd.
John of Antioch	Joh. Ant.
John Malalas	Joh. Mal.
Jordanes	Jord.
Libanius	Lib.
Marcellinus Comes	Marc. com.
Merobaudes	Merob.
Minutes of the Senate	*Min. Sen.*
Nicephorus Callistus	Nic. Call
Nestorius	Nest.
Notitia Dignitatum	*Not. Dig.*
Novellae Theodosianae	*Nov. Theod.*
Novellae Valentinianae	*Nov. Val.*
Olympiodorus of Thebes	Olymp.
Orosius	Oros.
Paulinus of Nola	Paul.
Paulinus of Pella	Paul. Pell.
Paulus Diaconus	Paul. Diac.
Philostorgius	Philost.
Prosopography of the Later Roman Empire	PLRE
Possidius	Poss.
Priscus, *Chronica*	Prisc. *Chron*
Priscus, *Romana*	Prisc. *Rom.*
Procopius	Proc.
Prosper Tiro	Prosp.
Pseudo-Augustine	Pseudo-Aug.
Renatus Profuturus Frigeridus	Ren. Prof.
Saint Jerome	Jer.
Salvian	Salv.
Scriptores Historiae Augustae	*Scrip. His.*
Sidonius Apollinaris	Sid. Ap.
Sirmondian Constitutions	*Sirm.*
Socrates Scholasticus	Soc.
Sozomen	Soz.

Suidas	*Suid.*
Theoderet	Theod.
Theophanes	Theoph.
Vegetius	Veg.
Victor of Vita	Vict. Vit.
Zosimus	Zos.

Chapter 1

Historical Background and Early Years

HISTORICAL BACKGROUND

At the time of the birth of Aetius, some time around the year AD 391,* the Roman Empire had been in existence for many centuries.[1] During that time the empire had constantly evolved and although most changes had been slow and complex only about 100 years before Aetius' birth there had been dramatic upheavals in its nature. In 284 Diocletian became emperor. His reign began at the end of a long period of instability and confusion caused by revolt and invasion. Although his predecessors had done much to help stabilize the empire, it was Diocletian's reign that saw the return of a more stable government under a long-lived emperor. There were still periods of instability, but his longevity allowed the empire a period in which to recover.

It is Diocletian and his (eventual) successor Constantine who are credited with overseeing a period of major political and military reform, although it should be acknowledged that in many cases they simply accepted and regularized the changes that had been ongoing throughout the third century, and that slow change would continue to occur after their deaths.

One of the most important changes had been the inauguration of the Tetrarchy. The Tetrarchy had divided the empire in half, each half being ruled by an *Augustus* (emperor). Each *Augustus* had his own *Caesar* (deputy and successor) to help run his half of the empire. As part of the bureaucratic system, each of the four co-rulers had a *Praefectus Praetorio* (Praetorian Prefect) to help with the administration of his 'quarter' of the empire. Each *Praefectus* wielded great power and could readily influence military affairs, as he retained control of the main logistical system of the empire. Although abandoned on the death of Diocletian, the system of using four *Praefecti* was revived under Constantine. As time passed the position of prefect became more influential, especially that of the two prefects in charge of the two imperial capitals.

Rome was now only the nominal capital of the Roman Empire. Two new cities had emerged as the major political centres of the empire: Milan in the west and Constantinople in the east. In both cases this was in large part due to their strategic locations. Milan, at the head of the Italian peninsula, was strategically placed to allow western emperors to defend Italy and campaign along the Rhine, whilst Constantinople, at the crossing point between Europe and Asia Minor, allowed

---

* Unless otherwise stated, all dates are AD.

eastern emperors to command personally Roman armies either in the east or in the Balkans.

The End of the Fourth Century

The sons of Constantine divided the empire between them, after which there was a series of costly civil wars. The eventual victor, Constantius II (d. 361), came to the conclusion that as the empire was being threatened in both east and west it was too big for one man to control. Emulating Diocletian, he enrolled his cousin Julian as *Caesar* (vice-emperor) with control in the west. When the two men disagreed, another civil war was triggered, but Constantius died in 361, before the two rivals could meet. Julian (360–363), known as 'the Apostate' because of his support for paganism, gathered his troops and led an ill-fated invasion of Persia, during which he died. The death of Julian in 363 effectively ended the Constantinian dynasty.

Jovian (363–364) was proclaimed emperor but soon afterwards died on the way to Constantinople. His successor was Valentinian (364–375), who, after being acclaimed by the army and close officials, quickly acclaimed his brother Valens (364–378) as joint-Augustus, with Valentinian taking the West and Valens the East. Diocletian's decision to divide the empire was now taken as the norm. Valentinian spent his reign repairing and reinforcing the defences of the west and attempting to enforce his will on the turbulent tribes across the Rhine and upper Danube. Valens, meanwhile, was given the task of minimizing the damage to the east from the unfavourable treaty with the Persians signed by Jovian.

In an attempt to secure the new dynasty, in 367 Valentinian declared his son Gratian as *Caesar* and successor. When Valentinian died in 375 Gratian prepared to take control of the west. However, the troops in Pannonia declared Gratian's half-brother, Valentinian II, as emperor and Gratian was forced to accept only Gaul, Spain and Britain, while Valentinian II ruled in Italy, Illyricum and Africa. Valens retained sole control of the east.

In 376 a large band of Goths under Fritigern appeared on the banks of the Danube seeking sanctuary from the Huns. Valens allowed them entry to the empire, but they were badly treated and broke into open revolt. In 378 Valens gathered an army together and led them to face the Goths in battle. Contrary to expectations, Valens was defeated and killed by the Goths at the Battle of Adrianople. Gratian was now the senior emperor. To rule the east, Gratian chose Theodosius, the son of a man also called Theodosius who had displayed military ability in the west before being arrested and executed in 376.

With Theodosius in the East and Gratian and Valentinian II in the West, the empire was slowly able to recover. After being defeated in a second battle against the Goths Theodosius led his forces in a campaign aimed at restricting the Goths' access to supplies and, in 382, his strategy was proved to be effective: the Goths capitulated. Although the Goths were beaten and forced to accept a treaty, they had not been crushed and remained united under their own leaders: an unprecedented move.

The Battle of Adrianople

Although the significance of the Battle of Adrianople is debated, one major factor had changed: after the battle, the Goths were a permanent political and military force within the empire. Their presence changed the way in which the Roman government dealt with barbarians. At first, this change was only visible when the Romans dealt with the Goths, but this quickly changed until it became the manner in which the court dealt with all barbarian leaders.[2]

For the barbarians outside the empire the treaty was a revelation. The Goths had been allowed to settle under their own leaders. Prior to this, invading barbarians had been defeated and their leaders either executed or deployed on the far edges of the empire, away from their own men. The earlier attitude of barbarian leaders – that the empire was too large to defeat but was a tempting target for raids – changed. Now it appeared possible for barbarian leaders to enter the empire and coerce it into giving them lands and military positions at the head of their own troops. The emphasis of barbarian attacks slowly changed from being attempts to gain plunder, to attempting to force the empire to grant them lands and military posts within it. This change of emphasis was to have dire consequences for the west.

Theodosius and Civil Wars

Imperial neglect of Britain resulted in a man named Magnus Maximus being proclaimed as emperor by the British troops. When he crossed to Gaul, Gratian's troops deserted and Gratian was captured and executed. After a brief hiatus, Maximus invaded Italy against Valentinian II. This was unacceptable to Theodosius, who declared war and defeated Maximus, inflicting heavy casualties on the western army. Theodosius installed a Frankish general named Arbogast to support Valentinian, but instead Valentinian died in mysterious circumstances. Arbogast proclaimed a man named Eugenius as emperor of the West, and in a repeat of earlier events Theodosius invaded, heavily defeating the western army at the Battle of the Frigidus in 394 and removing Eugenius and Arbogast from power. He then proclaimed his son, Honorius, as western ruler, with Stilicho, the husband of Theodosius' adopted daughter Serena, as regent. When Theodosius died in 395 Aetius would have been about four years old.

Conclusion

Despite the fact that the reigns of Diocletian and Constantine are credited with halting the calamities of the 'third-century crisis', the establishment of the Constantinian dynasty hides the fact that civil wars continued to be fought. Further, the advent of succeeding 'dynasties' gives a misleading impression regarding a continuity of peace and a return to the quieter times of the second century.

In reality, change had been enormous. The empire now had two permanent courts, one in the east and one in the west. Although the emperors were quick to maintain the appearance of unity, the courtiers were intent upon maintaining the division and so preserving their positions and lifestyles. Furthermore, the losses suffered during the wars of the fourth century left the empire significantly weaker militarily, especially in the west. Yet at the time these weaknesses were hidden. The empire was now reunited under the dynamic leadership of an emperor who had been successful in war.

THE EMPIRE AT THE TIME OF AETIUS

Early Life

Unfortunately, the date of the birth of Flavius Aetius is unknown, but was around the year 391, as he is described as a 'young adolescent' in the year 405.[3] More accuracy is impossible. He was born in Durostorum, in Moesia Secunda (Lower Moesia – see Map 1).[4] His father was Gaudentius, a 'member of one of the leading families of the province of Scythia'.[5] Little is known of Gaudentius. Born in the east, he was most likely a high-ranking eastern soldier who adopted the imperial family name – Flavius – as a sign of his loyalty to Theodosius and his heirs. After the death of Honorius in 395 Gaudentius accepted service in the west with Stilicho.[6] His political status in the west was such that early in Honorius' reign he was able to marry the daughter of a prominent Italian family. Unfortunately, the fact that Aetius' mother was a rich Italian noblewoman is the only information we have.[7] That Gaudentius married her is probably an indication that he was following Stilicho's policies of fusing eastern military command with western political influence, although it should be noted that romance may have had a very large part to play in the arrangement.[8]

Stilicho controlled the army in the west between 395 and 408 and was commander during several military campaigns against the Goths under Alaric. Gaudentius probably began his service in the west as a *protector domesticus* (household guard), but in 399, shortly after the defeat of the revolt in Africa led by Gildo, he was given the post of *comes Africae* (Count of Africa) by Stilicho.[9] This promotion was both a reward for his continuing loyalty and a sign that he was trusted by Stilicho to keep the grain shipments to Italy moving.

Having a father who was serving in the army, according to the law Aetius would spend his early years in the Roman military service. In his early life he would also be a witness to the political and military policies of Stilicho.

Like Stilicho (and possibly Constantius III) before him, Aetius appears to have begun his career in the elite corps of the *protectores*.[10] The *protectores* began in the third century and over time became a bodyguard unit, reserved for individuals who were earmarked for rapid promotion. At an unknown time, and again like his older contemporary Stilicho, Aetius was transferred to the *Tribunus Praetorianus (Partis Militaris)* ('Military Praetorian Tribune', a tribune and notary on the imperial general staff).[11] It is difficult to be exact about the nature of this post, mainly because very little information has survived in the sources. Unfortunately, the little we know of the *Tribunus Praetorianus* suggests that this may have been an honorary title, 'the significance of which is not clear', but which is known to have come with several privileges.[12]

The latter promotion would have resulted in the acquisition of a relatively large amount of political rank for one so young. As will be seen, this would be important for the next stage in Aetius' career, but the appointment also demonstrates the high rank and political influence of Gaudentius.

The Civil Service

Following in his father's footsteps, Aetius was placed in a military post. This is significant since during this period the 'bureaucracy' of the empire had earlier been divided between the 'military' and the 'civil'. Despite the change, the civil service, or *militia officialis*, was always classed as part of the army, wearing military uniform, receiving rations, bearing the old, 'non-commissioned' ranks of the army and being entered on the rolls of 'fictive' units. For example, all clerks of the praetorian prefecture were enrolled in Legio I Adiutrix, a unit that had long ago ceased to exist as a military formation.[13] The top civilian post was the *Praefectus Praetorio* (Praetorian Prefect). The Prefects acted as the emperor's representatives, governing in his name with legal, administrative and financial powers. Yet these were not the only powerful individuals at court.

The earlier *consistorium* ('consistory', council) had consisted of any individual ministers that the emperor wanted to consult about a specific topic. Probably by the date of Aetius' birth this had become more of a formal body with specific duties.[14] It was replaced by the *proceres palatii* ('notables of the palace'), sometimes simply known as the *palatium* ('palace'). As its name implies, this was formed largely from those individuals whose employment kept them in close proximity to the emperor. Closest to the emperor, at least physically, was his personal household. Included in this category were the *protectores et domestici* ('corps of officer cadets'). From an early age Aetius was at the heart of the imperial court.

Of more importance were the principal imperial ministers whose support and advice would be of great consequence to the emperor. Amongst the most powerful of these men were the *magister officiorum* ('master of offices') and the *comes sacrarum largitionum* ('count of the sacred largesses'). The *magister officiorum* had many duties, including command of the *agentes in rebus* ('imperial couriers') and control of the *scholae* ('imperial bodyguard'). He also controlled the *officia dispositionum* and *admissionum*, and so managed the emperor's timetable and audiences. The *comes sacrarum largitionum* was in charge of finances, controlling the precious metal mines, the mints, and all revenue and expenditure in coin.[15] These individuals each commanded a large number of men who served as *rei privatae* ('private secretaries'). They tended to be fiercely competitive and protective of their powers, rights and privileges.

All or any of these men could expect to be consulted by the emperor on important issues concerning their special field, and in the case of the most powerful individuals with regards to the whole running of the empire. Yet the delineation between these posts, especially at the top, was relatively narrow, and as a result often overlapped. This tended to cause friction between the top ministers of the empire.[16]

The Army

The civil service accounted for only a tiny fraction of the population of the empire and a career in it appears to have been seen as a means of self-promotion and security. The same cannot be said of the army. The army was restructured at the same time as the civil service. Although sometimes perceived as a precursor to modern military hierarchies, care must be taken when looking at the organization and the apparent modernity it represents.

This is nowhere borne out more than in the *Notitia Dignitatum*.[17] This massive document lists the postholders of the Roman army in a very hierarchical structure, with lower ranks apparently responsible to their superior. Although this is a very easy assumption to make, in reality things were not necessarily as they appear.

The emperor was the undisputed head of the armed forces. However, as events of the third century had shown, he could not be at all points where danger threatened, and from the reign of Valentinian and Valens the empire was permanently ruled by two different emperors at separate courts in the east and west. In the West, as time passed the command of the army moved away from the emperor and devolved upon the newly created *magister peditum* ('master of the infantry') and *magister equitum* ('master of the cavalry'). In the course of time the *magister peditum* became the more senior of the two posts. Yet the *magister peditum* had a major problem. The series of civil wars fought by Theodosius I at the end of the fourth century had greatly weakened the western army. Stilicho, Constantius III and their successors would always be short of the manpower necessary to re-establish fully the dominion of the West.

Finance and Taxation

In the fifth century inflation was still rampant in the West, despite the reforms of Diocletian (284–305) and Constantine I (306–337) and other attempts to calm matters by later emperors. Although these had resulted in the stabilization of the gold economy, lower-denomination coins continued to be debased. Furthermore, the coins for the West were being produced by only six official mints: Trier, Lyon and Arles in Gaul, Sirmium in Pannonia, and Aquileia and Rome in Italy.

In earlier centuries coins had been common items, their distribution largely being initiated by payments to the army, from where they had spread throughout the local economy. However, the cost of the army had taken its toll and in this later period there is some evidence of units not being paid, whilst in the late fourth century the troops began to be paid in kind rather than in coin.[18] The change from a monetary system to one based upon agricultural production would have aggravated the pre-existing economic instability and so ensured that many individuals became disenchanted with Roman rule.

To exacerbate further feelings of unhappiness, many of the larger landowners – including some of the richest people in the empire – were exempted from the payment of many of the taxes. It would have been galling for the poorer members of society to note that the rich avoided having to pay taxes. Even where they did have to pay, the taxes were not progressive: the rich paid the same amount as the poor, leading to a further increase in the sense of disenfranchisement amongst the lower and middle classes.

Yet despite these difficulties, the empire continued to survive. This was thanks largely to the fact that a proportion of the state's income came from public lands. These lands, either deserted thanks to the passage of war or confiscated from 'traitors' and pagan temples, or lying intestate or unexploited, were appropriated by the state and leased out by bailiffs to peasants, so ensuring a slow, steady trickle of money into the imperial coffers.[19]

This money was supplemented by taxes on mines, quarries and on the mints themselves, but these provided only a limited amount of revenue. As a result, the empire was forced to rely on the taxation of the poor and the middle classes, and only attempted to coerce the senatorial aristocracy to provide funds at times of dire emergency, as will be seen during the course of this book.

The Citizens

It is possible to see the later empire as one in which the divisions within society contributed to the fall of the West. Over time the rich became wealthier. This was partly because many farmers were forced to sell their lands or their service to the rich to fulfil their tax obligations. Consequently, the rich greatly increased their holdings and wealth whilst many of the poorer people were forced into poverty and entered a patron–client arrangement with local political or military officials. The officials came to be given the name *potentes* to distinguish them from their clients. The net result of these developments was the creation of a 'submerged economy' and 'the formation of social groups no longer in contact with the state'.[20]

Where the more powerful individuals also lost faith in the empire, or where service was deemed worthless, they turned to the church. This is the period during which the church cemented its position of authority and also copied the administrative structure of the empire, an organization that exists to this day. The civilian bureaucracy (*militia officialis*) and the army (*militia armata*) were joined by the (*militia Christi*) 'soldiers of Christ'.[21] Although this helped the church to prosper and grow, the result was a loss of manpower to both the bureaucratic and military arms of the empire. Individuals wishing to evade their responsibility as functionaries of the state instead joined the clergy, sometimes as bishops and men of great ecclesiastical and political power, but where these options were not available simply as monks.[22]

There were two main outcomes to these changes. One was that the wealthy came to hold power greatly disproportionate to their numbers. Once ensconced in their position, these same men tended to use their influence to protect their own interests rather than those of the state. An example of their influence may be seen in the repeated elevation of usurpers in outlying provinces to the role of 'emperor'.

Linked to this change is the fact that over a long period of time there was a transfer of loyalty. In the earlier empire bonds of loyalty had run from the poor to the wealthy to the aristocracy and finally to the emperor. In the late third and early fourth centuries many of the wealthy and the aristocracy entered the church.

The bonds then ran from the poor to the wealthy to the church. The emperor was eliminated from the equation and loyalties reverted from the abstract empire to the more concrete person of the local bishop. The church replaced the empire as the focus of people's lives.

At the opposite end of the spectrum is the rise of the *bacaudae* – by the fifth century the term *bacaudae*, rather than usurpation, was used for any uprising against the empire where there was no leader aiming at becoming emperor – in the West. The origin and nature of the *bacaudae* remains unclear, but it would seem that when it began the phenomenon was mainly one of armed 'uprisings' by peasants in the less-Romanized areas of Gaul and Spain. The movement may have been enlarged, if not started, as a result of poorer peasants taking up arms to protect themselves and/ or survive. The first uprising under the name *bacaudae* was c.283–284, when Gallic peasants rebelled against their treatment.[23]

The main cause of unrest may have been the laws that tied people to their places of residence and jobs.[24] In Gaul there was another reason for dissatisfaction. In the early fifth century the Praetorian Prefect moved from Trier in the north to Arles in the south. The move alienated a large part of northern Gaul and all of Britain, since it reinforced the concept that the emperor and his court were more concerned with the core of the empire and that those provinces on the northern periphery would, as a consequence, be neglected.[25] Furthermore, the emperor moved his court from Milan, where it was easily accessible from Gaul, to Ravenna, where access from northern Gaul and Britain was poor. The move helped to alienate the indigenous aristocracy of the north west of the empire who were already tempted to join the church rather than serve the empire.

The result of unpopular laws, civil wars, movements of political centres and barbarian invasions, was a tendency for the poor and unprotected to begin to cluster more tightly to the heads of their families, and they in turn to their aristocratic master or to the local warlord.[26] As a result, it is logical to assume that the *bacaudae* were uprisings where the local inhabitants, probably including members of the local lower aristocracy, decided to secede from the empire and follow their own path, much as the British had done during the earlier reign of Honorius.[27]

As the empire slowly began to withdraw its influence from the northern borders, the Germanic tribes slowly began to increase theirs. The Franks, for example, were beginning the gradual widening of their influence over northern Gaul, yet for the most part this was a very gradual process and the full effects would not be felt until some time in the future.

CONCLUSION

During the course of the early-fifth century the empire in the west came under increasing pressure from three sources. Possibly the least of these was the risk of usurpations within the empire, since the loss of Britain, the major source of usurping generals, greatly reduced the threat. The second was that barbarians both inside and outside the empire no longer took part in raids simply for financial gain. Instead, their leaders were intent on gaining land and prestige within the empire. In hindsight, this was the greatest threat to the survival of the west. Finally, there was the growing danger of large parts of the west seceding from the empire and following their own courses. The loss of Britain in this way provided a model for secessionists, but Britain had never been vital to the security of the empire: Africa, Gaul and Spain were.

Chapter 2

Aetius the Hostage*

STILICHO

In 394 Theodosius I won the Battle of the Frigidus and re-united the empire. Following Theodosius' death in 395 Stilicho took control of the West. He disbanded the *foederati* ('foreign' troops, especially Goths: see Chapter 4) who had fought for Theodosius at the battle. Feeling that their services deserved more reward, almost immediately these troops rebelled under the leadership of Alaric. Alaric and the Goths would remain free agents for the remainder of Stilicho's rule.

After twice fighting Stilicho, Alaric took service with the East, being given the post of *magister militum per Illyricum*. However, feeling that he was becoming politically isolated, in 401 Alaric invaded Italy. After laying siege to Aquileia and Milan, Alaric attempted to cross the Alps into Gaul. Before he could do so he was caught outside Pollentia and narrowly defeated by Stilicho. Alaric agreed to a peace treaty and retreated across the north of Italy towards Illyricum. When in the neighbourhood of Verona Alaric made one last attempt to cross the Alps and reach softer targets further in the west. Stilicho acted quickly and this time Alaric was defeated more heavily. With many of his men defecting and joining Stilicho, Alaric was forced to resume his march to Illyricum, finally being settled in the West's portion of the diocese in a minor military post.

Illyricum

In 404 Stilicho, who from the start had wanted to be guardian for Arcadius in the East, was forced to accept that this would never happen. Instead, he sent envoys to Constantinople with the lesser claim that Theodosius was planning to return the whole of the prefecture of Illyricum to the West before he died.[1] Needless to say, this damaged East–West relations.

As relations deteriorated, Stilicho began to make plans for the forcible annexation of Illyricum. Part of these plans involved using Alaric's forces to help in the invasion. There followed negotiations between Stilicho and Alaric concerning the possible invasion. Obviously, Stilicho wanted to be sure that once Alaric was in Illyricum he would not simply devastate the prefecture on his own initiative, claiming that he was acting under orders from Stilicho. Conversely, Alaric wanted to ensure that this was not simply a plan by Stilicho to get rid of Alaric. After all, once Alaric had invaded Illyricum, Stilicho could easily announce that Alaric was a traitor and that the invasion was nothing to do with the west.

---

* It is recommended that this chapter be read in conjunction with the Chronology to aid understanding.

It would appear that agreement was reached, and to secure the arrangements hostages were exchanged. The names of the hostages given by Alaric are unknown, but Alaric specifically demanded that he was given Jason, son of Jovius (an extremely powerful individual, as will be seen), and Aetius, who was probably in his mid teens.[2]

The taking of hostages now has an extremely negative association. Modern-day hostages are taken against their will and held to ransom, usually for either money or for political gain. In the ancient world the exchange of hostages was a standard method of demonstrating that the two parties were in full accord and that they were intent on keeping to the agreements made. As a result, it was expected that hostages were individuals of rank and distinction, demonstrating the two parties' faith in each other. That Aetius was asked for by name reveals that Gaudentius, like Jovius, was a highly respected and powerful individual within Stilicho's private circle.

For the Romans, the taking of hostages in such matters was an extremely important factor in 'international' relations. Rome expected to receive important hostages, and especially the sons and heirs of the leading men within the opposition forces. In this way the Romans hoped to be able to impress and educate the next generation of barbarian leaders in the superiority of Rome, so making political allies for the future.

Radagaisus

Over the winter of 405–406 the two armies prepared for an invasion that did not happen. In late 405 the Goth Radagaisus led a large number of people – allegedly 400,000 – over the Alps into Italy.[3] The empire was paralyzed with fear, and for a time Stilicho remained with the troops at Ticinum.[4] Once in Italy, Radagaisus divided his forces into three. When the campaign season of 406 began Stilicho moved against him.[5] Taken by surprise, Radagaisus was forced to retreat to the heights around Faesulae, where he was captured and executed. The other two groups were quickly defeated and the remnants driven out of Italy.

Stilicho returned to his plan for an attack upon Illyricum. He promoted Alaric to the post of *magister militum per Illyricum*, and Jovius, of whom little is known prior to this, was made *praefectus praetoriano Illyrici* and sent to join Alaric. In early 407 Stilicho ordered Alaric to march to Epirus before awaiting the arrival of Stilicho with troops from the Italian army.[6] The plan was for the combined force to annex the whole of the prefecture of Illyricum for the West. Aetius doubtless accompanied Alaric, but Stilicho would never join the invasion.

Before he could set sail Stilicho received a letter from Honorius forbidding him to go.[7] Not only was Honorius unhappy with the concept of invading the East, but there had been a new development in the west: barbarians had crossed the Rhine into Gaul.[8]

The Invasion of Gaul[9]

On the last day of 406 a large number of barbarians crossed the Rhine frontier into Gaul. They consisted of Asding Vandals under Godigisel, Alans under two 'kings', Respendial and Goa, and a separate group of Siling Vandals and Sueves. Goa the

Alan immediately offered his services to the Romans and, along with the people he led, appears to have crossed into the empire unhindered. He is later attested as serving Aetius.[10] After a battle against the Franks the main body of the barbarians crossed the frontier and the news of the invasion was sent to Honorius. Once he received it, he immediately ordered the invasion of Illyricum to be cancelled.

The British Revolt

Unknown to Stilicho and Honorius, towards the end of 406 the British had revolted and elected a man called Marcus to be the new emperor.[11] He was quickly assassinated and his place taken by Gratian, a British native.[12] The news of the invasion of Gaul reached Britain early in the new year.[13] When it was realized that Gratian was not going to act he was replaced by Flavius Claudius Constantinus, better known as Constantine III.[14]

Meanwhile, the Vandals, Alans and Sueves attacked the cities of northern Gaul.[15] Constantine quickly collected an army together and crossed to Gaul, landing at Bononia (Boulogne). He sent his newly appointed generals, Nebiogast and Justinian, to secure Lyon, the capital of the Gallic prefecture. His troops ignored the barbarian invaders. However, shortly after the capture of Lyon, Constantine opened negotiations with the barbarians.[16] By a combination of force and diplomacy Constantine brought the invaders under control and used them to swell his own ranks.[17] To make matters worse for Stilicho, Spain also recognized Constantine.[18]

The Fall of Stilicho

News of Constantine's landing caused a crisis and Stilicho now had no option but to cancel the proposed campaign in Illyricum.[19] He ordered the Roman troops to move from the east coast of Italy to Pavia, yet by the time the army had been moved it was too late in the year (407) to take any action. In the meantime, Alaric returned to the western-controlled part of Illyricum and demanded 4,000 pounds of gold to pay for his troops' invasion of Epirus.

Constantine sent envoys asking to be made a colleague of Honorius, a move that was rejected. Instead, early in 408 the Goth Sarus was given a small army by Stilicho and attacked Constantine, defeating Constantine's forces and killing Justinian and later Nebiogast before besieging Constantine in Valence. However, new forces from northern Gaul arrived to support Constantine and Sarus fled back over the Alps.

It was now clear that a major expedition was needed to defeat Constantine. Over the protests of the Senate, Stilicho appointed Alaric to command in Gaul, despite the fact that the Senate had only just been forced to give in to Alaric's demands for 4,000 pounds of gold. The move alienated many to Stilicho's domination and opposition began to mount to his control.

At this point news arrived that Emperor Arcadius had died in Constantinople. Although Honorius wanted to go to Constantinople to supervise the care of the new emperor, his nephew Theodosius II, Stilicho intervened and declared that he would go himself. Tensions mounted, but for unknown reasons Stilicho remained stationary in Italy.

Finally, in mid August 408, as the emperor inspected the troops in Pavia prior to the Gallic expedition, Olympius, Honorius' *magister scrinii* (master of the imperial secretaries), instigated a mutiny of the army. Many leading men of Stilicho's regime were seized and killed, and the emperor himself feared for his life.

News of the mutiny was quickly carried to Stilicho, who at this time was in Bononia. He fled to Ravenna, and Olympius, who was now master of the emperor, ordered the troops in Ravenna to put Stilicho under house arrest. When news reached Stilicho of his impending arrest he sought sanctuary in a church. At day-break on 22 August 408 the soldiers, led by one Heraclianus, entered the church and swore an oath before the bishop that they had been ordered by the emperor not to kill but to arrest Stilicho.[20] Once Stilicho was out of the church, however, Heraclianus

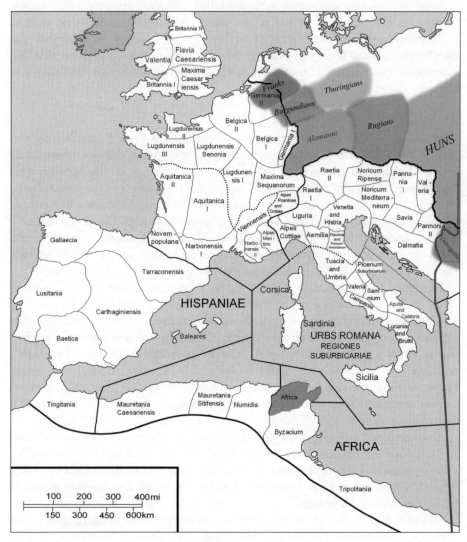

Map 2. The Western Empire c.408

produced a second letter condemning him to death for his 'crimes against the state'.[21] At this point Stilicho's servants and loyal federates made to rescue him from execution, but Stilicho stopped them with 'terrible threats and submitted his neck to the sword'.[22] On his death, chaos and anarchy broke out in Italy.

AFTER STILICHO

Resentful of Stilicho's employment of barbarian troops and of their loss of prestige, the regular Roman army in Italy turned upon the federates. However, the barbarian troops were not at hand, so in an orgy of bloodlust the Romans killed or enslaved the families of the allied troops.[23] This was a huge mistake, since the federates immediately joined their forces to Alaric.

Some of Stilicho's supporters were also killed, but such executions only appear to have been at the start of the revolt: many of Stilicho's supporters, such as Constantius, survived and later rose to high rank. Amongst the survivors was Gaudentius, although why he was spared is unknown. The suggestion that this was due to the influence of his rich and possibly powerful wife is a possibility, but remains conjecture.

ALARIC

With his new reinforcements Alaric was once again in a position to invade Italy, this time without Stilicho to oppose him. Surprisingly, Alaric did not immediately invade Italy, instead releasing the hostages he had been given in 405. Aetius and his fellows were allowed to return home. There followed a series of embassies between Alaric and Honorius. As part of the negotiations Alaric asked for a new exchange of hostages, specifically that Aetius be one of those given to him. Honorius refused.[24] At an unknown date, but probably between 408 and 410, Aetius was sent to the Huns as a hostage, almost certainly as part of an agreement to ensure that the Huns did not invade the West during the period when Alaric was at large in Italy.[25]

Frustrated by Honorius' refusal, Alaric once again invaded Italy.[26] Without an active leader, the Roman army was powerless to resist. Realizing that Honorius in Ravenna was safe, Alaric laid siege to Rome. When the citizens of Rome agreed to support his demands Alaric raised the siege. Olympius fled into exile and his place was taken by Jovius, who now began negotiations in an attempt to prevent war,[27] reaching an agreement with Alaric.[28] However, when the proposal was put to Honorius, the emperor refused to ratify any of it, declaring that he would never have a Goth as *magister militum*.[29] Alaric immediately made a more moderate offer, but again Honorius rejected it.[30]

Alaric returned to Rome and in 409 placed the city under siege for a second time. In December 409 he persuaded the *praefectus urbis Romae*, Attalus, to become his puppet emperor. It is probable that it was at this time that Galla Placidia was taken captive by the Goths, as it was only now that she is mentioned by Zosimus as being a hostage of Alaric, not before.[31]

Emperor Attalus and Alaric moved to Ariminum, from where they hoped to put pressure on Honorius. Talks began, but at this vital moment 4,000 troops arrived from Constantinople to help Honorius. Gaining confidence from their unexpected arrival, Honorius stood firm and the talks broke down.[32]

In summer 410 Alaric deposed Attalus in the hope that the concession would encourage further negotiations, and was advancing towards Ravenna in preparation for the opening of talks when he was unexpectedly attacked by Sarus.[33] Although victorious, Alaric saw the attack as being ordered by Honorius. Furious, Alaric returned to Rome, and on 24 August 410 his troops were allowed to enter the city at the Salarian Gate: for the first time in 800 years, the Eternal City was sacked by barbarians.[34] The event shocked the Roman world and doubtless when the news reached him Aetius was just as appalled.

After the sack Alaric marched his troops south and began to gather ships for an attempt to attack and conquer Africa. Unfortunately for Alaric, storms destroyed the fleet he had gathered. At this point he became ill with an unknown disease and died. His successor was his brother-in-law, Athaulf.

GAUL, SPAIN AND CONSTANTIUS

Whilst this was happening in Italy, in 409 Constantine III's new *magister militum* Gerontius had rebelled and proclaimed a man named Maximus as emperor.[35] As support for his new regime was poor in Spain, Gerontius decided to employ the barbarians currently in Gaul. After devastating Gaul, in early autumn 409 the Vandals, Alans and Sueves crossed the Pyrenees and entered Spain to serve with Gerontius.[36] They were allocated land by Gerontius, deciding which tribe received which area by the means of lots when they could not reach an amicable agreement.[37] The Asding Vandals received the southern parts of the province of Gallaecia while the Sueves took 'that part of Gallaecia which is situated on the very edge of the western ocean';[38] the Siling Vandals were granted lands in Baetica; the Alans received territory in Lusitania. Gerontius himself retained Tarraconensis and Carthaginiensis.

In 411 the remainder of the Spaniards 'in the cities and forts surrendered themselves'.[39] Finally assured of his position in Spain, and with the barbarians overcoming local opposition to their settlement, Gerontius attacked Constantine in Gaul. He quickly defeated Constantine's forces and killed Constantine's son Constans at Vienne, after which he placed Constantine under siege in Arles.

CONSTANTIUS III

Unfortunately for Gerontius, Honorius had finally appointed a new *magister militum*, an energetic and capable soldier by the name of Constantius, who had been a supporter of Stilicho. Constantius took an army across the Alps and advanced on Arles. Gerontius' Spanish troops deserted him and he fled back to Spain, where shortly afterwards his troops mutinied – no doubt unhappy with his settlement of the barbarians in Spain – and he was executed. In the meantime, Constantius continued the siege of Arles. Eventually, the city surrendered, and Constantine III was arrested and beheaded. The military exploits of Constantius triggered a new feeling of optimism in Rome, as evidenced by the list of buildings repaired in Rome after the sack of the Goths. The sense of renewal was echoed by Olympiodorus, whose history reveals a story of decline and renewal between 407 and 425.[40]

BRITAIN

When Constantine III had crossed from Britain to Gaul the inhabitants of Britain would have been hoping for the renewal of a strong empire under the dynamic leadership of a British-nominated emperor. They were to be quickly disillusioned. After rapidly advancing to the south of Gaul, Constantine's rule stagnated, even allowing his own *magister militum*, Gerontius, to rebel. As events in Gaul deteriorated into total confusion, with usurper replacing usurper, Britain came under pressure from external threats, especially from the Saxons across the North Sea.[41] Unable to obtain help from the continent, the British finally gave up hope and decided to defend themselves. At some point between the years 408 and 411 Britain left the empire for the last time.[42]

ATHAULF AND WALLIA

Athaulf, the new leader of the Goths after Alaric's death, remained in Italy during 411. In 412 he led his forces into Gaul, taking with them the emperor's sister Galla Placidia, and declared his support for yet another usurper called Jovinus. However, Jovinus and Athaulf quickly fell out. Reaching agreement with Honorius, Athaulf attacked and captured Jovinus, who was quickly beheaded. Despite this, Athaulf could not count on Honorius' full support, since the Romans did not keep their side of the agreement, mainly because Galla Placidia remained a Gothic captive. Consequently, Constantius began to put military pressure on the Goths. Notwithstanding this, in January 414 Athaulf married Galla Placidia.[43] She quickly bore him a son named Theodosius. Unfortunately, Theodosius died soon after, and Athaulf himself was assassinated in 415.

Athaulf was succeeded by Sarus' brother Sigeric, who humiliated Galla Placidia by making her walk in front of his horse. Fortunately for her, he was assassinated after a rule of only seven days and the new king, Wallia, soon came to an agreement with Honorius and Galla Placidia returned to Italy – where she was forced to marry Constantius, despite the fact that she loathed him intensely. As part of the agreement the Goths were ordered to attack the Vandals in Spain, the date of the attack probably being 416.[44]

SPAIN

The attack came as a complete surprise. Earlier, probably in 411, the Vandals, Alans and Sueves appear to have reached an agreement with Honorius, although the accuracy and dating of this claim is still a matter of debate.[45] Since that time, the barbarians in Spain appear to have remained peaceful.[46] However, they were still harbouring the usurper Maximus, who, following the defeat of Gerontius, had fled to them for safety, and since then they would appear to have refused to return him to the empire.[47]

In 416 Wallia led the Goths against the Vandals in a campaign the Goths completed to great effect. The huge losses suffered by the Vandals appear to have been enough to convince Constantius to order the Goths to withdraw. It was now clear that, having lost so much of his potential support, Maximus was no longer a threat, and it is probable that Constantius was worried that a complete elimination of the Vandals would encourage Wallia to abandon the new treaty and instead attempt to take the place of the Vandals in Spain. On their return, in 418 or 419, the Goths were allowed to settle in Aquitania in Gaul.[48] Their long wanderings were finally over. Unfortunately for Wallia, he died shortly afterwards and was succeeded by Theoderic.[49] Either before his elevation, or more likely shortly afterwards, in an attempt to cement his position, Theoderic married Alaric's daughter.[50]

THE SETTLEMENT OF THE VISIGOTHIC KINGDOM

The treaty by which the Visigoths were settled in Aquitania in 418 has been the subject of much debate. The argument is based upon the ambiguous phrasing used in the sources, which can be interpreted to either mean that the Visigoths were allocated money and treated as soldiers or that they were granted land and its associated revenues.[51] However, it is probably best to follow Philostorgius and accept that the Visigoths were granted land to farm in return for supplying troops when required.[52] It is unlikely that they were individually allocated land by the Roman bureaucracy, although this remains a possibility. It is more likely that the Goths simply moved in and took land in different regions depending upon local conditions.[53]

The concept that the Visigoths were granted land is reinforced by a review of the personalities involved in the treaty. Wallia was the leader of a large group of people who had been harassed out of Italy and forced, usually on the verge of starvation, along the southern coast of Gaul before being compelled to fight in Spain for the empire. There can be little doubt that, shortly before his death, the offer of land to farm for his people would have been accepted with a minimum of hesitation. On the other hand, the *magister militum* Constantius (later Emperor Constantius III) had been a follower of Stilicho. Constantius had taken a leading role in having Olympius killed for his actions in inciting the mutiny against Stilicho.[54] It is likely that Constantius used both Stilicho and the Emperor Theodosius I as his military and political role models. As a result, Constantius followed the example set by Theodosius, settling the Visigoths in Gaul and imposing similar terms as Theodosius had applied in 382. Due to the hardships of their years fighting against Rome it is clear that the Goths were in poor condition, since they seem to have been given a tax exemption in order to help them recover after the initial settlement.[55]

The decision to settle the Goths in Gaul may seem strange, given that Stilicho had taken great pains to keep them out of the trans-Alpine region. Yet it simply reflected political and strategic reality. At no point could the Romans have evicted the Goths from Gaul and forced them to return east. The Romans did not have the surplus manpower for a campaign carried out in the teeth of fierce Gothic opposition: after their long suffering, the Goths would have resisted to their utmost any attempt to return them to their starting point in Illyricum. Furthermore, since the battles against Alaric in 402, conditions had changed in Gaul. By settling the Visigoths in Aquitania Constantine could set them to guard against any attempt by the Vandals, Alans or Sueves to re-enter Gaul from Spain. Moreover, they were now perfectly placed for campaigns against the barbarians in Spain, as well as against insurgents, usurpers or *bacaudae* in Gaul itself.[56]

It also seems certain that the Roman government did not expect the Visigoths to remain independent for long. The fact that the Roman administrative system continued to function normally implies that the Visigoths were perceived as a 'friendly and obedient force' on Roman territory.[57] However, at least in part this was due to the fact that the Germanic peoples entering Roman territory had no political agenda of their own and no ideology that they wished to impose. As such, they found it 'most advantageous and profitable to work closely within the well-established and sophisticated structures of Roman life'.[58]

It is common to find modern historians criticizing Theodosius, Constantius and their successors for their policy concerning the settlement of barbarians on Roman soil. The main problem that is addressed is that the new settlements, unlike those of earlier centuries, retained their political leaders, rather than being settled on Roman terms under Roman supervision and governed by Roman prefects.[59] This was the major flaw in the Roman plan: although the Visigoths were settled on land according to Roman terms, they remained a people apart with their own leader. Additionally, their new king, Theoderic, was only recently crowned and needed to boost his own standing with his followers if he was to strengthen his hold upon his people. Although it is likely that Constantius believed that he could weaken the Visigoths politically and militarily over time, he was not to be allowed that time to fulfil his plans.

The other criticism of these settlements is due to the loss of revenue from the settled areas to a government whose coffers were already rapidly shrinking.[60] With the settlement of the Goths these complaints reach their apogee. Unlike earlier (and later) settlements, the treaty with the Goths appears to have placed two-thirds of the income of the forfeited territory into their hands, leaving only one-third in the hands of the Romans.[61] Usually, only one-third of the income was granted to the settled barbarians, following the traditional Roman method of quartering soldiers on the owners of land, known as *hospitalitas*.

Although interpreted in a negative light, there is some validation for Constantius' policy. Firstly, and possibly of foremost importance, the Goths were transformed from enemies into friends. This allowed Constantius to withdraw troops facing the Goths to fight in other theatres. As a result, he was not compelled to begin either a new recruiting drive or to allocate funds to pay for troops to garrison areas facing the Goths. This saving in part negated the extra cost of allowing the Goths to settle in Aquitaine. Secondly, the great majority of the taxes collected were used to pay for the army. In theory, the Goths were now part of the army, and as such were simply receiving their pay as usual. The loss of revenue needed to pay the army was in effect being used to pay the 'army'. Thirdly, there were huge problems with tax collecting, with many landowners being members of the aristocracy, who were immune from some aspects of taxation. Although the number of individual aristocrats who owned land in Aquitaine may have been small, the settlement in effect transferred them from being immune from tax to being tax payers. Finally, as will be seen in Chapter 6, the consequences of the civil wars fought by Theodosius I against western usurpers and the continuous warfare following the 'rebellion' of Alaric and the crossing of the Rhine in 406 were huge. Analysis has revealed that between the accession of Theodosius in the East and the compilation of the *Notitia Dignitatum* (dating to c.420) in the West, about half of the Western field army had been lost.[62] Constantius needed to end the wars against the Goths as otherwise the army could easily enter a process of rapid collapse. Furthermore, by bringing the Goths within the structure of the army, he would help to alleviate the problems of manpower shortage and, hopefully, be given time in which to recruit and rebuild.

Finally, the settlement would give respite to the war-weary provinces of Gaul and allow them the time they needed to recover, although the concept that the settlement allowed 'normal life to resume its course, though under new masters' may be a little too optimistic.[63] Following the treaty of 418/419 a degree of stability again appeared in the West, despite the tremendous losses previously suffered.[64] Further, the sparse written record demonstrates that in many cases the local 'Roman' aristocracy benefited from the change, since their new masters settled in Toulouse and so gave them readier access to influence and power than was available under the Italo-centric empire.[65] There can also be little doubt that for some the settlement was simply a change of masters, with Gothic landowners taking the place of imperial tax collectors. Yet for many – and especially those on the borders, where both small-scale and large-scale warfare continued – the settlement was a further blow to their dwindling prosperity.

As a consequence, despite the fact that the settlement should probably still be seen as detrimental to the affairs of the empire, at the time the benefits may have been seen as outweighing the shortcomings. In fact, the adoption of the policy of creating *foederati* out of the invaders may have been the main reason why the West survived the invasions and civil wars of the early-fifth century.[66] It is largely with the benefit of hindsight, and the knowledge of what ramifications the policy would have in the long term, that the negative aspects of Constantius' decision can be seen as outweighing the positives.

SPAIN

The attack by the Goths had seriously weakened the Siling Vandals and the Alans. As a result, they decided to leave their territories and place themselves under the command of Gunderic, the king of the Asding Vandals.[67] At an unknown point in time the king of the now-combined Vandals and Alans took the title 'King of the Vandals and the Alans', a title later attested to Gelimer due to a silver *missorum* with the legend *Gailamir Rex Vandalorum et Alanorum*. As Gelimer ruled from 530 to 534, this illustrates that the Alans kept a separate identity within the Vandal kingdom.[68] Yet these are not the only peoples who joined forces under Gunderic. According to Possidius, 'There were Vandals and Alans, mixed with one of the Gothic peoples, and individuals of various nations'.[69] Without realizing it, the Roman plan to weaken the Vandals and Alans instead resulted in their coalescing to form a new Vandal 'supergroup' that could rival that of the Goths themselves.[70]

Gunderic's new 'alliance' was far more powerful than the army he had previously commanded. In 419 he led his troops against the Sueves and besieged them 'in *Nerbasis montibus*' (the Erbasian Mountains).[71] It is possible that Gunderic was attempting to force the Sueves to join with his forces, so making him undisputedly the strongest military leader in Spain.[72] Unfortunately for him, a Roman relief force under Astyrius, *comes Hispaniarum*, broke the siege and foiled Gunderic's ambition.[73] Shortly after this, as a reward for his services both before and after this campaign, Astyrius was made *patricius*. This was not the end of the matter, as the Vandals retreated south, and Maurocellus, the Spanish *vicarius*, only escaped from Bracara after the loss of some of his men.[74] The new Vandal army was at war with Rome and remained a major threat to the security of Spain. They were now set on finding new territories, since the conflict at Bracara is the first sign of them expanding their influence towards the south of Spain.

THE HUNS

Aetius was probably not fully aware of the complex military and political manoeuvring being carried on during this period of extreme confusion, since for most – if not all – of the time he was a hostage with the Huns.[75]

It is extremely difficult to draw a clear picture of the nature of the Huns at this time. The sources are very vague and where information is given it is often used to provide an overarching view of Hunnic rule that is contradicted by other sources.[76] For example, due to events later in Aetius' career, it is often assumed that the king of the Huns at this time was Rua. Unfortunately, this association is far from secure, as Rua is not attested as king of the Huns until 424.[77] It is more likely that Aetius was sent to the Hun king Uldin, who at around this time dominated the Danube frontier. Uldin had invaded Thrace in 405 and had helped in the defeat of Radagaisus in 406.[78] In 408 Uldin had invaded Thrace again. Unfortunately for him, on this occasion the Romans had used 'promises and bribes' to cause many of his followers to abandon him.[79] It is almost certain that it was Uldin who secured Aetius as a hostage following this 'defeat'. An exchange of hostages after negotiations would on one side allow Uldin to save face and on the other help to guarantee that he would not attack the empire again. This was especially important during the years from 408, when Italy was under extreme pressure from the Goths (under Alaric and later Athaulf) and from the usurper Constantine III in Gaul.

Yet it is clear that although Uldin was pre-eminent in the region of the Danube, he was not a supremely powerful sole leader of the Huns: there are many examples of Hunnic forces taking service with the Romans, and to a large degree they appear to have followed the 'traditional' barbarian practice of following strong leaders until they felt that these were no longer serving their own best interests, after which they defected and served somebody else.[80]

GOTHIC AND HUNNIC INFLUENCES ON AETIUS

There is very little evidence for the nature and appearance of Aetius except for what can be deduced from the sources. However, Gregory of Tours, quoting Renatus Frigidus, actually describes Aetius:

> Aetius was of medium height, manly in his habits and well-proportioned. He had no bodily infirmity and was spare in physique. His intelligence was keen, he was full of energy, a superb horseman, a fine shot with an arrow and tireless with the lance (*contu inpiger*). He was extremely able as a soldier and he was skilled in the arts of peace. There was no avarice in him and even less cupidity. He was magnanimous in his behaviour and never swayed in his judgement by the advice of unworthy counsellors. He bore adversity with great patience, was ready for any exacting enterprise, he scorned danger and was able to endure hunger, thirst and loss of sleep.
>
> *Greg. Tur. 2.8*

It is almost certain that his skill as a horseman and at archery was picked up whilst with the Huns. Yet what is more notable is that during his time amongst the Goths and Huns, Aetius missed the major confrontations between Stilicho and his enemies. He also missed the campaigns fought by Constantius against both usurpers and Goths in Gaul. It is interesting to note that Stilicho and Constantius III displayed a preference for the strategy of manoeuvre and blockade to that of direct military confrontation. In this they followed the habits of the later imperial army, recognizing that a defeat would drastically reduce the manpower available to the army. By contrast Aetius, being exposed for a long period to the slightly more aggressive Goths and the far more aggressive Huns, may have learned far more adventurous strategies and tactics from his barbarian mentors.

Furthermore, by being removed from the court and army at an early age, Aetius was less susceptible to the traditional Roman ethos of relying largely on the Roman army for defence. His time amongst the barbarians may have taught him that, far from being inferior to the Romans, these people were at least the equivalent of their 'cultural superiors' within the empire. Far more importantly for his near future, his time amongst the Huns allowed him to build personal relationships and alliances that would help him in the years to come.

Yet in the long term, and possibly of equal importance to his absorption of the 'barbarian' willingness to fight, Aetius' time amongst the Goths and Huns would result in him being able to speak at least a little Gothic and Hunnic.[81] When it came to later negotiations with Huns and Goths, both on the diplomatic side as well as with negotiations with *foederati*, Aetius would not have need of an interpreter. It is likely that such linguistic skills would have impressed opposition ambassadors and spokesmen.

AETIUS RETURNS HOME

There is absolutely no indication in the sources as to the date when Aetius was released from his time as a hostage to the Huns. Analyzing the sparse evidence, several possibilities emerge. For a very early date, it is possible that upon the death of Uldin Aetius returned to the empire. However, this would not allow Aetius time to build long-lasting, stable relationships amongst the Huns. It is far more likely that he remained a hostage after Uldin's death.

The difficulty here lies in the fragmentary nature of the history of the Huns. It is known that Uldin invaded Thrace in 408 and was forced to retire. It is also known that in 412 the king of the Huns was Charaton.[82] Unfortunately, we do not know whether Charaton was the successor to Uldin or a king of a completely different group of Huns in a different location.

Assuming that Charaton was the successor to Uldin, the latter must have died at some point between 409 and 412. It would follow that at this point Aetius remained as a hostage to secure the treaty first agreed with Uldin. In this way Aetius became known to the next generation of Huns, who were probably of around his own age. Included amongst these were Rua, Octar and Mundiuch, the brothers who were to lay the foundation of a genuine Hunnic empire under the control of one individual, Attila, son of Mundiuch.[83] Although conjecture, it is likely that Aetius remained with the Huns for a long time, at least until the death of Charaton, which dates most likely to the end of the 410s or possibly as late as the early 420s.

The extended stay would allow several years for him to forge strong personal relationships with the boys who would become the next generation of rulers. It is possible that Aetius was returned following the death of Charaton. After all, his contemporaries and friends Rua and Octar were now beginning their 'joint' rule. His presence was not needed, since the brothers had no intention of invading the west or of placing the court in Ravenna under pressure. Their greatest priority in the following years was to unite the Huns under their own leadership. After that, they would aim at Constantinople for glory. Details are few and unclear and there can be no certainty about the political circumstances surrounding the rise of Rua and Octar. However, from the limited evidence available it is possible that Rua took control of the Hunnic tribes facing the western empire whilst Octar took control of those facing the east.[84] Yet although it is possible that the death of Charaton was the reason for Aetius' return, there is one further major event that could have signalled the end of Aetius' time as a hostage to the Huns. This concerned the Emperor Honorius.

CONSTANTIUS III AND HONORIUS

On 1 January 417, prior to the settlement of the Goths in Aquitania in 418, the *magister militum* Constantius had married Galla Placidia, half-sister of Honorius.[85] They had two children, a daughter named Justa Grata Honoria – usually known simply as Honoria – and a son, Valentinian, who was born on 2 July 419.[86]

Constantius' rise now reached towards its apogee. In imitation of Stilicho, after his marriage Constantius received the title *parens principum* (first parent, parental guardian) in 420, and then on 8 February 421 he was appointed co-emperor with Honorius whilst Placidia was declared *Augusta* and their son Valentinian was declared *nobilissimus* (most noble).[87] Although no doubt an honour, Constantius soon regretted the elevation, since after he became emperor his movements were heavily circumscribed and he no longer had the freedom he had enjoyed as *magister militum*.[88] It is possible that this assertion was to affect the generals who came after him, since the vast majority of them had no wish to place themselves upon the throne, possibly due to the knowledge that once emperor they would be heavily tied down by bureaucratic red tape, so unable to lead the army in person and so risk losing the army's support.

Yet even aside from Constantius' own dismay, his elevation to emperor did not meet with universal approval: his elevation – along with those of Placidia and Valentinian – was not recognized by Theodosius II in the East.[89] Allegedly, Constantius was so angered by this refusal to recognize his rule that he began preparations for war with the East.[90] Unfortunately for him, but possibly fortunately for the empire, these came to nothing as he died on 2 September following a short illness after reigning for only six months. Following his death, relations between his widow Galla Placidia – who had been declared *Augusta* by Honorius and Constantius in 421 – and her half-brother the Emperor Honorius quickly deteriorated and she fled to Constantinople.[91]

Honorius himself was not to enjoy the pleasures of sole rule again for very long. On 15 August 423 he followed in his father's footsteps and died of oedema (dropsy).[92] The West now needed a new emperor. Of more importance to Aetius, the death of the emperor signalled the end of the treaty that Honorius had signed with the Huns. Although he may have returned to Ravenna prior to this (see above), it is almost certain that with the end of the treaty all of the hostages that had been exchanged with the Huns now returned home. Aetius headed for Ravenna.

GAUDENTIUS

The reunion of Aetius and Gaudentius was doubtless joyful. Aetius had spent several years with the Huns and, although his position as a hostage gave him a protected position and meant that he was unlikely to be harmed, there were still many other dangers that could have taken his life.

Whilst Aetius had been in the east, Gaudentius had remained in the west. Unfortunately, there is no mention of him in any of the sources. Everything about his life is completely unknown. Yet it is almost certain that he continued to serve both Constantius III and his successors as *magister militum* in a military capacity. Honorius had died without leaving any heirs. Gaudentius, and to a lesser degree Aetius, would now be in a position to influence events.

Chapter 3

Aetius Takes the Stage

CASTINUS, BONIFACE AND AETIUS

When Aetius returned to the court in Ravenna he found that politically the atmosphere was highly charged and the court divided into at least two camps. Earlier, in either 420 or 421, Honorius had appointed an individual by the name of Castinus to be the *comes domesticorum* ('Count of the Household').[1] In this position Castinus had led a campaign against the Franks.[2] Probably at the beginning of 422, after the death of Constantius III, Honorius had elevated Castinus to be a *dux*, before shortly afterwards making him *magister utriusque militiae* ('Master of all the Troops').

The elevation of Castinus was to have political consequences. Placidia, a very forceful woman, appears to have aimed at becoming the power behind Honorius. Brought up in the household of Stilicho and Serena, in all likelihood she aimed to emulate their political and military domination of Honorius as *parens principum*. On the other hand, women were usually subordinate to men in Roman society, and so any attempt by her to gain control of the court will have been resented by those men who would have expected to be in her place. She quickly came into opposition with Castinus, who as the *magister militum* saw himself as the natural heir to Stilicho and Constantius III.[3] The scene was set for a bitter rivalry. Although the advantage may have been with Castinus, since he controlled the army, Placidia was known to be ruthless: in 408, when Rome was being besieged by the Goths under Alaric, she had allegedly approved the Senate's decision to kill Serena, the adopted half-sister who had raised her. Sentiment was not a strong part of Placidia's personality.

In 422 Castinus was ordered to lead a campaign against the Vandals in Spain, being given a mixed force of Romans and Visigothic *foederati* (allies) from the new settlement in Aquitania.[4] In an unexpected turn of events, another Roman general was ordered to accompany him. Boniface had risen to fame as early as 413, when the Goths under Athaulf had attacked Marseilles during the conflict between Athaulf and Constantius III. During the attack Boniface had managed to wound Athaulf himself, a feat for which he was 'fêted by the citizens'.[5] Following this moment of fame Boniface successfully commanded troops in Africa in 417 and entered into correspondence with (Saint) Augustine, in the course of which Augustine allayed his Christian fears that fighting wars and killing was against God's will and would ensure 'eternal damnation'.[6]

The reasons for Boniface's appointment as the companion to Castinus in 422 are unknown. However, later in his career he was firmly loyal to Placidia, and it is likely

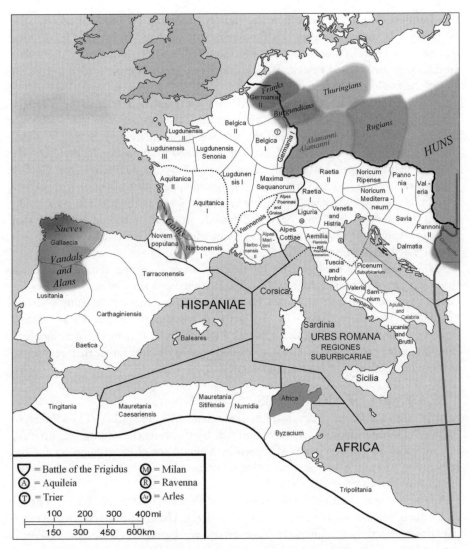

Map 3. The Western Empire c.423

that he was appointed upon advice by Placidia as a counterbalance to Castinus should he become too successful. Unfortunately, having two opposing commanders has never been an effective strategy, and things did not go according to plan. Even before the expedition had sailed for Spain Castinus and Boniface quarrelled.[7] The reasons are unclear and may relate to Castinus being unhappy at Boniface's appointment by Placidia. On the other hand, Prosper claims that it was because Boniface decided that following Castinus would be 'dangerous to himself and degrading'.[8] Whatever the cause, the argument was strong enough to make Boniface fear for his life – at that time Castinus was far more powerful than himself. The net result was that Boniface fled to Africa, which was rapidly becoming his personal power base, for safety.[9] At some time after this Boniface's wife died and in his grief he decided that he should enter a monastery. He was dissuaded from this and shortly after met a Gothic 'princess' named Pelagia, who, although an Arian, was persuaded to convert so that he could marry her.[10]

In the meantime, Castinus continued with the campaign against the Vandals. After initial successes, including the final capture of the usurper Maximus – who was later executed – he managed to pin the Vandals in one place and, having 'reduced them to starvation by siege so that they were prepared to surrender, he precipitously engaged them in open battle and, being betrayed by his auxiliaries [the Goths], suffered defeat and fled to Tarragona'.[11] It would appear that Castinus had become overconfident, possibly antagonizing his Gothic *foederati* in the process. As a result, the Goths deserted him and he was defeated, although it should be noted that Hydatius 'hated' the Goths, and so his statement that they deserted Castinus needs to be treated with some caution.[12]

Rather than taking the blame for the defeat, Castinus claimed that his failure was the result of a plot against him by Placidia, Boniface and the Goths.[13] Whether his claim was true or not is unknown but in the circumstances it remains a strong possibility. This is reinforced by the fact that when news of the defeat reached Ravenna, Honorius and Placidia quarrelled and Placidia fled to Constantinople.[14] Boniface, however, secure in Africa, remained loyal to Placidia rather than Honorius, and even helped her by sending her money.[15]

THE DEATH OF HONORIUS

Shortly afterwards, in August, Honorius died, like his father Theodosius of dropsy.[16] Despite the modern conviction that by this time the empire was divided, in contemporary society it was still seen as a single entity, even allowing for the convention of having two separate rulers, so the west waited for Theodosius II, emperor of the east, to make a decision regarding its rule.

Amongst those awaiting developments was the newly returned Aetius. Thanks to his long sojourn with both the Goths and the Huns, it is likely that Aetius' personal connections at court were fragmentary, and based largely upon the political connections of his father. As a result he was an unknown quantity to many. However, despite this, he was to be caught intimately in the events that were to follow.

At first Castinus appears to have wanted Theodosius to accept the role of sole emperor. This would have been an ideal situation, since in this event Castinus would become the effective ruler of the west. However, Placidia was haranguing Theodosius into accepting the rights of her son Valentinian, who was now four years old, to become the next emperor in Italy. Castinus heard of Placidia's attempts to promote Valentinian in Constantinople. If Valentinian was installed as emperor, Placidia would become the effective ruler in the west. Castinus had earlier claimed that Placidia had conspired with Boniface to bring him down. If Placidia rose to power, Castinus' future looked bleak.

There will have been many who supported Placidia in her attempt to restore the 'House of Theodosius'. Into this group fell Boniface, largely due to his apparent personal connections to Placidia. No doubt he, and others, also felt that they would profit from Placidia's gratitude when her son was set upon the throne. In fact, Boniface was to benefit from his support of Placidia almost instantly. Before deciding upon the identity of the new emperor, and possibly as a reward for his loyalty to Placidia, it would appear that Theodosius appointed Boniface *Comes Africae* (Count of Africa). It was now certain that Boniface would maintain his support for the Theodosian dynasty. Castinus would have been dismayed by Boniface's promotion in Africa, as it signalled that Theodosius was inclined to champion Placidia's claim for Valentinian by promoting her supporters in the west.

JOHN

Theodosius II failed to make a quick decision. Castinus decided to take a fateful step. As the *magister militum* Castinus was the senior military official in the West, and, emulating Western *magistri* of the past, he decided to act on his own initiative. On 20 November 423 he appointed John, the *Primicerius Notariorum* (Head of the Secretaries), as the new Emperor of the West.[17] Placidia's supporters no doubt fled from Rome and took refuge either in the East or on their own estates. Their places would be taken by loyal supporters of Castinus and John.

Castinus' part in John's claim of the throne is sometimes doubted. Yet although Castinus maintained a low profile throughout this period, and ensured that there was no direct link between himself and the elevation of John, there can be little doubt that, as *magister militum*, he had a major part in the appointment. Without his support, John, who was not the most senior civil servant in the West, would not have been crowned emperor. Furthermore, opposition from Castinus would certainly have resulted in the instant removal of John from power. With the tacit support of Castinus, John was crowned in Rome, before travelling to Ravenna.[18]

John's first act was to send an embassy to Constantinople in an attempt to gain recognition for his elevation. At the same time, the embassy was to propose Castinus as the West's nominee as consul for 424: the embassy failed.[19] Furthermore, the ambassadors were badly treated and exiled around the east.[20] It was clear that Theodosius was intent on removing John from power.

Exuperantius and Aetius

Before the reply from Constantinople arrived it is clear that John made several appointments to the senior positions of command in the West. Following his return from the Huns, Aetius had been thrust into the political turmoil surrounding the death of Honorius and the elevation of John. It is clear that he gave his support to John in opposition to Theodosius and Boniface. The reasons are unknown and open to speculation. However, there is one possibility that has remained unexplored.

As early as 399 Aetius' father Gaudentius is attested as being a *comes* in Africa.[21] Merobaudes notes that he was later made '*comitis a militibus in Galliis*' ('Count of the troops in Gaul'), possibly a poetic term for the post of *magister militum per Gallias*.[22]

However, Renatus Frigeridus claims that Gaudentius eventually became *magister equitum*.[23] Although the dating of these appointments is insecure, it is possible that they date to John's usurpation, and imply that both Gaudentius and Aetius joined in wholeheartedly with John's claim to the throne in 424. As reward for their support, Gaudentius was promoted to the post of *magister equitum* and sent to Gaul, almost certainly supplanting Boniface as the second in command to Castinus. Aetius was given the post of *cura palatii* ('Controller of the Palace').[24]

Unfortunately, although this hypothesis would explain much, there is no supporting evidence in the sources for it. On the other hand, no other reason is given for Aetius' support for John and the promotion of Gaudentius helps to explain the similar promotion of Aetius, and also explains why Aetius was so willing to support an unknown usurper.

There is one further detail that may support the appointment of Gaudentius as *magister equitum* during John's reign. Castinus was undoubtedly wary of the reaction to John's crowning in the West. He knew that if the East disagreed with John's appointment then there would almost certainly be a civil war. Unfortunately, the West was no longer strong enough militarily to oppose the East. Although again speculation, the appointment must have been approved by Castinus for a specific political reason. With Gaudentius as *magister equitum*, Castinus could transfer all responsibility for the appointment of John to Gaudentius' shoulders. In this way, if John won, Castinus would remain the senior general. If John lost, Castinus could claim that it was not his fault that John was elevated as emperor: instead, it was clearly simply a plot on the part of John and Gaudentius. In this way, although he could be implicated in John's appointment, he could avoid the full responsibility in the event of John losing.

At an unknown date Aetius married the daughter of a man named Carpilio. Otherwise unknown, Carpilio is attested as being *comes domesticorum* at some time in his career.[25] The couple had one son, named Carpilio after his maternal grandfather.[26] No date is given either for the elder Carpilio's holding of office or for the marriage. The only clue we have is that Gregory, quoting Frigeridus, dates the marriage to after Aetius' time as a hostage with the Huns.[27] The most obvious time was during the reign of John. Indeed, it is tempting to claim that Carpilio was another of John's appointees and that the marriage was an attempt to bind the 'conspirators' together and ensure their loyalty. However, there is no actual evidence to support this claim.

The only other appointment of which we can be certain is that of an individual named Exuperantius, who came from Poitiers in the centre of Gaul and was appointed as *Praefectus Praetorio per Galliarum* ('Praetorian Prefect of Gaul').[28] The promotion of a Gaul to the post may have been intended as an attempt to ensure Gallic loyalty, since it paved the way for further appointments of Gallic nobles to positions of power in the new regime.

Reaction to John's Appointment

Unfortunately for John, alongside these developments the continued animosity between Castinus and Boniface also had immediate repercussions. Unsurprisingly, in Africa Boniface refused to accept John's claim to be emperor. Declaring his loyalty to Theodosius, Placidia and the young Valentinian, Boniface immediately cut the supplies of grain from Africa to Italy.[29] This was bad news, especially for the citizens of Rome, as prolonged lack of supplies from Africa could easily lead to famine. There was now no doubt that there would be a civil war.

In a similar manner, in 398 Gildo, the commander in Africa, had rebelled against Stilicho and attempted to attach himself to the eastern emperor Arcadius. Stilicho had sent Gildo's brother Mascezel to Africa and in a lightning campaign Gildo had been defeated.[30] It would appear that John attempted the same sort of campaign, dispatching a picked force – including Huns – from Italy to recapture Africa.[31] However, the main effect of the campaign being sent to Africa was to leave John too weak to consider any further pre-emptive manoeuvres in Italy.[32] Instead, he was forced to remain on the defensive as soon as the expedition left.

In Gaul, John's attempt to curry favour by the appointment of Exuperantius failed. Although many will have been opposed to John's position as an usurper, John's decision to submit clerics to secular jurisdiction also caused offence, and may imply that he had 'Arian tendencies'.[33] Furthermore, Castinus' abortive campaign in Spain in 422 now caused further complications. The Visigoths under king Theoderic appear to have refused to support the new regime. Instead of supplying troops for Castinus, Theoderic appears to have seen the impending civil war as an opportunity to enlarge his dominions in Gaul. In the confusion the army in Gaul decided to mutiny and the troops in Arles, presumably declaring their loyalty to the Theodosian house, killed Exuperantius.[34] Furthermore, the Gallic Chronicler in the entry for 425 states that 'Count Gaudentius ... was killed by the soldiers in Gaul.' Although brief and possible to interpret in different ways, the account implies that Gaudentius had only recently been killed in a 'military uprising', and the most obvious reason for this is the Gallic 'rebellion' against John.[35] As an eastern 'foreigner' and a supporter of a regime that was clearly failing, Gaudentius was an obvious target for troops loyal to the House of Theodosius. No doubt the troops involved hoped that by killing Gaudentius they would gain favour with the soon-to-be-restored Theodosian imperial court. Unfortunately for John, he had no troops to spare to avenge either Exuperantius or Gaudentius, and he was forced to remain inactive.[36] It was now certain that there would be no help from the west for the army of Italy.

Boniface, Valentinian and Aetius

At some point in 424 the west's expedition to Africa set sail. Far from regaining Africa and giving John a military victory, the campaign ended in defeat, and one of the major outcomes was to ensure that the forces that John had at his disposal to face the upcoming war against Theodosius II were weak.[37] The other was to weaken military and political support for John's reign in the West.

Furthermore, Theodosius now confirmed his backing for Placidia and Valentinian. They were sent to Thessalonica and, reversing his decision in 421 to not accept Valentinian as *nobilissimus* and Placidia as *Augusta*, Theodosius officially invested

Valentinian as *Caesar* on 23 October 424.[38] As a further sign of the new-found concord between Theodosius and Placidia, Theodosius belatedly recognized the appointment of Constantius III as emperor of the west in 421, three years after the event, thus ensuring Valentinian's recognition as the son and heir of the deceased emperor.[39] To command the expedition against John, Theodosius appointed Ardabur, the eastern *magister utriusque militiae*, along with his son Aspar.[40] With them was Candidianus, possibly a fellow *magister militum* to Ardabur.[41]

Ardabur was an experienced and able commander. He had been in command of the East when war broke out between Rome and Persia in 421. He had led an extensive and successful campaign into Persian territory in 421 and in 422 had ambushed and killed seven Persian generals.[42]

In late 424, and in desperation, John turned to Aetius. Recognizing the need for large numbers of reliable troops, John ordered Aetius to go to the Huns with a large sum of gold in the hope that Aetius could obtain their support.[43] Aetius had faith in his relationships with the new Hunnic kings Rua and Octar, having grown up alongside them for many years. Further, his status as a high-ranking hostage with the Huns would result in Aetius being viewed as the representative of a legitimate government. If John had sent another envoy it is unlikely that this would have been a success, mainly due to the Huns not wishing to waste their time and manpower supporting an unknown usurper. Aetius accepted the mission and began the long journey back to the Hunnic lands.[44]

The Campaign in the West

Whilst Aetius travelled to the Huns, Theodosius ordered Ardabur and his son Aspar to lead their forces into Italy and defeat John. Accordingly, Ardabur and the eastern army marched through Pannonia and Illyricum to capture Salona.[45] Based on the coast, Salona was an ideal strategic point from which to launch a two-pronged attack on Italy. Placidia and Valentinian joined Ardabur at Salona, ready for the proposed invasion.

At the beginning of the campaign season of 425 Ardabur contemplated the actual invasion of Italy. He decided to divide his forces, Ardabur himself leading the naval forces, whilst Aspar and Candidianus led the rest of the army by the land route into Italy.

Aspar now led his troops into Italy. He appears to have taken the cavalry ahead of the main force in an attempt to catch John by surprise. The remainder of the army under Candidianus followed at a slower pace. In this way Aspar managed to surprise John and before a warning could be sounded he captured the city of Aquileia. Placidia and Valentinian joined him there.[46]

For Ardabur, events took a completely different path. Whilst at sea he was blown off course and his vessel, together with two other triremes, was captured by forces loyal to John.[47] John, still hoping for recognition from Theodosius, decided to treat Ardabur well, as otherwise it was certain Theodosius would continue the war. Hearing of the capture of Ardabur, the Eastern army's morale fell, but Candidianus managed to capture several cities in northern Italy, helping to dispel the gloom.[48]

Ardabur took advantage of the situation. Allowed to wander at will, he began talking to John's senior officers. These men had probably already begun to regret their support for John. After all, his campaign in Africa had failed and now news arrived that Aspar had already taken Aquileia.[49] Yet there may be one further reason for their change of allegiance. Olympiodorus claims that Ardabur 'suborned the generals that had been retired from their commands'.[50] It would appear that, alongside the promotion of Exuperantius and Aetius, John had promoted trusted men to senior posts within the army. The men who had been replaced remained with the army but, obviously, their loyalty to John had been damaged. Although an alternative translation, this explains the willingness of these officers to come to an agreement with Ardabur.

Their co-operation was vital. In the knowledge that the army with John was not totally loyal, Ardabur sent a message – probably with the aid of at least some of these officers – to his son Aspar telling him to travel 'as though to a victory assured'.[51] Aspar followed his father's orders, travelling quickly to Ravenna with a picked force. In order to conceal Aspar's movements, Candidianus continued his campaign of subduing the cities of northern Italy.[52] It would appear that Aspar was then guided across the marshes that surround Ravenna and so was able to reach the city undetected.[53] Finding the gates open, Aspar took control of the city, doubtless helped by the army under John, which at this point almost certainly decided to change its allegiance.

John himself was captured in Ravenna and was then sent under guard to Placidia and Valentinian, who had remained in Aquileia when Aspar attacked Ravenna. Once in Aquileia John was taken to the hippodrome, where he was mutilated by having his hand cut off, and was then paraded on a donkey, before finally being executed by decapitation.[54]

THE ARRIVAL OF AETIUS

Three days after the execution of John, Aetius returned to Italy leading a large force of Huns.[55] His orders from John had been to 'fall on the rear of the eastern army after it had entered Italy'.[56] Acting upon his orders, and likely unaware of John's death, Aetius immediately attacked the eastern army. After heavy losses on both sides a truce was agreed, probably after messages reached Aetius that John and Gaudentius were dead.[57] Aetius was enough of a realist to acknowledge that his position as a rebel was hopeless. In the circumstances, he did the only thing that he could: he used the threat of the Huns as a bargaining point to negotiate with Placidia, now acting as regent for her son.

Discussions with Placidia and Valentinian followed. Although unattested, alongside Aetius' use of the Huns as a bargaining counter it is possible that the prestige accorded to his mother's family also played a part. If the sources are correct in saying that she was rich, it is probable that she had strong ties to the western Senate. In that case, Placidia would not wish to simply execute Aetius, as this could provoke unnecessary resentment in the Senate. Placidia would need the wholehearted support of the Senate to ensure a smooth transition of power to her son Valentinian.

Aetius accepted the position of a high-ranking military officer in the new regime.[58] In return, he negotiated a treaty with the Huns. They were paid a large amount of gold as compensation for their travel and losses, and after an exchange of hostages and oaths the Huns departed for home. The concept that Aetius also ceded territory in Pannonia to the Huns at this time is mistaken and belongs to a later episode in his life.[59]

However, Placidia would never forget that Aetius had supported John against her son: the two would remain political opponents and she would not hesitate to manipulate him in her attempts to 'foil the ambitions of any general who showed signs of becoming too powerful for her liking'.[60]

Having secured the West, Placidia and Valentinian travelled to Rome where on 23 October 425 Valentinian was proclaimed emperor by Helion, cousin of Theodosius II. Valentinian was now just six years old. Theodosius had wanted to preside at the ceremony himself, but had been prevented by illness.[61] Upon securing the throne Placidia made a man named Felix the new *magister militum praesentalis*, at the same time giving him the title *patricius*.[62] Nothing is known about Felix before this appointment. The lack of information suggests that he was not an outstanding military leader. As a result, it is likely that his appointment was due to him being well known and trusted, at least by Theodosius II in Constantinople, and that he was seen as a loyal individual who would not pose a threat to Placidia.

One of the first decisions of the new regime was to send Castinus into exile rather than have him executed.[63] Castinus' decision to maintain a low profile during John's reign saved him from death.[64] In the hope of gaining support, and in recognition that Rome had still not fully recovered from the sack by the Goths, in early 426 one of the main taxes on the city of Rome and the Senate, the *aurum oblaticium*, was remitted by the new emperor.[65]

The senior post given to Aetius was, in the circumstances, an extremely important one, and one in which he would be allowed to demonstrate his military abilities to the full. He was made *magister militum per Gallias*.[66] However, it should be noted that at some time in the past, and presumably during John's usurpation, Aetius' father Gaudentius had been killed by an uprising of the troops in Gaul.[67] Although the promotion was a major advancement for Aetius, it is possible that Placidia and Valentinian may have been hoping that Aetius' ambition would be held in check, or that he might even be assassinated, due to animosity felt by the troops for his father being carried over to Aetius. Aetius' acceptance of the risky appointment can be seen as his accepting that he needed to prove his loyalty to the imperial court, even at the risk of his own life. Just as importantly, the appointment also removed Aetius from the court in Italy, allowing Felix time to consolidate his power as *magister militum* without interference from Aetius and his relatives.

Aetius' rise to power had been remarkably fast. In under two years he had gone from being the *cura palatii* of an usurper to the *magister militum* of an accepted emperor. However, his meteoric rise had one major drawback: he was now in political opposition to Galla Placidia, who would find it hard to forgive him for his support of John, and of the other two major players in the west: Felix, the new *magister militum praesentalis*, and Boniface. In return for his undying loyalty through-out her troubled time, Galla Placidia promoted Boniface to *comes domesticorum et Africae* (Count of the Household and of Africa), ordering him to stay in Africa – possibly to ensure that the vital province remained peaceful and trouble free.[68] Both of these men had more influence than Aetius with Galla Placidia. Yet in reality she was forced to play the three men off against each other in an attempt to maintain a level of independence for herself and Valentinian, and it would not be long before Aetius was thrust once again into the centre of imperial politics. In the meantime, he prepared for life as the army commander in Gaul.

Chapter 4

The Late Roman Army[1]

COMMAND HIERARCHY

Modern historians analyzing the *Notitia Dignitatum*, and especially those with a military background, have tended to relate the linear, rigid hierarchy apparent in its pages with the modern armies of the 'advanced' nations.[2] This fails to take into account the fact that the *Notitia* may be depicting an ideal, and reality is rarely this organized. For example, in many cases the posts depicted may have been only intended to be occupied for a short period under a specific emperor, or they may have been created by an emperor for a personal favourite but then left vacant after the individual retired from service.

Unfortunately, it has been relatively common in the past to take the titles given in the *Notitia* and link them to the titles given to individuals in other sources. On the other hand, it should be remembered that ancient writers were not usually interested in applying strict military rankings according to an accepted hierarchy: in many cases the writer was more concerned that the terminology follow the flow of the narrative or the metre of the poem to consider such niceties. As a result, the use of titles such as *magister peditum*, *magister equitum*, *magister utriusque militiae* and so forth may all actually represent the same post, depending upon the authority, accuracy, mode (history, poetry and chronicle) and sources used by the ancient author in question. Furthermore, there are numerous examples in the sources of individuals with the title *magister militum vacans*. Although sometimes given to military commanders conducting specific campaigns beyond the remit of the usual *magistri*, such as the campaigns in Spain under Aetius, the title could also be used simply to reward a loyal follower with the prestige and privileges attached to the post of *magister militum*.

Furthermore, the *Notitia* describes the standing army in time of peace. During a military campaign *ad hoc* command structures would have been utilized, rather than a strict adherence to the peacetime organization.[3] Some of the 'promotions' may then have continued in existence as a form of reward from the emperor for a job well done. However, these did not fit easily into the command structure represented in the *Notitia* and may account for some of the confusion both in the document and in the existing written sources.

There are two final warnings with regard to the *Notitia*. The first is that the original was a working document. The political and military complexities inherent in the West in the early fifth century mean that, almost without doubt, the *Notitia* was out of date when the final list was completed. This explains why there are doublets and omissions from the text.[4] The second is that this is not a document from the fifth century: it is a copy of a document, and as such may contain many errors and omissions that were not in the original.

Yet with all of these caveats, the *Notitia* is still of vital importance to the historian, since it is one of the very few documents that, whatever its failings, gives an insight into the intended working of the Roman military and bureaucratic infrastructure.

REFORMS

The reign of Constantine I (306–337) saw the *praefecti praetoriani* lose their military powers. These tasks were assumed by the newly created *magister peditum* ('master of the infantry') and *magister equitum* ('master of the cavalry'). By at the latest the mid-fourth century a third, subordinate *magister*, plus attendant troops, was added in the West, the *magister militum per Gallias* (Master of the Troops in Gaul). These three *magistri* controlled the *comitatenses* (on the troop types and other ranks, see below) and in theory had authority above the provincial *duces* ('dukes'), who controlled the *limitanei* in the provinces. However, the *duces* retained the right to correspond directly with the emperor, so the commonly perceived linear hierarchy is not actually present.

Since the new *magistri* commanded large bodies of troops, for his own security the emperor retained control of the elite *scholae* via the *magister officiorum*.[5] These troops would act as the nucleus for an army that would defeat any *magister* unwise enough to raise the standard of revolt.

Below the various *magistri* was an assortment of *comes* (counts) and *duces* (dukes). Attempts to maintain the illusion of a linear hierarchy are doomed to failure, as it seems likely that the designations *comes* and *dux* were given by different emperors depending upon the individual circumstances surrounding the appointment.

There is one last proviso that needs to be remembered. The fluid nature of the ranks and titles allotted within Roman Empire was not hidebound by modern preconceptions of 'amateur' and 'professional' soldiers. The result was that in an emergency almost any imperial official could act as a military commander, regardless of whether he was of the 'correct' rank, or even if he was a soldier.[6]

With these observations in mind, it is clear that great care needs to be taken before deductions are made based on the specific titles held by military commanders. Due to the improvisational nature of many appointments, it may be possible to draw up a table showing the chain of command under one or possibly two consecutive emperors. To attempt to do the same for the entire fourth and fifth centuries would be impossible.

UNIT HIERARCHY[7]

During the third and fourth centuries the army was divided into two main components: the *comitatenses* and the *limitanei*. The *comitatensis*, usually translated as 'field army', was stationed to the rear of the borders and was, at least theoretically, a 'mobile' army that could be used at any point within the empire. The *comitatenses* were further divided into two, with the 'ordinary' units of *comitatenses* being slightly lower in rank than the *palatina* or 'palace' troops. Furthermore, some units appear to have been divided into *seniores* and *iuniores*, with the seniores having superior status.

The *limitanei* were troops stationed permanently on the *limes* (borders). The *limitanei* are given different names in the sources, being known as *riparienses*, *ripenses*, *castellani* or *burgarii*. Although in theory these names may indicate a differentiation in the nature of the troops, what differences there were between them remains unknown. Whatever the nature of the troops, the terms *legiones* and *cohortes* appear to have been used for the infantry, with *ala* and *equites* being used for the cavalry.[8]

To add to the complexity, over the course of time many of the *limitanei* were taken from the frontiers and transferred to the 'field army', being given the title *pseudo-comitatenses*, and units could be punished by being downgraded from *comitatenses* to *limitanei*.

Slightly outside this two-tier system were the *scholae*, guard cavalry units under the personal control of the emperor. However, since during the course of the fifth century the western emperor no longer went to war in person, over time the *scholae* gradually lost their martial status and became ceremonial units. Finally, the emperor himself chose individuals from among the *scholae* to form the *candidati*, his personal forty-man bodyguard.[9]

DISTRIBUTIO NUMERORUM

Included within the *Notitia Dignitatum* is a document with the title *Distributio Numerorum* ('Distribution of the Army Units'). This attempts to list the distribution of the army throughout the West.[10] A close analysis of the *Notitia*, and especially of the *Distributio*, has suggested that between the years 395 and 420 nearly fifty per cent of the western 'field army' was lost.[11] This was due mainly to the civil wars at the end of Theodosius I's reign (379–395) and the civil wars and invasions from 401 until the settlement of the Goths in Aquitaine in 418–419.[12] The losses in manpower, due to fighting, desertion and possibly the disbanding of rebellious units, combined with the loss of tax revenues caused by the continuous wars, decimated the 'field-armies'. To plug the gaps, Stilicho and Constantius III had transferred many units of the *limitanei* to the field army as *pseudocomitatenses*.[13] The result was that some areas of Gaul and Africa were virtually stripped of *limitanei*. Although the consequences of these actions were to be dire, this is only apparent in hindsight. The treaties with tribes along the frontiers in Gaul, and especially the Franks, plus the fact that Africa was not exposed to any serious military threats, meant that the withdrawal of troops did not result in any immediate repercussions.

Despite these problems attempts have been made to estimate the size of the Roman army in the fifth century, and especially of the 'field armies' that faced the barbarian invaders, and sometimes each other, in the field. This is one estimate of the size of the different armies:

WEST

Western Illyricum	13,500
Gaul	34,000
Praesental	28,500 (by the time of Aetius there was usually only one *magister* in the west)

EAST

Thrace	24,500
Illyricum	17,500
Oriens	20,000
Praesental	42,000[14]

It should be remembered that these are 'paper' strengths according to the *Notitia Dignitatum*. They do not take into account the fact that the *Notitia* was by the mid 420s becoming obsolete. It is possible that many of the units of the *limitanei* that were listed may have had no existence outside the *Notitia*, especially in Africa and Spain, since at least some of these troops had been called to the 'field army' during the earlier rebellions and invasions and never returned to their places of origin. Further, there would be constant attrition due to losses in battle, by accident, from troops being ill or hospitalized, or even troops being deployed on non-military duties away from the main body of the army. The figures also do not take into account difficulties with recruitment. It is possible that in extreme cases the troops available for combat could be as low as half- to one-third this number, although this may be taking too negative an approach.

NON-ROMAN UNITS

The terminology used for non-Roman units is extremely confusing. This is in part because the Romans appear to have used the same terms for units of widely differing origin. Furthermore, as the sources do not use the terms in a strict, military sense, but often use whichever word fits with the style or meter of the work being written, certainty is impossible.[15]

Foederati

A major example of this is the use of the term *foederati*. Originally the term was applied to non-Romans serving in regular army units under the terms of a *foedus* (treaty), possibly such as that signed by Constantine I (306–337) with the 'Ripuarian' Franks, or that signed by Julian (355–363) with the 'Salian' Franks.[16] Many of the barbarian units listed in the *Notitia* probably began their existence as wholly barbarian units, yet it should be noted that these were 'regular' Roman units, trained, supplied and equipped by the empire. As time passed they almost certainly lost their 'barbarian' status due to the enlistment of non-barbarian troops in their ranks.[17]

However, over time the term *foederati* came to be applied more loosely. As a result, when the words *foederatus* or *foederati* are used by the sources, the full context needs to be determined before any deductions are made concerning the exact nature of the troops being described. Therefore, for the purposes of this book, the term *foederati* will be used exclusively with regard to barbarian troops serving under their own leaders in non-Roman units, whether these are 'internal' forces such as the Goths or 'external' forces such as the Huns.

Bucellarii

During the reign of Theodosius I (379–395) the *magister militum* Stilicho and the *praefectus praetorio Orientem* Rufinus were probably the first individuals to begin recruiting *bucellarii*, barbarian troops serving as personal bodyguards to military and political leaders as well as the emperor.[18] Indeed, the employment of *bucellarii* quickly became fashionable and Stilicho was forced to pass a law restricting the size of these 'personal' armies.[19] As a result, during the lifetime of Aetius such troops were still limited in number. It is only later, and especially in the reign of Justinian I (527–565), that large numbers began to be recruited by powerful individuals.

The tendency of late Roman military commanders to supplement their forces with barbarian mercenaries is understandable, although it was contrary to the aristocratic belief that Rome should be defended by Romans. *Magistri* such as Stilicho and Aetius may have understood that employing mercenaries was in many ways beneficial to Rome. Rather than entering the army, Roman civilians were able to continue their trades and pay the taxes needed to employ mercenaries. Furthermore, the troops employed by the empire were denied to the barbarian leaders, reducing their effectiveness whilst simultaneously increasing the power of the defending forces.

UNIT STRENGTH[20]

Along with the change in structure came a change in the organization of the units within the army. Although figures remain conjectural and different authorities have different ideas, modern estimates of the strength of the various units is roughly as follows: Guard units (*scholae*[21] etc.) 500 men; *auxilia palatinae* 800–1,200 men; legions (*comitatenses*) 1,000–1,200men; legions (*limitanei*) 3000 men; *limitanei/riparienses* 300–500 men; cavalry (*comitatenses*) 480–600 men; cavalry (*limitanei*) 350–500 men. However, the units entitled *milliary* in the *Notitia* possibly numbered c.750–1,000 men, as they had in the third century, and some legionary units may have retained their earlier strength of c.5,000 men until much later.[22] An additional factor is that, in an army covering such a vast area as the Roman Empire, there would also be regional differences between units.[23] Finally it should be remembered that on campaign units could easily be as low as two-thirds strength due to illness, injury and the need to leave a depot garrison behind at the unit's base for administrative and recruitment purposes.[24] Any numbers given for Roman troops in battle must remain hypothetical.

RECRUITMENT

There would appear to have been four methods of recruitment for the regular army in the later empire: legal requirement, the enrolment of volunteers, conscription, and levies from 'barbarians' settled either as prisoners of war or as normal Roman farmers with a duty to provide troops for the army when a levy was demanded.[25]

Yet a career in the army was unpopular. In the fifth century there were many barbarian invasions of the West and a high level of brigandage, banditry and civil wars. Joining the army could mean a recruit being posted to a province far away, so leaving his family to the attention of a variety of enemies, as a result of which many men preferred to stay and defend their own homes.[26] Furthermore, taxation was high, and there was a growing resentment of the actions of the army, who were now billeted around towns and cities. As a result, there is evidence of citizens siding with invaders in the expectation of better treatment and booty.[27] However, it is likely that here, as elsewhere, regional variations and political pressures played a large part in the attraction of the army as a career, since especially in 'peaceful' provinces such as Egypt a career in the army would offer secure employment at relatively low risk.

One of the other main methods of recruiting for the army, and the one most often mentioned in the *Codex Theodosianus*, was conscription. However, the fall in population numbers and the fact that a relatively high proportion of the population lived in towns resulted in competition between the army and the landowners in the Senate for able-bodied men. Although in times of war conscription may have been thought necessary, in times of peace the situation was different. In peacetime, provinces were allowed to pay a tax known as the *aurem tironicum* ('gold for recruits') instead of supplying men. Since the Senate of Rome used every means possible to avoid having men from their estates conscripted into the army, conscription was regularly commuted into the *aurem tironicum* and the money raised used to pay for Germanic mercenaries, who did not need training and who generally equipped themselves. Furthermore, the system was open to abuse, because emperors often found themselves to be short of money since the income from taxes rarely covered the expenditure needed to maintain the empire. When this happened, it was tempting to pass a decree calling for conscription simply in order to commute this to the *aurem tironicum* to boost the treasury.[28] The vicious cycles these measures created was a major factor in tensions between emperors and Senate remaining high.

Having looked at the difficulties of recruiting troops from large areas of the West, it should be noted that other provinces, especially those on the frontiers where life was harder, continued to supply recruits. In this period the Balkan provinces continued to be good recruiting grounds until after the collapse of the West, following which eastern emperors began to recruit in Asia Minor.[29]

Whatever the origin of new troops, whether conscripts, volunteers or mercenaries, it was the task of the *duces* to supervise recruitment and the assignment of individuals to units. This also included the weeding out of men unsuitable for a military career.[30] Unfortunately we are not given any details as to how this functioned.

TRAINING

Until recently it was accepted by many historians that, following Zosimus, training of the army had declined and that this was accompanied by a commensurate loss of discipline.[31] The quality of the troops within the Roman army was always proportional to the quality of leadership, yet the question of leadership is rarely raised in relation to the Late Roman Empire.[32] Ammianus gives accounts where leaders did not lead their troops effectively.[33] Following the enlargement of the army and the inaugurations of many new units under Diocletian and Constantine, large numbers of new commanders had been required and it must be accepted that there is the likelihood that overall the quality of army commanders had declined. This factor is important, in that the training of troops depended upon the efficiency – or otherwise – of their commanding officers. The predominant factor in troop training is the quality and enthusiasm of the officers. If the officers were of high quality, the troops would receive regular training wherever they were stationed; if not, they would not be trained. If the officers were poor, training was most likely neglected.

ARMY EQUIPMENT*

The equipment used by the troops was still regulated by the government and manufactured in *fabricae*, state-owned arms factories whose workers were actually classed as part of the military establishment. Seven of these *fabricae* were located in Gaul and it is probably indicative of the confusion prevalent in Britain and Gaul in the early-fifth century that at some point it was recognized that the supply of military equipment to Britain would fail. Although the precise date and circumstances are unknown, it is interesting to note Gildas' claim that the empire recognized that Britain would no longer be an integral part, instead giving 'energetic counsel to the timorous natives' and leaving them 'patterns by which to manufacture arms'.[34]

The nature of the equipment used by the later Roman army has been the source of much debate, since Vegetius claims that the army no longer wore armour:

> From the founding of the city down to the time of the deified Gratian, the infantry army was equipped with both cataphracts (body armour) and helmets. But upon the intervention of neglect and idleness field exercises ceased, and arms which soldiers rarely donned began to be thought heavy. So they petitioned the emperor that they should hand in first the cataphracts, then helmets.
>
> *Vegetius, 1.20*

Coupled with the lack of archaeological findings that can be specifically dated to the period and the confusing picture painted by surviving monuments and funeral *stelae*, the statement was taken at face value and used as evidence that the later army was no longer equipped with metal armour.

However, more recent work has overturned this acceptance, and has, for example, shown that the sculptures in many cases have small holes drilled in them to make the appearance of mail armour.[35] Furthermore, it is possible that Vegetius is describing an actual petition from the *scholae palatinae*, a guard unit, that they be excused from wearing armour.[36] However, the remains of copper alloy scales found at Trier, along with remnants of mail found at Trier, Weiler-la-Tour and Indepenţa, the latter of

---

* This section on the arms and armour of the Late Roman Army is virtually the same as that previously included in the book *Stilicho: the Vandal Who Saved Rome* (Pen and Sword, 2010). Readers with the previous book may wish to skip this section.

which date to the late-fourth or early-fifth century, shows that armour was still being used in the late empire, a point reinforced by Ammianus Marcellinus, who gives many references to individuals wearing armour.[37]

Finally, there is the evidence in the *Notitia Dignitatum*. There are drawings in the manuscript that illustrate the insignia of some of the office holders, and in some instances these depict some of the equipment made in the *fabricae*. These include the items such as helmets and body armour previously thought to be no longer in use. As a result, it is now generally accepted that the late Roman army wore heavy equipment equal to that of their predecessors.

However, it should be remembered that the process of production was time-consuming and expensive and consequently items that were no longer 'fashionable' would continue to be issued until stockpiles were used. Therefore, many items of equipment from earlier periods may have continued in use on a small scale, remaining invisible in the archaeological and sculptural records. This is especially the case when it is noted that Synesius, Themistius, Libanius, Ammianus, Vegetius, the 'Abinneus Archive' and the Law Codes all attest to the fact that imperial laxity resulted in troops facing a lack of equipment, as well as arrears in pay and the supply of food.[38]

MISSILES

Long Range: Bows, Slings (*fundae*), Staff-slings (*fustibali*), Crossbows (*arcuballistae*), Artillery

The Romans used a wide variety of long-range missile weapons, although knowledge of some of these can only really be attributed to scenes found on murals and mosaics, and so may only have been used for hunting. The most common form of missile weapon was the **composite bow**, as attested by the title *sagittarii* (archers) in the *Notitia Dignitatum*. These were the standard missile weapon of the Roman army and were similar to those in use by the Persians and other eastern enemies of the empire.

Slings and **staff-slings** (slings attached to a 4 foot-/1.18 metre-long stave) were also used. However, they never appear to have formed a large proportion of the military establishment, probably being restricted to a few skirmishers supporting the combat troops.

A little-used weapon in military circles is the **crossbow**, which may be the weapon described by Vegetius as *arcuballistae*.[39] Other versions of the weapon included the *cheiroballista* described by Heron, which was loaded by placing the end on the ground and pressing on the stock until the string was drawn and a bolt/arrow fitted into the weapon. The crossbow is often portrayed in hunting scenes in murals and mosaics, but does not appear to have formed a major part of the army's arsenal.

Artillery had been used by the Roman army since at least the second century BC. Later variants included the *manuballista* of Vegetius, a torsion engine capable of accurately firing projectiles for a long distance.[40] The army also produced a version mounted on a cart for ease of transport, known as the *carroballista*, which is shown on Trajan's column. There is little doubt that these weapons were used in the field, but the regularity and form of their deployment remains open to doubt. There was also the artillery used for siege warfare, such as the *onager* ('wild ass'), which was too large and difficult to set up for use in the field.

Short Range: Darts, Javelins*

There appear to have been a variety of **darts**, including types called *plumbatae*, *mattiobarbuli/martiobarbuli*, *plumbatae tribolatae* and *mamillatae*. These were carried by the infantry and thrown as the range closed. The *plumbatae* had a lead weight behind the head to aid in penetration, whilst the *plumbatae tribolatae* is claimed to have had three spikes emerging from the lead weight so that if it missed a target it still posed an obstacle by presenting a sharp point to an unwary foot or hoof.[41]

There were a variety of thrown weapons that come under the loose category of **javelin**. These include types called the *spicula*, the *hasta*, the *pila*, the *iacula*, the *verruta* and the *tela*. Despite prolonged investigation, it is clear that the differences between these weapons are unknown.[42] Vegetius suggests that each man should be issued one heavy javelin (*spiculum*) and one light javelin (*verrutum*).[43] However, it should be noted that these different names may be describing weapons that are almost identical. For example, it is known that the older *pilum* existed in a variety of forms, with some being heavier than others. It is possible, therefore, that Vegetius' report of a *spiculum*, which is usually accepted as the newer name for the *pilum*, actually describes the heavier variety, whilst the *verrutum* is referring to a lighter version of the same weapon. Certainty in these matters is impossible.

Combat Weapons: Swords, Spears, Others[44]

Earlier Roman infantry had been heavily trained in the art of using the short **sword** known as the *gladius hispaniensis* whilst the cavalry had been issued with the *spatha*. For unknown reasons, by the time of the later empire the whole army appears to have used the *spatha*. Vegetius also attests to the use of a shorter sword, which he calls the *semispatha*.[45] Although there have been a variety of swords found in the archaeological record that are smaller than the *spatha*, Vegetius tells us nothing about the weapon, so any correlation between archaeology and Vegetius remains speculation. The *spatha* was a long, double-edged sword that varied from between 0.7 to 0.9 metres in length.[46] Although such weapons are usually described as being used in a 'slashing' motion, the *spatha* had a point that made it suitable for thrusting as well.

It is commonly assumed that hand-held, shafted weapons can be divided into those used as missiles and those retained for use in hand-to-hand combat. However, it is clear from ancient sources and modern re-enactors that there was little, if any, difference between the two types of weapon. This leads to the obvious conclusion that whether they were used as missile or hand-to-hand weapons was determined more by circumstances than by weapon typology. Therefore, any of the weapons described in the section on close-range missiles as javelins could also be used in

---

* See also 'Spears'.

combat, should circumstances dictate. Furthermore, spears such as the *spiculum*, which had a large part of its shaft encased in iron, would be ideal in combat, as the iron would protect the wooden shaft from being sheared by enemy swords. Alongside these types of dual usage are types classed simply as 'spears', used by both infantry and cavalry and ranging between 2 and 2.5 metres in length.[47] Yet even these could either be thrown a short distance or retained for combat.

Many burials include a short, single-edged **knife**, which by this time appears to have replaced the earlier broad-edged dagger, the *pugio*. The change in the design of the dagger may simply have been recognition that its use as a utility tool far outweighed its employment as a weapon. As a consequence, it became simpler and was only sharpened on one side.

Alongside traditional Roman weapons were others that were either of unknown origin or were Germanic imports. For example, there is evidence that some at least of the Roman cavalry used conventional **axes**, as mentioned by Ammianus and Procopius and shown in the *stela* from Gamzigrad and the Column of Arcadius.[48] Unfortunately, these examples of the use of axes are very rare and so the distribution of these weapons remains a mystery. There is also the use of **maces**, as mentioned by Theophylact.[49] Germanic imports included weapons such as the *sax* (a single-edged long knife) and the *francisca* (throwing-axe), which were slowly being introduced into the empire, and attested later is the use of the **lasso**, following Hunnic practice.[50] Again, the extent of their use in the Roman army remains unknown.

Defensive Equipment: Helmets, Mail, Scale, 'Muscle Cuirasses', Lamellar, Shields, Other

The earlier use of helmets with single-piece bowls spun from a single piece of metal disappear before the middle of the fourth century. Their place is taken by two new forms. The most common of these are the styles termed **ridge helmets**. Possibly deriving from Persian helmets, they are first found in archaeological deposits dating to the early fourth century, possibly c AD 325.[51] This date is confirmed by a coin from the reign of Constantine I (306–337), which appears to show Constantine wearing a 'stylized Berkasovo helmet', and by the sculpture found at Gamzigrad dating to the end of the third century (see Illustration 3).[52]

There are several slightly different styles, all – as in the 'Berkasovo' example just cited – named after the place where they were found. There are many finds from around the empire, but probably the most important were the up to twenty examples found at Intercisa (modern Hungary). There was a variety of styles involved, including the extraordinary version with an integral metal crest known as Intercisa 4. Yet all of these were made using a similar technique, which was to manufacture the bowl as two separate pieces before joining them with a strip of metal along the crown, which gave them their distinctive 'ridge' appearance.

It would appear that many of these helmets had attachable crests, and it may be that the 'integral crest' of Intercisa 4 was either cheaper than buying a separate crest or may have been a way of distinguishing officers from other ranks.[53]

At some point in the fourth century, if not earlier, the Roman army adopted another form of helmet, the *spangenhelm*. Named after the *spangen*, the plates that joined the separate parts of the bowl together, they may be dated as early as the Tetrarchy (c.293–312), although this date is uncertain and they may only have been introduced in the fifth century.

The reason for the change from one-piece bowls to ridge helmets (and possibly *spangenhelms*) is unclear. Earlier claims that this was due to the expansion of the army under Diocletian and the need to supply equipment that was cheaper and easier to make have recently been questioned.[54] It has been pointed out that the new manufacturing method required accuracy in order to join the two halves of the bowl properly, so making them difficult to manufacture. Furthermore, the fact that many of them have traces of silver, gilt and/or paste gemstones attached results in the end product actually being quite expensive.

These claims do not take into account the fact that the process of spinning iron can both weaken it and lead to irregularities in the bowl. This may account for the need to reinforce earlier, one-piece bowls across the brow. Furthermore, unless the manufacture was extremely well controlled, the ensuing bowl could be slightly off-centre and so weak down one half. This would have resulted in a high wastage of material as sub-standard bowls were returned to the forge for remaking. The new methods produced bowls that did not need brow reinforcement and were of a more uniform thickness and quality, since they are easier to work and toughen than the one-piece skull.[55] Although looking to modern eyes, with computer-driven accuracy, as if they are a step back, in production and quality they may actually have been an improvement on earlier helmets.

Although a little strange in appearance, there are artistic representations of troops wearing **coifs**.[56] These appear to be allied to extremely long coats of mail. How they were manufactured or what form they took in reality is unknown, as none have ever been found in the archaeological record.

A final piece of protective headgear was the ***Pilleus Pannonicus*** (Pannonian hat). This was a round, flat-topped cap. The earliest depiction is from the coins of Constantine I and from the Arch of Constantine. When seen in detail it is depicted as being 'brown and furry' and was probably made of felt.[57] Of little defensive value in itself, its use amongst the military may have started due to its being used as a helmet lining. It may then have become a symbol for members of the army who were not wearing their helmets. In the porphyry sculpture of the four tetrarchs in Venice, the four emperors are wearing the *Pilleus Pannonicus*, possibly as a sign of their affiliation with the army.

It is unfortunate that due to decomposition or rust the vast numbers of helmets that were once in use have been reduced to a mere handful. The case is even worse when it comes to body armour. Therefore, what follows is largely conjectural and could be supplanted at any time by new archaeological finds.

Simply put, **ring-mail** armour was made by making lots of small rings of iron and joining them to make a flexible, but rather heavy, form of protection.[58] Although there have been isolated finds of mail dating to the fifth century (see above), there is enough to show that it was certainly still being made. Monumental evidence suggests that the mail came in two lengths: either a 'short' version covering the shoulders and coming down to around mid thigh, or a 'long' version, which reached to the elbow and the knee.

Scale armour was made by lacing small overlapping plates of metal on to a fabric or leather structure. The result was a form of protection roughly equivalent to that of mail, but without the large amount of flexibility that mail offered. It would appear that the shape of the scale 'shirts' took the same form as those of the mail shirts already described.

It is common for depictions of **muscle cuirasses** to be represented on large monuments in this period, such as the Column of Arcadius. There are difficulties with accepting depictions of muscle cuirasses on such monuments at face value. The most obvious of these is that the monuments probably owe more to traditional Hellenistic forms of carving rather than representing contemporary models. Many of the items depicted refer back to ancient hoplite practices rather than reflecting what troops of the time actually wore.[59] Furthermore, a close analysis of the monuments has shown that some of these representations of muscle cuirasses actually appear to represent scale or mail armour. This would reinforce the theory that such monuments were carved with an eye more to the Hellenistic traditions of the past than to the accurate representation of contemporary armour.[60] As a result, it is likely that muscle cuirasses, being tailored to the individual, would be expensive to manufacture and so be used only by those of higher rank, not the average soldier.

A surprising absence during this period is that of *lamellar* armour. Made of longer strips of metal wired to a forming-garment of cloth or leather, these long scales ran vertically in the armour, producing a very firm but extremely stiff protection. Attested both before and after the period, it is curious that between c.350 and 425 there is no evidence at all for this armour. The most obvious explanation is that it continued in use but that there is no written, architectural or archaeological evidence for it. However, the lack of evidence is puzzling.

The common form of **shield** used by the Romans was a large oval shape, although the depiction of round shields on monuments has led to confusion. There is evidence that the Roman army was being influenced by Germanic shields, and it is possible that the use of round shields was restricted to guardsmen such as the *scholae*.[61]

The *Notitia Dignitatum* lists many shield patterns and labels them as though they were associated with specific units within the army. Although the accuracy of the *Notitia* in this regard is open to question, it is interesting to note that according to Ammianus at the Battle of Strasbourg the Germanic tribesmen recognized Roman units by their shield devices.[62] Although the patterns allocated by the *Notitia* may be of dubious accuracy, the theory that units had specific shield designs appears to be correct.

The use of **segmented** armour for the arms and legs of heavily armoured horsemen, the *catafracti* and *clibanari*, is attested and evidenced in the drawings of armour produced by the *fabricae* in the *Notitia Dignitatum*. However, there is no evidence of its use by the infantry, although this should not be ruled out if the occasion arose. The *catafracti* and *clibanari* also had armour for their horses. The exact nature that this took is unclear, although evidence from before and after this period suggests that it could be linen, horn, copper alloy or iron scales, or even possibly mail, though the latter would be extremely heavy.

Finally, it should be noted that **greaves** for troops' legs were now extremely uncommon, although again they are depicted both before and after this period, so it is likely that they continued in use.

THE NAVY

In modern states the navy is a separate establishment with its own hierarchy of command. In the Roman Empire the navy seems to have been regarded as part of the army. The *Notitia Dignitatum* has the various fleets being commanded by *praefecti*, yet in reality whenever they were used in large numbers the fleets were commanded by *magistri* or similar senior members of the military establishment.

The *Notitia* has a number of fleets stationed in the western empire. The ports used include Ravenna, Misenum, Arles, Aquileia, Como and the mouth of the Somme. There would appear to have been two major types of ship in the fleet. For combat the fleets had warships, the standard galleys as used throughout the later period of the empire. For transport and supply, a number of merchant vessels were maintained with each fleet.[63] A third type of vessel was also used: specialized transport ships for the carrying of horses. However, the number of vessels in each fleet is usually unknown, although the strengths of some fleets may give an indication of overall numbers. For example, the fleet stationed in Skythia had 125 *lusoriae* (light boats) and 119 *iudicariae* and *agrarienses* (varieties of light boats) built in 7 years.[64] As will be seen later, when large fleets are gathered together for a single campaign, a figure is given in the sources for the combined might of the Roman navy.

There were also small fleets of riverboats based on the Rhine and the Danube to patrol and secure the rivers. As with the main, sea-going fleets, these were classed as being part of the army, and in these cases they were part of the *limitanei* (*riparienses*) stationed on the borders.[65]

WARFARE

Although often ignored by historians, there was a fundamental change in the nature of warfare during the later empire: 'In a period characterized by defensive strategy and low-intensity warfare associated with the ongoing maintenance of imperial security, the dangers of defeat in a large-scale action far outweighed the benefits of victory.'[66] It is often overlooked that Theodosius was defeated by the Goths after the Battle of Adrianople. The defeat saw the end of Roman attempts to inflict heavy defeats on their external enemies regardless of the costs. Instead, they resorted to using blockade and siege. It is only when confronting usurpers that Roman commanders still attempted to defeat the enemy in pitched battles.[67] This outlook remained prevalent amongst Roman military commanders, being promoted by

Maurikios in his famous *Strategikon* dating to the late-sixth century, although outright victory was still expected by the aristocracy until after the Fall of the West.

The desire to avoid pitched battles whenever possible and the change to a more low-level form of warfare led many historians to dismiss the late Roman army as inferior to its predecessors. They interpreted the change as being one of quality: whereas the early army was well trained, well led and well equipped, the later army was poorly trained, poorly led and, at least according to Vegetius, poorly equipped.[68] Modern historians have reassessed the information available and come to the conclusion that the later army was as well equipped and led as that of the earlier empire. Unfortunately, in some cases the argument has now swung too far. Army efficiency was, to a large extent, based upon location. Warfare was extremely rare in places such as Africa and Egypt, where the main task of the army was policing the local population and repelling low-scale raids from across the frontier. The troops in these places were not equivalent to the armies of the previous centuries. Troops on more warlike frontiers, such as the Danube, the Rhine and the areas facing Persia, were doubtless better trained, better equipped, and more likely to be led by able and experienced officers.

Yet this does not mean that the armies of these areas reacted to invasion and war in the same way as earlier armies. Advocates of the concept of late-army efficiency sometimes ignore the fact that, however good the army was, army leaders remained constrained by the difficulties of raising and equipping troops. Having the best army in the world is of little value if it is wasted in unnecessary battles and worn out of existence.

There is another aspect to the late-Roman practice of using blockade and siege more often than battle. The chance of forcing the enemy to surrender without inflicting large losses was a priority. The standard Roman method of dealing with enemy prisoners of war was to separate them into smaller contingents and then disperse them around the empire. In this way the barbarians could farm territories left vacant by war as well as providing recruits to the army. The enemy commanders would either be separated from their men and, if competent, enrolled in the Roman army, or executed.[69]

Yet ironically the employment of barbarian troops could politically weaken the Roman commander. Both the Senate and the regular Roman army were opposed to the mass employment of barbarians. The need to balance the requirements of defence and the political opposition to the employment of large numbers of mercenaries and federates would remain a worry for all *magistri* until the last decades of the West, when the army was no longer strong enough to mount serious opposition to their use.

Chapter 5

The Barbarians

THE 'GERMANIC' ARMIES OF WESTERN EUROPE[1]

Information concerning the Germanic armies of the fifth century is sparse. Although ancient writers have left descriptions, they are based more on *topoi* (traditional literary themes) and a desire to differentiate between the tribes than they are reality. An example of this is the *francisca*. This classic Germanic throwing-axe is portrayed in the sources as being used almost exclusively by the Franks. However, archaeology has shown that it was distributed over a very wide area, being employed, for example, by the Alamanni. As a result, it should be remembered that our descriptions of the various Germanic 'nations' conform more to ancient historiography and the desire to find a way of differentiating between the tribes than it does to reality. With this observation in mind, it is possible to investigate the German armies.

Organization

Later records show that once the Germans had settled down in their own kingdoms they used a decimal system to organize their armies.[2] The theory that this is a technique derived from before their settlements is reasonable, but prior to their establishment in the new, large kingdoms, their armies were formed only from whatever forces were available. These are unlikely to have been conveniently numbered, and so specific organization may have been rare. It is more likely that these armies were based upon a very informal adoption of the decimal system, with plenty of leeway allowed to take into account tribal and even village loyalties.

Most western barbarians were farmers. When called upon to serve in the army the majority would have been equipped only with a spear and shield, and possibly with missile weapons such as the *francisca* or the javelin.[3] One man usually owned the loyalty and the services of a cluster of farms and villages, which were known as *cantons*.[4] The number of men that cantons could raise would vary, but it is estimated that the largest would be able to muster at most 2,000 men, with the average more likely to be around 1,000.[5] This would tie in with the later military official, the *thusundifath* (leader of 1,000).[6] However, each leader would have had a small retinue, his *comitatus*, which served him in military matters.

Command

In theory, the leader of each canton would have a political alliance with a more powerful leader who was likely to have dominated several such cantons. In turn, many of these leaders would serve a yet more powerful individual. The outcome is described by Ammianus Marcellinus:

> Now all these warlike and savage tribes were led by Chnodomarius and Serapio, kings higher than all the rest in authority (*potestate excelsiores ante alios reges*) ... these were followed by the kings next in power (*potestate proximi reges*), five in number, by ten princes (*regalesque decem*), with a long train of nobles (*optimatum*), and 35,000 troops levied from various nations, partly for pay and partly under agreement to return the service.

> *Ammianus Marcellinus, 16.12.23–27*

Ammianus struggled to translate the German terms into Latin, with *reges* being the only word he felt was suitable. There can be little doubt that the ten 'princes' were the leaders of cantons, and that the 'nobles' were their *comitatus*. These ten warlords owed service, or at least some form of loyalty, to the five men 'next in power' and these five followed the orders of Chnodomarius and Serapio.

This system left little room for formal command and control as practised by the Romans, with each commander knowing his place in the line of battle. Although the warlords may have gained experience in inter-tribal or anti-Roman warfare and raids, they would have little practice of fighting in large armies alongside unknown commanders.

Although this description seems to follow to some degree the feudal system of the Middle Ages, this is not quite true. In fact, there is a distinct lack of tribal structure, as shown by the ability of groups to move from tribe to tribe. The new barbarian social formations that settled in the west 'were not simply imported from the woods of Germania': they were 'new social forms of identification in a complex environment'.[7] In other words, 'kingdoms' such as those of the Visigoths and Vandals were not simply the mass migration of whole tribes from outside the Roman empire into the empire to settle on new lands: they were a combination of many different tribesmen from a variety of origins deciding, under different stimuli, to serve under one leader.[8] A major example of this lack of unity comes from the invasion of Gaul by the Vandals, Alans and Sueves in 406–407. What is commonly overlooked is that one of the tribes, under their king, Goa, immediately abandoned the invasion and took service with Rome. It is clear that any of the warlords from the canton upwards only owed loyalty to their superiors out of common interests or fear. Each canton was its own political unit with its own, individual agenda. In theory, one could change allegiance whenever desired. The Romans had in the past exploited these divisions for their own political purposes and after Adrianople this factor had allowed Theodosius to slowly strip the Goths of men. Theodosius had negotiated with individual cantons and when agreement was reached had moved them away from the Balkans. In this way he continuously weakened the Goths' ability to fight. Political disunity was one of the major failings of the Germanic peoples at this time.

Once within the empire the situation changed. The barbarian kingdoms had no administrative institutions of their own and so used Roman administrative institutions. As a result the barbarians immediately adopted urban lifestyles and their main urban centres developed into capitals. For example, the Visigoths had Toulouse, the Ostrogoths had Ravenna, the Franks had Paris, the Burgundians had Geneva and the Sueves had Braga. This resulted in an increased tendency for the Romans to regard the leaders in these cities as kings and helped to give these kings the military power to dominate their kingdoms.[9]

Training and Discipline

As already noted, the Germanic armies were divided into two. The first is the trained and disciplined *comitatus* of the individual warlords, retained on a permanent basis with plenty of free time in which to practice the art of warfare, although the level of their skills would depend upon the skill and personality of their warlord. However, it is unlikely that they practised warfare on a larger scale, so the Roman legions tended to have the strategic and tactical advantage in large-scale battles.

The other part of the army was formed of the farmers who made up the bulk of the German population. The majority were equipped with spears and shields, although the better off would be able to afford a sword.[10] Thrown weapons such as axes and javelins were relatively common. These men would have had some training, but this would have varied, and its inconsistency would help to explain their reputation for ferocious charges but inability to keep pace with the Romans in a long fight.

Only the warlords and the *comitatus* would have had the finances available to buy horses. This would explain two stereotypes of Germanic cavalry. Firstly, their paucity in numbers: modern estimates suggest that a Germanic army would at the most have a third of its forces mounted. More often than not, the proportion would be lower, probably at around one-fifth.[11] The vast majority of the army were farmers relying on subsistence agriculture who could not afford to buy a horse. Secondly, the high quality of German cavalry: Vegetius himself comments that the Romans had progressed in their cavalry arm thanks to the example set by the Goths, Alans and Huns.[12] Yet the quote only refers to the tribes in the east, where the cost of horses was lower and more individuals could afford to own one.[13] Eastern horses were also of higher quality. Earlier, Caesar sometimes had to supply his German mercenaries with horses, since their own were too small for the task.[14] Yet the situation had improved during the intervening centuries, with the Alamanni being renowned as a people 'who fight wonderfully from horseback'.[15] Moreover, some of the tribes that had broken through the frontiers in the early-fifth century, such as the Vandals, the Goths and the Alans, were from the east. As a consequence, the number and quality of their cavalry was almost certainly greater than that of the indigenous Germans. This would help to explain why these tribes had greater success against the western Roman army than did, for example, the Franks or the Alamanni.

Barbarian society had metalworkers of great skill and finesse and the quality of the goods they produced matched anything that could be made in Rome. However, there were not many such workers, with the result that many items, such as swords, were available in smaller quantities and at a higher price. The majority of Germanic warriors could not afford a sword.

Still less could they afford protective equipment. It is interesting to note that a slightly later series of Frankish laws assessed a mail shirt as being equivalent in value to two horses or six oxen and a helmet the equivalent of one horse.[16] This helps to explain why the Romans forbade the sale of weapons and armour to the Germans and why Germanic tribes were so poorly armed. Unlike the Romans, they simply couldn't afford the equipment.

Equipment

Missiles   The majority of missiles used by Germanic troops appear to be of the hand-thrown variety. Although bows were in use, they were not composite bows as used by the Romans, Alans, Sarmatians and Huns. Instead, they were simple bows made from a single piece of wood.[17] Archery does not appear to have been an important part of Germanic warfare, and so the evolution of the bow in the west was very slow when compared to the east. Agathias even goes so far as to claim that the Franks did not know how to use the bow.[18] Furthermore, unlike the Huns and the Alans, the Germans did not employ the bow as a mass weapon from horseback. Only individuals used the bow when mounted in the west.[19] Unfortunately, there is also little conclusive evidence for the carrying of more than one spear by the cavalry. Representations in art show only a single spear, and ancient authors do not mention the use of javelins by German cavalry. As a result, it may be that German cavalry did not practice missile warfare, instead relying on advancing quickly to close combat and using the spear as a thrusting weapon. This is certainly the impression given by Procopius when describing the later warfare as practiced by the Vandals and Goths.[20]

As with the bow, although there can be little doubt that the sling was known to the northern tribes, there is very little evidence for its use during the period in question. Therefore, although a possibility, whether it was used by troops in battle remains a mystery.

Alongside the variety of 'javelins' and their heavier equivalents (see below), the main missile weapon favoured by the Germanic tribes along the Rhine was the *francisca*, a throwing axe carried by a large number of warriors. The axe was possibly first called the *francisca* by Isidore of Seville (c.560–636), who claimed that it was given that name by the Spanish because of its extensive use by the Franks.[21] It is notable that slightly earlier than this Gregory of Tours (c.538–594) called it either the *securis* or the *bipennis*,[22] therefore only by the later time of Isidore was it used extensively by the Franks. Prior to this, it was used by many of the Germanic tribes, and examples have been found in Britain, Alamannia and further east.[23]

One area where the Germans were poorly served was in siege warfare. The tribes of the west did not know how to build artillery or other siege weapons with which to take cities. Instead, they were forced to rely on subterfuge and the betrayal of cities by sympathetic individuals within them.

Combat Weapons   The sword used by the Germans was their own version of the *spatha*, the long, double-edged sword that varied from between 0.7 to 0.9 metres in length.[24] Unfortunately, although the German smiths were adept at making these weapons, the results were expensive and so restricted the distribution of swords among the poorer classes of warrior. As a result, the most common weapon was the spear. As was stated in the section on Roman equipment, it is commonly assumed that hand-held, shafted weapons were either used as missiles or retained for use in hand-to-hand combat, whereas in reality there was little difference between spears and javelins.

Many of the spears used by the Germans were similar to those used by the Romans, doubtless through the extensive contacts over the centuries and the employment of German warriors by the Roman army. Items such as the Roman *pilum* and its derivatives such as the spiculum found their equivalent in the German *angon* and its equivalents, as excavated in places such as Vimose and Illerup (third century) and Ejsbøl and Nydam (fourth century).[25] These items were widespread and not the dominant weapon of a specific group. The *angon* is found as far apart as Britain and the upper Danube.[26]

However, as with the Romans, the most common item appears to have been a simple spear, which could be used either underarm or overarm by both the cavalry and infantry, and which was about 2.5 to 3.5 metres in length with a variety of metal heads fixed to the top of the shaft.[27] These were the most common weapons used by the Germans, being found in large numbers throughout *Germania*.

One distinctive item of equipment carried by German warriors was the *seax*, a 'short-sword' or 'dagger', depending on the dimensions of the individual weapon.[28] This was a single-edged blade of various lengths, and as time passed it gradually became longer and developed into a short sword. However, in this early period it is probably best thought of as a dagger for when the primary weapon, either spear or sword, was lost or rendered unusable. Like the *francisca*, although later identified with a specific people, in this case the Saxons, in the earlier period it was found throughout *barbaricum*, not just in Saxony.[29]

Finally, as with the Roman army, there were a number of other weapons that appear to have been used in limited numbers, according to the personal taste of the warrior. Amongst these are axes, clubs and 'warhammers', yet it should be remembered that none of these weapons were common.[30]

Defensive Equipment   Metal helmets were extremely expensive and beyond the means of the vast majority of warriors, being restricted to the wealthier nobles and *comitatus*. What little evidence there is suggests that they were similar to the spangenhelms and ridge helmets used by the Romans. As a cheaper alternative, Ammianus mentions the use of leather helmets which, whilst imperfect, would no doubt be an improvement on going bareheaded.[31]

It appears that the few individuals who could afford armour wore either mail or scale styles. As is to be expected, these were extremely expensive: they are rarely found in burials, suggesting that they were considered valuable heirlooms rather than items for deposition.[32] Although over time these items slowly became more common, the process was slow. One of the greatest rewards for a German leader would be acceptance as a Roman officer, with access to Roman arsenals for himself and his followers. This was to become an increasingly common demand from Germanic invaders.

The shields used by the German tribes appear to have been mainly round or oval in shape and could be anywhere from around 60 centimetres to 1 metre in height (2–3 feet), probably based on personal preference.[33] The traditional hexagonal shape associated with the German cavalry employed within the empire during the first centuries BC and AD was still in use, but to a lesser degree than other styles. Although other styles of shield are depicted on monuments, in general they appear to be variants of the oval or octagonal types and may have been relatively uncommon.

In the mid to late twentieth century and earlier there was a form of shield known as the 'coffin' shield, which was traditionally assigned to the Goths. Although this is now firmly fixed, it has proved impossible to find any examples in either the sculptural or archaeological record. It is possible that some of the monumental evidence was interpreted as proof of the existence of these shields but that these examples have since been re-interpreted as stylistic conventions caused by the problem of perspective. As a result, although it is has proved impossible to determine whether these forms actually existed, the likelihood is that they did not.

It is interesting to note that during this period there was a change in the shape of the boss on Germanic shields. The metal boss was used to cover the hole in the shield made by the hand-grip. Before and after the period of the migrations the boss was usually a simple dome shape. During the migration period, although the dome shape persisted, there was a shift to a more pointed shape of boss. Warriors would always have punched with the shield when opportunity arose, but the earlier and later dome shape of the boss implies that the shield retained a more important role as a defensive item. The change in boss shape to a point suggests that the shields were now used in an offensive capacity for punching, indicating that for a short period of time during the migrations Germanic warriors adopted a more aggressive attitude to warfare.

Germans and the Empire

The people of the empire had a standard of living, especially amongst the higher echelons, that was unheard of in *Germania*. During the previous 400 years there had been many examples of German warriors who had entered the empire and risen to high rank, gaining along the way comparatively fabulous wealth. The empire was 'a land of opportunity with great ease of living'.[34] The availability of goods that they could not otherwise obtain accounts for the large number of raids and attacks launched against the empire by German cantons.

Many Germanic attacks, such as the invasion of Italy by Alaric in 401 and the invasion of Gaul in 406, took place in winter.[35] This was probably due to the fact that the farmers who comprised the bulk of the army had little to do agriculturally at this time of year. Further, the harvest in autumn would supply the attackers with food for the campaign.

The superior lifestyle of the Romans also explains why the Germans were determined to settle within the empire. Their leaders could demand military positions, the pay for which would allow them to live to standards they would be unable to achieve at home. Even the peasant farmers would benefit by the move, since there were large areas of agricultural land within the empire that was of far better quality than that across the Rhine. It is little wonder that as the empire declined German pressure on the frontiers increased.

Strategy and Tactics   By the time that Aetius came to power German strategy can be defined as putting pressure on the emperor to allow the Germans to settle on imperial soil and to give the Germanic leaders posts within the Roman military hierarchy that would elevate their prestige amongst their followers, as well as giving them the money with which to maintain – and even expand – their *comitatus*. The practice of cantons raiding the empire seems to have been in decline. Instead, the peoples along the frontiers, especially the Franks, began their slow, inexorable and permanent infiltration of the imperial borders.

In war, although the individual leaders of Germanic tribes may have been more sophisticated than their predecessors, the fact that the troops remained virtually untrained peasant farmers restricted their abilities. With little training and co-ordination, German tactics on the battlefield could not become too convoluted, as the troops would easily become confused. As a result, in battle the infantry formed a single line with the cavalry on the flanks. However, the Battle of Strasbourg shows that ambushes were a possibility when an opportunity arose.[36]

When defeated, many of the western Germans simply fled as best they could, but the eastern Germans, such as the Goths, adopted the wagon laager of the nomadic peoples to the east. This gave them a secure place to which they could retreat. Furthermore, it acted as a military camp and could be used as a fortification if needed, as happened at Adrianople and later in Greece.[37]

Germanic inability to build siege engines resulted in their being unable to capture cities unless by stealth or treachery. As a result, they had to resort to blockade and threat. When circumstances were favourable, as after the victory at Adrianople, these tactics could work. If the circumstances were unfavourable, such as when cities were strongly defended, the Germans tended to bypass them to reach softer targets such as villas. Their lack of siege ability remained a constant weakness in the arsenal of the German tribes, even after their founding of new kingdoms on Roman soil.

In conclusion, it would appear that there were very few changes in tactics or strategy between the first and the fifth centuries. However, the fact that many individual Germans took service in the Roman army no doubt had the effect of very slowly transforming their organization and outlook. Unfortunately, the nature of any such transformation is not documented by the Romans, who believed that they were facing the same type of foes as their ancestors had faced under Augustus and Marcus Aurelius.

The Huns

The political institutions of the Huns appear to have been similar to those of the western Germans. A group of families owed allegiance to a noble or warlord, who in turn gave service to a superior noble. As with the Germans, this resulted in a fluid society where allegiance could easily change unless loyalty or fear kept lesser nobles in their place. The fragmentary nature of Hunnic society is demonstrated by the large number of Huns who, with their leaders, entered service with the Roman army. In some cases this was doubtless to avoid serving an unpopular leader at home who had established a large powerbase and sought to expand it by dominating those tribes around him.

In warfare, the Huns were renowned for their superior skills at horse archery, the majority of their troops being lightly equipped horse archers. Some of the nobles may have employed helmets and body armour, in which case they most probably used the same styles of equipment as their neighbours. If this is the case, then at least some of their forces may have been equipped with simple *spangenhelm* helmets and either traditional chain- or scale-mail, or possibly *lamellar* armour. It is probable that scale mail and lamellar predominated, since both of these styles were easier to make and maintain. They were also lighter and easier to tailor to the needs of mounted troops using a bow.

Hunnic swords would probably have been eastern versions of the *spatha* design, as used by the eastern Germanic tribes and more especially by the Persians. We have no information on additional equipment such as greaves and vambraces. Since the main role of the Hunnic warrior was as a light horse archer, if these items were used at all it is probable that it would have been amongst the nobles, yet even here they would be rare.

The main weapon of the Huns was the asymmetrical composite bow, the lower limb being shorter than the upper limb. The result is a bow that is easier to fire from horseback, since the lower limb tends to make less contact and be less interfered with by the horse. Extensive research by modern bowyers and archers has established that, although the asymmetrical bow requires much more skill and is much harder to master than the symmetrical bow, the end result is an archer that is far superior to one using the symmetrical bow. The asymmetrical bow excels in really high poundages (the amount of power needed to draw back the string), which gives greater range and power, is faster to fire, and performs far better with a thumb ring. In tests a fair degree of accuracy and power can be achieved even with flightless arrows by an archer trained in the use of the thumb ring.[38]

The Huns did not have regimented training regimes such as those found in the Roman army. Yet this was not necessary. They relied on manoeuvrability as their main tactic:

> When provoked they sometimes fight singly but they enter the battle in tactical formation, while their medley of voices makes a savage noise. And as they are lightly equipped for swift motion, and unexpected in action, they purposely divide suddenly in scattered bands and attack, rushing

about in disorder here and there, dealing terrific slaughter; and because of their extraordinary rapidity of movement they cannot be discerned when they break into a rampart or pillage an enemy's camp.[39]

The Huns relied on the superior horsemanship gained from many years of riding horses to enable them to manoeuvre so rapidly in front of their enemies. This skill also allowed them to employ one of their favourite battlefield tactics – the 'feigned flight'. By pretending to rout, the Huns would make the enemy believe that the battle was won, coaxing them into chasing after the retreating Huns. Once the enemy formation was broken the Huns would quickly reverse direction and attack the disordered pursuers, usually with devastating effect.[40] The 'hit and run' tactics employed during both raids into enemy territory as well as large-scale battles was hard for their enemies to counter because of their relative immobility. The prospective losses in booty and the need to maintain troops to face the Huns means that in reality it was probably cheaper to pay 'tribute' to the Huns than oppose them. Furthermore, the lack of permanent settlements may have made the Huns particularly difficult for the Romans to fight, since the usual Roman response to a raid was to lead a counter-attack, which devastated the enemy homelands. It is only later that the Huns under Attila appear to have made semi-permanent home-steads. When this happened, they in turn became vulnerable to strikes against their families.[41]

There was no single king amongst the Huns. Division was by tribe, with each tribe following its own leaders. Although tribes could easily form temporary alliances against mutual enemies, it should not be thought that all Huns were a single 'people' with the same aims and ideals. The Huns appear to have been a large collection of tribes who had slowly moved west in a combination of small groups and large armies. Nor was there the concept of a 'Hunnic empire'. In fact Hunnic mercenaries may have served Gothic kings against their fellow Huns in the fourth century.[42] The modern concept of a single, unified horde is mistaken. The only time when the Huns ever approached unity was under the leadership of Attila, and even this was only temporary as after his death his empire quickly collapsed.

For a long time these warriors would be allied to Aetius and be the basis of his military and political standing. Yet towards the end of his rule they would be turned against him and the most renowned point of Aetius' career would be a fight against these formidable warriors, led by Attila, their most famous leader.

Chapter 6

Magister Militum per Gallias

THE ARMY OF GAUL

After coming to an agreement with Placidia, Aetius was given control of the field army in Gaul. Unfortunately, the actual condition of the army there is unknown at this late date, and is a matter of some debate. As was noted in the introduction, it is possible to use the *Notitia Dignitatum* as a basis for analysis, but in reality the *Notitia* is of uncertain reliability.

There is little other recourse for anyone attempting to reconstruct the nature of the fifth-century army. Consequently, the figures that follow, although highly speculative, at least give an impression of what Aetius expected to lead upon assuming command.

The *Notitia* lists either fifteen or sixteen *Auxilia Palatina* units, one *Legionis Palatina* unit, nine *Legiones Comitatenses* units, ten *Legiones Comitatenses* and twelve other units whose status is unclear. This gives a theoretical total of 45,600 men if all units are at full paper strength, or the lower figure of 30,400 if a two-thirds strength is assumed.

For cavalry, the Notitia lists four *Equites Palatina* units and eight *Equites Comitatenses* units. Again, at theoretical full strength this would give a mounted arm of 7,200 men, whilst the two-thirds estimate would give 4,800 men.

Although in theory these forces could have been supplemented by taking *limitanei* from the frontiers and using them in the field army, in this period the move would have been risky, as weakening the frontiers could have invited yet further attacks from across the Rhine.

It is possible that Aetius also had with him some *foederati*, but if so the nature and numbers of these troops is completely unknown. Finally, he would almost certainly have maintained a small force of *bucellarii* for his personal use. Again the composition and numbers are unknown, but it is reasonable to assume that he would have had a small bodyguard of Huns, provided by Rua but paid for by Aetius himself.

The total force that Aetius could command can, therefore, be assumed to muster between 35,200 and 52,800, although it should be acknowledged that illness, injury, the need to deploy troops away from the main field army as garrisons, plus the need to leave an administrative core at the unit's base, will have further reduced the numbers available.[1] As a result, it can be assumed that Aetius could command troops numbering around 20,000–30,000 foot and 3,200–4,000 horse, an average of approximately 29,000 men. However, as noted above, it is possible that the number was much less, as some of the units may now have been part of the *praesental* army in Italy, whilst others may only have existed on paper.

When Aetius succeeded to the command the troops were most probably stationed at various points around Gaul. Immediately upon his appointment in Italy it is most likely that the only troops Aetius had control of were a small number of Huns retained for his personal service after the dismissal of the main body. These would form the core of his personal *bucellarii*. It is highly unlikely that he would have been given troops from the army of Italy as this would be needed to guarantee the newly won position of emperor for Valentinian III and, in any case, would not be given to the recently defeated leader of a rebellion in case he decided to renew the conflict. Furthermore, a large part of the army that had won the civil war was from the East and would ultimately have to return home. Finally, before he could take control of

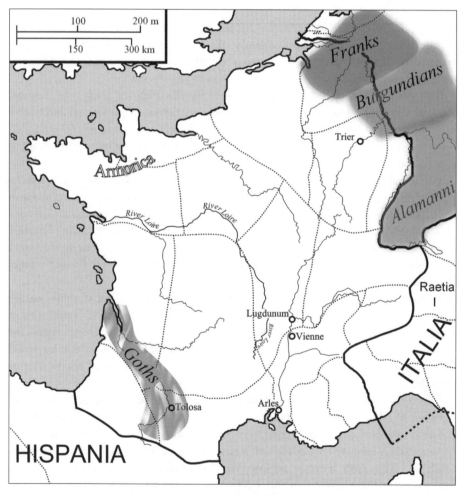

Map 4. Aetius in Gaul

the Gallic army, Aetius would need intelligence on recent events in Gaul prior to departing from Italy to gather his army in person.

Conditions in Gaul

> The barbarians above the Rhine, assaulting everything at their pleasure, reduced both the inhabitants of Britain and some of the Celtic peoples to defecting from Roman rule and living their own lives disassociated from the Roman law. Accordingly the Britons took up arms and, with no consideration of the danger to themselves, freed their own cities from barbarian threat; likewise all of Armorica and other Gallic provinces followed the Britons' lead: they freed themselves, ejected the Roman magistrates, and set up home rule at their own discretion.
>
> *Zosimus 6.5*

> Gaul and Spain were demolished and utterly destroyed by the barbarian nations of the Vandals, Sueves, and Alans.
>
> *Narratio de imperatoribus domus Valentinianae et Theodosiane*

The greatest difficulty facing Aetius when he became the commander of the army in Gaul was the confusion prevalent in the West. The rebellion in Britain and the constant usurpations in Gaul and Spain, coupled with the invasions of the Vandals, Alans and Sueves and the later arrival of the Goths, had all overwhelmed large areas of Gaul. Where the barbarians had not actually plundered the countryside, the army's lack of ability to maintain order had allowed several areas of Gaul, such as Armorica in the north, to become practically self-governing under the aristocrats who had remained in the area. However, the departure of the Vandals, Alans and Sueves to Spain and the settlement of the Goths in Aquitania allowed time for the restoration of order. The campaigns of Constantius III (d. 321) had no doubt ensured that in most areas, and especially in the south around Arles, peace was restored.

Yet conditions had not been restored to those that had existed prior to 406. The seat of government was now permanently in Arles rather than Trier, and the post of *Praefectus praetorio Galliarum* was now firmly in the hands of the aristocracy of southern Gaul. Whereas before 406 it had tended to be in the hands of Italian senators – probably individuals who had large land-holdings in the south of Gaul – it was now held by Exuperantius and possibly Amatius after him.[2]

Furthermore, although the Gallic upper classes could still hold imperial office in the traditional manner, there were distinct problems in Gaul. One was that with the movement of the capital to the south and the withdrawal of the imperial court to Ravenna there was a lack of opportunities for men of ambition. The resultant lack of economic and political power resulted in the beginning of a steady decline in traditional education, such as rhetoric, for all but the highest echelons of society.

Coupled with this was the lack of enthusiasm of all but a few to enter imperial service. In imperial service the hours were long and except possibly at the very top levels the financial rewards were not seen as being equal to the workload imposed. As a result, instead of serving the empire, those of more modest means began to transfer their ambition to the church, another piece of evidence for the gradual fragmentation and transferral of loyalties in the West.[3]

This may seem surprising, in that the church was an imperial institution and had intentionally copied imperial forms of administration. Yet the influx of influential members of the higher and lower aristocracy resulted in the church growing ever greater in prestige. As imperial power withdrew, the removal of traditional sources of patronage and influence resulted in the church becoming the local expression of imperial government. As a result, the local bishops soon came to be ranked higher than other imperial representatives: for example, the Bishop of Arles soon began to wield social and political power far beyond his status as a bishop.[4]

The hierarchical ties to the emperor broke. The local loyalties that had earlier focused upon the hierarchy's ties to the imperial person were transferred to the local bishop, who became the trusted spokesman at court.[5] Rather than focusing upon the empire or the province, all ranks of the local Christian community began to give their loyalties to the much smaller division of the diocese. As a result, bishops became increasingly more autocratic.

The process had been given a major boost by a scandal in the late fourth century. In 390 Bishop Ambrose of Milan had excommunicated Emperor Theodosius I after Theodosius had ordered a massacre of civilians in Thessalonica. Theodosius had been forced to undergo several months of public penance before being allowed back into the church. The episode had major implications. The impression given was that bishops could have authority over the emperor himself. (It should be remembered that in this period the Pope was revered as being senior, but had not yet been acknowledged as the infallible 'God's representative on earth' of the Middle Ages.) In theory, any bishop could use Ambrose's actions as a model in his dealings with the emperor, although it must be noted that later emperors were less likely to pay attention than the pious Theodosius and not all bishops were as forceful as Ambrose. Yet the benchmark had been set: in some instances the church was mightier than the emperor.

The imperial government was aware of these developments. The inauguration of a new 'Council of the Seven Gauls' can be interpreted as a major political statement by the government. Although the settlement of the Goths in Aquitania could easily be seen as the break up of Gaul into non-Roman 'kingdoms', the Council was to represent the whole of Gaul and was a declaration that the whole of Gaul, including both the areas settled by the Goths as well as the north, was still part of the empire, with the Goths as a small people within it.[6]

The usurpation of John in 424 had resulted in yet another civil war in the West when it really needed time to recuperate and restore itself. The news that the army of the *magister militum praesentalis*, and possibly units of the army of Gaul, was being withdrawn to defend Italy meant that some outlying areas of northern Gaul, especially Armorica, continued their drift away from the empire, seeing no benefit in paying high taxes to an empire that was totally incapable of fulfilling its duties with regard to protection.

There was one further development that was to affect seriously Aetius' time as commander in Gaul. Economically and politically, the provinces of Gaul were becoming increasingly divided between the north and the south. In the south, Arles (Arelate) was being developed until it could be described as *Gallula Roma Arelas* ('Arelas, small Gallic version of Rome') by Ausonius.[7] The town had become important largely thanks to its river harbour, which was mainly concerned with the transport of the *annona*, receiving goods from the Mediterranean and sending them on to Trier and the rest of Gaul. With the settlement of the Praetorian Prefect of Gaul in the city, Arles became even more important than previously, in the fifth century rebuilding the walls for greater protection, probably against the combined threat of the Goths in Gaul and of the Vandals in Spain. The government was also under pressure from the Senate to keep the south of Gaul inviolate and safe, who had large landholdings in the area. Economically, militarily and politically, southern Gaul was seen as vital to the welfare of the empire.

In the north of Gaul, however, and especially north of the Loire, things were different. Under constant threat of invasion, the landowners of large estates had withdrawn and landholding had reverted to small, peasant plots, possibly under the control of local aristocrats. The removal of the court and large sections of the army caused a loss of income that resulted in a reduction in the import of, for example, fine pottery from southern Gaul, northern Italy and Spain.[8] As the distinctive services of the empire withdrew, so the forces of self-government grew. The north was to become a centre of resistance to Roman rule in Gaul.

Despite this, even in the north the aristocracy spent much of its time and resources on the building of religious centres. As a result, the towns of Gaul were 'transformed largely from centres of Roman civilization to the cores around which the Christian religion flourished and kept alive some of the imperial values and structures'.[9]

However, for Aetius, the immediate problem was that John's policies in Gaul had resulted in the death of the newly appointed Praetorian Prefect Exuperantius and possibly of Gaudentius, Aetius' father, both of whom had been killed by the troops.[10] It was clear that the imperial and personal policies of John and his predecessors had done much to alienate the population of Gaul from imperial rule. As he took up his post of *magister militum per Gallias* Aetius was faced with the need to counter the growing sense of disunity in Gaul. He was also faced with the Goths under their king, Theoderic.

The Goths

Although there is a tendency amongst modern historians to call the Visigothic territories in Gaul a kingdom from the moment of their settlement in 418–419, this is a mistake.[11] The designation 'kingdom' has unavoidable associations, bringing to mind the more settled monarchies of the early to high medieval period. The reality in fifth-century Gaul was far different. The title kingdom is also one given in hindsight, built largely upon the claim to the title *rex Gothorum* by Alaric and his successors.[12] Yet there are two problems with this interpretation. The first is that the title of *rex* was not Germanic. It was of Roman origin and was used in an attempt by Roman writers to identify the military and political leaders of the barbarians. Alaric was possibly the first Germanic leader to use the title himself, employing it as a political tool to place pressure on the court at Ravenna. The actual date at which Gothic leaders stopped using the title as a political tool and began to use it as a firm claim to total dominion over their fellow Goths is unknown. Secondly, although the Visigothic leaders were using the title '*rex*', they accepted that the more powerful Germanic title of '*thiudans*' was still only to be borne by the reigning emperor in Ravenna.[13]

Furthermore, it is unclear what, if any, difference there was between the earlier settlement of the Goths in 382 and the later settlement of 419. Although it can be claimed that the main difference was that the later settlement had a leader who claimed the title *rex*, the lack of information concerning the settlement of 382 means that there remains the possibility that this settlement, too, recognised the dominance of a single Gothic leader. Yet the earlier Gothic settlement is not referred to as a kingdom.

Apart from this, the two settlements may be more similar than expected: in the east the Goths had been allocated a specific territory but their dependence upon Roman generosity remained and there were distinct limits on their freedom; in the west, in the new 'proto-kingdom', they were settled in a specific territory and there was a similar limit to Visigothic power, since they were excluded from the Mediterranean and the Romans maintained full control of the land routes to Spain.[14]

The similarities are not surprising, since in both cases the Roman victories that achieved the treaties were almost identical: the Goths had achieved 'unbelievable' triumphs – the Battle of Adrianople in 378 and the Sack of Rome in 410 – before being blockaded into submission. It is likely that in both cases the Goths were settled according to the principles of *receptio* and the provision of recruits for the army.[15] As in the east, there was thus no guarantee – and probably little hope – that the Goths would establish their own rule and break free from the domination of Rome.

The history of the Goths from the rise to power of Alaric in 396 to their settlement only twenty-two years later in 418 shows that, far from being an unitary force under a settled king, the Goths were in fact a conglomeration of forces and tribes who had agreed to follow the lead of Alaric and his successors.[16] At any time of their choosing, the Visigothic aristocracy always retained the right to leave the main body and strike out on their own, either to move out of the empire or to join with imperial forces in the hope of employment and promotion. Naturally, the men that owed allegiance to the aristocracy would follow their leaders in whichever way they chose to go.

It would be unrealistic to assume that the Visigothic aristocracy gave up this right the moment that the Romans allowed them to settle in Gaul. It is far more likely that they continued to act in an independent manner. Even a century later powerful

Gothic nobles caused intense dynastic instability. Not only that, but the Goths were not the only component of the new kingdom. At some later point during the Gothic siege of Bazas their Alan allies had a change of heart and defected to the Romans defending the town.[17] If the Gothic nobles and allies could defect later in their history, the possibility would be especially the case immediately after the settlement in Gaul.

Yet the seeds were quickly sown for the growth in power of the Gothic king. The fact that the Romans had granted the Goths land in the three provinces meant that, in effect, the Gothic aristocracy assumed the role of the now-vacant Roman aristocracy. The only way that the Goths could control their new lands was by the use of Roman administrative systems. The result was that the Gothic aristocracy immediately began to settle in the towns. Theoderic himself settled in Toulouse and all Roman political exchanges with the Goths was via the new Gothic 'capital'. The role of Theoderic as the sole leader of the Goths was important to the Romans, as it made dealing with them easier for the imperial government. Theoderic was treated as the sole leader, but in return he was expected to control all of the Goths and maintain his part of the treaty with Rome.

The fact that the Romans tended to channel their diplomacy through Theoderic resulted in Toulouse becoming effectively the capital of the Visigothic proto-kingdom. The increased political power of the king no doubt contributed to an increase in internal political control.[18] Furthermore, it is likely that from this time onwards Theoderic established a 'standing army'. He was able to use this army to defend himself from internal rebellions, as well as protecting his people from external threats.[19]

However, those aristocrats who had been given land away from the capital no doubt ignored the commands of the new king in distant Toulouse whenever it suited them. In effect, rather than being the anointed king, it is better to see Theoderic as an individual who has continually to prove himself in order to retain control of his most powerful subjects. Only by exerting his full power and demonstrating that he was in control would he ensure that the majority of the aristocracy would look to him for guidance. Otherwise, they would continue in the old traditions of independence.

In this context, the outbreak of a Roman civil war was of inestimable value to Theoderic. As a recently created king, his hold on power was likely to be relatively tenuous. After all, two of his immediate predecessors had been killed by disaffected factions that remained within Theoderic's following. In order to avoid this happening to himself, Theoderic needed to demonstrate that he had the ability to support those who followed him.

Consequently, as the conflict between John and Valentinian began, Theoderic attempted to augment and demonstrate his strength. It is possible that he sent forces to capture many small towns, especially those at strategic points. However, only one city is mentioned directly in our sources. At the time when Aetius was appointed to the command in Gaul, Theoderic and the Goths were busy laying siege to Arelate (Arles).[20]

The Visigothic siege of Arles, the capital of Gaul and the seat of the newly founded Council of the Seven Provinces, is usually interpreted as an attempt by Theoderic to extend Visigothic influence to the Mediterranean.[21] However, this is almost certainly too simplistic an interpretation. The decision to lay siege to Arles was probably the combination of many factors. One of these is that the deaths of Gaudentius and Exuperantius demonstrate that Gaul was not going to support John. By promoting his actions as those of a loyal representative of the 'true' imperial government, Theoderic could join the Gallic forces in besieging the agents of the usurper. After all, Theoderic's treaty was with the members of the Theodosian dynasty, and he may have been able to claim that he was simply fulfilling his obligation by attacking disloyal elements.

A second factor is that financially the city was of huge importance to the empire, as it was the main commercial centre of Gaul through which the majority of trade passed to the Mediterranean. Its loss would be a serious blow to the financial affairs of Ravenna, which were already in a perilous condition.[22] Furthermore, Arles was now the capital of Gaul and was of inestimable political importance to Rome. Given the fact that the north of Gaul was beginning its slow slide away from the empire, the loss of Arles would result in the imperial hold on Gaul becoming extremely tenuous. If he could take the city, whichever of the two sides won the civil war would be forced to make concessions to Theoderic for the return of the city, and if the Theodosian claim was victorious they may also have felt obliged to reward him for his loyalty.

On the other hand, taking Theoderic's attempt to capture Arles as evidence of a Gothic attempt to expand their influence to the Mediterranean is unrealistic. Arles was an extremely important city and the chance of the Goths taking Arles and of being allowed simply to keep it were extremely remote. Theoderic would have known this. If the city was taken and held, it was far more likely that a major Roman expedition would be sent to recapture Arles at the first opportunity, and the past twenty years of conflict had shown that the Goths simply could not win. Therefore, it is unlikely that Theoderic seriously contemplated annexing the city on a permanent basis.[23]

Additionally, political treaties were usually seen as being signed between individuals such as Theoderic and Constantius, not between political entities such as Rome and the Goths. The death of Honorius almost certainly meant that there would need to be a new treaty signed with whoever won the civil war. It is more likely that the move to lay Arles under siege was a declaration of loyalty to the Theodosian government in the hope that they would change the terms of the treaty of 418.

It is probable that Theoderic wanted two amendments to the original treaty. The first would have been concerned with extending the land personally held by him. An increase in his personal landholdings would result in an increase in revenue for Theoderic. This in turn would finance an enlarged personal *comitatus* (personal following). As a result, he would be able to begin the process of firmly establishing himself as undisputed leader of the Visigothic kingdom, since his increased military power would allow him to bring the aristocracy under ever-tighter control.

The second was related to the past. In order to be compared favourably with Alaric – the Visigoth who had, after all, sacked Rome itself – Theoderic needed a military post high in the hierarchy of the Roman army. In this way, he would gain the financial benefits from his new position, as well as holding an official rank to use in his dealings with the local aristocracy in Aquitania. He would also gain prestige from being the first of Alaric's successors to gain an official post in the imperial infrastructure.

As a result of these deliberations, when civil war again broke out within the empire Theoderic acted without hesitation and laid siege to Arles.

AETIUS' FIRST CAMPAIGN

Once Aetius had learned of events in Gaul he would have known what to do. He left Italy with his bodyguard and advanced into Gaul with the intention of gathering his forces for a campaign against the Goths. This doubtless took some time, as only a short time previously he had been part of John's regime and had only recently accepted service under Valentinian. Initially the troops stationed in Gaul would have been wary of Aetius' motives and strategies and of following his orders unquestioningly. Having gained the trust of most of the Gallic army, and learning of the composition of the enemy, Aetius collected his forces before advancing towards the Visigothic siege lines.

It is unclear exactly what happened at Arles when Aetius reached the city. The two sources that tell of the siege give only very brief notices of events:

> Arles, noble city of Gaul, was assailed by the Goths with great violence, until, threatened by Aetius they withdrew not without losses.
>
> *Prosper Tiro. s.a. 425*

> Arles was freed from the Goths by Aetius.
>
> *Chron Gall 452 102 s.a. 427*

Prosper's statement that the Goths withdrew 'not without losses' is ambiguous. It could mean either that Aetius' forces attacked and forced the Goths to withdraw after taking casualties, or more likely, if the statement that Arles had been 'assailed by the Goths with great violence' is accurate, that the Goths had taken losses whilst attempting to storm the city. The Gallic Chronicler's statement is completely uninformative on the point. The only thing that is certain is that Theoderic was unwilling to face Aetius in a pitched battle.

It is most likely that Theoderic withdrew without battle, having taken losses only during the course of the siege. As the Roman forces approached, Theoderic's forces were probably dispersed around the city in order to enforce the siege. Needing time to collect and order his forces, Theoderic would have had little choice but to withdraw.

Yet there is another factor. Aetius was the legitimate representative of the new Theodosian government, and his previous role as a hostage with the Goths attested to his political importance. As the son-in-law of Alaric, it is certain that Theoderic was already acquainted with Aetius due to Aetius' tenure as a hostage between 405 and 408. Theoderic could not maintain his stance of supporting the House of Theodosius if he continued the siege in opposition to Aetius.

After the Visigothic departure, Aetius and Theoderic conducted negotiations, during the course of which an exchange of hostages appears to have been arranged and peace terms agreed, possibly with increased benefits in return for continued loyalty to the Theodosian dynasty, although the details are unknown.[24]

The raising of the siege of Arles was of inestimable value to the regime in Ravenna. A military success would have helped to secure Valentinian on the throne, a position that was still precarious. The fact that Aetius had won a victory over the Goths was a sign that after the confusion of the civil war the new regime was asserting itself and the opponents were now working together.

It should be noted that the actual dating of Aetius' campaign is open to question. Prosper dates it to 425, whilst the *Gallic Chronicle of 452* dates it to 427.[25] Although certainty is impossible, given the nature of events it is possible to reconstruct a viable timeline.

In 425 Aetius was made *magister militum per Gallias* and travelled to Gaul. However, he was unable to act instantly as he needed time to re-establish control there. He would need to convince all of the local commanders that he was now the loyal servant of Valentinian and that he had no intention of leading the Gallic army in another civil war. He would also need to demonstrate that he was not going to take reprisals for the death of his father. After this he would need to collect his forces, during which time, and claiming to be unaware of the change in circumstances, the Goths launched their attacks upon the besieged city.[26]

It will have been at the earliest in 426 when Aetius led the Gallic army to relieve the siege of Arles and forced Theoderic to retire. The necessary negotiations needed to conclude the war will most likely have continued into 427, especially as at this early stage in his rehabilitation Aetius would not have had the power to sign the treaty on his own. A lot of time will have been spent waiting for Valentinian and his ministers to ratify the new treaty. Therefore it was only in 427 that a treaty was agreed between Aetius and Theoderic and hostages were exchanged.

Although only a theory, the timeline does allow a reasonable passage of time for all of the events to take place, as well as explaining the confusion in the different chronicles.[27] Following the conclusion of the campaign, and possibly accompanied by an embassy from Theoderic to ratify the treaty, in 427 Aetius returned to Ravenna to report in person on the Gallic campaign.

THE DISGRACE OF BONIFACE

When Aetius returned to the court in 427 it was to find himself embroiled in a political tangle. Felix appears to have been taking steps to ensure that he remained the sole military power in the West. According to Prosper, either during or shortly after Aetius' campaign against the Goths, a tribune by the name of Barbatus had attacked and killed Patroclus, Bishop of Arles, for which Felix was held responsible. It is possible that Aetius was recalled in part to explain the circumstances surrounding Patroclus' death. Furthermore, a deacon in Rome was also attacked, again allegedly upon the orders of Felix.[28] It would appear that Felix was reacting to religious dissent against his rule, and this may reflect a broader sense of unrest.

However, the crisis came when Boniface, Placidia's supporter for several years, was accused of wanting to set up his own empire in Africa.[29] The accusation was made by either Aetius or Felix – unfortunately, our sources differ. Procopius, John of Antioch and Theophanes all claim that Aetius was responsible for the accusations.[30] However, as a note of caution, it should be remembered that Procopius was writing in the sixth century, John of Antioch in the seventh and Theophanes in the eighth. Unfortunately, we do not know what their sources were for these allegations, so it is uncertain how accurate they are likely to be.

Prosper, however, implies that it was Felix who was responsible for the accusations.[31] Given that Prosper was a contemporary who was also antagonistic towards Aetius, it seems possible that he is more accurate in his allegations. Yet, as usual, certainty is impossible. The claim would tie in to the 'aggressive' stance apparently being taken by Felix with regard to any opposition, as shown by the deaths of the clergymen. Furthermore, it is unlikely that Placidia would listen to any accusations made by Aetius, a man who had until recently been the supporter of a usurper. Aetius was not yet in a position where his word would be accepted against Placidia's staunchest ally.

As a consequence, it seems highly probable that it was Felix who made the accusations against Boniface.[32] Coming from the *patricius* and the leader of the army that was supporting her in power, Placidia had to take the accusations seriously. Since Aetius had just returned to report on his actions in Gaul, it would make sense for Placidia to request that Boniface should report on affairs in Africa in person. It would also be a chance to all three of the most important men in the West together to formulate plans for the West's restoration.

Consequently, Placidia was persuaded to summon Boniface to Ravenna, but she was also told that he would not come as he was turning against her. In the meantime, word was sent to Boniface warning him of a plot and advising him not to return to Italy.[33] When Boniface refused to return, Placidia declared him a rebel and ordered Felix to send an army to take control of Africa.[34]

According to his (no doubt welcome) instructions, Felix sent Mavortius and Gallio, both of whom may have been *comes rei militaris*, and Sanoeces, who may also have been a *comes rei militaris* but who could instead have been the leader of a contingent of Huns, to Africa.[35] It would appear that the army was besieging Boniface when Mavortius and Gallio were killed, being betrayed by Sanoeces, although the precise details are unknown. Shortly afterwards Sanoeces himself was killed. When the news reached Italy, the *comes rei militaris* Sigisvult was sent to Africa to conduct the war, which he proceeded to do for the next two years.[36] It is almost certain that Sigisvult was a Goth and that when he was ordered to go to Africa he took a contingent of Gothic troops with him, possibly in accordance with the new treaty signed between Aetius and Theoderic, although the context is extremely insecure.[37] What is more certain is that Sigisvult was an Arian and that he took with him the Arian bishop Maximinus. Shortly after landing, Maximinus was sent to dispute with Augustine in Hippo.[38]

PANNONIA

In the meantime, either late in 426 or early in 427, Felix set out to fight the Huns, who had allegedly held Pannonia for fifty years.[39] Interestingly, Jordanes also notes the attack on the Huns, claiming that the Roman army was accompanied by Goths.[40] Although the entry in Jordanes is suspect, and doubtless there were many groups of Goths who were unattached to the settlement in Aquitaine seeking employment, it is intriguing to note that this tallies with the possibility of the employment of Goths by Sigisvult mentioned above. Consequently, it is almost certain that immediately after the treaty with Theoderic there is evidence for the Goths supporting Rome. It is also evident that the Huns did not have any large settlements in Pannonia, their presence being restricted to smaller settlements and the pasturing of flocks across the River Save. As a result, the campaign was a success, and the Huns, who had probably only lightly held areas in Pannonia, were forced out.

Politically and militarily the successful campaign would be important to Felix. He had led the Italian *comitatensis* against the enemy in his first military operation as the senior *magister*. The 'victory' over the barbarians established his credentials and helped to cement his grasp on power. Felix would be able to broadcast a large amount of positive propaganda about his leadership qualities, if only to act as a counterbalance to the victories Aetius was winning in Gaul.

THE CAMPAIGN ON THE RHINE

It is unlikely that Aetius was involved in this campaign, since his presence was needed in Gaul, where a lot of work was still needed in order to restore the whole of Gaul to the empire. He is likely to have spent the remainder of the year of 427 returning to Gaul and preparing for the campaign of the following year.

When the campaign season of 428 began Aetius gathered his forces and advanced towards the Rhine.[41] The Franks had used the opportunity given by the Roman civil war to extend their territories along the river. It is likely that the Franks had not conducted a military campaign, but that there had been a peaceful settlement on abandoned farmland along the frontier, in a similar manner to the Huns in Pannonia. Surviving farmers may also have employed cheap illegal immigrants rather than Romans, helping the Franks to recognize where Roman lands were becoming deserted.[42] Advancing with his army, Aetius forcibly evicted the trespassing Franks, making them retire from Roman territory and probably taking the opportunity to re-negotiate agreements with the recognized leaders of the Franks which had been annulled by the death of Honorius.[43] At the same time, Aetius reinforced the concept that the empire was now strong and reunited once more, and that the Franks were again subject to Roman commands.

Aetius now had two successful campaigns to his credit against two of the dominant barbarian groups of Gaul. It was fitting that the newly appointed *magister militum per Gallias* was responsible for restoring Roman authority by defeating the Goths and the Franks. Furthermore, the speed at which he was intimidating barbarians and recovering Gaul was no doubt appreciated in Ravenna. He was quickly gaining credibility. Furthermore, the involvement of the Gallic aristocracy in the usurpations of 411 and 413 had damaged their influence at court. In response they changed to taking religious careers, during which they could rise to the point where they could wield a great deal of religious and political power.[44] However, those who were still hoping that they could regain their political influence saw Aetius as the ideal man to support. His success in Gaul and his political power in Ravenna resulted in him being seen by the Gallic aristocracy as the man to follow. However, political events in Africa and Ravenna were to have far-reaching consequences, both for Aetius and for the empire.

BRITAIN

Aetius' successes in Gaul may have had an impression on the peoples of Britain. The resurgence of the empire on the continent appears to have resulted in an increase in contact between Britain and Gaul. The attempt by the empire to reassert its control of northern Gaul may have resulted in an expectation that the empire would soon be restoring its government in Britain.[45] Accordingly, the Catholic leaders of the island sent messengers to Rome asking for a mission to be sent to combat the rise of Pelagianism on the island.[46] There was a synod held in Gaul and 'on the recommendation of the deacon Palladius, Pope Celestine sent Germanus, bishop of Auxerre, as his representative'.[47] By restoring the links between Gaul and Britain via the church the government was able to declare that the British provinces were once more part of the empire.

THE VANDALS

As was mentioned earlier, whilst all of this activity was occurring in Gaul and Italy, in Spain the Vandals had not been idle. They and their allies moved into the south of Spain and in 425 and 426 captured Carthago Spartaria (early Roman Carthago Nova, now Cartagena) and sacked Hispalis (Seville), following which Gunderic, king of the Vandals, died. His successor was his brother, Gaiseric.[48] It is likely that with their capture of Carthage the Vandals captured a large number of sea-going vessels in the harbour. Using these, in 425 they ravaged the Balearic Islands and also raided Mauretania.[49] It is likely that they faced little opposition in Mauretania, a fact that Gaiseric would remember.

Normally, the Romans would have gathered a fleet together to oppose the Vandals' use of ships, but at this time the fleet from the western Mediterranean was either in Gaiseric's own hands after the fall of Cartagena, or was being used to transport, guard and supply the forces being used by Sigisvult for the war against Boniface. However, the capture of a Roman fleet and the lack of Roman opposition

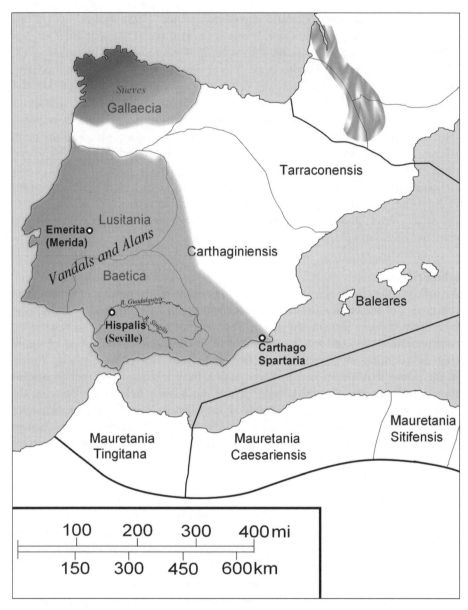

Map 5. Spain c.429

gave Gaiseric the chance to implement a move that would prove fateful for both the Vandals and for the Romans. Access to the sea gave him the opportunity to cross the Straits of Gibraltar and land in Africa.

Realizing that an alliance with the now Mediterranean-based Vandals could help to defeat the enemy, either Felix or Sigisvult made a complete U-turn and attempted to recruit at least some of the Vandals to their cause. At the same time, and possibly with more hope of success, Boniface may also have attempted to gain the alliance of at least some of the Vandals:

> Thereafter access to the sea was gained by peoples who were unacquainted with ships until they were called in by the rival sides to give assistance.
>
> *Prosper Tiro s.a. 427*

It was unlikely that the Vandals would agree to fight alongside the Goths, who had only the decade before so ravaged the Vandals themselves. However, in the case of Boniface, the recruiting of Vandals was an obvious measure to offset the opposition's use of Goths. Furthermore, following the attack of the Goths in 416–418, it is likely that the opportunity to fight the Goths would be taken by at least some of the Vandals. It would appear that at least some agreed to join the Roman army and fight for Boniface against Sigisvult and his Goths. They would have represented those individuals who were unhappy at the total dominance of Gaiseric in Spain.

Yet Gaiseric retained command of the majority of the Vandals and was still intent on capturing more territory in Spain. In 428 they captured, and this time held, Hispalis.[50] They now had large parts of the south of Spain under their control.[51]

The Vandals Cross to Africa

Despite his successes in Spain, it was clear to Gaiseric that his people would always live in fear of a Roman and Suevic attack as long as they remained in Spain. Furthermore, following his acquisition of ships, there was now within his reach a Roman province that was untouched by war and of vital importance to the Romans. With the Roman fleets in use elsewhere, and so unable to stop him, in 429 Gaiseric gathered his people together and prepared to lead them in a wholesale migration across the Straits of Gibraltar to Tingitania.

It is usually accepted that Gaiseric led the whole of the Vandals and Alans to Africa. However, it is possible that some of them had no desire to fight yet another long war with the Romans and instead wished to remain in Spain. These may have now separated from the main body of the Vandals under the leadership of an individual named Andevotus.[52] It should be noted that Andevotus is otherwise unknown and may not have been associated with the Vandals, instead being an (Ostro)Goth.[53]

With his heart set on a move to Africa, Gaiseric received disturbing news. Hermenegarius, described by Hydatius as 'king of the Sueves', although more likely either a son of Hermeric or an unrelated noble, was plundering Lusitania.[54] Gaiseric did not have enough ships to ferry the Vandals to Africa in one crossing: it would take many journeys before they were all safe in Africa.

Gaiseric realized that to attempt a crossing now would leave those Vandals still in Spain awaiting the return of ships vulnerable to attack by the Sueves. Gathering his forces, he led his army in pursuit of the Sueves, finally catching them at Emerita. Defeated in battle, Hermenegarius fled, drowning in the River Ana.[55] Returning south, Gaiseric finally led his people across the Straits into Africa.

There has been much debate concerning the dating of the crossing to Africa and regarding the claim by Procopius and Jordanes that Boniface invited the Vandals in return for aid against his Roman enemies.[56] The dating of the crossing is insecure. However, on this occasion it is possible that Hydatius, living in Spain, is closer to the mark, especially as he may be referring to an unknown source when he dates the crossing specifically to May of 429.[57] Furthermore, 429 allows time for all of the other events chronicled to happen without undue speed of action being required.[58] Consequently, it will be assumed that it was in May 429 that the Vandals crossed to Africa from Spain.

The claim that Boniface was responsible for inviting the Vandals into Africa is also extremely unlikely.[59] Although in revolt against the government in Ravenna, he will have suspected that it was not Placidia herself that was responsible but Felix: Boniface's loyalty had been rewarded in the past and his faithful service would expect continued loyalty from Placidia. Such an invitation would have been seen as the ultimate treachery in Ravenna. However, the strongest argument against Boniface inviting the Vandals into Africa is the complete silence of contemporaries, who in reality would have made the most violent complaints had this been true.[60]

Furthermore, as an experienced commander, Boniface will also have known the perils associated with inviting such a large body of barbarian troops into a relatively undefended province, especially without military supervision. The scenes of his battles against Felix's commanders in the province of Africa were a long way from the Vandals' crossing point. Unsupervised, the Vandals would almost certainly begin to devastate the country around them in the hope of extorting large subsidies and land for their families. As a result of these deliberations, it is possible to theorize that both Procopius and Jordanes knew of Boniface's employment of small numbers of Vandals in the civil war and so assumed that the price for their use was the invitation to cross into Africa.[61] As a final point, at this time Boniface's friends at court were by now enlisted to help clear him from the accusations that had started the war. It would be foolish of Boniface to risk his hope of clearing his name by inviting the Vandals into Africa.

It has also been suggested that Aetius was responsible for the suggestion that the Vandals cross to Africa after the loss of the unnamed battle alongside the Sueves in Spain.[62] This is extremely unlikely, as at this point he was not in a position either to travel to the south of Spain, being embroiled in events in Gaul and Ravenna, or to negotiate with the Vandals, since his office was that of *magister militum per Gallias*. In this context it should be noted that the concept of reaching Africa had proved a lure to the Gothic leader Alaric shortly before his death in 410, and his successor Wallia had also contemplated the crossing in 415:[63] that Gaiseric should consider it with his newly acquired fleet is only natural.

In May–June 429 Gaiseric used his available ships to transport his peoples across the Straits of Gibraltar. The only source for the number of people who crossed is Victor of Vita. He notes that, in an effort to cause fear in Africa, Geiseric ordered a count of his people, 'even those who had come from the womb into the light that very day'.[64] This produced a figure of 80,000 men, women and children. Procopius later noted the claim that there were 80,0000 Vandals in the crossing to Africa, but that the actual number was 50,000.[65] This suggests a viable fighting force of no more than around 20,000 men. Although sometimes questioned by modern historians, it is interesting to observe that Victor himself notes that 'news of this [number of 80,000] had spread widely', and that he was informing people of the true nature of the crossing.[66] It would appear that the rumour had spread that the Vandals had crossed with 80,000 fighting men.

Landing in Mauretania Tingitana, Gaiseric might have expected to face the local army in battle, but since the *comes Tingitana* had a maximum of 5,000–7,000 men, of whom at the most 1,500 would have been capable of facing Gaiseric's battle-hardened veterans, it is unsurprising that the local commander made no move to stop the overwhelming might of the Vandals.[67] With the Vandals now at large south of the Mediterranean and with the important province of Africa under direct threat, Boniface's position was looking extremely insecure.

Chapter 7

Magister Militum Praesentalis[1]

FELIX, BONIFACE AND AETIUS

Stilicho (who controlled the West between 395 and 408) had used the term *comes et magister utriusque militum praesentalis* and *parens principum* to denote his power in the West up to his death in 408.[2] Following his lead, Constantius III had combined the titles *comes et magister utriusque militum praesentalis* and *patricius* (patrician) to demonstrate his position of dominance in the West.[3]

In 425, after the defeat of John, Felix had probably been given the title of *comes et magister utriusque militum praesentalis* and *patricius* in emulation of Constantius III.[4] In theory he was now in the same position as Stilicho and Constantius: effective ruler of the West. Yet this was not so, as, unlike Stilicho or Constantius, Felix had no known backing from the aristocracy of the West and had two challengers to his authority. The first was Boniface, who had supported Galla Placidia during her time of need, and the other was the latecomer Aetius.

Due to Felix's (successful) attempt to have Boniface disgraced, it is clear that early in Valentinian's reign Felix understandably perceived Boniface as the greater threat. This is supported by the fact that during this early period it would actually have been easier for Felix to invent a claim that Aetius was planning on rebelling, since his loyalty to Valentinian would have been a cause for concern. That this was not attempted implies that Aetius was too weak politically and militarily – especially once the Huns had been sent home – to be seen as a threat, although it is possible that even at this early date he had a reputation for being a man of his word and so unlikely to rebel. Furthermore, unlike Aetius, Boniface had been appointed by Honorius and supported by Theodosius II. He had no reason to support Felix as a benefactor. It is likely that Felix would have liked to remove Boniface and replace him with one of his own supporters. Recent history had shown that the commander in Africa wielded great power, as he could cut the supply of grain to Rome and Italy. Felix would not want this position occupied by a political opponent. Yet although the plan to disgrace Boniface had apparently succeeded, the situation was about to be turned on its head.

The year 429 began with two very different reports. Aetius returned to Ravenna bringing news of victories in Gaul and what looked like the beginnings of a complete Roman recovery in the north west. On the other hand, the Vandals were ravaging the western Mediterranean and the war with Boniface looked like it would last indefinitely. However, at some point during the course of the war Placidia had decided that it was not in character for Boniface to attempt to establish his own empire, especially as his loyalty had previously been faultless. As a result, she sent some of Boniface's friends to Africa to open talks with him.[5] At this point the envoys were shown the evidence, and especially the letter telling Boniface not to return to Rome if so ordered.[6] When she heard this Placidia ordered a halt to hostilities and under the guidance of a negotiator from Rome by the name of Darius, who was a senator, Sigisvult and Boniface concluded a peace treaty.[7] Boniface was re-instated in favour at the court.[8] With peace declared, either in late 429 or early in 430 Sigisvult returned to Italy, and Celer, an individual who had previously been *vicarius* of Africa, was appointed Proconsul of Africa.[9]

This was none too soon, as it will have been in mid–late summer 429 that messengers arrived in Carthage with the news that the Vandals had crossed the Straits of Hercules and landed in Tingitania. After Sigisvult had returned to Ravenna, probably early in 430, Boniface began to martial his forces for a campaign against the Vandals. Furthermore, if in Italy they had not heard before, Sigisvult returned to Ravenna with the disastrous news that the Vandals were in Africa and heading towards Carthage. Alarmed at the news, messengers were sent from Ravenna to Constantinople telling of the Vandal invasion and asking for help.[10] Darius headed west in an attempt to negotiate with the Vandals.[11]

comes et magister utriusque militiae

The fact that Felix had used his influence and power to disgrace Boniface, who up to that point had been Placidia's loyal supporter, no doubt turned Placidia against Felix. Recognizing that Felix's position as the only *comes et magister utriusque militiae* gave him almost unlimited power, Placidia decided to set up a rival to counterbalance his presence. This could not be Boniface: politically, appointing him as *comes et magister utriusque militiae* would be unacceptable, since it was clear that he and Felix were now enemies. Such a move would be interpreted – correctly – by Felix as specifically aimed at himself. Although his reaction would be unknown, it would almost certainly result in another civil war.

However, appointing Aetius was a possibility. He was certainly in opposition to Felix. In fact, Felix may have recognized that Aetius was quickly becoming a threat, with his power-base in Gaul. As a result, Felix may have attempted to undermine Aetius' popularity in Gaul by appointing a Gaul named Theodosius, who is otherwise unknown, as *praefectus praetorio Italiae et Africae* (Praetorian Prefect of Italy and Africa).[12] Felix may have hoped that fostering clients in Gaul would help to counterbalance Aetius' popularity there. On the other hand, it is possible that the appointment was made by Valentinian and Placidia and was simply an appointment by the new regime of an individual known to be loyal to Valentinian.

Although the appointment of Theodosius has sometimes been interpreted as a part of Aetius' political manoeuvring, this is almost certainly false. Theodosius was promoted to the post prior to February 430, when Aetius was still only *magister militum per Gallias* and so unable to make such high-level appointments.[13] Even if Aetius had suggested the appointment, Felix would naturally have blocked such an obvious attempt by Aetius to curry favour in Gaul. The political attempt to undermine Aetius ensured that there would be no co-operation between him and Felix.

The appointment of Aetius as *magister militum praesentalis* could be justified: his military achievements in Gaul had gone a long way to recovering Rome's authority in the area. If his skills could be employed in larger areas of the West, it would help to secure Rome's recovery. However, as *magister militum per Gallias* he did not have the authority to interfere in Spain and possibly at a later date Britain. For that he needed a post that allowed him to move freely between prefectures. As a result, on his return from Gaul Aetius was given the post of *comes et magister utriusque militiae*, although this would have been related to the junior post of *magister equitum*: Placidia was not strong enough to oust Felix, who retained the more senior post of *magister peditum*.[14] It is possible that in her desire to raise Aetius to be *magister militum praesentalis* Placidia was trying to emulate the situation in the East. Since the time of Theodosius I there had been five nominally equal *magistri*.[15] Unfortunately, this was against all of the traditions of the more conservative West, and any attempt to enforce such a reform would doubtless help to cement opposition to her plans. This was even more the case since she was not the ruling emperor.[16] Although as *magister peditum* Felix still retained seniority, there can be little doubt that Aetius' promotion was against his wishes. Placidia had decidedly raised the stakes by making Aetius a real rival to Felix, rather than just a potential one.[17]

430*

Aetius' appointment could not come too soon. The west was still in dire straits with enemies both internal and external roaming at will. Probably his first task in the new year was to counter a large band of Visigoths led by an individual named Anaolsus who were wandering in Roman territory near to Arles. It is unknown whether this attack was ordered by Theoderic or was simply one of his nobles acting independently. If it was Anaolsus acting on his own initiative, then given the recent defeat at the hands of Aetius this was a dangerous move and liable to incur the displeasure of Theoderic, since it could easily be interpreted in Ravenna as Theoderic re-opening the earlier conflict. It is more likely that Theoderic had instigated this manoeuvre in order to test the strength and readiness of the empire: by the campaign season of 430 the news that the Vandals had invaded Africa had doubtless spread across the western Mediterranean. By employing Anaolsus, if the campaign went badly Theoderic could claim that Anaolsus was acting unilaterally and so avoid further conflict. If it went well, Theoderic could expand the attack using 'royal' forces. In the event, Theoderic did the right thing in distancing himself from Anaolsus' attack. Leading the Gallic army, Aetius attacked Anaolsus and annihilated his forces, Anaolsus himself being captured.[18]

---

* Events in the years 430–439 are extremely confusing and open to very different interpretations. To help simplify the narrative, at this point the text will be divided annually in order to make the analysis easier to follow.

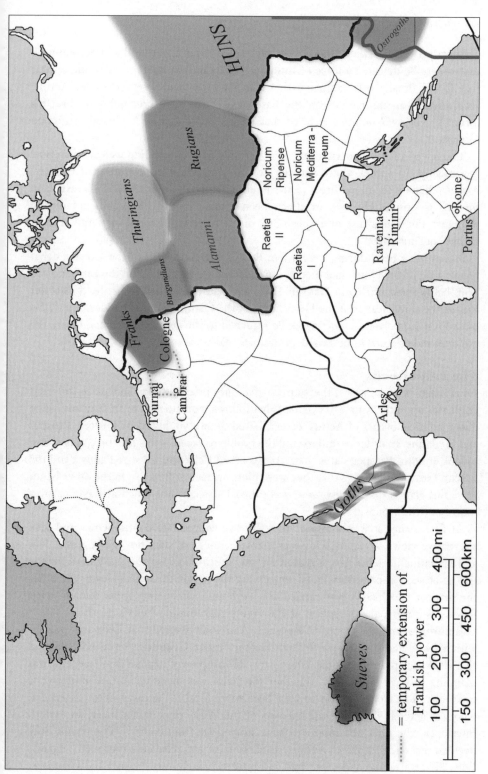

Map 6. Aetius' Campaigns in Gaul, Raetia and Italy

Shortly after defeating Anaolsus Aetius turned the army around and headed back east, where he defeated a force of Iuthungi (Alamanni) in Raetia.[19] It would appear that it was during this campaign that Flavius Merobaudes served under Aetius, according to an inscription on the base of a statue to Merobaudes in Trajan's forum.[20] The two victories ensured that Aetius' reputation as a general continued to grow.

The speed of the two victories demonstrates one outstanding aspect of Aetius' generalship. In an era where manoeuvre and blockade were the order of the day, Aetius relied on the more direct tactics of either ambush or direct battle. The reason for this is simple. He had, in effect, been trained by the Huns and not by the Romans. The Huns' use of ambush and direct force is mirrored in Aetius' tactics throughout his career.

It may have been during his time in Raetia that Aetius heard the sad news that Octar, king of the Huns, had died.[21] He had been leading a raid on the Burgundians – probably those settled in Gaul in 413 – and had been killed in battle.[22] This left Rua as the single leader of the Huns north of the Danube. Aetius had lost one of his most loyal supporters. Undeterred, he returned to the court at Ravenna, where the political stakes were to be raised in dramatic fashion.

The Fall of Felix

As is usual in these cases, the sources give only brief outlines and place different emphases upon the course of events. What follows is an attempt to analyze one of the major political events of Aetius' career, based upon two divergent sources, Prosper and Hydatius. In order to understand the problems faced at this juncture, it is useful to look at both. Prosper states that: 'Aetius killed Felix and his wife Padusia and the deacon Grunitus, sensing that they were plotting against him.'[23] On the other hand, Hydatius claims that: 'Felix, who was called Patrician, was killed at Ravenna by a mutiny of the troops.'[24]

At first glance it would appear that the two sources are contradictory and give alternative views of events. However, Prosper does not state how Felix was killed, and Hydatius does not give a reason for the 'mutiny'. Close analysis allows for the two to be seen as complementary, one giving the reason for Felix's death, the other the manner in which it was carried out. Although uncertainty must remain, what follows is a rational description of the events surrounding Felix's death.

Returning with the troops to Ravenna, Aetius discovered that Felix was present with his wife Padusia. Also with them was the deacon Grunitus. Aetius now claimed that Felix was plotting against him, just as he had plotted against Boniface, and was planning to have him killed. Whether the claim was made on Aetius' initiative is unknown. The troops appear to have been more loyal to Aetius, a Western general who was actively defeating the enemies of the West, rather than Felix, an eastern interloper who does not appear to have strayed far from court.[25] The troops duly decided that their loyalty to Aetius was paramount and rebelled – mutinied – against Felix. They attacked and killed him and his party, including Padusia and Grunitus.

It is also possible that Placidia had a hand in these events. Boniface had been loyal to her throughout his career and she had been made to look extremely foolish when she had been tricked into declaring him a traitor and waging war against him. It was now clear to her that Felix was not going to simply serve Valentinian in the interests of the empire, but was intent on becoming the sole military officer of any standing. She may have approached Aetius in order to have Felix removed, but there is no evidence for this in the sources, and the fact that Aetius had only recently been opposed to Valentinian suggests that Placidia may not have trusted him fully. As a result the theory remains interesting but unproven and improbable.

The hypothesis that Aetius acted on his own and that the troops supported him has the benefit of uniting the two sources as well as giving a reasonable sequence of events, at the end of which Aetius could be accused of 'killing' Felix and his wife. Aetius was now the sole *comes et magister utriusque militiae*. The man who had been the rebel of 425 had risen to be the supreme military commander of the west.

The question remains as to whether Felix was really plotting to overthrow Aetius or whether Aetius invented the plot as a means of eliminating one of his two major rivals to power. It was only the year before that Felix's machinations against Boniface had come to light, no doubt to the anger of Placidia. As a result it is almost certain that Felix would not begin a new plot to remove Aetius, since Placidia and the rest of the civilian government would be alert to such a move and so be in strong opposition to the measures. Yet there remains the possibility that, prior to the plot against Boniface being uncovered, Felix had set in motion plans to remove Aetius and that Aetius found out about this in either 429 or early in 430.

Yet on reflection it is more plausible that Aetius viewed his inferior status to Felix as undeserved and so used Felix's reputation against him. By accusing Felix of a plot in front of the troops, who were no doubt heavily sprinkled with his supporters, Aetius could leave it to the troops to decide the truth of the matter. Given that Felix had earlier plotted to overthrow Boniface – another popular Western general – the matter would be in little doubt. In due course, the troops faithfully killed Felix and Padusia, removing one of the two barriers to Aetius' complete control.

Africa

In Africa, the Vandals were slowly advancing along the northern coast, hampered by the slow pace of the women, children, elderly and the baggage animals. Although the actual route of their advance is unknown, it is likely that it followed the main routes east towards Carthage. Although Victor of Vita accuses the Vandals of the mass destruction of cities and buildings, it is clear from other evidence that he exaggerates their destructive impact, since little if any literary or archaeological evidence survives that supports his view.[26] Possibly the only direct evidence for the Vandals' march is an inscription found at Altava, dating to August 429, which includes the mention of the deceased being wounded by a 'barbarian':[27]

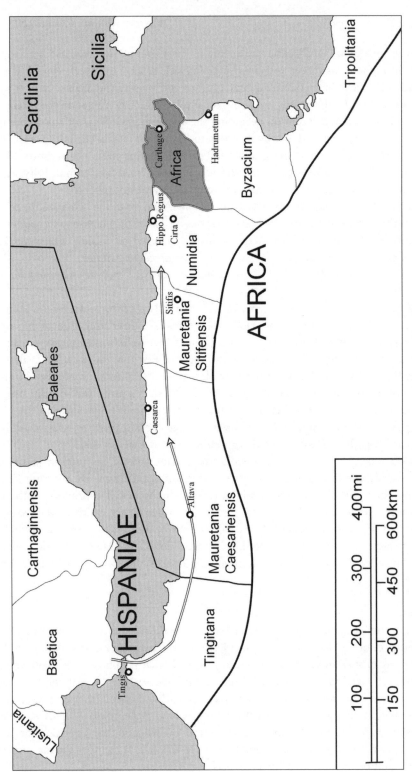

Map 7. The Vandals in Africa

       -- -- --
1   KALSEM
    ANNOPROCCCXC
3   GLADIOP*ABARBAROS

- - - discessit - - -]
Kal(endas) se(pte)m[bres]
Anno pro(uinciae) cccxc
Gladio p(ercessus) a barbaros

Although the attribution is insecure, it is possible that these 'barbarians' were the Vandals on their long journey across north Africa.[28]

At an unknown date either shortly before or shortly after the 'attack' at Altava, Darius, the man who had negotiated a peace between Boniface and Sigisvult, convinced the Vandals to accept a truce and halt their advance.[29] In the meantime, freed from the burden of fighting a civil war, Boniface gathered his forces ready to oppose any further advances by the Vandals. When the Vandals resumed their march east early in 430, no doubt much to the disappointment of Darius, Boniface led his men out and met the Vandals in battle somewhere to the west of Hippo Regius.

The size and deployment of the opposing forces are unknown. According to Victor of Vita, the Vandals at the crossing into Africa were organized into eighty *thusundifaths*, each of 1,000 people. However, he also states that the organization was inaccurate, being an attempt to convince onlookers that the forces crossing to Africa were larger than they actually were.[30] Therefore, the whole population that crossed to Africa numbered substantially less than 80,000, perhaps in the region of 70,000, possibly even lower. At the most, this should have given the Vandals an army of around 20,000 fighting men.[31]

Opposing the Vandals were the troops under Boniface. According to the *Notitia Dignitatum*, the commander in Africa should have had thirty-one *comitatenses* (field) units and twenty-two *limitanei* (garrison) units stationed in Tripolitania and Numidia. This gives a total of approximately 35,000 men, although the actual strength may have been much lower.[32] However, these troops were used to dealing with minor border raids and the supervision of the movement of nomadic tribes through the provinces. These men were not of the same quality as the Vandal and Alan warriors who had been fighting across western Europe for the previous twenty years. Furthermore, it is likely that Gaiseric was a far better commander of troops than Boniface.[33]

Gaiseric also had under his command a force of Goths.[34] Unfortunately, the number of Goths is completely unknown, as is their origin. Most likely is that they were a group of Goths who had joined the Vandals earlier, in Spain. It is also claimed that they were the entourage of Boniface's wife Pelagia, who is described as a 'Gothic princess' by both Merobaudes and Sidonius Apollinaris.[35] As such, upon her marriage she was probably followed by a small band of loyal retainers. These may have rebelled and joined Gaiseric, for an unknown reason. However, the

Goths could also be a contingent left behind by Sigisvult when he returned to Italy to help in the defence of Africa and who rebelled and joined the Vandals. The claim that they were followers of Sanoeces, who was most likely a Hun, has also been proposed, but this can be deemed the least likely of the four hypotheses.[36]

Despite Boniface' undoubted skills as a general, his men were defeated, and the survivors – including Boniface – retired to the safety of Hippo.[37] The victorious Vandals followed and in May or June 430 Boniface was laid under siege in the city.[38] The siege soon became a desperate affair. Thanks to their ships, the Vandals were able to cut completely all supply lines into the city.[39] As the siege lengthened the priests in the city, including (Saint) Augustine, held prayers pleading for relief from the siege.[40] However, in the third month of the siege Augustine died, probably of a fever, on 28 August 430.[41] With their great religious leader dead, the citizens of Hippo began to lose all hope of salvation. Despite this, Boniface himself continued to lead the brave resistance to the siege.

However, the Vandals themselves also began to suffer. This was not an army intent upon sacking the city before retiring with the booty. The Vandals besieging the city included very large numbers of the old, women and children, non-combatants who weakened the attackers by using any surplus supplies that would have allowed the besiegers to last longer than the besieged. Soon, the Vandals began to feel the effects of the siege as much as the citizens of Hippo. Despite these problems, they continued to press the siege. Stretched on all fronts, and unsure of events in Africa, the West was unable to send troops to help Boniface. Instead, they relied on their appeals to the East to supply the troops needed in Africa.

Spain
Although the Romans had helped the Sueves to retain their independence from the Vandals in 420, by 430 they, under their king Hermeric, had reverted to type and were pillaging the central areas of Gallaecia.[42] Although there do not appear to have been Roman troops in the area, there was still strong resistance from the native inhabitants, especially from 'people [*plebem*] who remained in possession of the more secure forts'. Due to this fierce resistance, Hermeric appears to have called off the raid, instead renewing the peace treaty and returning the captives he had taken.[43]

431
Almost certainly due to the confusion caused by the news that Felix had been killed, and augmented by the news that the Vandals were at large in Africa, warfare and rebellion erupted again in 431. The first reports that arrived in Ravenna were that at least some of the peoples of Noricum – probably the Vandals settled there by Stilicho in 400–401 – had rebelled. Situated guarding the northern approaches to Italy, these two provinces (Noricum Ripense and Noricum Mediterraneum) were of vital importance to the defence of Italy, and so needed to be pacified as quickly as possible. Aetius wasted no time. He led the *praesental* army north from Italy and quickly crushed the rebellion before it could become widespread.[44]

Following this victory, Aetius prepared for a campaign against the Franks under Clodio, who had invaded Roman Gaul and captured Tournai and Cambrai.[45] It is unclear whether these were the same Franks that had been forced to retreat in 428 or whether this was a different group.[46] Since the earlier canton(s) had been given notice that the West was recovering after the civil war, the latter is more likely. However, there was not enough time left in the campaign season to allow for the campaign to be concluded. As a result, Aetius crossed the Alps into Gaul and prepared his forces for a campaign against the Franks early in 432.

Before he left for Gaul, as a reward for defeating so many enemies in such a short space of time, Aetius was nominated for the consulship of 432. The nomination implies that Placidia was either not too distressed by the recent death of Felix or that the political strength of Aetius was such that she had no choice but to accept the nomination. It is more likely that it was a combination of the two. What is more surprising is that the nomination was accepted by the East, since Felix would appear to have been an Eastern nomination – or at least accepted by Theodosius. The East's nominee for the year was Valerius, brother of the Empress Eudoxia.

Very late in the year an embassy led by Bishop Hydatius of Aquae Flaviae arrived from Gallaecia in Spain and informed Aetius that, once again, the Sueves under Hermeric had broken their treaty and were plundering the area.[47] It is also possible that Hydatius informed Aetius that an individual named Vetto, who is otherwise unknown but who may have been an envoy sent by the Goths, had arrived in Gallaecia for talks with the Sueves.[48] Unfortunately for Hydatius, Aetius was preoccupied with the upcoming campaign against the Franks. It is probable that Aetius felt that the news of a successful campaign in Gaul would help to dampen the enthusiasm of the Sueves for continuing their depredations and possibly deter them from making an alliance with the Goths. In any case, Aetius could not move south into Spain until after the Franks had been defeated. As a result, the bishop was forced to wait until the new year for a satisfactory response.

Interestingly, although by 431 Britain is usually seen as being isolated from the rest of the empire, Prosper records that a bishop named Palladius, 'having been ordained by Pope Celestine, was the first bishop sent to the Scots believing in Christ'.[49] It would appear that, even at this late date, some at least amongst the clergy believed that the fate of Britain was as yet undecided, and that they were determined to ensure the continuation of Christianity in the farthest reaches of the empire.

Africa

After fourteen months of siege, hunger and the inevitable diseases were ravaging both the city inhabitants of Hippo and the Vandals outside the city walls.[50] However, the Vandals appear, like most German tribesmen, to have been poor in the art of siege warfare. Running out of provisions themselves, and with disease spreading amongst their dependents, in July or August they raised the siege.[51] Shortly after there was an unexpected twist. Unannounced, the Eastern *magister utriusque militiae* Aspar arrived with reinforcements from both East and West.[52] Aspar's arrival is evidence of detailed contact between East and West concerning the condition of Africa, possibly under Aetius' direction, and illustrates that the two halves of the empire still saw themselves as being united in their rule.[53]

432

In early 432 Boniface and Aspar led their troops to meet the Vandals. Somewhere to the west of Hippo Regius the two sides met in battle. The Vandals were again victorious, forcing the Romans to retreat.[54] It is after this defeat that the future emperor Marcian was captured by Gaiseric.[55] According to later legend, Gaiseric witnessed an omen that Marcian was destined to be emperor and as a consequence was released after having promised never to attack the Vandals.[56]

Unlike the previous battle, on this occasion Boniface, followed by Aspar, did not retire to Hippo, probably as he did not want to experience being placed under siege by the Vandals again. Unfortunately, the decision left Hippo undefended, and the city was taken and sacked by the victorious Vandals.[57] No doubt this was particularly savage due to the suffering caused amongst the Vandals by its earlier refusal to surrender. The Vandals then went on to attack the whole of the Prefecture except Cirta and Carthage.

The Franks

Whilst Boniface was being forced to retreat in Africa, early in 432 Merobaudes was in Gaul delivering a panegyric to Aetius on the occasion of his first consulship, which has unfortunately not survived.[58] Shortly after, Aetius once more led his troops north to the Rhine. Success appears to have been rapid, and after retaking the lost cities of Tournai and Cambrai a treaty with Clodio was agreed.[59] With the threat from the Franks overcome, Aetius turned his mind to the matter of the Sueves in Spain.

It is very likely that Aetius knew of the attempt by the Goths to form an alliance with the Sueves. It is also virtually certain that he was quickly made aware that the overtures of the Goths had been rebuffed: Vetto 'returned to the Goths having achieved nothing'.[60] No action was yet needed against the Goths.

Unexpectedly, neither did Aetius lead his forces into Spain to engage in battle with the Sueves. Instead, he sent *comes* (count) Censorius as an envoy to the Sueves, and on the journey Censorius was accompanied by Bishop Hydatius. The mission was a success and the Sueves halted their attacks.[61] Although Aetius may have wanted to lead the army to face the Sueves, events elsewhere halted any planned campaign.

The removal of Felix as *comes et magister utriusque militiae* in 430 would have been a surprise to Placidia. Having learned in 429 that her loyal supporter Boniface was innocent of the claims laid against him, there is little doubt that she would have wanted him as the senior military official to work alongside her. Aetius' actions had removed the greatest obstacle to her wish. Moreover, Aetius' assumption of the consulship for 432 was most likely against her wishes and forced upon her by his strong position in Italy. It is possible that Aetius becoming consul was the final straw for Placidia and made her decide that he must be removed from power before he had established an unassailable position.

Aetius' long absence on campaign gave Placidia the chance she needed. In early 432 she sent messengers to Boniface in Africa ordering him to return to Italy.[62] Arriving shortly after his defeat by the Vandals, it will have been a relief for Boniface to receive the order. He took ship for Italy, probably accompanied by a sizeable force of loyal troops, or at least his *bucellarii*. Aspar remained in Africa commanding the remnants of the Western force, as well as the troops sent by Constantinople.[63]

The Battle of Rimini

Boniface landed in Italy, probably at Portus, and travelled the short distance to Rome. Upon his arrival he was endowed with the title of *comes et magister utriusque militiae*.[64] Marcellinus claims that at the same time he was invested with the title of *patricius*.[65] When combined with the title of *magister militum*, this usually denoted the individual with the greatest military and political power in the West.[66] Boniface had supported Placidia throughout her 'exile' in Constantinople due to the quarrel with her brother Honorius. He had also stood by her when John had usurped the throne in 424. There can be little doubt that Placidia wanted her most loyal supporter to be in command in Italy. The fact that Placidia arranged for the promotion to happen in Rome, rather than waiting for Boniface to travel to Ravenna, implies that there was a need for haste. This is confirmed by Hydatius, who specifically states that Boniface was recalled and that Aetius was then 'deposed' (*depulso*).[67] Aetius was to be ousted from his command and from court.

Aetius was most likely preparing for the campaign against the Sueves in Spain when the news arrived that Boniface had landed in Italy and promptly been invested with the above titles. It is possible that Boniface's son-in-law Sebastian (Sebastianus) was made *magister equitum*, a post junior to that of Boniface. No doubt Aetius feared for his safety and decided that the best form of defence was attack. This was the reason he sent Censorius as an ambassador to the Sueves and led his own troops across the Alps and into Italy.

In the meantime, Boniface gathered all of the troops that he could find in Italy and prepared to meet Aetius in battle. That he was able to meet Aetius on at least equal terms indicates that Boniface was held in high esteem by the troops. Although the army that had been serving Aetius remained loyal to him, others in the West appear to have preferred Boniface, the long-standing supporter of Placidia and Valentinian, rather than an ex-rebel, to be in control of the army.

The two forces met in the proximity of Rimini.[68] It is extremely frustrating that there is no detailed account of the battle that followed. Instead, what little information can be gleaned comes from the Chronicles.[69] It would appear that Boniface, supported by his son-in-law Sebastian, was completely victorious and Aetius was forced to surrender. It is even possible that Aetius and Boniface met in personal combat on the field, with Aetius wounding Boniface with a 'long spear', although this is uncertain.[70] Following the defeat, Aetius agreed to relinquish power and to retire to his estates in Italy.[71]

Unfortunately, Boniface had been wounded in the battle (whether by Aetius or another individual is unknown), and between a 'few days' and three months later he either died directly from or by complications caused by his wounds, or from an illness.[72] It was extremely unfortunate for the empire that Boniface and Aetius had been opponents. Boniface was later praised for his bravery and honesty, and it is possible that an alliance of the two men may have resulted in a very different history for the Western Empire.[73]

It is surprising to note that Aetius, who had now twice been in opposition to Placidia (425 and 432), was allowed to retire to his own estates after losing the battle rather than being either executed or exiled.[74] There are at least two possible reasons for this. One is that Aetius had very powerful supporters who were prepared to stand by him. Rather than alienate these men, Placidia and Boniface agreed that Aetius should be allowed simply to retire. A second is that a large part of the army was still loyal to Aetius. By allowing Aetius to retire, Placidia, and especially Boniface, may have hoped to allow Aetius' forces to integrate more easily with the victorious army under Boniface.

Whichever it was, one major factor is conspicuous: it was assumed that Aetius would remain true to his word to retire. This implies that both Placidia and Boniface accepted an oath that Aetius would not continue to fight. Furthermore, it appears that Aetius accepted his defeat graciously and also accepted Boniface's word that he would be safe. It would appear that Aetius, despite the defeat, did not instantly fear for his life and so either flee into exile or commit suicide. The fact that these two opponents seemed to trust each other in any way is quite remarkable.

Not long after the battle, the situation changed. With the death of Boniface his son-in-law Sebastian 'inherited' the post of *comes et magister utriusque militiae*.[75] Unfortunately, it would appear that he was unwilling to allow Aetius to remain at large in Italy. Sebastian's supporters – or possibly followers of Boniface angry at his death – made a sudden attack on Aetius' home in an attempt to kill him.[76] Aetius fled to Rome, possibly in an attempt to seek support. When this was not forthcoming, at least on the scale needed to defend himself, he escaped and travelled, via Dalmatia and Pannonia, to the lands of the Huns (see Map 6).[77]

433

Aetius arrived at the court of the Hunnic king Rua.[78] His long-standing friend again agreed to help him, although upon what terms are unclear. It is possible that Aetius agreed to recognize Hun control of territory that they were already occupying in Pannonia, or that he took with him a sum of gold that, along with his friendship, sufficed, or that he agreed to an alliance and, less likely, to the payment of subsidies. It is possible that it was a combination of all three of these factors. Unfortunately, there are no details in any of our sources, and all suggestions about the terms agreed are speculation, not fact.[79]

Following the agreement, Aetius returned to the West.[80] Although it is often assumed that he was accompanied by a large force of Huns, this is nowhere speci-fically stated in the sources and it is also possible that he was simply accompanied by an embassy that threatened war if he was not restored to his former position. The threat of an attack by the Huns may have been enough to intimidate Placidia into accepting Aetius' return.[81] Aetius was restored to his previous position as *comes et magister utriusque militiae* without having to fight a battle, although a cryptic mention in the Gallic Chronicle of 452 suggests that Sebastian was preparing to fight Aetius by summoning Visigoths to his aid.[82]

Yet there is one further factor in Aetius' quick return to power. We have only a few glimpses into the character of Sebastian, and these come from later in his life. Although 'an able advisor and an active soldier', he later allowed his men to engage in 'piratical' activities.[83] It is possible that his conduct during his brief role as senior general resulted in Sebastian losing popular support very quickly in Rome and Ravenna, so that when the news arrived that Aetius was being supported by the Huns and was on the point of return, the army refused to support Sebastian, who was thus in no position to face Aetius. Although speculation, this would explain Aetius' rapid return to power.

Aetius quickly re-established himself in the court at Ravenna. One of his first acts was to secure the dismissal of Sebastian, who sought refuge in Constantinople.[84] He was also now in a position to continue the diplomatic activity that he had begun prior to Boniface's recall from Africa. At an unknown date in 433 Censurius returned from his embassy to the Sueves and Aetius was able to ratify a new peace treaty, including an exchange of hostages between the Sueves and the Gallaecians.[85] When Censurius returned it would appear that he was accompanied by bishop Symphosius, who is otherwise unknown, who attempted to reach an agreement with Aetius. The nature of the discussions is unclear, but it is most likely to have been an attempt by Hermeric, king of the Sueves, to gain a military post in the higher hierarchy of the empire. Unfortunately for Hermeric, the petition failed.[86]

For Aetius, the disaster of losing the Battle of Rimini had been completely reversed. There was now no military figure of any standing capable of opposing him in the West. In 424 he had been a rebel against Valentinian III and Galla Placidia. By 433 he was in a position to achieve total dominance of the Western Roman Empire, but on both of these occasions he had needed the support of the Huns to retain his power.

Aetius' return and total dominance of political and military affairs had a negative aspect for at least two people. One was the young Emperor of the West. In 433 Valentinian 'came of age' – being fourteen – but there was little prospect of his learning how to function as emperor on his own.[87] The other was Valentinian's mother Placidia. She had raised Boniface to power in opposition to Aetius, but in the end Aetius had been triumphant. With her loyal supporter Boniface dead, Placidia doubtless had serious concerns for the future, especially in the matter of Aetius' ambitions.

Chapter 8

Undisputed Leadership

Sebastian, Boniface's son-in-law, had been removed from office and had fled into exile. Restored to power, Aetius now made a quite startling political move: almost immediately upon his return he married Pelagia, Boniface's widow. This was allegedly upon the advice of Boniface himself, and it gave Aetius control of Boniface's name, his wealth and his *bucellarii*.[1] This implies that despite their political opposition, there does not appear to have been any deep-rooted animosity between Aetius and Boniface – simply a question of earlier divided loyalties. This hypothesis has one further major implication: if Boniface had approved of his son-in-law taking power Aetius would certainly have been either exiled or killed. It would seem that Boniface felt that Aetius was more fitting to lead than Sebastian. The fact that Sebastian was so easily removed from his position suggests that this low opinion had quickly come to be shared by the people of Rome.

Pelagia herself was probably a Goth and had been brought up as an Arian. Although she converted to Catholic Christianity before her marriage to Boniface, it was alleged that she had had their daughter baptized by an Arian priest.[2] Whatever the circumstances surrounding the new marriage, she appears to have been loyal to Aetius, even 'praying assiduously' for his return from war in 451.[3]

Sadly, there is no mention of what happened to Aetius' first wife, the daughter of Carpilio. The fact that Boniface allegedly advised Pelagia to marry Aetius implies that she had died by this time.[4]

The marriage may have been useful to Aetius in another way. Pelagia's origin as a 'Gothic princess' may have given him useful connections to the Gothic nobility.[5] As well as marrying Pelagia, Aetius also bought all of Boniface's property.[6] This combination ensured that no one else could aspire to replace Boniface and so challenge Aetius.

434

All of these developments took time, and it is likely that Aetius spent the whole of the year 434 arranging his marriage, adjusting to his new role as sole military leader, settling affairs in Italy, negotiating with Placidia and Valentinian, appointing trusted men to positions of power and beginning the process of linking all of the various offices of state to himself.[7] He also dispatched political embassies to a large number of people in an attempt to establish peace in at least some quarters of the West.

In many cases the negotiations failed. The outbreak of yet another civil war and the recall of large numbers of troops to Italy, coupled with the ensuing lack of military activity elsewhere, had resulted once more in the various barbarian tribes both within and outside the empire testing the limits of Roman power by attempting to expand their spheres of influence, nominally by supporting one of the two sides in the civil war. The quelling of these invasions and uprisings would take up most of Aetius' time for the next few years.

435

However, in one area Aetius had an early success, and one that would potentially give him the breathing space he needed to begin the recovery of the West. In 434 he had sent Trygetius to negotiate terms with the Vandals. Trygetius was a man of some importance and had previously been *comes rei privatae* in 423.[8] In the years since 431 and Boniface's campaigns against the Vandals, Aspar, the Eastern *magister militum*, had been conducting a campaign of containment.[9] It is a testament to his skills that, despite being defeated by the Vandals in his first battle, the Vandals do not seem to have been able to make any permanent settlements in Africa. This can be compared to Gaiseric's ability to defeat Boniface on two separate occasions.

Over the winter months of 434–435 Trygetius managed to convince Gaiseric that a peace treaty was preferable to continuing the war, and on 11 February 435, at Hippo, a treaty was announced. The Vandals were given 'a part of Africa to live in'.[10] As a reward for his efforts in Africa, Aspar was awarded the post of consul for the year 434. Despite being an Eastern general, in recognition of his services to the West he was the West's nomination.[11]

It is unfortunate that we do not have any clear indication of the actual terms of the treaty with the Vandals. Procopius claims that in return for land in 'Libya', the Vandals agreed to pay a yearly tribute and Huneric, son of Gaiseric, was sent as a hostage to Ravenna.[12] Yet as Procopius makes no other mention of a treaty, it is certain that he has conflated the treaty of 435 with the later treaty of 442 (see Chapter 12).[13] Although some of the details given might be an accurate representation of the treaty of 435, which these were is unknown. It should be noted, however, that Procopius' statement that the Vandals were given only some areas in Africa, and not Africa Proconsularis itself, certainly relates to the earlier treaty.

Alongside Procopius, Prosper states only that the Vandals were given 'a part of Africa'.[14] As a result, modern interpretations of the specific territories allocated differ. For example, there is the claim that the Vandals were given 'Numidia and the Mauretanias'.[15] Another hypothesis is that they were given 'the province of Africa – except the city of Carthage – the province of Byzacena, and a part of Numidia'.[16] A further suggestion is that they were allocated territories 'probably along the coast of Numidia'.[17] They might even have gained control of 'large areas of Numidia and Mauretania Sitifensis, including Calama and Sitifis'.[18]

These differing suggestions can lead to confusion, yet it is possible that slightly more detail can be inferred from a later entry by Prosper, where he notes that: '[Gaiseric] persecuted some of our bishops, of whom the most famous were Possidius, Novatus, and Severianus.'[19] This entry is supported to some degree by the Novels of Valentinian.[20] It has been suggested that Possidius was bishop of Calama, Novatus

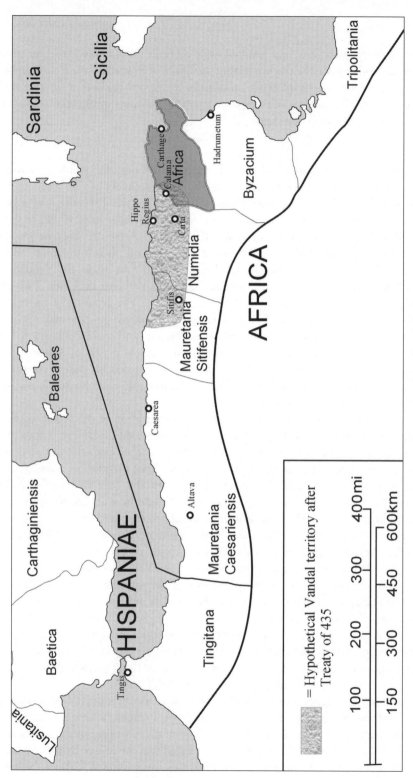

Map 8. The Vandal Settlement of 435

Labels visible on the map:

Sardinia
Sicilia
Lusitania
Baetica
Carthaginiensis
HISPANIAE
Baleares
Tingis
Tingitana
Mauretania Caesariensis
Altava
Caesarea
Mauretania Sitifensis
Sitifis
Numidia
Cirta
Hippo Regius
Calama
Carthage
Africa
Hadrumetum
Byzacium
AFRICA
Tripolitania

= Hypothetical Vandal territory after Treaty of 435

100   200   300   400mi
150   300   450   600km

of Sitifis, and Severianus of Cera.[21] This implies that the Vandals were settled in parts of Mauretania Sitifiensis, Numidia and Africa Proconsularis, but beyond this the exact nature of their settlement is unknown.[22]

The references to the treaty also imply that Gaiseric was given an official post within the empire, since he appears to have had the rights of a military commander and Roman official to order ecclesiastical affairs.[23] The suggestion is possibly supported by a famous passage in Victor of Vita:

> In his cunning duke Geiseric [*Geiserici ducis*], intending to make the reputation of his people a source of dread, ordered then and there that the entire crowd was to be counted, even those who had come from the womb into the light that very day.
>
> *Victor of Vita, 1.2*

Although the majority of interest in the passage concerns Victor's claim concerning the number of Vandals who crossed to Africa, it is interesting to note that he calls Geiseric *Geiserici ducis* (*dux*, duke), not *rex* or a similar Latin term.[24] The most likely explanation for this is that in the treaty of 435 Geiseric, following the example of previous barbarian leaders such as Alaric, had demanded an official post as part of the peace agreements. He was given the title *dux*, probably with responsibility for the areas of Africa allocated to the Vandals. Victor, who hated the Vandals, used his title anachronistically to highlight the treacherous nature of Geiseric in later 'invading' Roman territory as a Roman officer. If this hypothesis is true, then it is almost certain that the Vandals were given land and billets according to traditional Roman methods.[25]

The treaty would appear to be similar in many respects to that accorded to the Goths in Aquitaine in 419, where the Goths were given territory in return for military service as *foederati*. However, there was one major exception: due to the weaker status of the empire Gaiseric, unlike Theoderic, appears to have been given a military post.[26] However, it should be remembered that this is only conjecture based on very limited evidence.

Despite the appalling circumstances, the peace treaty was a welcome piece of news, since when the information arrived in Italy Aetius was already campaigning against the Burgundians in Gaul. It would appear that during the confusion of Aetius' return to power the Burgundians had seized the opportunity to raid one of the Belgic provinces.[27] However, it is likely that another main cause for the war, as with the other tribes in the west, was the slow spread of Burgundian families into deserted agricultural areas nominally under the control of the empire.

Whilst in Gaul Aetius received news of a major rebellion. In 'Farther Gaul' an individual named Tibatto was leading a *bacaudic* revolt of *servitia* (the 'servile order').[28] The origins and nature of the revolt are unknown. Although many different theories are possible, it is most likely that it was part of the slow fragmentation of Gaul that had been occurring since the start of the fifth century. The slow drift of northern Gaul away from imperial control may have resulted in a desire in those areas to set up their own government to govern their affairs without the need to pay taxes or to consult with the emperor. However, there was little or no aristocratic support for the rebellion, and the army remained loyal. As a result, the uprising is classed in the sources merely as '*bacaudic*' rather than being seen as a revolt.

Fortunately for Aetius, help was near to hand. Litorius, who was either already a *comes rei militaris* or who was promoted to the post specifically for the campaign, was sent to Armorica to put down the *bacaudae*.[29] It is possible that even at this early date Litorius was appointed as *magister militum per Gallias*, but unfortunately the only source for this period is Prosper, who simply calls Litorius *comes*.[30] Taking with him a contingent of Huns, Litorius headed north.[31]

With matters in hand, Aetius continued his campaign against the Burgundians, probably using only the *praesental* army of Italy, estimated at around 28,500 men.[32] After a very fast campaign the Burgundians were crushed and their king, Gundichar, forced to agree to a treaty favourable to Rome.[33] Unfortunately, later events would show that the campaign did not quell the spirit of rebellion amongst the Burgundians. One possible reason for this is that, due to the tumultuous state of affairs in the West, Aetius may have rushed the negotiations for the treaty and so imposed terms that were far too stringent on the Burgundians.

In the midst of the wars in the West, Aetius had one small piece of good news concerning the internal politics of the empire. On 30 July 435 a statue of Merobaudes was erected in the Forum of Trajan, built at Aetius' suggestion (according to Merobaudes as thanks for his earlier panegyric). The inscription on the base of the statue has survived:

> *Dedicata III Kal(endas) Aug(ustas) conss(ulibus) dd(ominis) nn(ostris) /*
> *Theodosio XV et Valentiniano IIII // [Fl(avio) Merob]audi v(iro)*
> *s(pectabiili) com(iti) s(acri) c(onsistorii) / Fl(avio) Merobaudi aeque forti*
> *et docto viro tam facere / laudanda quam aliorum facta laudare praecipuo /*
> *castrensi experientia claro facundia vel otiosorum / studia supergresso cui*
> *a crepundiis par virtutis et elo / quentiae cura ingenium ita fortitudini ut*
> *doctrinae / natum stilo et gladio pariter exercuit nec in umbra / vel latebris*
> *mentis vigorem scholari tantum otio / torpere passus inter arma litteris*
> *militabat / et in Alpibus acuebat eloquium ideo illi cessit in praemium / non*
> *verbena vilis nec otiosa hedera honor capitis / Heliconius sed imago aere*
> *formata quo rari exempli / viros seu in castris probatos seu optimos vatum /*
> *antiquitas honorabat quod huic quoque cum / augustissimis Roma principibus /*
> *Theodosio et Placido Valentiniano rerum dominis / in foro Ulpio detulerunt*
> *remunerantes in viro / antiquae nobilitatis novae gloriae vel industriam /*
> *militarem vel carmen cuius praeconio gloria / triumfali crevit imperio*

> CIL VI 1724 v.2 = ILS 2950= Hubner 748

The text states that Merobaudes was renowned as both a warrior and a poet. Moreover, in an unrelated text Hydatius implies that other statues were erected to Merobaudes.[34] Although many of these others may also have been erected at the instigation of Aetius, some at least were doubtless proposed by the Senate without his involvement. The acclamation given to Merobaudes no doubt was taken by Aetius to be a reflection of support for his regime: after all, Merobaudes was clearly one of Aetius' more powerful supporters and had written and delivered the earlier panegyric for him in 432.

Britain
Whilst these developments had been taking place on the continent, Britain was once again being converted to Pelagianism. In response, probably in 435, Germanus, Bishop of Auxerre, was sent to Britain for the second time, winning back the converts and this time taking the preachers of Pelagianism to exile on the continent.[35]

Although sometimes overlooked, in the context of the time the military campaigns of Aetius and the spiritual campaign of Germanus can be interpreted as a 'careful co-ordination of the political and military policies of Felix and Aetius with the ecclesiastical activities of [Pope] Celestine'.[36] Although tempting, the idea must remain open to doubt. The activities of Germanus may possibly have been initiated by the Pope, but it is more likely that the two missions in 429 and 435 were instigated by the islanders. Furthermore, the pressure on the frontiers and in Gaul was such that the policies and actions of Felix and later Aetius would appear to have been reactive rather than proactive. As a result, it is probably better to see these activities as separate and linked to 'external' activity rather than being the formulated policies of the military and spiritual leaders working in tandem to regain control of the west.

Patricius
Upon returning from the wars against the Burgundians, Aetius received the greatest confirmation that his position was secure, at least for the time being and as long as he was being successful. On 5 September 435 he was honoured with the title *patricius*.[37] This is not surprising. Although opposed by Placidia up to the death of Boniface, Aetius had shown that he was determined to maintain his position, probably since he thought he was the best man for the task.

Although Placidia may have been loath to appoint Aetius as *patricius*, it would have been difficult for her to refuse: he was clearly the only general with power at the time, and whatever she thought of him, realistically she could not do anything else. On the other hand, his record was actually quite good. Since 425 he had fought in two civil wars, 'drawing' the battle in 425 and losing to Boniface in 432. But these were his only failures. He had also fought seven campaigns against barbarians within the empire, winning them all. His energy and willingness to fight almost certainly marked him out from most of his contemporaries and set an example moulded on the guides set by Constantius III and, to a slightly lesser degree, by Stilicho.[38]

Yet despite the fact that Aetius had obtained the title of *patricius* against the odds and could be expected to be fiercely jealous of his titles and power, it should be noted that he was now mentally secure in his position: secure enough to allow other individuals to use the title *patricius*. When this happened Aetius – and possibly Constantius III before him – adopted a more grandiose title: in the case of Aetius, *magnificus vir parens patriusque noster* instead of the more modest *patricius noster*.[39] As the empire became more desperate in its attempts to survive and the West disintegrated, the most powerful individuals were striving to invent ever more complex titles with which to emphasise their importance.

436

No doubt the celebrations concerning the title of *patricius* lasted for a long time. As a result, it was not until the new year that Aetius prepared to meet the fresh challenges that awaited him. The first of these was that Theoderic, king of the Goths, 'confounded the peace agreements and seized many towns in the vicinity of their settlements, attacking the city of Narbonne most of all'.[40]

At the same time, the Burgundians were again attacked by the Romans. Although the reference to a second war against the Burgundians by Hydatius is sometimes seen as a doublet, simply repeating the war of 435, the information given by Prosper confirms that this was a second war:[41]

> At the same time Aetius crushed Gundichar, who was king of the Burgundians and living in Gaul. In response to his entreaty, Aetius gave him peace, which the king did not enjoy for long. For the Huns destroyed him and his people root and branch.

Prosper, rather than dating the conclusion of the war to 437, keeps the information under one entry, a relatively common occurrence in the chronicles.[42] Yet information in Hydatius also suggests that the war was not begun by Aetius:[43]

> The Burgundians, who had rebelled, were defeated by the Romans under the general Aetius.

Hydatius' claim that the Burgundians had 'rebelled' may refer to the war of 435, but it is just as likely that he is noting that in 436 the Burgundians had rebelled against the recently signed treaty.[44]

The reason for the combined rebellion is unknown. Yet given the context it is possible, although unfortunately impossible to prove, that the reason for the renewal of war was Gothic and Burgundian discontent with the peace treaties of 426 and 435 respectively. Since Gundichar had 'entreated' Aetius for peace, it is almost certain that the treaty of 435 was to the detriment of the Burgundians, and so unhappiness may have continued to fester. Yet the fact that war again erupted so quickly is surprising, unless there was an external stimulus. The cause may have been an alliance in 436 between the Goths and the Burgundians, probably proposed by the Goths, instigated by their respective unhappiness with the extent of Roman domination. It is also feasible to conjecture that the Goths had been preparing for this war for a long time. It is feasible that the envoy to the Sueves named Vetto, who had in 431 travelled to Gallaecia, was attempting to enrol the Sueves in a general uprising of 'barbarian nations' within the Western Empire.[45]

It is also within the realms of possibility, although extremely uncertain, that it was in 436 that Theoderic arranged an alliance with the Vandals in Africa. This would ensure that no Vandal troops would be sent to Gaul to support the Romans against the Vandals and Burgundians. To cement the alliance Theoderic's daughter, who is unfortunately not named, was married to Gaiseric's son Huneric.[46] Although the dating and true nature of this event is uncertain, and it may be dated to 431 alongside the similar attempt to enrol the Sueves by Vetto, it is at this date that the circumstances would best fit such an alliance.[47]

Although the rebellion may primarily have been caused by a desire to renegotiate the earlier treaty, a secondary cause may have been Theoderic's attempts to establish himself as the dominant political leader in his new kingdom. In a later entry dated to 439, Prosper states that Vetericus was 'considered loyal to our state and renowned for the frequent demonstration of his skill in war'.[48] Vetericus is otherwise unknown, but was most likely a Gothic noble who had decided to take employment with Rome rather than serve under Theoderic. The reason for his choice, and his opposition to Theoderic, is unspecified, but may be the result of a disagreement with Theoderic's policies. As a result Vetericus may have left the Gothic area and taken service with Rome as a result of his opposition to Theoderic. His desertion of Theoderic and his taking part in the war on the Roman side would explain his 'loyalty' to Rome. It may also be evidence that not all Gothic nobles were happy with Theoderic's leadership and may have resented his attempts to force them to obey him.

The Gothic and Burgundian Rebellion

Possibly taking advantage of the fact that the Romans were distracted by events in Armorica, the new rebellion broke out.[49] The two simultaneous rebellions forced Aetius on to the defensive. During 436 Litorius was completing the suppression of the *Bacaudic* revolt in Armorica, probably with the Gallic army, and it would appear that Aetius was using the *praesental* forces to simply contain the combined Gothic and Burgundian rebellion. Unwilling to face the Goths with his thinly stretched forces and so leave other areas open to attack by the Burgundians, Aetius was forced to remain inactive whilst the Goths moved into Roman territory and laid siege to Narbona (Narbonne).[50] The rest of 436 was spent ensuring that the rebellion did not spread and that the Goths and Burgundians did not break out from their already-conquered areas to spread devastation around Gaul and possibly Italy.

Aetius and the Huns

However, Aetius was not idle. He could not afford to allow the Goths to become independent in any way, shape or form. If the Goths were allowed to break the treaty they had agreed with Rome, Rome would lose both the revenues that the Goths currently enjoyed as well as their military service. The loss of both money and service, along with the need to garrison permanently the suddenly unfriendly frontier with the Goths, would stretch the resources of the empire to breaking point.

Accordingly, Aetius dispatched at least one emissary in the hope of receiving help in Gaul. For over a decade he had received support from the Huns whenever it was needed, especially in 424 and more recently in 433. Furthermore, analysis of the years between and after these events illustrates that the army of the West now had a large number of Huns fighting alongside the Roman army. However, rather than receiving small numbers of reinforcements, Aetius realized that a larger force was necessary. Although the dating is uncertain, it is very likely that it was in 436–437 that he formally ceded parts of Pannonia near to the River Save to the Huns.[51]

The formal cession of territory in Pannonia was not in reality actually giving away land ruled by Rome. Priscus does not say 'the whole of Pannonia' but 'the part of Pannonia close to the River Save which became subject to the barbarian by the treaty with Aetius': the treaty only alienated marginal lands along the borders to the Huns. In 427 Felix had led a campaign to evict the Huns from Pannonia, but it is clear that in the intervening period they had simply re-crossed the river to graze their herds again.[52] By formally allocating lands they already controlled in reality to the Huns, Aetius was able to boost the political power of Rua. In response, Rua agreed to lead his main army against the Burgundians as soon as the weather allowed.

Although interpretations differ and many see the cession of Roman territory as 'un-Roman', it is clear that as *de facto* leader of the West Aetius was determined to maintain his personal ties with the Huns. They in turn responded by providing him with the *foederati* and other troops he needed to maintain himself in power. Furthermore, it is possible that Aetius was using the Hunnic *foederati* to offset the lack of new recruits being provided by the imperial court, and especially the Senate. It is feasible that Aetius was becoming increasingly reliant upon the Huns to help bolster his own rather precarious military position within the empire. Without their aid, the lack of recruits would severely limit his freedom of action. By accepting the reality of the Huns' penetration of Pannonia, Aetius ensured that for a long time his armies in the West would continue to be supported by Hunnic allies.

437

The siege of Narbonne by the Goths continued over the winter of 436–437. Fortunately for Aetius, at the end of 436, or possibly early in 437, Litorius was finally able to capture Tibatto, leader of the *bacaudae*.[53] With their main leader captured and their other leaders either captured or killed, the rebellion in northern Gaul collapsed.[54] Litorius was at last free to move south.

Narbonne was by now in the last stages of the siege, since the inhabitants were starving. Marching through the Auvergne district, Litorius arrived unexpectedly outside Narbonne.[55] Caught by surprise in their siege positions and unable to form a coherent battle line, the Goths were quickly routed.[56] Fortunately for the inhabitants of Narbonne, every man in Litorius' army had been ordered to carry two measures of wheat, which was now used to ease the problem of starvation in the city.[57]

However, Litorius' limitations were also exposed during this campaign. On the march through the Auvergne some of the Huns in his army broke away and plundered the region until stopped by a force led by Eparchius Avitus,[58] a Gallic senator of distinguished family who had become a favourite of the Gothic king Theoderic during the 420s.[59] He had served in the army under Aetius during the campaigns against the Norici and Iuthungi in 430–431, after which Aetius may have promoted him to be *magister militum per Gallias*, although this is uncertain.[60] He would appear to have been in control of forces stationed near to the Gothic siege lines at Narbonne, possibly in an attempt to restrict their ability to forage and so limit their capacity to maintain the siege indefinitely. He defeated the renegade Huns in a battle near Clermont before joining Litorius, probably shortly after the latter's entry into Narbonne.[61]

It may appear surprising that Litorius did not halt his advance and turn to deal with the Huns, yet given the fact that the city of Narbonne had been under siege for a long time he may have thought that raising the siege was of more importance than losing the element of surprise. He decided not to waste time bringing the Huns back under control. Furthermore, he might have lost the advantage of surprise if he had turned to deal with the Huns and allowed news of his arrival to reach the Goths.

At roughly the same time as the siege of Narbonne was being raised, the Huns under Rua arrived in Gaul and attacked the Burgundians. The attack was devastating: according to Hydatius, 20,000 Burgundians were slaughtered, including the king.[62] Although no doubt the numbers were exaggerated, the scale of the defeat is echoed by the Gallic Chronicler, who notes that 'almost the entire people with their king were destroyed'.[63] This historical event may be the origin of the *Nibelungen* cycle, upon which Wagner later based his epic *Der Ring des Nibelungen*.[64]

Spain and Northern Gaul

Yet it would appear that the confusion and war in southern Gaul had resulted in further attacks and rebellions. In Spain the Sueves resumed their attacks on the native inhabitants. Censurius and Fretimund, who is otherwise unknown, were sent as ambassadors, but this time it would appear that Aetius was unwilling to rely on politics alone.[65] It is probably at this date that Aetius sent an unknown commander into Spain with orders to defeat the Sueves. Jordanes notes that Aetius had been successful, since by 'inflicting crushing defeats he had compelled the proud Suevi and barbarous Franks to submit to Roman sway'.[66] Furthermore, Merobaudes in his first surviving panegyric alludes to Aetius' successes in Spain.[67] It should be noted, however, that this campaign is otherwise unrecorded and of dubious dating.

The note in Jordanes also points to a further war, this time with the Franks. As is usual, the events described are extremely difficult to confirm or to date, yet it is known from Salvian that at some time prior to 440 the Franks had attacked Gaul and captured Cologne and Trier.[68] It seems that another force had been sent by Aetius to face the Franks in the north and had defeated them. However, it is possible that due to the ongoing war with the Goths the campaign against the Franks was merely one of containment, and that the Franks were not actually evicted from Roman territory at this time, since the dating and context of this war are very difficult to establish.

Valentinian and Licinia Eudoxia

Aetius was not present during the campaigns against either the Goths or the Burgundians. Instead, he was involved in a series of major diplomatic coups with regard to the East. In 437 he travelled east to Constantinople with Valentinian for Valentinian's marriage to Licinia Eudoxia, daughter of the Eastern Emperor Theodosius II, in October 437.[69]

The party arrived in Constantinople on 21 October 437[70] and appears to have included Merobaudes and Sigisvult, who at this date may have been *magister equitum*, and so the most senior military figure behind Aetius, although the date of Sigisvult's appointment is insecure.[71] However, it is certain that he must have held an important position due to the events that then occurred.

The marriage took place on 29 October 437.[72] In an attempt to ensure continuing good relations, to foster a sense of the continuing unity of the empire, but mainly in the spirit of sharing engendered by the marriage, as part of the marriage celebrations Theodosius made major political concessions to the West. In the spirit of goodwill and rejoicing, Aetius was granted his second consulship.[73] At the same time, Sigisvult was made a consul.[74] This was an exceptional occurrence, since it was traditional that one consul was nominated by the West and one by the East. The allocating of both consulships to the West was a major concession and is almost certainly connected with the marriage.[75] It is also evidence that by 437 the regime of Valentinian and Aetius in the West was seen as being successful by the East, a concept that is re-inforced by Socrates when he states that Valentinian had 'made the western regions safe'.[76] The achievements of Valentinian and Aetius were highly appreciated.

Furthermore, in a continuation on the theme of awarding 'Eastern' posts to the West, it is possible, but by no means certain, that at the same time Merobaudes was declared *patricius* by Theodosius, almost certainly on Aetius' recommendation, although the post was in the East and was no doubt only honorary.[77]

Gaiseric

Yet amidst all of the rejoicing and happiness, the first signs of a coming catastrophe were appearing in the West. In 437 Gaiseric, King of the Vandals, began to persecute the Catholic priests in his dominions in Africa.[78] Despite the Catholic sources' dismay at such actions, it is almost certain that other Christians in Africa would have found the treatment of the Catholic Christians ironic, since it was only twelve years previously, in 425, that a persecution of non-Catholic Christians in Africa and an empire-wide ban on non-Catholics in cities had been ordered by Valentinian.[79]

Nor was this the only sign of the storm to come: 'In the same year barbarian deserters of the federates took to piracy.'[80] Although the meaning was no doubt obvious to contemporaries, this is now a very cryptic entry, which could mean many things. However, given the context and with the benefit of hindsight, the entry almost certainly refers to the Vandals. Gaiseric, having learned of the revolt in Gaul, and possibly having arranged a marriage alliance with the Goths, was intent on expanding the boundaries of his proto-kingdom, or at least of enriching himself in order to pay his *comitatus*. It is likely that he ordered members of the Vandal aristocracy to begin raiding the West using the ships already used for the crossing to Africa, hence the reference to 'deserters' and 'piracy'. The move would allow his kingdom to gain in wealth, but at the same time if necessary he would be able to deny involvement to the Roman government, declaring that these 'pirates' were 'deserters'. He could also claim to his Gothic allies that he was doing something to help the war effort. Using these methods Gaiseric could benefit from the raids, test the readiness of the West to punish further aggressive action, avoid responsibility for the attacks if the West proved too strong, and show faith with his allies.

438

When it became clear that the West was unable to hinder these acts, in 438 the Vandals began to spread their activities. They now started to raid the western Mediterranean, focusing their attention on the undefended island of Sicily.[81]

The reason for the continued neglect of the Mediterranean was that Aetius was focused upon the war against the Goths. Although the Burgundians had been decimated by the Huns, the Goths continued to fight. It would appear that their anger at their treatment was such that they were willing to continue the war unaided, even though alone they were unable to defeat the armies of the West.

Returning to Ravenna after the marriage in Constantinople, it is probably in 438 that Aetius made slight alterations amongst the commanders in Gaul. Avitus, who had probably been *magister militum per Gallias*, was appointed *praefectus praetorio Galliarum*.[82] His removal from a military post may have been a consequence of his failure to defeat the Goths in person during the earlier siege of Narbonne, instead relying upon the arrival of Litorius. On the other hand, the new post was a position for which Avitus was supremely suited. A Gallic senator, his appointment could be used as proof that Gaul and its senators remained central to the concept of imperial unity. Further, his intimate knowledge of Gaul and its resources would ease the burden of supplying the army during the Gothic war.

Interestingly, the appointment of Avitus as first a general and then a civilian bureaucrat demonstrates that the hypothesis that military and civilian posts were now definitely separate is mistaken. As with the earlier empire, talented individuals would be given whichever post suited their abilities, regardless of whether this meant changing between military and civilian status.

Avitus was probably replaced as *magister militum per Gallias* by Litorius, who had clearly demonstrated his military ability during the suppression of the *bacaudic* revolt and by the raising of the siege of Narbonne.[83] However, for the campaign season of 438 Aetius once again personally assumed command of the armies in Gaul. In a great battle he won a significant victory, allegedly slaughtering 8,000 Goths.[84] This may be the Battle of Mons Colubrarius referred to by Merobaudes in his panegyric.[85] The battle demonstrates that Aetius was not content to arrange traditional, set-piece battles with the Goths:

> All the forces of the Goths ... had sallied forth with their king to ravage Roman territory ... At the mountain that the ancients call ... Snake Mountain [Mons Colubrarius]... he surprised – as is his custom – and killed the greatest part of the enemy; once the infantry units, which were very numerous, were routed, he himself followed hard on the scattering

cavalry troops and overwhelmed those standing fast with his might, and those fleeing with his eager rapidity. Not long afterwards the king himself was on hand with the remainder of his forces, and, stupefied with sudden horror near the trampled bodies ... [here the text finishes].

Merobaudes, Panegyric 1, fragment IIA, 10f

The claim that Aetius preferred to use surprise 'as his custom' rather than pitched battle not only demonstrates his skill as a general, but also implies that he could not risk losing the large number of men that would be engaged in a formal battle. At the same time, he may have been employing traditional Roman military doctrine coupled with Hunnic concepts of 'hit-and-run' to ensure success in battle. Although the scale of the victory and the number of losses suffered by the Goths are no doubt exaggerated by Merobaudes – since this is a panegyric – it would appear that Theoderic had experienced a fairly heavy reverse. Yet it was not catastrophic, since he refused to accept defeat and the war continued on into 439.

In the same year Aetius was to receive a welcome piece of good news. In Spain peace had once again been established between the Sueves and a 'section of Gallaecians'. Yet in part at least this had been forced on the Sueves by an internal problem. Their king, Hermeric, was extremely ill at this time and after the peace treaty had been agreed he abdicated in favour of his son, Rechila.[86] Rechila immediately set the tone for his new reign, crushing the Vandal Andevotus near the River Singilis in Baetica and capturing his treasury.[87] The southerly location reinforces the possibility that Andevotus was the leader of the remnants of the Vandals in Spain (see Chapter 7). The aggressive start to his reign also implies that Rechila was seeking to negotiate new treaties that were more advantageous to the Sueves.

The *Codex Theodosianus*

In the East there was a further cause for celebration. In 438, after ten years of compilation, the *Codex Theodosianus* was finally published.[88] A major work of civil law, the *Codex* was commissioned in 429 by Theodosius and listed all of the laws that had been promulgated since the year 312. A copy was sent to Valentinian in the West and was laid before the Senate in Rome for acceptance. In 439 it was accepted as law by the West, so ensuring the continued legal unity of the whole empire.[89] Interestingly, the Code implies that the dominance of Aetius was not yet complete by 439. In the *Gesta Senatus Urbis Romae* (Minutes of the Senate of the City of Rome), which outlines the procedure in the Senate by which the laws were accepted, there were cries for Faustus, Paulus and Aetius to be made consuls.[90] However, the fact that neither Paulus nor Faustus ever gained their hoped-for consulships and that Aetius had to wait a further seven years for his third suggests that Valentinian and Placidia may have still retained a large degree of autonomy at this date, although the extent of this is uncertain.[91]

By 438 it was clear that the financial situation in the West was deteriorating. In July of that year Valentinian was forced to accept that some of the outstanding taxes he so desperately needed were never going to arrive due to the financial straits of his subjects. As a consequence he agreed to a remission of delinquent taxes, almost certainly in the hope that this sign of grace would encourage the taxpayers to then keep up with their newly levied taxes.[92]

439

It would appear that political circumstances in Ravenna demanded that Aetius leave the conduct of the Gothic war in the hands of Litorius, not least because Aetius may have needed to be present when Merobaudes delivered his second panegyric.[93] He would almost certainly have wanted to be at the ceremony when he was honoured

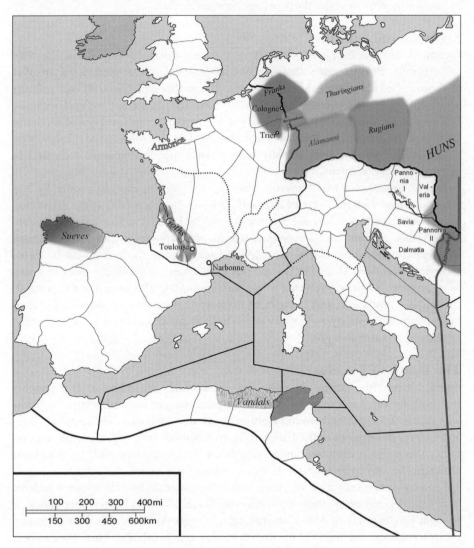

Map 9. The Western Empire c.439

with a statue erected by order of the emperors.[94] The evidence suggests that Aetius was the most aggressive, talented and – above all – successful military leader in the West. However, with generals of the calibre of Sigisvult and Litorius, plus the fact that the Goths had just suffered a great defeat, Aetius probably felt that there was no need to remain in Gaul and take command himself. As time passed and Aetius began to feel secure in his position, it is notable that he came to rely more and more on his subordinate generals, such as Litorius and Sigisvult, to do the actual fighting whilst he remained in Italy. From a fixed position it would be easy for him to provide strategic direction: messengers would know where to find him without having to chase a campaigning army and as a result he would have all of the intelligence he needed to be able to make the most appropriate decisions.

Sigisvult and Litorius

Questions have been raised concerning the posts being occupied by Sigisvult and Litorius. Prosper states that in 439 Litorius held a post 'second only to that of Aetius'.[95] Since other evidence suggests that at this date Sigisvult was *magister equitum*, what Prosper probably means is that Litorius was 'second' in Gaul, meaning that he was *magister militum per Gallias*: the military leader in Gaul would no doubt only have to answer to Aetius for his actions. On the other hand, it has been suggested that he may have actually been given a special temporary command as *magister militum* of Spain.[96]

It is almost certain that Sigisvult was *magister equitum*, especially since he had been honoured with the consulship in 437. It has been proposed that the promotion of individuals to be *magistri militiae* was ordered by Placidia in an attempt to undermine Aetius' position.[97] However, Aetius at no point appears to have felt threatened by these appointments, and he certainly did not attempt to defeat them by force, as he had Boniface. Moreover, he did not even change his military titles in a way to emphasize that he was superior to the *magistri militiae* who were being appointed. Instead, it is probably nearer to the mark to interpret these promotions as being based upon the military ability and loyalty of the individuals and to them being appointed on Aetius' recommendation.[98]

The Death of Litorius

Sigisvult's activities during the campaign season of 439 are unknown. It is possible that both he and Litorius were involved in attacks upon isolated groups of Goths who had been despatched around Gaul in an attempt to extend Theoderic's power, and so were not present at the Battle of Mons Colubrarius in 438. Sigisvult appears to have been a more cautious commander than Litorius, and hence has received little notice in the surviving histories and chronicles of the period.

Litorius, however, was a far more aggressive commander. He appears to have been experiencing great success, pushing the Goths back into the territory allocated to them by the treaty of 418. Unfortunately, his success resulted in him becoming complacent about the ability of his Roman troops, along with their Hun allies, to beat the Goths.

The Goths, now forced on to the defensive, were retreating into their original territories, pursued by Litorius. Sigisvult may also have been involved, although he may instead have remained in Italy. Litorius decided to end the campaign by fighting one last glorious battle near to the Gothic 'capital' of Toulouse.

After seeking the advice of soothsayers, possibly demonstrating that he was a pagan, Litorius led his army into battle with the Goths. After a long fight, with heavy losses on both sides, Litorius led his Huns – probably meaning his *bucellarii* – in a personal attack, but the Huns were killed and he himself was captured.[99] Shortly afterwards he was put to death.[100]

In the emergency conditions that followed, it would appear that the Goth Vetericus was temporarily placed in charge – at least if that is the meaning of Prosper's very short statement 'in the same period, Vetericus was considered loyal to our state and renowned for the frequent demonstration of his skill in war'.[101] Vetericus stabilized the situation following the potentially disastrous defeat.

In this emergency, Aetius himself left Ravenna to take control of the Gallic army.[102] Fortunately for him, the losses suffered both in this battle and in the previous years of the conflict had weakened the resolve of the Goths. In fact, according to Salvian, 'The Goths sought peace and we denied it; they sent bishops to make terms and we rejected them; they honoured God even in the person of alien priests and we despised him in our own.'[103]

There can be little doubt that Aetius wanted to conclude the war with a significant victory, which would help raise morale in the West as well as deter the Goths from renewing their attempts at expansion. As a result, he personally led a campaign against the Goths. Advancing towards Toulouse, Aetius began the siege of a Gothic military camp near their capital. After a brief pause in which to build siege towers, his men breached the walls of the camp and slaughtered the defenders, who were unable to flee.[104]

Shortly after the siege Aetius sent Avitus to the Goths to negotiate.[105] The end result was a peace treaty that in many ways appears to have left the situation unchanged from before the war started.[106] The treaty was most likely unsatisfactory in some details to both the Goths and the Romans. However, in two areas it was beneficial to the Goths: firstly, the Goths needed time to rest and recover their strength after their defeats, although the Romans also needed the peace in order to deploy the freed troops to other theatres of war. Secondly, although the evidence is inconclusive, it is possible that this treaty was the first in which the two sides treated each other as 'sovereign entities', and in which Theoderic was recognized as 'king' in return for controlling his subjects.[107] The impression is reinforced by the fact that, unlike in the previous decade, Theoderic appears to have observed the terms of this treaty until the death of Valentinian, suggesting that one of his main aims – that of being acknowledged in Rome as king and equal – had been fulfilled.

Following the peace treaty with the Goths Aetius' reputation, especially in Gaul, was at its height. The Gallic aristocracy especially appear to have been supporting Aetius and his policies in Gaul.[108] After the treaty had been arranged, Aetius returned to Italy.[109] It is most likely at this time that he learned three pieces of news. The first was not good: in Spain Rechila, the new king of the Sueves, taking advantage of the long war between the Romans and the Goths in Gaul, had captured Emerita.[110] The second also was bad and concerned affairs across the Danube.

The Huns

Following the agreements with Aetius in 433 and 435, and no doubt encouraged by having a secure peace agreed with the west, Rua turned his attention to the Eastern Empire. Although details are few and no dates are given, it would appear that at some point after Aetius' visit in 433 the Huns and the East were at war.[111] This seems to have been a success for the Huns. However, Rua now achieved a domination north of the Danube, which was not accepted by some of the subordinate tribes. At some point in the late 430s large numbers of the 'Amilzuri, Itimari, Tounsoures, Boisci, and other tribes who were living near to the Danube were fleeing to fight on the side of the Romans'.[112]

Disturbed by the idea that these men could defy him, Rua sent an embassy to Constantinople threatening to renew the war if the Romans did not return the 'fugitives'. After a flurry of exchanges, conducted by Eslas for the Huns and Plinthas for the Romans, a meeting was set in the town of Margus. Alongside the Roman and Hun delegates were assembled the 'kings of the Scythians', probably the leaders of the tribesmen who were defecting to Rome.[113]

The East did not want a war and so in the Treaty of Margus agreed to the terms set by the Huns. At least some of its details are preserved by Priscus: the Romans would no longer accept service from individuals fleeing from Hunnic territories; those who had already crossed to Roman territory were to be returned; Roman prisoners-of-war from the previous conflict who had returned home were to pay eight *solidi* each to their previous captors; the Romans were not allowed to make alliances with any tribes upon which the Huns were about to wage war; the Huns and the Romans were to be treated equally at 'safe' markets; and the treaty was to last as long as the east paid 700 pounds of gold annually to the Huns, whereas previously they had paid only 350 pounds of gold.[114]

In order to put the tribute into perspective, it is possible to note the annual income of some Roman families: 'Many of the Roman households received an income of four thousand pounds [of gold] per year from their properties, not including grain, wine and other produce which, if sold, would have amounted to one third of the income in gold. The income of the households at Rome of the second class was one thousand or fifteen hundred pounds of gold.'[115] Although appearing a considerable sum, the subsidy was only half the annual income of a family household 'of the second class' in Rome. On the other hand, in 434 the cost of supplying the whole of the city of Constantinople with grain was 611 pounds of gold.[116] Although a relatively small amount for the rich, the sum was a vast amount for the poor.

The treaty was a major coup for the Huns and demonstrated to all of their subjects that even the mighty Roman Empire was not beyond their control. Furthermore, even within the Roman Empire the might of the Huns was now an accepted fact:

Aetius, in the West, had been restored to power by the threat of Hunnic intervention whilst the East had been forced to accept a treaty imposed by the Huns.

The power of the Huns was now such that individuals other than Aetius felt that it would benefit their careers if they could establish strong political ties with them. During the negotiations for the Treaty of Margus, the imperial side had been represented by the ex-general and ex-consul Plinthas, who had employed a variety of devious schemes to ensure that he would be the main envoy and so gain influence with both the Romans and the Huns, possibly in an attempt to emulate Aetius' position in the west.[117]

However, the treaty was not concluded with Rua: early in the proceedings he died, possibly as the result of being hit by a thunderbolt.[118] Although the date of Rua's death is stated by the Gallic Chronicler to be 434, other evidence makes this unlikely.[119] The major factor is that during the long war with the Goths between 437 and 439 the West was helped by large numbers of Hunnic allies.[120] The fact that these Huns continued to serve Rome implies that the political situation amongst their fellows across the Danube had remained unchanged. Although it is possible that Rua's successor had continued to supply mercenaries to the West, or that these Huns were simply mercenary bands, this is unlikely.

The rule of the Huns passed jointly to the sons of Mundiuch, Rua's brother.[121] One of these was called Bleda, and apparently he assumed control of the Hunnic tribes facing the Eastern Empire. The other, and the one who inherited control of the tribes facing the Western Empire, was called Attila.[122] Following the signing of the Treaty of Margus, in a display of power Attila and Bleda marched through Scythia and fought the Sorosgi, an otherwise unknown tribe.[123] The martial attitude of the new rulers was immediately being displayed, although according to Socrates it may have been tempered by the outbreak of a plague, but this is otherwise unattested.[124]

Yet even though the news of the death of Rua, his ally, and the accession of Attila, who was of the next generation and so did not have the same personal ties to Aetius, was bad, it was the third piece of news that would have caused the worst shock to Aetius and the court at Ravenna. Either late in 439 or early in 440 news arrived in Italy that a major disaster had happened: the province of Africa Proconsularis, the source of much of the grain for Italy and especially Rome, had been lost.

Chapter 9

The Fall of Africa

AFRICA

When talking about Roman rule in Africa there is, understandably, sometimes confusion concerning the meaning of the term. Although Africa is now the name for the whole continent, for the Romans Africa was more usually applied to the province created in 146 BC after the defeat of Carthage. Shortly after this the Romans conquered more areas of the North African coast and these became the provinces of Tripolitania, Byzacium, Numidia, Mauretania Sitifensis, Mauretania Caesariensis and Tingitana. Tingitana eventually became part of the Diocese of Hispania, but the rest were included as part of the Diocese of Africa with its capital at Carthage. As a result, it is easy to become confused, so wherever applicable the term 'Africa' applies to the whole Diocese, and the term Africa Proconsularis will be applied to the province (see Map 10 for further clarification).

The province of Africa was known as Africa Proconsularis. Along with Egypt, it was the breadbasket of the early Roman Empire. Grain had been taken, as part of Africa's tax, to feed the citizens of Rome and Italy. Egypt had also supplied grain, but after the foundation of Constantinople this had been diverted to Constantine's new city. Since then, Rome had come to rely almost completely on the African grain supply to feed its citizens, and two-thirds of Africa's annual harvest was exported to Rome. Control of the grain shipments to Rome was vital and from early in the empire's history the governor of the province – and a few other provinces (see Map 1) – was a proconsul rather than a senator, hence the name Africa Proconsularis.

Although in the earlier empire the main commodity exported from Africa had been grain, from the late second century olive oil had become important, with the interior of the provinces of Numidia, Byzacena and Tripolitania, and especially the territories of Lepcis Magna, Oea and Sabratha (See Map 11), being used for olive production. In fact, the anonymous author of *Expositio totius mundi et rerum* noted that Africa was wealthy in all things, including grain, fruit, trees, slaves and textiles, but 'it virtually exceeds all others in the use of the olive'.[1] The other major commodity exported from Africa was African red-slip ware, a distinctive form of pottery that is now used by archaeologists as evidence for trade patterns from Africa to the wider Mediterranean area. However, in the early-fifth century all of these goods were mainly destined for the market of Rome and Italy.

The fact that the city of Rome was dependent on African grain was of great benefit for the citizens of Africa. Not only did they have a ready market, but the imperial government ensured that all of the transport facilities in Africa and its surrounding provinces were of the highest standard to ensure quick delivery of the grain. This infrastructure was highly beneficial to those wishing to export other goods. Thanks to the favourable lease laws employed in Africa there was a huge production of surpluses and these were transported along government-maintained highways to the Mediterranean for shipment to Rome and throughout the Mediterranean. Apart from agricultural surpluses, traders were also willing to take African red-slip ware on their journeys, stowing these smaller items between the larger loads of foodstuffs.

A final reason for the prosperity of the African provinces was that they were not exposed to war. Although there may have been local troubles in the area, the troops stationed in Africa were mainly there to control the movement of the local nomadic tribes as they migrated between their winter and summer pastures, ensuring that they did not stray on to settled lands and cause damage.

Yet Africa was not exempt from the changes being seen in the other parts of the west. In Africa, as elsewhere, the local councillors were becoming reluctant to serve on their local councils since financially the burden was very high. Commercially, in many areas the *forum*, the centre of towns and cities, had either fallen out of use or at least had become much reduced in size. Furthermore, temples and some bathhouses were starting to fall into ruin. The functions of the *forum* were now being replaced by buildings connected to churches, signalling the rise in attachment to Christianity and the loss of emphasis of pagan institutions. Additionally, large houses were now beginning to be divided into smaller units and shop fronts were appearing along street frontages, replacing the shopping area of the forum.[2]

There were also areas of dispute. The main one of these was Christianity. There was a large community of Donatists in Africa, who were in opposition to the Catholic majority. The disagreement went back to the previous century, when Diocletian (284–305) had ordered a persecution of Christians in the empire between 303 and 305. Many Christian clergymen had been killed in the persecution, but some had surrendered, giving up their copies of the scriptures and in some cases betraying fellow Christians to the authorities. These men were known as *traditores* ('the ones who handed over').

After the persecution, and particularly following Constantine the Great's edict of toleration, many of these men had been allowed to return to their former positions. A large number of Christians refused to accept their authority, seeing them as traitors to the faith. When a new Bishop of Carthage was consecrated by a *traditor*, his opponents refused to accept him. Eventually, in 313, a man named Donatus (after whom the movement was named) was elected as bishop and the controversy broadened due to the fact that Donatus was an anti-*traditor*.

As Bishop of Carthage, Donatus wielded great power and was able to appeal against the appointment of *traditors*, but in 313 a commission found against the Donatists. Despite this, the movement continued, especially in Africa, leading to widespread division even after Donatus' death in 355. This was largely due to the Donatist priests being local men who spoke local languages and dialects, so endearing them to the provincial population outside the big cities. On the other hand, Catholic priests tended to speak only Latin, and so had more of a following in the cities.

The Donatist cause was not helped by the rise of the *Circumcellians*. These were groups from the lowest levels of society who developed anti-Roman biases and were prone to rebellion. They were usually Donatists and their infamy resulted in Donatism being associated with rebels and bandits. As a result, in the early-fifth century there began a persecution of the Donatists in Africa, which Saint Augustine thought to be harsh and ill judged.[3]

In June 411 in Carthage a conference took place that found against the Donatists. Slowly, under pressure, Donatist adherents began to convert to Catholic Christianity. Yet by the 430s there were still many strong adherents to the cause who were unhappy with the course of events: religious division continued.

As a final point, although Roman Africa tends to be studied as a single entity, it should be noted that only in Africa Proconsularis was Latin a common language. The other provinces were not the same and there were at least three languages in use in the area. Furthermore, there was a distinct cultural division between Romanized Carthage and the rural countryside.[4] These divisions meant that although the Vandals arrived as barbarian outsiders, and are so described by Catholic and aristocratic literature, they may have been seen as 'saviours' by those members of the population unhappy with Catholic imperial rule.[5]

Despite these changes, the province was peaceful and relatively prosperous, so the Vandal invasion in 430 was doubtless a major shock for the inhabitants. Not only were they under threat of war for the first time in several generations, but the troops in the area were unused to having to fight set-piece battles. Probably as a result of their lack of experience and suitable training, the Roman army in Africa was defeated, first under Boniface, and then under Boniface and Aspar reinforced with the East Roman forces.

The treaty of 435 was in many ways unwelcome in the area, since it was now clear that the empire was not in a position to evict the Vandals, or defeat them and ensure their compliance with the treaty (see Map 8). However, given the fact that the resources of the West were becoming increasingly strained from both internal and external threats, the treaty had one major advantage: it saved most of Numidia, Byzacena and Africa Proconsularis – including Carthage, the point of export for most African grain – from the Vandals.[6] Although there was political and religious confusion following the Vandal invasion, the actual damage to the economy was limited, and there is little doubt that after 435 grain exports to Rome were resumed.

Carthage itself was the third-largest city of the empire, only Constantinople and Rome itself having greater populations. By the end of the fourth century it has been estimated that it may have had a population as high as 100,000.[7] The main task of Carthage was to act as the administrative centre of Africa Proconsularis and as the main port for the distribution of goods brought from the interior and from smaller ports along the coast. Anyone in control of Carthage would be able to impose taxes on the goods being exported, so becoming fantastically rich.

The net result of these factors was that the provinces of North Africa had extremely high productivity but were low on maintenance, and so were the major net contributor to the financial stability of the West. Furthermore, surplus revenues from Africa were vital to the maintenance of the armed forces.[8] However, this should not be overestimated. The largest estates were owned by relatively few men, who were the most powerful and influential in Italy. These individuals did not want men from their estates being conscripted into the army, nor did they want to pay the taxes necessary to furnish new recruits. Although Africa was vital to the economy, the political power of the major landowners was a source of constant friction between the emperor, the *magister militum* and the Senate.

THE VANDALS

The Vandals had now achieved a position superior even to that of the Goths in Gaul. Gaiseric had a military position, his followers were settled in some of the most prosperous areas of the West and, most importantly, the main armies left in the West were focused upon the defence of Gaul rather than on opposing the Vandals in Africa. The improvement in the fortunes of Gaiseric's people since the attack of the Goths in 416 was immeasurable. Yet as has already been noted, Gaiseric does not appear to have been content with this new-found security. From 437 he began to test the preparedness of Aetius to face the Vandals. The piracy of 'barbarian deserters' implies that Gaiseric was looking at the possibility of extending his influence in Africa, a theory reinforced by the fact that he began to persecute Catholic priests and the local nobility.[9] Both of these actions suggest that Gaiseric had not fulfilled his ultimate ambition, especially since the persecution of clergy and nobles suggests that he was aiming at removing all of those individuals who could lead indigenous resistance to his aims. He replaced the departing Roman nobles and clergymen with Vandal nobles and Arian clergymen.[10]

THE FALL OF CARTHAGE

When it was clear to Gaiseric that Aetius' attention was focused upon the war against the Goths in Gaul, Gaiseric decided that, if he did not act whilst the Roman army was occupied, he might never again get the chance. He had twice defeated the army of Africa, once when it had been reinforced by troops from the East, so confidence would have been high. It is almost certain that by 439 the Eastern troops had returned home with Aspar. Furthermore, it is unknown whether the troops Boniface took to Italy to face Aetius in 432 were ever returned to Africa. Consequently, it is clear that Gaiseric was facing a very weak army in Africa, but one that could be reinforced from Italy should the war against the Goths be won. With these considerations in mind, he now took the last, fateful step on the journey of the Vandals. In an act of supreme political daring, he led his army out of the areas allotted to them and advanced towards Carthage, breaking the treaty of friendship he had agreed with Rome.[11]

On 19 October 439 Geiseric arrived outside the walls of Carthage.[12] There is little primary information for the manner of Geiseric's attack on the city, the main evidence being that he took it by a 'stratagem' or 'trickery'.[13] As a military official of the empire, there can be little doubt that he could easily gain entry to the city with a small bodyguard, after which the opening of the gates would have been a simple matter.

Whatever method he used, once inside he unleashed the Vandals. The Vandal sack of Carthage is usually seen as being a vicious episode. Prosper claims that Gaiseric:

> Put its citizens to various kinds of torture and took all their wealth as his own. Nor did he refrain from spoiling the churches. Emptying them of their sacred vessels, and depriving them of the attention of their priests, he ordered that they no longer be places of divine worship but quarters for his people. He was harsh towards the entire captive population but particularly hostile to the nobility and clergy so that no one could tell whether he was waging war more against man or God.
>
> *Prosper s.a. 439*

This passage is illuminating, if interpreted correctly. It is clear that the aristocracy were targeted by Gaiseric in order to remove them and replace them with his own nobles.[14] Many of the landowners fled to Italy. Those who left had their lands confiscated by the Vandals.[15] The events are similarly described by Victor of Vita, who notes that the 'old class of freemen, freeborn, and noble' were condemned to slavery.[16]

Prosper also states that Gaiseric wanted his people to settle in abandoned churches. In this context it is likely that the phrase 'his people' should really refer to the Vandal Arian clergy. The claim is reinforced by Hydatius, who claims that Gaiseric immediately began a persecution of the 'Catholics'.[17]

These accounts combine to paint a picture of a violent sack of the city, yet this may be misleading. The dual attack on the Catholic Christian church and the aristocracy probably had three aims. One was to remove the leading clergy and aristocrats who could lead resistance to Gaiseric's takeover. A second was to release lands that could then be used to reward Gaiseric's loyal followers, including the Arian priests. Thirdly, the persecution of Catholic clergy would result in the Donatists, and other Christian sects who had been recently persecuted, transferring their loyalty to Gaiseric.

Consequently, it is probably far better to accept that on the whole the 'sack' of Carthage was more of an exercise in evicting the clergymen and the aristocracy – the potential leaders of resistance – from Carthage rather than a wholesale destruction of the city, although the Vandal warriors were no doubt let loose to enter the city and spread terror and disruption, so ensuring that there would be no attempt at defence by the population.

After the first attack was over the troops at large gained at least some of its booty for themselves, but not too much: Gaiseric was able to pass a decree ordering 'that each person [citizen of Carthage] was to bring forward whatever gold, silver, gems and items of costly clothing he had', hardly necessary or successful if the city had been ransacked as described since the vast majority of these goods would otherwise have been taken by the Vandal troops.[18]

Many of the Catholic clergy and Roman aristocracy fled from Africa and arrived in Italy as refugees.[19] No doubt their horror stories heavily influenced Prosper's account of the capture of Carthage. In the meantime, the lands in Africa Proconsularis owned by absentee landlords who had always lived in Italy were also seized by Gaiseric and divided as he thought best fit.[20] However, there is little evidence that once the initial conquest was over Gaiseric ordered a full persecution of Catholics.[21]

RAVENNA

The capture of Carthage was a major blow to the empire. In one fell swoop Gaiseric had stripped the West, and especially Italy, of its major grain supplies and a large part of its tax base. Since the capture of Carthage took place on 19 October 439, it is unlikely that news of the event reached Ravenna until early in 440, and a *novel* issued by Valentinian concerning the employment of *decurions* (city officials) in January 440 makes no mention of the loss of Africa.[22]

Although unrecorded, there can be little doubt that panic swept Rome when the news of the Vandal success arrived. Aetius and Valentinian now had to secure alternative sources of grain for the imperial city. The likelihood is that in the first instance Aetius followed the example set by Stilicho during the 'Revolt of Gildo' in Africa by arranging for emergency supplies of grain to be transported to Rome from Gaul and Spain.[23] However, a series of *novellae* were now issued in order to prepare the west for the emergency.

The first of those still extant is dated to 2 March 440 and was concerned specifically with the military aspects of the crisis, as it ordered a conscription of troops to meet the emergency. With the Vandals at large in the Mediterranean, there was a need to enlarge the number of troops at the empire's disposal, and in an attempt to strengthen the army a simultaneous *novel* was issued, entitled *De Tironibus et de Occultatoribus Desertorum* (*Concerning Recruits and those Hiding Deserters*), announcing that all landowners should furnish the correct number of recruits for the army and declaring the punishment for those who did not do so and instead harboured these deserters.[24] It is also possible that a lost *novel* calling for a new conscription of troops, which is referred to in a *novel* of 444, also dates to this period.[25]

The further *novel* was concerned with the logistical aspect of the loss of Africa.[26] Up to this time Greek merchants had been allowed to trade only under severe restriction in the West, no doubt in an attempt to protect the economy in the face of strong Eastern competition. With the loss of Africa the markets of Rome were opened to Greek merchants, and an attempt was made to fix the price of goods, no doubt especially grain, to ensure that prices remained stable. The need to avoid fluctuating prices was made even more important by the fact that the West had lost the most important tax base for its financial stability.

As has already been noted, the surplus revenues from Africa were a major factor in the maintenance of the armed forces. Without Africa, the west would struggle to maintain its army. To make matters worse, tax collectors were collecting double the amount of taxes required by law and keeping the surplus half. This was obviously causing huge levels of resentment and also destroying the tax base. In an attempt to stop the practice, a law was passed specifically ordering tax collectors to stop, although the law appears to have had little effect.[27]

In the same *novel* in which Greek merchants were allowed into Italy it was ordered that the walls of Rome were to be repaired to defend against any attack by the Vandals.[28] At the same time it would appear that attempts were made to repair and upgrade the fortifications of Naples.[29] These measures to defend the West were necessary. Prior to the seizure of Carthage the Vandals had captured a small fleet when they had moved into the south of Spain, probably the one based at Cartagena. Although this had allowed them to begin raiding the western Mediterranean, the West still had enough ships to pose a threat to them if they attempted to raid either Sicily or Italy. With their rapid seizure of Carthage the Vandals had captured the Roman fleet that was permanently stationed there. Although the fleet was most likely transport ships rather than warships, this instantly made the Vandals a naval force to be reckoned with as it allowed Gaiseric to transport a much larger force anywhere in the Mediterranean. Moreover, it simultaneously reduced the ships available to the West, so making it harder for Valentinian and Aetius to counter Vandal moves. Gaiseric now determined to use his newly won fleet.

When news was received in Ravenna that Gaiseric 'had led forth from the port of Carthage a large fleet' it was suddenly realized that with their new fleet the Vandals could strike anywhere along the coast, and having troops in the correct place to defend against them would be extremely lucky. As a result, a *novel* entitled *De Reddito Jure Armorum* (*Restoration of the Right to use Weapons*) was issued, countermanding a law of 364 that declared that 'No person whatever, without Our knowledge and advice, shall be granted the right to employ any weapons whatsoever':[30]

> Genseric, the enemy of Our Empire, is reported to have led forth from the port of Carthage a large fleet, whose sudden excursion and fortuitous depredation must be feared by all shores. Although the solicitude of Our Clemency is stationing garrisons throughout various places and the army of the most invincible Emperor Theodosius, Our Father, will soon approach, and although We trust that the Most Excellent Patrician, Our Aetius, will soon be here with a large band and the Most illustrious Master of Soldiers, Sigisvuldus, does not cease to organize guards of soldiers and federated allies for the cities and shores, nevertheless, because it is not sufficiently certain, under summertime opportunities for navigation, to what shore the ships of the enemy can come. We admonish each and all by this edict that, with confidence in Roman strength and the courage with which they ought to defend their own, with their own men against the enemy, if the occasion should so demand, they shall use those arms which they can, but they shall preserve the public discipline and the

moderation of free birth unimpaired. Thus shall they guard the provinces
and their own fortunes with faithful harmony and with joined shields.

Nov. Val. 9.1 (24 June, 440)

The same *novel* also demonstrates that along with ordering the citizens to arm
themselves other measures were being taken for the defence of Italy. Aetius had
been recalled from Gaul and was gathering troops prior to marching to the defence
of Italy, and the *magister militum* Sigisvult was deploying those troops stationed in
Italy to defend against the impending attack.[31] The *novel* also proves that by June
440 the scale of the emergency was so great that envoys had already been sent to the
East and Theodosius II had instantly agreed to send troops. Unfortunately, the fact
that the East was under great pressure from the Huns would result in a delay in the
arrival of the promised reinforcements.

In other areas too things were not going as smoothly as Valentinian would have
hoped. In particular, Aetius was having difficulty in Gaul. The main cause of this is
likely to have been a decision made by Aetius: 'abandoned country properties of the
city of Valence were given over for division to the Alans who were led by Sambida
(Sangiban)', possibly the same Alan 'king' known as 'Sangibanus' who was to feature
later in Aetius' life.[32] The decision may have been the cause of an argument between
Aetius and Albinus, who was probably the *Praefectus Praetorio Galliarum* (Praetorian
Prefect of Gaul).[33] The mutual hostility only appears to have been soothed and the
'friendship restored' by the intervention of Deacon Leo, later to become the Bishop
(Pope) of Rome.[34] It is possible that the settlement of the Alans was also the cause
of the 'disturbances' in Gaul that Aetius was forced to pacify before he was able to
return to Italy.[35] Whatever the nature of these disturbances, by June 440 Aetius was
expected to arrive in Italy.

Earlier, in January, a *novel* had been issued that abolished all tax exemptions.[36]
This was doubtless aimed specifically at the aristocracy and was a demonstration
that the financial condition of the west was becoming alarming and that the loss
of the revenues of Africa was a crippling blow. Equally certain is that opposition to
the law will have arisen amongst the aristocracy.

Aetius did indeed return to Italy in June. Once there a *novel* was issued, dated
4 June, aimed at halting the abuses of tax collectors by allowing complaints against
them to be judged by the Praetorian Prefect, rather than the *comites* (counts) of the
treasuries.[37] It would appear that this measure may have been attempting to stop
the abuses of imperial tax collectors in Gaul, Aetius' main power base.[38] The
measure was proposed by Petronius Maximus, the *praefectus praetorio* himself. It was
opposed by Paterius, a man famous for his influence at court.[39] There now began
a long struggle between Aetius and opposing factions at court.[40] Paterius himself
later became *Praefectus praetorio Italiae* and repealed the law in a *novel* issued on
27 September 442.[41] The most likely cause of opposition to Aetius' policies was the
unhappiness of the Senate with the new *novel*. This stopped the flow of income to
the bureaucratic elite involved with the collection of taxes, who were either members
of, or intimately connected to, the Senate.

GAISERIC

Gaiseric had become a major threat to the security of the West. Yet this was not the only danger. With a fleet at his disposal, even the court at Constantinople feared attack.[42] Although the nature and the dating of the building work on the Sea of Marmara has been questioned, the fact that it could be associated with the Vandal threat by the author of the *Chronicon Paschale* demonstrates the alarm that was caused in the East by the Vandal seizure of Africa.[43]

In the meantime, Gaiseric did not remain idle. Unwilling to allow the West to regain the initiative and determined to put pressure on the government in Ravenna to reach a compromise, he gathered his fleet and set sail for Sicily, laying siege to Panormus, the island's main naval base.[44] Taking the city would not only allow him to force the emperor to accede to his seizure of Carthage: it would also allow Gaiseric to capture yet more ships to add to his fleet.

At least one group of Vandals crossed the Straits of Messina to raid Bruttium.[45] However, Gaiseric's campaign in the island was to end without permanent gain: in a strange irony one of Aetius' major enemies gave him, and the West, an unexpected relief from Vandal attacks.

SEBASTIAN

In 432, after the death of Boniface, his son-in-law Sebastian had taken the position of *magister militum* before being driven out upon the return of Aetius. Sebastian had fled to Constantinople, but once established he had allowed his followers to engage in 'piratical' activities in the Hellespont and Propontis.[46] With his position becoming insecure, Sebastian had finally fled from Constantinople, attempting to take refuge with Theoderic and the Goths in Aquitaine.[47] Rebuffed, he had fled to Barcelona, but being declared a public enemy had left and travelled to Africa.[48]

When Gaiseric was informed that Sebastian had landed he feared that he was intent on using his father-in-law's reputation to raise an army and retake Africa. Gaiseric was doubtless aware of the loyalty of Africa to Boniface. Furthermore, by the end of the year Gaiseric must have been aware that Theodosius had promised to send aid to the West, as claimed in the *novel* already mentioned from June 440.[49] The double threat of a Roman commander in Africa and an invasion from Constantinople ensured that Gaiseric returned to Carthage.

Either late in 440 or early in 441 Gaiseric left Sicily. The actual date is unknown, but a letter from Paschasinus, Bishop of Lilybaeum, to Pope Leo I implies that the date may have been early in 441.[50] However, at least some of Gaiseric's fears were unfounded: Sebastian had actually gone to Gaiseric in the hope of gaining asylum from his Roman enemies.[51] This hope was to be mistaken. Fearing his military abilities, a short time after his arrival Gaiseric had him executed.[52]

It would have been a great relief to the emperor and Aetius when Gaiseric left Sicily. Yet it was not all good news: the damage caused by the Vandals forced Valentinian to lower the assessment of taxes in Sicily and the surrounding islands to one-seventh of their pre-attack level.[53] The *novel* also notes that Syracuse, Aetna,

Lilybaeum, Thermae, Solus and other places were to be treated differently, but unfortunately the text after the word 'Solus' has been lost and so their treatment is unknown.

At some point early in 441 Aetius learned the news that the east was finally sending an army to help in the reconquest of Africa.[54] This piece of good news was echoed by a second, more personal one. Either in late 440 or early 441 Pelagia gave birth to a son, Gaudentius.[55] Possibly prior to this Aetius also had a daughter, although whether her mother was Carpilio's daughter or Pelagia is unknown. She appears to have been married to Thraustila, who was either a Hun or a Goth who served Aetius, probably as a *bucellarius*. Thraustila later joined Valentinian's body-guard and was to play a major part in events after the death of his father-in-law.[56]

Buoyed by the news that he now had two sons and that the east was sending an expedition to help the west, Aetius began to prepare for the upcoming campaign, which would begin when the weather cleared in the spring to allow the eastern fleet to sail the Mediterranean in safety.

Chapter 10

The Treaty of 442

440

Although the Vandal seizure of Africa remained the focal point of activities throughout 440, other events continued to unfold. One of these was the renewal of hostilities with the Sueves in Spain. The cause of the war is unknown, but Aetius at once resorted to the tried-and-tested tactic of sending Censurius as an envoy to the Sueves. On this occasion the tactic failed: instead of negotiating a peace treaty, Censurius was forced to take refuge in Martylis (Mertola) and endure a siege by the Sueves. Eventually he was forced to surrender under terms and was taken prisoner.[1] It would appear that he remained a captive with the Sueves until 448, when he was murdered at Hispalis by a man named Agiulfus.[2]

441

Throughout 441 and into 442 the attention of the Western court remained fixated on events taking place in Africa and Sicily and on the financial measures needed to support the army. In March 441 a series of *novels* was passed enforcing taxes upon the rich and upon the guilds, who were claiming many exemptions due to the privileges given to them by earlier emperors.[3] Yet although the focus was to the south, pressure remained on the remainder of the West. At some point either late in 440 or early in 441 Aetius received news of a major *bacaudic* rebellion in Tarraconensis. With the Goths in Gaul now at peace, and with the troops from the East expected, Aetius decided to send an expedition to Spain. Accordingly, Astyrius, the father-in-law of Merobaudes, was promoted to the post of *comes et magister utriusque militia* and sent to Spain to suppress the revolt.[4]

The appointment as *magister utriusque militiae* is attested by two separate sources. The first is Hydatius, where Astyrius is called 'a general of both services'.[5] The second is by an ivory diptych found at Liege:

> *Fl(avius) Ast<e = Y>rius v(ir) c(larissimus) et inl(ustris) com(es) ex mag(istro) utriusq(ue) mil(itiae) cons(ul) ord(inarius)*
>
> *CIL XII 10032.2 = ILS 1300*

The appointment is unusual in that both before and after this date Sigisvult is attested as *magister utriusque militiae*, implying that he held the post continuously under the supreme command of Aetius. Therefore, either Sigisvult remained in post and Astyrius was appointed to a special, one-off command for the campaign in Spain, or Sigisvult stood down and was replaced for a short period before being

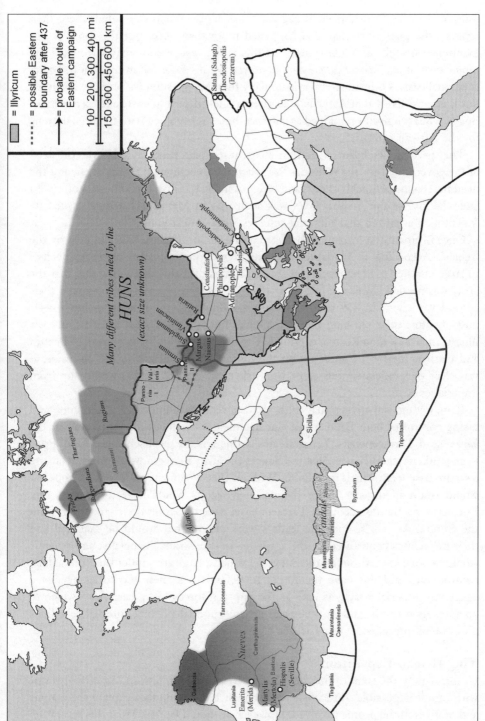

Map 10. Africa, Spain and the East

reinstated to his former post. If Sigisvult was replaced and reinstated, there then remains the possibility that this happened more than once, but the event is not mentioned by the surviving sources. If this is the case, Aetius may have used the junior post of *magister utriusque militiae* to reward his loyal followers on a periodic, rotational basis. Unfortunately, it is unlikely that this question will ever be resolved, but it is most likely that Astyrius was given a one-off post to ensure his seniority in Spain, whiles Sigisvult remained as *magister*, but was occupied with the preparations for the African campaign.

The speed at which the expedition was sent to Spain probably relates to the need of the government for the revenues lost when the 'rebellion' in Spain began and the need to reconquer quickly the area in order to help replenish the imperial coffers. In fact, the loss of the African taxes was such that in March 441 a *novel* issued by Valentinian admitted that imperial reserves were almost gone.[6]

Once in Spain Astyrius quickly began a savage campaign in order to destroy the 'rebels'. According to Hydatius he 'slaughtered the Bacaudae of Tarraconensis in large number'.[7] The savagery of the attack was probably due to the fact that the army was needed elsewhere in Spain. The Sueves were attempting to expand their control yet again. In 439 they had captured Emerita, and at some point in 441, possibly after their old king Hermericus had finally passed away after a four-year illness, their new king Rechila captured Hispalis (Seville) and took control of Baetica and Carthaginiensis.[8] Coupled with the loss of Tarraconensis to the *bacaudae*, it was clear that unless serious steps were taken Spain, like Africa, would slip from imperial control.

It may seem surprising that with the Sueves expanding their dominions and taking control of both Baetica and Carthaginiensis the focus of Aetius was on the *bacaudae* of Tarraconensis. Yet strategically this was the most sensible option. Prior to any military campaign against the Sueves the army in Spain would need to ensure a secure base from which to operate. Without this, a campaign that ended in defeat would result in disaster, since the defeated troops would have nowhere to go. Furthermore, the dissidents in Tarraconensis were declaring their separation from the empire. As rebels, once the leaders were caught they would be executed and their belongings confiscated by the emperor. In dire straits financially, any revenue would be welcome. Although the Sueves now had a large area under their immediate control, they did not have the forces to defend these new territories against a concerted imperial attack, as long as the imperial forces had a base from which to operate. As a result, and as was usual in late imperial politics, internal rebellions always took precedence over barbarian invasion.

The African Expedition
Unfortunately the sources for the African expedition are few and brief. However, with care it is possible to reconstruct a sequence of events that explain the actions and motives of the people involved. However, it should be noted that this recreation is hypothetical and other interpretations are possible.

At an unknown date in 441 a large fleet was dispatched from Constantinople, bound for Sicily.[9] The equipping and organization of the campaign was allocated, according to Evagrius, to Cyrus, the *Praefectus Praetorio Orientis*.[10] It appears that an otherwise-unknown individual named Pentadius was the man who actually ensured that the army was well equipped once it had arrived.[11] Both Prosper and Theophanes give a few details concerning the expedition.

> Theodosius opened hostilities with the Vandals by sending the generals Ariobindus, Ansila, and Germanus with a large fleet. They deferred the business with long delays and proved to be more of a burden to Sicily than a help to Africa.
>
> *Prosper s.a. 441*

> Theodosius sent out 1100 cargo ships with a Roman army commanded by the generals Areobindus, Ansilas, Inobindos, Arintheos, and Germanus. Gizerich was struck with fear when this force moored in Italy and he sent an embassy to Theodosius to discuss a treaty.
>
> *Theophanes 5941*

Surprisingly, Aspar, the *magister militum* who had campaigned in Africa against Gaiseric between 430 and 434, remained behind when it could be expected that he lead the campaign. This was probably due to rising tensions between Constantinople and both the Persians and the Huns, demanding the attention of Theodosius' most trusted general.[12] He may also have manipulated events so that he remained near the capital: the example of Aetius and his predecessors in the West may have provided a model that the generals in the east still had hopes of emulating, however remote.

Of the generals mentioned, Ariobindus was *magister militum*, and probably the senior officer as *magister militum praesentalis*.[13] Germanus was almost certainly the *magister militum vacans* mentioned in the Code of Justinian.[14] Since Ansila is included in both lists it is possible that he also was a *magister militum*, but otherwise he is unknown.[15] Inobindos and Arintheos are only mentioned by Theophanes and not by Prosper, implying that they were of lesser rank. Neither is known beyond Theophanes' reference.[16] This list of commanders, along with the number of vessels carrying the troops, suggests that this was a significant military expedition, probably comprising the bulk of the *praesental* army stationed in Constantinople as well as elements of the field army of Thrace. The commanders would expect to receive further reinforcements from the West.

Despite their orders to invade Africa, the expedition reached Sicily and then stopped. Once ashore, according to Prosper, they 'deferred the business with long delays and proved to be more of a burden to Sicily than a help to Africa'.[17] There are at least two likely causes for the delay. The first is the need to co-ordinate the forces of East and West, for example deciding who would lead which units and formations, and most especially who would be in overall charge of the army. In a similar manner, Belisarius, in his campaign against the Vandals almost a century later in 533, took advantage of delays in the sea voyage from Constantinople to Sicily to order his troops and to allocate commands.[18]

The second is that it is almost certain that orders to stop the attack swiftly arrived from Constantinople whilst negotiations were entered into with Gaiseric's envoys. Since the reign of Arcadius the East had preferred to husband its armies, instead using diplomacy and its seemingly endless supplies of money in order to 'subsidize' potential attackers. The prospective attack upon Gaiseric had caused Gaiseric to panic and send envoys. Gaiseric had been able to defeat the armies in Africa, but he knew that he could not defeat the combined *praesental* armies of East and West. At the same time, following their traditional policy, if at all possible the East would prefer to reach a peaceful solution to the problem of Africa.

Yet there was a more pressing reason for Theodosius to want a quick ending to the war against Gaiseric. In 441, even as the expedition was setting sail, the Persians had attacked Theodosiopolis (Erzerum) and Satala (Sadagh) in the east (see Map 10). The cause of the war was simple. The Romans had begun building and strengthening the defensible frontier system in the east. Furthermore, earlier, the Romans had agreed to subsidize Persian defences at the Caspian Gates, the main area of weakness where the Huns had in 395 crossed into Persian and Roman territory. For internal propaganda purposes the Persians referred to these subsidies as 'tribute' and Theodosius, unhappy with the claim, stopped the payments. With Roman defences being built and the subsidy being withheld, the Persians attacked. Aspar and Anatolius may have been sent to deal with the invasion.[19] Although the war was of short duration, ending in June 441, it was clear that any attempt to evict the Vandals from Africa could result in the Persians invading the east.[20]

Unfortunately, the war against the Persians was not the worst event for the East in 441. Whilst the majority of the *praesental* and Thracian armies were in Sicily, the Huns attacked Thrace.[21] When an embassy was sent to ask for the reasons for the attack, Attila and Bleda complained about the actions of the Bishop of Margus, who had allegedly robbed the royal tombs across the frontier. They demanded restitution and that the bishop be handed over.[22] When this did not happen, they invaded Thrace, capturing the cities of Viminacium, Singidunum and Naissus in the process (see Map 10).[23] The Huns may also have captured Sirmium at this time, although this is not certain.[24] When the Bishop of Margus realized that he was about to be handed over, he went to the Huns and offered to betray Margus to them in exchange for his safety. They accepted the deal and duly captured Margus.[25] The Huns went on to 'devastate' Illyricum.[26]

At the same time internal rivalries within the Eastern command system also appear to have raised their head. John, a Vandal who was *magister militum per Thracias*, was 'treacherously killed by Arnegisclus', one of his subordinates.[27] It is possible that one reason for his death is that he was a Vandal and that his death was a reaction to the Vandal invasion of Africa. However, it is more likely that the execution was part of the internal political fighting in the East and may have been sanctioned by the court in Constantinople.[28] His position as *magister militum* suggests that he was an able soldier, and his death is a clear indication that the war effort against the Huns was to be hampered by internal politics.

Despite the internal problems, Anatolius and Aspar gathered their armies and faced the Huns.[29] At this point, and for an unknown reason, Attila and Bleda decided to accept a one-year truce and withdrew from Illyricum.[30]

Theodosius was now under intense pressure and could not afford to fight a war on more than one front, especially as the war against the Vandals would be fought with troops withdrawn specifically from Thrace. Accordingly, he was willing to agree terms with Gaiseric that would otherwise have been unacceptable. Furthermore, unable to muster enough forces to reconquer Africa on his own due to the ongoing wars in other theatres, Aetius would be forced to accept any treaty agreed by Theodosius.

The Treaty of 442

It is unfortunate that no comprehensive list of the terms of the treaty of 442 still exists. Instead, estimates of the terms have to be made from the fragments that remain in existence. Two of the most important of these are to be found in Prosper and Procopius. The statement in Prosper's chronicle is very brief:

> The Augustus Valentinian made peace with Gaiseric and Africa was divided between the two into distinct territories.
>
> *Prosper s.a. 442*

The report in Procopius is slightly more detailed, but unfortunately, as seen earlier, it is also slightly confused. It would appear that he has conflated the treaties of 435 and 442, which, given the timescale between the treaties and Procopius' writing, is understandable:

> [Gaiseric] made a treaty with the Emperor Valentinian providing that each year he should pay to the emperor tribute from Libya, and he delivered over one of his sons, Honoric, as a hostage to make this agreement binding.
>
> *Procopius 3.4.13*

The use of the term 'Libya' is clearly from the earlier Treaty of 435, since there is no mention of the Vandals taking Africa Proconsularis and Carthage. However, the paying of 'tribute' and the sending of Huneric (Honoric) as 'hostage' both appear to refer to the Treaty of 442.

The specific nature of the 'tribute' is unknown. However, given that when Gaiseric had first captured Carthage he had cut the supplies of grain to Italy, it is almost certain that the term refers to the restoration and continuation of the grain supply from Africa. Since the provinces in Africa produced a very large excess of grain, this was a small price for Gaiseric to pay in return for being accepted as the ruler of Africa.[31]

To help cement the treaty, Gaiseric's son, Huneric, was sent as a hostage to Ravenna. His time in the capital was to be very well spent. Merobaudes describes this period as a success, especially since it resulted in Huneric becoming attached to the imperial family.[32] Prior to the reading of Merobaudes' poems, which occurred some time around the year 443, Huneric had become engaged to Eudocia, daughter of the emperor Valentinian.[33] Interestingly, this was in direct contravention of the law passed by Valentinian and Valens and only recently ratified by its inclusion in the Theodosian Code.[34] This would not be the first time that a female member of the imperial family had been forced to marry a barbarian: Galla Placidia had been married to Athaulf in 414. It is possible, however, that the betrothal was not a serious proposition but was merely a ruse aimed at ensuring that Gaiseric continued to adhere to the terms of the treaty. If that is true, the betrothal was a counter-balance to Huneric becoming a hostage. Gaiseric may have asked for a daughter of the emperor as counter-hostage to Huneric, but as the imperial family did not exchange hostages from its members, the betrothal did give a modicum of assurance to Gaiseric that his son would be safe.

Although this was most likely a separate agreement from the treaty and represents Huneric's acceptance at court as much as his father's capture of Carthage, the betrothal had one immediate side-effect: Huneric's marriage to the daughter of the Gothic king Theoderic was annulled. Possibly in an attempt to place the blame on her, she was accused of attempting to poison Huneric. In retaliation, she was mutilated – her nose and ears were cut off – and sent back to her father.[35] Much to the approval of Aetius, the alliance between the Vandals and the Goths had ended in dramatic fashion. However, since Huneric would now be theoretically in line for the throne, Eudocia's claim to inheritance was declared ineligible to avoid a barbarian being Valentinian's heir. Pulcheria thus became the heir apparent in the West.[36]

Merobaudes may also give a further detail on the nature of the agreement, although this is slightly more conjectural. In the second panegyric he 'uses the adjective *socius* [which] with other tenuous evidence suggest that the Empire bestowed on Gaiseric the ancient status of *socius et amicus cum foedere*' (ally and friend by treaty).[37] This would help explain both the fact that the empire could accept the Vandals' occupation of Africa and the fact that Gaiseric continued to honour the treaty in the future, since he was now being acknowledged as virtually the equal of the emperor. This impression would have been reinforced by the prospective marriage between Huneric and Eudocia.

Africa
Secure in his position, Gaiseric was now able to distribute lands and positions of power as he thought fit, steadfast in the knowledge that he was safe from attack by the empire.

> Byzacena, Abaritana and Gaetulia, and part of Numidia he kept for himself; Zeugitana and the proconsular province he divided up as an

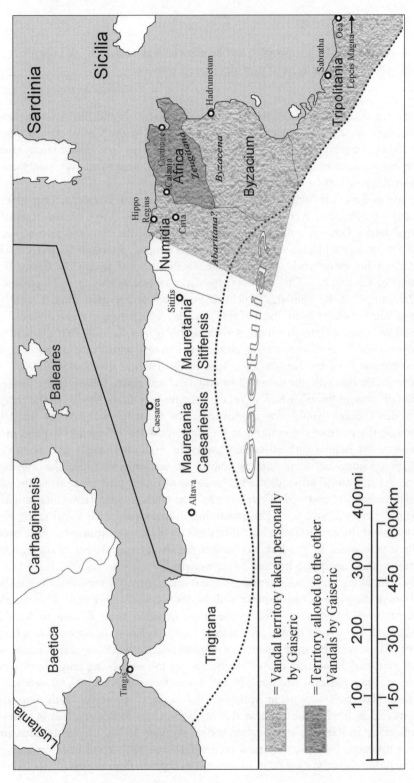

Map 11. The Vandal Settlement of 442

allotted portion for his people'; and he allowed Valentinian . . . to take for himself the remaining, and now devastated provinces.

Victor of Vita, 1.13

The fact that the parts of Numidia, Mauretania Caesariensis and Sitifensis that had been returned as part of the treaty had been 'devastated' by the Vandal occupation is reinforced by the novels of Valentinian, which mention the large reduction in taxes that the regained provinces had to pay in order to allow them to recover – only one-eighth of the pre-Vandal assessment.[38]

The remainder of the African territory, Africa Proconsularis, Byzacena, Tripolitania and parts of Numidia, were now ruled by the Vandals. Most of the territory remained under Gaiseric's direct control, but he 'gave the best and richest land [Africa Proconsularis] to his sons and the Vandal people', although Carthage itself remained in his own hands, and he established his royal palace on Byrsa, the Acropolis of Carthage.[39] This territory was later known as the *sortes Vandalorum* ('lot'/'allotment' of the Vandals), which, despite modern interpretations, is used by Victor of Vita simply to mean 'land of the Vandals'. The nature of these divisions is confused and open to interpretation, with some historians claiming that the land of the dispossessed Roman senators was given to the troops, whilst others claim that it was the income from the land, not the land itself, that was distributed.[40]

It is probable that only the income from the land was given, following the Roman tradition of '*honesta missio*', which in return brought hereditary service in the army, a fact which Gaiseric would have approved.[41] The net result was that the Vandals simply took the place of the empire, as the Vandal nobles 'effectively stepped into the shoes of the Roman authorities that had ruled Africa previously and took over the existing administrative regime, including the tax system', whilst the warriors received the traditional stipends of regular Roman troops, plus land out of the *fisc* (imperial exchequer) and *agri deserti* (uninhabited lands), whilst remaining billeted in towns – mainly Carthage.[42] The remaining Romans paid their usual taxes, but to the king, not the emperor: the only difference in these cases appears to have been that the leases issued by the Vandals were dated by the regnal year of the Vandal king, rather than using the Roman dating system.[43]

If the Vandal warriors took the place of the Roman army, Gaiseric and the Vandal nobility took the place of the emperor and the aristocratic landowners. This simple change of 'landlord' doubtless eased the transformation from Roman to Vandal Africa, as well as proving simple for the new Vandal rulers to understand and keep track of. However, the maintenance of Roman institutions can easily result in the suffering and dislocation caused by the Vandal takeover being minimized. The takeover was not peaceful and doubtless involved forceful evictions and deaths.

In fact, Gaiseric's actions in annexing the lands of powerful, rich absentee landlords and in forcing the resident Roman landowners to flee resulted in a large pressure group in Ravenna agitating for the recovery of Africa. Under the constant threat of invasion, Gaiseric doubtless retained a large proportion of his troops in Carthage rather than allowing them to disperse in order to farm personally. It should be noted, however, that once the immediate threat of invasion had passed the attitude of Gaiseric to the dispossessed Romans did in some respects relent. Later some of them returned to Africa and at least some of their property was returned.[44] At this time some of the Vandal troops may have been released from immediate service, especially those who had been involved in the fighting since before 429, who may have been close to retirement age, to begin their new lives as farmers and landholders, and the likelihood is that at the end of the Vandal kingdom the only difference between the Vandals and the 'native' Romans was that the Vandals served in the army.

Catholic churches were given to the new Arian clergy, as was some of the land confiscated from the Roman aristocracy, no doubt in order to make them self-sufficient and a powerful force to support the king. When Gaiseric later allowed some of the Roman aristocracy to return, the land 'donated' to the church was not restored to the returning Romans.[45]

Furthermore, despite the ancient portrayal of a rigid demarcation between the Vandal conquerors and the native Romans, close analysis of the sources suggests that there was a 'much more porous border between Arian and Nicene and much more traffic across it than our sources are willing to disclose'.[46] Although there was always a divide between the Arian Vandals and their Catholic Christian and Nicene subjects, laws enforcing a separation between Arians and – especially – the Nicenes explain why later kings ordered persecutions of Catholics: the law may have been needed in order to maintain Vandal identity and stop them being absorbed into the majority population.[47]

In one way, however, Gaiseric was able to change the nature of African society. The vast majority of the production of Africa was geared towards supplying Italy with necessities via the system of *annona* (supplying goods instead of tax). After the Vandal conquest, Africa was freed from this burden, and although the Vandals themselves must have appropriated some of the *annona* for themselves, their demands were less than those of Rome and Italy. Despite the fact that the 'tribute' will have continued to siphon goods, especially grain, for the empire, African traders were now allowed to trade a significant proportion of the surplus produce in other markets, including southern Gaul, Spain, north-western Italy and Sicily.[48] Alongside these, trade continued with Rome and Southern Italy, although now the customers were expected to pay for the goods they received rather than relying upon government 'donations' due to the *annona*.[49] Taxes from these activities will have helped to finance the embryonic Vandal kingdom.

The treaty was a landmark in Roman affairs. Although Valentinian and Aetius saved face by claiming that the Vandals had settled in Africa under Roman rule, the reality was that the government in Ravenna had agreed to the 'permanent' loss of territory to a barbarian king and acknowledged that they did not have the troops to retake it without help from the East.[50] Yet probably contrary to popular expectations, the Vandals did not attempt to further enlarge their realm until after the death of Aetius and Valentinian, after which time they believed that the treaty of 442 was invalid.

In part this was due to the fact that the Vandals, and especially Gaiseric, realised that they would provoke a further invasion from the East if they attempted to attack the West: after all, it was a matter of luck that the eastern expedition had been halted by the attacks of both the Persians and the Huns. There is no evidence, as suggested by some historians, that there was a political and military agreement between Gaiseric, Attila and Yezdigerd II. Furthermore, Gaiseric may have been following the 'standard barbarian policy' of attacking the West when it was weak or divided and of coming to terms with the emperor when the West was stronger and more able to defend itself.[51]

Yet there was a further factor in the protracted period of peace following the treaty of 442: Gaiseric was not yet totally secure in his 'kingdom'. Prosper notes that following the treaty:

> Some of Gaiseric's magnates conspired against him because he was proud even among his own people, due to the successful outcome of events. But when the undertaking was discovered, they were subjected to many tortures and killed by him. Whenever others seemed to venture the same thing, the king's mistrust served to destroy so many that he lost more men by this anxiety of his than if he had been overthrown in war.
>
> *Prosper s.a. 442*

As with the Goths, the modern perception that the Vandals were a unified 'kingdom' under the rule of Gaiseric conceals the reality of many different nobles and groups being unhappy with the rule of one man. Furthermore it is possible, though improvable, that Aetius and Theodosius had been able to send agents to Africa who had managed to provoke the conspiracy.[52] As a consequence, it would have been very risky of Gaiseric to provoke another war with the West, since it was possible that many of his own followers would change allegiance, so weakening his forces and giving a greater chance of victory to the Romans.

Italy

Despite the focus on the negative aspects of the treaty with the Vandals, at least one area actually profited from the loss of Africa. In the north of Italy the rural settlements continued their decline, mirroring the majority of the rest of the West and notwithstanding their function of supplying the 'imperial capital' of Ravenna. Yet the rural settlements in the south prospered. Apulia, Basilicata and Lucania began to supply Rome with the grain lost from Africa. Furthermore, Samnium and Lucania provided the old capital with animals, especially pigs, and the whole of the south now supplied the wine for Roman tables. This especially benefited the senatorial families who had large landholdings in these areas, since it naturally increased their financial and political importance.[53] It also resulted in these families wanting the Vandals to remain in Africa, as a Roman recovery would reduce their own income.

The Huns

Once the treaty was agreed, Theodosius recalled the forces in Sicily.[54] The timing was good, as the treaty with the Huns had expired and Attila and Bleda had renewed their attacks on Illyricum, capturing Ratiaria (probably Arzar-Palanca), Naissus (Niš), Phillipopolis (Plovdiv), Arcadiopolis (Lüleburgaz) and Constantia (Constanţa): only Adrianople (Edirne) and Herakleia (Marmara Ereğlisi) were not captured (see Map 10).[55]

Returning to Thrace, the Eastern army under Aspar, Areobundus and Ardegisclus met the Huns in battle, but was repeatedly defeated.[56] However, the Huns were unwilling to continue the conflict and probably in mid-442 a peace treaty was agreed, seemingly involving the payment of increased 'subsidies' by Theodosius to Attila and Bleda.[57] The reasons for the sudden acceptance of a treaty by the Huns when they obviously had the upper hand are unknown. They had devastated the Balkans and repeatedly defeated the armies that were sent against them. There can be little doubt that the increase in the 'subsidies' paid by the East were a factor, yet it is likely that there were more reasons for the decision.

One of these is the outbreak of a 'pestilence' in 442, which struck the empire.[58] If, as is likely, the disease first struck imperial cities, then it is certain that the Huns, who up to that time had been totally victorious, would be dubious about the wisdom of continuing the war. Attacking infected cities would increase their chances of catching the disease. It is likely that the decision divided the two brothers. Bleda, in control of the Huns facing the East, was the one who would be most at risk from a plague already apparent in the Balkans. Although the two joint rulers most likely usually ruled by consensus, on this occasion they may have been in complete disagreement. It is possible that Bleda forced Attila to accept the Eastern peace treaty in 442 simply by ordering his own forces to withdraw, despite Attila's desire to continue the campaign in order to extract more concessions. As is so often the case, certainty is impossible.

It should also be noted that, although they won the battles, the Huns are still likely to have suffered casualties. The manpower reserves of the East, unlike the West, were vast and in a war of attrition the Huns would simply run out of men. Moreover, the Huns needed to maintain a strong military base in order to maintain their grip on their 'empire'. They could not afford to go on fighting indefinitely. Their victories and the payment of tribute ensured that the Huns clearly emerged triumphant from the war and their high morale and aura of invincibility was maintained. This made certain that there would be no rebellions against their rule at home.

In Constantinople, Theodosius was unhappy with this state of affairs and set in motion a series of reforms in the Balkans. By September 443 the defences along the Danube were being strengthened until finally Theodosius felt that they had been improved to the point where there was no longer any serious threat from the Huns.[59] Either in the late 443 or in 444, and possibly reflecting Roman awareness of the increased division and tensions between Attila and Bleda, the payments to the Huns stopped.[60]

The outbreak of pestilence in 442 is an event that is sometimes overlooked, although it is extremely important. The fact that Hydatius, who usually focused on events in Spain, took time out to mention it demonstrates its severity. Although it is unknown which of the various diseases – cholera, diphtheria, smallpox etc. – it was, it is likely that a large percentage of the population, and of the army, died as a result. For the barbarians who doubtless also suffered it was a setback. For Aetius, who was already short of manpower in the army, it was a calamity.

Gaul

In Gaul peace with the Goths and Franks, and the earlier destruction of the Burgundians by the Huns, meant that only the *bacaudae* remained as a threat to the peace. Aetius probably realized that the easiest way to discourage yet another *bacaudic* rebellion was to station troops permanently in the area. Unfortunately, his Roman troops were needed for regular campaigns, yet there remained one alternative. The Alans under Goa had first entered the empire in the invasion of 406, when, in 'alliance' with the Vandals and the Sueves, they had crossed the Rhine into Gaul. However, unlike the other tribes, the Alans under Goa had quickly found employment with the empire and had continued to serve it for the ensuing twenty-five years. Since the majority of his men were nearing or beyond retirement age, Goa was undoubtedly asking Aetius for land upon which they could settle. Solving two problems with one stroke, Aetius decided to give them lands in 'Farther Gaul', which belonged to people associated with the *bacaudic* rebellions.[61] In this way the Alans received the lands they deserved for their faithful service, and at the same time their presence inhibited the activities of the *bacaudae*, lessening the likelihood of any rebellion within their specific area.

Learning of the decision, the Armoricans asked (Saint) Germanus of Auxerre to intervene on their behalf. As Goa was advancing towards Armorica fully expecting a fight with the natives he was met and stopped by Germanus. Allegedly Goa agreed to wait until Aetius had been informed of events and made a decision in the matter.[62] The reprieve was short lived. Unfortunately for the natives, Aetius confirmed his decision and the Alans and the natives fought for the land, the Alans emerging victorious.[63] From now on the *bacaudae* would operate in the knowledge that there was a veteran fighting force in the immediate vicinity willing to oppose them. Affairs in Africa and Gaul now appeared to be settled, although not necessarily to the complete satisfaction of Aetius.

Britain

Affairs in Britain at this late stage are extremely vague and the references given in the sources are of dubious accuracy and open to debate. However, the government's focus on Africa and, to a lesser extent, Gaul resulted in Britain continuing its slide away from the empire. However one event, dated to 441–442, is worth recording: 'The British provinces, which up to this time had endured a variety of disasters and misfortunes, were subjected to the authority of the Saxons.'[64] The exact meaning of this statement has been the cause of considerable debate, which it is not necessary to consider, but one factor seems clear: at some time in these years the rule of the south-eastern areas of Britain facing Gaul passed from 'Roman' into 'Saxon' hands.[65] From the early 440s onwards the south east of Britain no longer looked to the empire for guidance, instead looking across the North Sea to the Saxon and Jutish homelands, and turning its energies to the extension of 'Saxon' rule ever further west. The Romanized aristocracy in Britain began to be dispossessed and as a result in place of the rule of Roman law the rule of 'English' law began to emerge. Naturally, many of the islanders began to long for the security of belonging to the empire.

Chapter 11

After Africa

Although the treaty of 442 was not the desired outcome, and the aftereffects would be severe, it gave Aetius the breathing space necessary to continue his reclamation of other areas in the West. As an example, Astyrius, father-in-law of Merobaudes, remained on campaign in Spain suppressing the *bacaudae* of Tarraconensis.

Yet the troubles of the empire were not over. Even before the treaty had been signed a new disaster was overtaking the West: as noted in the previous chapter, in 442 a pestilence, the nature of which is unknown, began 'which spread over almost the entire world'.[1] The blow to an empire already suffering manpower and economic shortages was catastrophic. Fortunately for the empire, the barbarians both inside and outside it were also infected with the disease, so maintaining the balance of power.

On the other hand, it is possibly partly as a result of the disease – or at least the empire's failure to help those suffering – that in 442 there was yet another revolt of the *bacaudae* in the north of Gaul. In response, Aetius sent one of his personal staff, Majorian, with a small force of troops to deal with the rebellion.[2] No doubt Aetius expected the Alans of Goa, who had settled in the north, to join the imperial forces in their new conflict.

Majorian was the son of a *magister militum*, also named Majorian, who had served in the late-fourth century.[3] Also serving under Aetius at about this time was Ricimer, whose father was a Sueve and whose mother was the daughter of the Gothic king Wallia.[4] Both of these men would have a huge impact on the destiny of the West after Aetius' death, and it is interesting to note that they served alongside each other at this formative time in their lives.

443

The treasury, which had already been weakened by the loss of Africa, was now forced to take a humanitarian role in the treatment of the exiles from Africa. Thanks to the loss of income from their estates in Africa, the refugees were struggling to pay their taxes. In response, Valentinian issued a law giving tax relief and financial aid to the exiles.[5] Although it was hoped that this would be a temporary measure, it added to the drain on the imperial coffers. Furthermore, the loss of their income had forced the exiles to take loans in order to cover their expenses during their temporary stay in exile. When Valentinian and Aetius became aware of this, a law was passed that forbade the collection of interest on loans to 'Africans', and also stated that they should not have to repay any of their loans until their fortunes were restored.[6] It would appear that extended discussions were ongoing with Gaiseric to repatriate the refugees to their estates in Africa, with some of the refugees eventually being allowed to return.[7]

Aetius

After the disappointments of the previous year, and with the fighting in the north of Gaul continuing, in 443 Aetius continued with his attempts to settle affairs in those parts of the West that he still controlled in a manner that would hopefully reduce the tendency of parts of Gaul to rebel. Despite the level of recruiting almost certainly

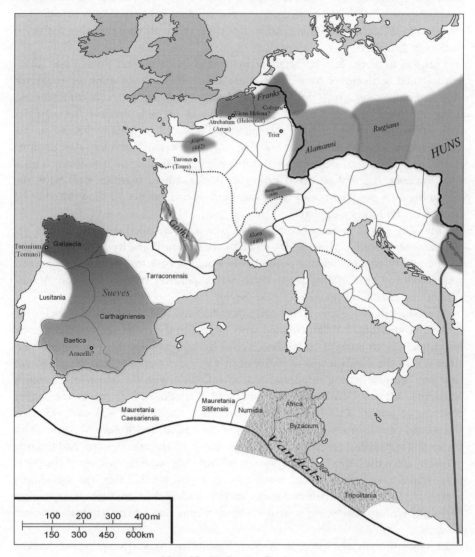

Map 12. Barbarian Settlements

being low, there was yet another attempt to levy recruits in the West.[8] Towards the end of the year a law was passed that reminded the *limitanei* of their obligation to work the lands assigned to them in order to reduce the liability of the taxpayer to feed them, as well as ensuring that the lands remained inviolate and free from purchase by other landowners.[9]

Faced with low levels of manpower, and willing to use any available source, Aetius now gave parts of Sapaudia (Savoy) to the remnants of the Burgundians to be divided with the native inhabitants.[10] By doing this he may have hoped to use the Burgundians as a garrison force facing the Alamanni, so allowing him to withdraw the regular garrison units to reinforce the field army. Moreover, the agreement doubtless contained a clause making the Burgundian troops liable to be called to serve in the Western army, along similar lines to agreements with the other barbarian settlers in the West.

This was to be the last deliberate settlement of barbarians on Roman soil: afterwards, such settlements were 'little more than official recognition of barbarian expansion and conquest'.[11] Furthermore, Aetius continued to rotate commanders, using the men he thought best fit to command in each theatre. Accordingly, Astyrius, who was a Spaniard, was recalled and replaced in Spain by his son-in-law Merobaudes. Unfortunately, the exact reason for Astyrius' withdrawal is unclear. Aetius may have been deliberately rotating his subordinates: he would not want a situation such has had occurred earlier in Africa, where Boniface had made the region his own personal power base, and there is no evidence to show whether he trusted his followers completely.

Following a brief period in command in which he 'smashed the arrogance of the *Bacaudae* of Aracelli', Merobaudes was also recalled to Rome by an imperial order 'at the urging of some jealous people'.[12] It would appear that factional issues had resurfaced and that at this point there was a political conflict between Aetius' supporters and their opponents in the Senate.

At roughly the same time Valentinian issued a *novel* that changed the rules for the ranking of senators.[13] When coupled with the political conflict the *novel* is usually interpreted as an attempt to weaken Aetius by undermining his main supporter, since it is to the disadvantage of Sigisvult.[14] The *novel* was largely to the advantage of a man who was rising to oppose Aetius' influence with the emperor: Petronius Maximus. Maximus had enjoyed a long and distinguished career in the higher echelons of power. This had culminated in his consulships in 433 and 443. It is the second consulship with which the law is concerned, and it gave Maximus with his second consulship precedence over Sigisvult, even though Sigisvult had the title *patricius*, since the latter had only one consulship. Although the issuing of the novel may indeed have been an attack on Aetius, it is possible that this was also simply a measure to reward Maximus for his service, rather than an attempt to weaken Sigisvult. Unfortunately, the sparse evidence means that a firm conclusion cannot be drawn.

In tandem with the perception that Valentinian was attempting to weaken Sigisvult's position, the suggestion by Hydatius that Merobaudes was recalled due to jealousy has often been echoed in modern works, in which the order is seen as another attempt to weaken Aetius.[15] It is certainly possible that in part the *novel* and the recall were against Aetius' wishes, and that Aetius found himself facing new opposition within the imperial court. The influence of the Senate on the allocation of military and civilian posts was always a restricting influence on the men in power, and the new law and the recall may simply signal a temporary swing towards a group of senators led by Maximus.

Yet there are other possible reasons for the recall of Merobaudes. One is the fact that yet again war broke out against the Franks. At some point in 443, possibly hoping that the imperial forces would be distracted by the *bacaudae*, Clodio, king of the Franks, attacked and captured Atrebatum (Arras).[16] He then went on to besiege the city of Turones (Tours), which was ably defended by Majorian. The attack may have been political. Clodio may have attempted to put pressure on Aetius to agree to the Franks keeping Arras in return for leaving Tours, rather than attempting to capture and keep Tours, which was a long way from Frankish territory (see map 12). The strength of the defence resulted in the siege lasting over the winter and into the new year.[17] Aetius may have wanted Merobaudes available to use in the face of this new conflict.

Another possible reason for Merobaudes' recall is that the West was about to enter into a new relationship with the Huns.

Attila*

With a new peace treaty in place with the East, in 443 Attila turned his attentions to the West. There is no doubt that he wanted the West to offer him the same sort of conditions that the East had offered. Yet he was a realist: his uncles had been close friends of Aetius and he respected the western general as an opponent. He also knew that the West was not in the same financial condition as the East, and so he was willing to demand less money.

With these conditions in mind, Attila sent envoys to Aetius demanding the opening of negotiations. Aetius, wary of Attila and half expecting an attack, sent Cassiodorus and Carpilio, his son from his first marriage, to the court of the Huns to arrange a treaty with Attila.[18] With large parts of Spain in the hands of the Sueves, Africa under the control of the Vandals, large areas of Gaul being controlled by the Goths, with an ongoing war with the Franks, and with other areas of Gaul in rebellion, Aetius knew that he could not afford a conflict, even if it was with only the western Hunnic tribes under Attila.

On the other hand, Aetius may have felt that a new treaty was necessary, since he had always employed Hunnic troops both as *bucellarii* and *foederati* and would not want the source of these troops cut off. Failure to deal with Attila could have resulted in large numbers of Hunnic warriors being recalled. Although many of these

* It should be noted that the dating of the events described here is extremely insecure. It is possible for this treaty to be dated to any year prior to 446, when it is mentioned by Merobaudes (*Pan.* 2.1-4). This date has been chosen as it allows other events the time to happen and so fits in best with the proposed chronology.

troops would have no reason to join Attila, since they were serving in the Roman army under their own, independent leaders, Attila could easily use their failure to leave the West as a pretext for war, or at least a devastating raid. Aetius had to be careful.

The two sides quickly came to an agreement. Aetius ceded territory in Pannonia to Attila, although the majority of Pannonia remained under Roman control.[19] It is also likely, mirroring Hunnic practice at other times, that the Romans agreed to pay 'subsidies' to Attila. Although this is nowhere explicitly stated it is possible that a *novel* issued by Valentinian in 444 relates directly to the need to pay money to the Huns.[20]

A major concession to Attila, and one probably meant to increase his enthusiasm for signing a treaty without declaring war, is that it is most likely during this treaty that Attila was awarded the honorary post of *magister utriusque militiae* of the West.[21] This was probably seen as a huge privilege by the Huns and was no doubt used by Attila to raise his standing to new heights amongst his people, and especially to increase his reputation over and above his brother Bleda. On Aetius' part, the granting of the title was a cheap way to give Attila imperial status without actually giving away anything substantial. In theory, Attila was now a 'friend and ally on equal terms with the other western *magistri*'.[22] As Attila needed to establish a new Roman military bureaucracy, as part of the deal Aetius sent Constantius to be Attila's *notarius* (secretary).[23] Finally, and to hopefully ensure adherence to the treaty, hostages were exchanged, with Carpilio remaining with the Huns for an unknown length of time.[24] Despite this, there can be little doubt that from this period onwards Aetius would be worried by the possibility of a Hunnic attack.

444

Yet the financial cost of the peace was to have a major effect on the West. The loss of revenue, especially from North Africa, where the richest provinces were in the hands of Gaiseric and the remainder had been devastated and were only able to pay a small proportion of their taxes, plus the need to maintain the various armies, placed a heavy drain on the exchequer.[25] In fact, it has been estimated that the loss of revenues from Africa may have been enough to equip and maintain up to 40,000 infantry or 20,000 cavalry. The impact on the army of Aetius was dramatic and disastrous.

Finally, in July 444 the emperor Valentinian was forced to accept that the treasury was empty:

> We have issued this decree only for the present time, because of the necessity of imminent expenses for which the resources of Our treasury cannot suffice.

> *Nov. Val. 6.3.1 (14 July 444)*

When even this was deemed insufficient, in either late 444 or early 445 Valentinian instituted a brand new tax, the *siliquaticum*, a payment of one twenty-fourth on all sales of goods.[26] Although this no doubt helped to raise extra taxes, it also resulted in the creation of a black market, where merchants attempted to sell their goods in secret in order to avoid having to pay the tax. The practice grew and necessitated a later law forbidding such activity.[27] Furthermore, early in 445 the inflation that was now rampant in the West forced Valentinian to issue a law laying down the value of a *solidus* (gold coin) at a set price, since merchants and moneylenders were attempting to devalue the coin.[28] This would mean even greater pressure on the depleted treasury.

In stark contrast to the West, and largely due to the strengthening of the Danube frontier and his refusal to pay any more subsidies to the Huns, in November of 444 the Eastern Emperor Theodosius was able to order a remission of taxes in Constantinople.[29] The fact that the East was slowly recovering from the turmoil of the early-fifth century was to have grave consequences for Aetius and the West.

Yet these lay in the future. For the remainder of 444 Aetius continued the struggle to regain Roman control of the West, especially Gaul. The siege by the Franks of Majorian in Tours finally ended. The reasons why the Franks raised the siege are unknown, but it is likely that it was due to Roman military activity authorized or led by Aetius aimed at both defeating the Franks and at putting down the *bacaudae*. The relief of the siege was probably accompanied by further manoeuvring by Aetius, yet the lack of funds in the treasury will have had a limiting effect on his options. Despite this, slowly, his efforts were starting to bear fruit.

The Huns

In one respect Aetius was helped by events outside the empire. Relations between Attila and Bleda appear to have been deteriorating. Finally, Attila acted: 'Bleda, king of the Huns, was struck down through the deceit of his brother Attila, who succeeded him.'[30] As usual, the dating is insecure: Prosper and Cassiodorus date the event to 444, Marcellinus to 445 and the Gallic Chronicler dates it to 446.[31] On this occasion it is likely that Prosper and Cassiodorus are correct, since the assassination would then take place shortly after the treaty of 442 with the East and the assumed treaty of 443 with the West. The variance in dates may simply be a case of sources reporting events when the news was received: it may have taken a year or more for news to be circulated outside the inner circles of the imperial government.

These treaties would have freed Attila from the threat of attack on the Huns' two major borders. These guarantees were necessary, as Attila would be contemplating the possible outbreak of a civil war following the assassination of his brother. As a final guarantee, and in order to maintain good relations with Aetius, it is most likely at this point that Attila gave Zercon, a dwarf originally belonging to Aspar, the Eastern general, to Aetius. Zercon had been captured and kept by Bleda, but after Bleda's death Attila had no use for him. Aetius returned Zercon to Aspar.[32] The exchange signifies that Aetius, Attila and Aspar all had at least informal relationships. The fact that Aetius and Aspar were in continuing communication is unsurprising, given that they shared equal power and were also potential allies. No doubt at the same time, Attila will have been campaigning to ensure his acceptance by the majority of the Huns.

445

445 was the year in which Aetius finally began to see some rewards for his hard work. The most important event of the year was the campaign in Gaul. Following the relief of the siege of Tours Aetius and Majorian continued to campaign in northern Gaul. During the campaign Aetius set an ambush at a village called Vicus Helena, possibly Hélesmes. The details come from Sidonius, who describes the 'battle':

> There was a narrow passage at the junction of two ways, and a road crossed both the village of Helena, which was within bowshot, and the river, where that long but narrow path was supported by girders. Thou (Aetius) wert posted at the cross-roads, while Majorian warred as a mounted man close to the bridge itself. As chance would have it, the echoing sound of a barbarian marriage-song rang forth from a hill near the river-bank, for amid Scythian dance and chorus a yellow-haired bridegroom was wedding a young bride of like colour. Well, these revellers, they say, he laid low. Time after time his helmet rang with blows, and his hauberk with its protecting scales kept off the thrust of spears, until the enemy was forced to turn and flee.

Sidonius, Carmen V. 214f

The poem goes on to note that the bride was captured. However, Sidonius does not explain why this battle was so important. It is most likely that the fighting involved Clodio himself, as well as his relatives, and that the outcome was that Clodio was willing to negotiate for the release of captives, and possibly his treasury, rather than continue the war. The other point to be made is the small scale of the warfare being fought most of the time in this period. Although in the earlier empire battles would be fought with large numbers of men, by the fifth century the majority of campaigns will have been fought using at most a few thousand men.

After the defeat of the Franks a peace treaty was agreed. It is possibly at this time that Cologne and Trier were finally returned to Roman rule after their capture by the Franks in 437 (see Chapter 8). In celebration of this military and political success, in 445 and 446 Aetius issued coins from the mint at Trier celebrating the victory.[33]

The treaty with the Vandals also began to bear fruit. In 445 there was a Vandal raid on Turonium in Gallaecia (see Map 12).[34] While this could possibly have been an attack by Vandals who had chosen to remain in Spain, the likelihood is that these Vandals were far too weak to launch an attack deep into Suevic territory. It is far more likely that it was a seaborne raid launched from Africa. It is also plausible that it was instigated by Aetius as part of his long-term strategy: the raid was 'so far from their African base and such an unlikely source of booty that one must suspect a

1. Possible diptych of Aetius. However, the attribution is uncertain, especially as the individual may be older than Aetius at his death.

2. The Sarcophagus of Stilicho. Despite its title, the identity of the burial is actually unknown and it has been suggested that it may be Aetius, although this is doubtful.

The Mausoleum of Galla Placidia in Ravenna, which contains three sarcophagi. The largest is attested as being Galla Placidia's. That on the left is attested as being Constantius III, whilst that on the right is either Valentinian III or Honorius. It is now a UNESCO World Heritage site.

4. The interior of Placidia's Mausoleum in Ravenna.

5. Painting of Galla Placidia from her Mausoleum in Ravenna.

. Medallions of Honorius and Galla Placidia.

7. Unpublished solidus showing the wedding of Valentinian III and Licinia Eudoxia. Theodosius II stands in the centre with his hands on the shoulders of the couple. The imperial couple spent the winter of 437438 in Thessalonica, at which time this coin was struck. (© CNG coins)

8. Honorius on the Consular diptych of Probus (406).

9. Diptych of Flavius Felix. Valentinian's first *magister militum*, he was killed by order of Aetius. *(By kind permission of Antiquité Tardive)*

10. An inscription from Altava. The inscription refers to 'barbarians' and may be the earliest evidence for the Vandals in Africa.

11. Inscription to Merobaudes recognizing his abilities as an orator.

12. The inscription to Aetius described in Chapter 13. *(Courtesy CIL)*

CN...VETMAGISTROMILITVM...ERG...ELLASQVASDVDV
...IVRABATBELLOPACEVICTORIASROMANOIMPERIO
REDDIDITMAGISTROVIRIVSQMILITIAEETSECVNDO
CONSVLIORDINARIOTOPATRICIO...SEMPERREIPVBLIC...
...LPENSOOMNIBVSQDONISMILITARIBORNATOQVIC
...ENATVSPOPVLVSQROMANVSOBITALIAESECVRITATEM
...VAMPROCVLDOMITISGENTIBPEREMPTISQVE
...RGVNDIONIBETGOTISOPPRESSISVINCENDOPRA...TI...
...VSSVPRINCIPVMDDDNN...HEONEDOSETPLACI...
...IANIPPAVGGINATRIOLIBERTATI...VAM...
...RENSESIGTIDILATATET...VI...TVRAEQVES
...AMCONLOCAVIT...IMPROBOOEVMREFVGODE...IC
...RVMVITVSTI...INIMICISSIMOVINDICILIBERTATIS
...PVDORISVLTOR...

13. Close-up of the inscription to Aetius. The length and details of inscriptions can sometimes add to our knowledge of important individuals. (*Courtesy CIL*)

14. Diptych celebrating the consulship of Astyrius, Merobaudes' father-in-law, in 449, preserved in Liège. (*Courtesy ILS*)

5. Silver disc: 'Aspar at the Games', made to commemorate Aspar's consulship in 434, probably a reward for his long and successful service in Africa.

6. The Roman amphitheatre at Arles. In the fifth century Arles became the 'capital' of Gaul, and the splendour of its buildings attest to the importance and wealth of the city. (© *Stefan Bauer*)

17. A coin allegedly produced for Aetius. Although its provenance is insecure, some have taken this coin as being proof that he was intending to seize the throne before he was executed. (*beastcoins.com*)

18. Coin minted by Boniface in Africa. It is possible to use this coin as proof of Boniface's treacherous intentions, yet as with many such artefacts the purpose is open to interpretation. (*beastcoins.com*)

19. A Siliqua (small silver coin) produced in Africa by Gaiseric. The use of such coins demonstrated the independence of the Germanic ruler, as well as being evidence that the Vandals (and other 'Germans') adopted Roman customs after settling within the empire. (*beastcoins.com*)

20. A coin minted by the usurper John. The advantage of studying coins is that these are sometimes the only representations that remain of short-lived usurpers, since their monuments were immediately demolished and defaced. (*beastcoins.com*)

21 and 22. Two coins minted during the reign of Valentinian III. Both emphasise the youth of the emperor, a factor that helped Aetius to dominate the west for so long. (*beastcoins.com*)

23 and 24. Coins minted for Aelia Pulcheria (*left*) and Aelia Eudocia (*right*). These may show two of the few remaining likenesses of these women and demonstrate the high standards of dress and comportment still expected of the imperial family despite the west's increasing bankruptcy. (*beastcoins.com*)

25. A bronze medal showing Attila. The 'demonic' wispy beard and the pointed ears emphasise his later reputation as the 'Scourge of God'.

26. 'Attila's Throne' in Venice. Although anachronistic (Venice wasn't founded until after Attila's invasion and death), this item demonstrates the exceptional hold that Attila has had on the western psyche.

7. 'The Feast of Attila' by Mór Than (1870). A stereotypical view of the court of Attila, all of which
re based on Priscus, the only description we have of him and his court.
lungarian National Gallery, Budapest)

8. Raphael's 'The Meeting between Leo the Great and Attila'. Based largely upon anachronistic
lescriptions of the meeting, this image is now widely accepted as a true picture of events.

29. De Neuville's depiction of 'The Huns at the Battle of Chalons'. This picture demonstrates that the image of 'eastern hordes' attacking Europe still strikes fear into the hearts of the west. It is interesting to note that there weren't too many women and babies at the Battle of Chalons.

30. The countryside around Troyes. This photo shows some of the typical countryside in the region where the Battle of the Catalaunian Plains took place. The manner in which the ground rises to a crest shows the importance for both sides in seizing such a dominant feature. (© *Sean Pruitt*)

31. Briullov's painting 'Genseric Sacking Rome 455'. The barbarism of the Vandals is emphasised by the impotence of the Pope, and although the historical accuracy is minimal, the treasures taken by the Romans during the sack of Jerusalem are now being taken by the Vandals.

Ste GENEVIEVE ET ATTILA

32. Maindron Hippolyte's 'Sainte Geneviève et Attila' in the Musée Beaux-Arts, Angers. Although a meeting between the two individuals is almost certainly imaginary, the production of such fine works of art emphasises both the longevity of Attila's reputation as well as the need in the Middle Ages to promote local heroes as saints. (*Didier Ryknerdes*)

Roman initiative behind this attack on Suevic territory'.[35] Vandal raids would force the Sueves to retain troops in Gallaecia to defend the coast from attack. In this way, Aetius could limit the activities of the Sueves in the rest of Spain, so helping him in future attempts at reconquest.

445–446

At the end of 445, and possibly in response to his recent successes, Aetius was heavily honoured in the West. For example, at some point in the 440s, and almost certainly dating to 445, a statue of Aetius was erected in the Atrium Libertatis:

> [Fl(avio) Aetio viro inl(ustri) comiti ... ne]c non et
> magistro militum per Gallias quas dudum [o]b iuratas
> bello pace victorias Romano Imperio reddidit, magi-
> stro utriusq(ue) militiae et secundo consuli ordinario
> at(que) patricio simper rei publicae [i]npenso om-
> nibusq(ue) donis militarib(us) ornato ...
>
> *CIL VI 41389 = AE 1950, 30*[36]

It was also in this period that Aetius' full title is used in a novel of Valentinian: '*comes et magister utriusque militiae et patricius*'.[37] However, the greatest honour was when Aetius was allowed to hold a 'victory procession' through the streets of Rome. In the first days of the empire the awarding of a triumph was a sign of the military victories achieved by a successful general. Unfortunately, the honour was now the exclusive prerogative of the emperor himself. Instead, Aetius was allowed to celebrate a *processus consularis* (consular procession), assuming traditional triumphal dress and marching in a 'festive procession' to the Capitoline Hill.[38] This was his reward for his recent victories and for his recent nomination for his third consulship, which was to take place in 446.

Although the third consulship may also have been awarded due to Aetius military activity, it is necessary to remember that one of the main themes of his time in command was the sharing of military, bureaucratic and civil powers with a relatively large group of senators. For example, Maximus, possibly one of Aetius' most powerful opponents, was made consul in 443. In the following year the honour was bestowed upon Albinus, an influential senator who had already been a Praetorian Prefect and who was later to be honoured as *patricius*. Throughout this period the imperial court acknowledged a large number of powerful individuals in the West. Although Aetius was doubtless wielding a large amount of military and civilian influence both directly and through his supporters, the appointment of 'outsiders' was almost certainly a necessity in order to limit the amount of opposition to Aetius' policies.

It is possible that Merobaudes' poem, the first surviving panegyric, was given at this time.[39] Despite being classed as a panegyric, it is more likely that this poem is instead a *gratiarum actio privata* (private thanks for deeds), a specific panegyric aimed both at promoting the patron and of thanking him for the writer's own career.[40]

The quality of rewards Aetius was receiving is mirrored in the level of his power. This can be measured by the fact that he was now in a position to intervene in all aspects of imperial government, not just the military. For example, in 445 he involved himself in the appointment of Gallic bishops, in the cases of children sold into slavery due to the poverty of their parents, and even concerned himself in the details of the supply of pigs to Rome.[41]

The Third Consulship

The height of the celebrations honouring Aetius was the panegyric delivered by Merobaudes on 1 January 446.[42] Given the fact that warfare had been a constant from 433, when Aetius returned, until 445, it is somewhat surprising to learn that 'the predominant theme of this composition is peace'.[43] Yet a close analysis of the poem, and a comparison of the poem with events in the West, leads to the conclusion that, in most respects, Merobaudes is actually correct.[44]

In lines 1–4 Merobaudes claims that the Danubian frontier is at peace. This is a true statement of affairs, since there had been a series of treaties with the Huns of Rua and Attila, and Aetius had not needed to campaign in the area since 431. In lines 5–7 he makes a similar claim for the Rhine frontier. Aetius had only the year before defeated the Franks and recovered much lost territory; the Burgundians had been heavily defeated and settled on Roman terms within the empire; and there is no record of fighting against the other tribes on the frontier. This too would appear to be a fair representation of events.

Lines 8–15 of Merobaudes' poem cover the pacification of Gaul. Although it had taken several campaigns over many years, by 446 the north seemed quiet, especially since the *bacaudae* had only recently been defeated and were as yet wary of renewing the conflict. Lines 16–22 focus upon affairs in the south of Gaul. After many years of fighting, following their defeat in 441 and the signing of the most recent treaty, the Goths appear to have remained quiet and made no further attempts to expand their dominions or their influence.

In line 24 Merobaudes begins his description of Africa and the treaty with the Vandals. In the early part of this section Merobaudes identifies the Vandals in Africa before, in line 27, he talks of the 'pacts' between Gaiseric and Valentinian. Merobaudes confirms the notion that in 435 Gaiseric had concluded a *foedus* with Rome concerning some of the western provinces of Africa. It also confirms that after the treaty of 442 Gaiseric was paying tribute to Rome, probably in the form of the grain supply that was so desperately needed in Italy. As has already been noted, when Merobaudes uses the term *socius* he is confirming that the Vandals are currently independent allies, rather than being subservient to Rome.

Before the end of the poem, in lines 98–104, it would appear that war was about to be resumed, although the enemy is unidentified. After this the poem returns to Aetius' martial abilities, yet as there are many large *lacunae* (missing words and phrases) in the text, the detailed content and the context are somewhat confused and the missing parts have to be reconstructed by hypothesis. The poem ends with a description of the victory over the Goths in 439, at the end of which Aetius appears to have surrounded an enemy camp before finally defeating the enemy – a fitting conclusion to the panegyric.

The reason for Merobaudes' panegyric was the bestowal upon Aetius of his third consulship. The importance of this is clear. For more than 300 years the honour of a third consulship had been reserved for members or prospective members of the imperial family. Aetius would never be a member of the imperial family, unlike his predecessors Stilicho (son-in-law and [adopted] brother of Honorius I) and Constantius (married to Honorius' sister Galla Placidia). As a result, the nomination of Aetius as consul for the third time should probably be seen as his desire to follow in their footsteps, and 'not to fall short of his predecessors in either distinction or power'.[45]

Overall, the panegyric and the bestowal of a third consulship offer the impression that, although things were not perfect, the empire would be in a worse condition without Aetius at the helm. This is an obvious thing for a panegyric to claim, but analyses of the events of 433 to 445 demonstrate that in some respects these claims are accurate. Yet the final emphasis of the poem on peace and security may also have been a way of underling the fact that although the financial condition of the empire was poor, as long as Aetius received the necessary funding and recruits for the army peace and prosperity would continue.

The main difficulty, both for Aetius himself and for Merobaudes' poem, was the loss of Africa to the Vandals. Even prior to 442 the West had been struggling financially; after 442 the situation had deteriorated to the point where by 444 the West was, effectively, bankrupt.[46] The question remained as to what Aetius could do to redress matters.

Britain

The peaceful condition of the empire and the 'renewal' of its power under the rule of Aetius may also have caused the Romano-Britons once again to hope for help from the continent. Gildas records that they sent messengers:

> To Aetius, now consul for the third time: the groans of the Britons . . . The barbarians drive us to the sea; the sea throws us back on the barbarians: thus two modes of death await us, we are either slain or drowned.
>
> *Gildas, Exc. Conq. Brit.* 20

Unfortunately, Aetius had no time or troops to spare for the help of Britain, especially as the routes north were insecure due to the *bacaudae* of Armorica. This last appeal to Rome for help failed, and the result was that the British either gave up hope and surrendered or decided to take up arms and fight for themselves:

> In the meantime the discomfited people, wandering in the woods, began to feel the effects of a severe famine, which compelled many of them without delay to yield themselves up to their cruel persecutors, to obtain subsistence: others of them, however, lying hid in mountains, caves and

woods, continually sallied out from thence to renew the war. And then it was, for the first time, that they overthrew their enemies, who had for so many years been living in their country.

Gildas, Exc. Conq. Brit. 20

Although this passage is of uncertain dating and its accuracy can be questioned, one thing is clear. At some point in the 440s, and almost certainly either during or after 446, the British finally gave up any hope of help from Rome.[47]

Chapter 12

The Calm Before the Storm

446

Following the panegyric, Aetius once again set to work. Appointing an individual named Vitus as his fellow *magister utriusque militiae*, Aetius sent him to Spain with an army comprising regular forces and an allied Gothic contingent, although it is likely that Aetius retained the majority of the *praesental* army in Italy in case of an attack by the Huns.[1] The purpose of the campaign is unclear, but since the main field of operations was Carthaginiensis and Baetica, it is likely that the aim was to restore Roman authority in these areas, as they had been under the control of the Sueves since 441 (see Map 12). This would tie in with the otherwise mysterious raid on Gallaecia by the Vandals in 445 (see Chapter 13). The campaign in 446 could expect to face less opposition, since many Sueves would be retained in Gallaecia to garrison strategic points along the coast. That there was no need to campaign in Tarraconensis implies that Merobaudes' campaign of 443 must have been a success.[2]

The strategy appears to have worked. Once in Spain Vitus 'oppressed the population of Carthaginiensis and Baetica'.[3] However, the oppression of the population took too long and Rechila was able to gather his troops to face the Roman attack. Somewhere in Spain the Sueves launched an attack on the Romans. The Goths were routed and Vitus fled with the rest of the army.[4] The Sueves re-established their rule over Carthaginiensis and Baetica.[5] The strategy adopted in Spain was not working out as expected.

447

Aetius' actions in the following years are unknown, since the remaining sources tell us little about events in the West between 447 and 450. With Gaul seemingly at peace, and with the Vandals keeping faith with the treaty of 442, it is most likely that any new military campaigns were again directed against the Sueves in Spain, although it is possible that, for the first time in many years, Aetius did not send out forces on military operations.[6] However, the extant sources focus on an event that occurred in the East.

On 27 January 447 there was a major earthquake and the part of the walls of Constantinople between the *porticus Troadensis* (near to the Golden Gate) and the *Tetrapylon* (near to where the Sahzade Mosque now stands) collapsed.[7] Almost certainly connected with the news that the walls had fallen and that Constantinople was vulnerable, and annoyed at the East's refusal to continue with its subsidies, in 447 Attila sent envoys to Constantinople.[8] These demanded the return of all of the

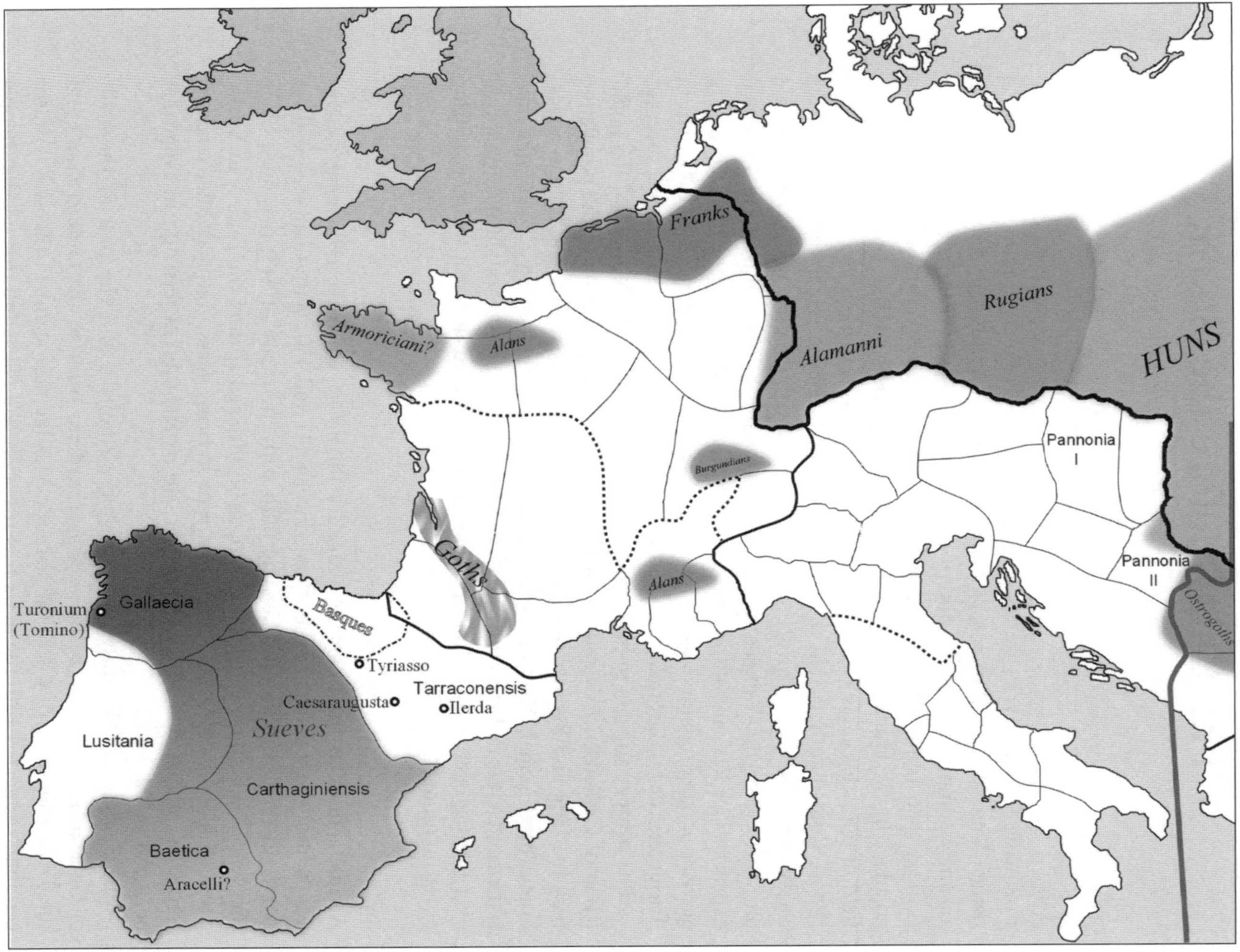

Map 13. Spain and Gaul 449–450

fugitives from the Huns who had fled to the empire for safety, as well as the tribute that had not been paid, otherwise Attila claimed that he would be unable to restrain the Huns.[9]

Analysis of the relevant passage of Priscus reveals the possibility that at this stage Attila had not yet brought all of the Hunnic tribes under his rule and that only the payment of tribute would enable him to restrain those he did not control.[10] This is an intriguing possibility, but it is just as likely that this was a piece of political posturing designed to allow Attila to pose still as the friend and ally of the Romans whilst making demands with menaces. The ploy did not work. The advisors to the emperor declared that war should be risked, and as a consequence Attila invaded Thrace.[11]

The new assault was devastating: 'New destruction broke out in the east. No less than seventy cities were laid waste by the plundering Huns, for no assistance was brought from the west.'[12] Callinicus goes further and claims that over 100 cities were captured.[13] The Gallic Chronicler's criticism that no help was sent to the East is surprising. With a shortage of manpower and barbarians occupying large areas of the West, it would seem impossible that Aetius could spare troops. An explanation of the claim may be that, for the first time in many years, the Roman armies of the West were not deployed on campaign. This would explain why the Chronicler was shocked by the fact that troops in the West remained idle whilst the East was fighting a savage war.

The claim that seventy cities were captured also illustrates the perceived savagery of the attack. The cities of Ratiaria, Athyras and Marcianopolis were amongst them, the latter after the defeat and death of the *magister militum* Arnegisclus in battle at the River Utus in Dacia Ripensis (see Map 1).[14] Attila advanced as far as Thermopylae, but by the time he had travelled that far the walls in Constantinople that had collapsed in the earthquake had been rebuilt under the direction of Flavius Constantinus, the Praetorian Prefect of the East.[15]

At this point the Huns rapidly withdrew from the Balkans: the Hunnic army had contracted 'sickness of the bowels', although fortunately for Attila the majority of the army was unaffected, probably thanks to their swift withdrawal from the affected areas.[16] With Thrace devastated, Theodosius sent the *patricius* and former *magister militum per Orientem* and consul Anatolius to Attila to negotiate a peace.

448

Over the winter of 447–448 the negotiations continued until a treaty was agreed. The terms were harsh. The arrears in the tribute had to be paid in full, amounting to 6,000 pounds of gold, and the new annual tribute was set at 2,100 pounds of gold.[17] But, and 'most dangerous for the future', a belt of land 'five days' journey wide and extending along the Danube from Pannonia to Novae in Thrace' was to be vacated by Rome,[18] implying that prior to this the Romans had been able to interfere in the workings of Attila's 'empire' even if only to spy on his movements and report them quickly to the emperor.[19] The net result was that the Huns now had a free crossing of the Danube without the possibility of interference from the Romans. Thrace was completely at their mercy. For Attila, the war was of even greater importance. In his first major campaign as sole leader of the Huns, he had smashed the Roman armies in Thrace and had forced humiliating terms upon the Eastern Emperor. His position as 'king' was assured.

The West

In the West the treaties with the Franks, the Goths and the Vandals were holding. Aetius did not have to concern himself with southern Gaul or Africa. However, in Spain there were still the Sueves and the *bacaudae* to worry about. Although the existing sources for the period tell us little about imperial campaigns in Spain, they do inform us that Rechila launched an attack upon the 'furthest reaches' of Gallaecia.[20] He was clearly still intent upon consolidating his sphere of domination. Shortly afterwards he died of natural causes and the rule passed to Rechiarus, his son.[21]

Although the situation in the West appeared to be stabilizing, it is possible that in 448 there was yet another *bacaudic* revolt in northern Gaul. The Gallic Chronicler states that 'Eudoxius, a physician by profession and of perverse, if well-developed, talents, fled to the Huns when implicated in the *bacauda* that took place at that time'.[22] Although otherwise unattested, and of dubious reliability, analysis of other sources shows that it is possible that a revolt took place.

The precise nature of events is insecure, but an entry in Jordanes suggests that at some point after 446 there was indeed a rebellion of the *bacaudae* in northern Gaul. Jordanes is not always the most accurate of historians, yet his testimony concerning events in 451 lists the peoples allied to Rome. Included in this list are the *Armoriciani*.[23] It is possible that these *Armoriciani* took part in the rebellion recorded by the Gallic Chronicler and that Eudoxius was the 'Gallic' leader of the revolt. Although the revolt of 448 was defeated, between 448 and 451 Aetius finally accepted that specific Roman control of the north of Gaul was now lost.

It is possible that Aetius' change of heart was due to the nature of these rebels. According to the British historian Gildas, at some date in the 440s the Britons sent an appeal to an individual in Gaul, either Aetius or to a later *Magister Militum per Gallias* named Aegidius: unfortunately, the name is unclear and so Gildas could be referring to either man.[24] If it was addressed to Aetius the claims went unanswered, probably because Aetius did not have enough troops to send aid to the Britons and to face the expected Hunnic attack.[25] In order to escape from the Saxons, in the fifth century many Britons fled from Britain to Armorica, augmenting the settlers who had allegedly arrived in the fourth century.[26] Indeed, so many eventually crossed the English Channel that the area in which they settled was renamed Brittany ('Little Britain').

The British nobles and their followers probably settled in Armorica in the mid to late 440s. Therefore, it is possible to suggest that during the *bacaudic* rebellion of 448 Aetius came into contact with these fresh settlers, whose manpower had swelled the forces in rebellion. Aetius was forced to accept that these new reinforcements meant that he would be unable to defeat any further rebellions using military force.

As a result, he entered into negotiations with the rebels. As part of the agreement the Gallic leader, Eudoxius, and possibly his leading followers, was forced to flee and Aetius confirmed the ascendancy of the incoming British aristocracy. In return, the new British leaders formed a military alliance with Aetius, becoming the *Armoriciani* of Jordanes. At least part of Aetius' willingness to accept the 'British' settlement may have been due to a feeling of guilt: he had been unable to send the help requested to Britain. The charitable actions of Aetius and Valentinian to the refugees from Africa demonstrate that they were aware of the failings of the empire and would take steps to help those who were suffering as a result. Furthermore, these people had shown clear evidence of a loyalty to Rome by crossing the English Channel to remain part of the empire. By accepting the incomers as allies Aetius ensured that the area would now be peaceful, discharged his moral obligations to the British exiles and released the troops campaigning in the area for other service. He will almost certainly have believed that in time the newcomers would retain their loyalty to the emperor in Italy.

Although pure speculation, this hypothesis does allow the sparse information that survives to be transformed into a logical narrative. It also gives an explanation for how the incomers were able to replace the local leaders, who were now in exile, and establish their own 'Little Britain'. It should, however, be noted that other chronologies can be constructed.

Whatever the cause and the nature of the inhabitants, the acceptance of the *bacaudae* as semi-independent was probably a necessity since the continuous wars in Gaul and Spain were keeping the treasury at a dangerously low level.

Sigisvult

One further event took place either in or shortly before 448. Contrary to (modern) expectations, by 448 Sigisvult had been made *patricius*.[27] This has resulted in speculation as to the nature of his appointment and the political motives behind it. Recent debate has questioned whether Sigisvult was even made *patricius*.[28] The argument revolves around the belief that a combination of the two titles of *comes et magister utriusque militiae* and *patricius* must result in the bearer being the 'supreme commander' in the west. Therefore, if Sigisvult – or indeed Merobaudes before him – was *magister militum* and *patricius*, then either Valentinian or Placidia must, at least in theory, have promoted him in opposition to Aetius.

This need not necessarily be the case. The concept that a combination of the two titles could only be borne by one man rests on the cases of two of Aetius' predecessors, Stilicho and Constantius. Yet in both of these examples the men involved were breaking new political ground with their appointments and no doubt were wary of competition. After fifteen years of undisputed leadership it is not surprising that Aetius finally relented and allowed his loyal and long-serving supporter Sigisvult to achieve the only title that had eluded him. By allowing Sigisvult to be made *patricius* Aetius both rewarded him for his loyalty and ensured that he received the recognition he deserved. The move also ensured Sigisvult's continued loyalty.

449–450

In line with Aetius' policy of rewarding his loyal followers with the highest status he could award, in 449 Astyrius, father of Merobaudes, was made consul in the West, at which point he was probably stationed in Arles. In commemoration, he was given a panegyric by Flavius Nicetus.[29]

Furthermore, Aetius appointed Firminus, a Gaul, as *praefectus praetorio Italiae*: for the first time since 430 the prefect was not from one of the powerful Italian senatorial families. This was to be only the second time between the years 426 and 465 that a non-Italian was made prefect.[30] The appointment has resulted in solemn debate regarding Aetius' policies concerning the empire and especially of the internal politics prevalent in Rome.[31] Unfortunately, these arguments rely on the fact that the previous non-Italian incumbent, Theodosius, was also an appointee of Aetius.[32] This is certainly a mistake, as Theodosius was appointed prior to February 430, when Aetius was only *magister militum per Gallias* and so unable to make such appointments. There are two more likely options. One is that the appointment of Firminus was simply a political ploy to maintain Aetius' popularity with the senators of Gaul, rather than a response to Aetius' political and financial requirements within Italy. The other is that the dire financial problems now facing the empire required an 'outsider' to force through legislation attempting to raise taxes and recruits from the senators who usually occupied the post of prefect and so could use their power to block or change any proposals.

In reality, it is more likely that the appointment was a combination of the two. The appointment allowed Aetius to reward the Gallic aristocracy who had long since been amongst his greatest admirers: Aetius 'was a hero to at least a large section of the Gallic aristocracy'.[33] This concept is reinforced by his appointment the following year of Opilio, another Gallic aristocrat, to the post of Prefect of the City of Rome, and his apparent seizure of the financial reins from Valentinian and the Senate.[34] Furthermore, Aetius' reliance on these two men and their combined success is supported by the fact that some time around the year 451 both men were elevated to the *patriciate*, whilst Firminus remained in the post of prefect until 29 June 452.[35]

The whole episode implies that prior to 450 there had been political opposition to Aetius that had been powerful enough to retain control of state finances. Yet this was now at an end. A *novel* issued in March 450 remitted all delinquent taxes prior to September 447 and then renewed the law of 440 limiting the authority of the *comites* of the treasury and declared that from this time forward the only tax inspectors allowed must be confirmed by either the *praefectus praetorio* or by Aetius.[36] With Firminus' support, Aetius began an attempt to break the dominance of the Senate of Rome over financial and military matters: the imperial court may have favoured Italians, who had a tendency to forgive each other their outstanding taxes.[37]

The West

However, things were again beginning to go wrong in the West. A possible sign that king Theoderic was beginning to resent Aetius' domination, early in 449, and doubtless after negotiations begun in 448, was his giving his daughter in marriage to

Rechiarius, king of the Sueves.[38] Although it is possible that this was the daughter mutilated by Gaiseric and Huneric, this is nowhere attested, and it is more likely that she was another, unnamed daughter.

There are most likely two major reasons for the marriage alliance. Firstly, there is Theoderic's desire to break from Roman control. Despite his attempts to break free, or at least establish himself as a political player at court, Theoderic was still confined to his nascent kingdom. An alliance with the Sueves, who were in a similar position to him, albeit with slightly more freedom, would strengthen his hand when dealing with Roman politicians, especially Aetius. Secondly, Theoderic's daughter who had been married to Huneric and who had been mutilated had returned home. The fact that this was done after the Vandals had made a treaty with Rome no doubt caused Theoderic to blame the emperor and Aetius, at least in part, for the fate of his daughter. Theoderic will have been unhappy to remain in the same subservient position to people who had caused his family such grief.

Reassured that the Goths would not now attack him under orders from Aetius, in February 449 Rechiarus plundered the territories of the Vasconiae (Basques).[39] At around the same time, Censorius, the envoy who had been captured by the Sueves in Martylis in 440, was 'assassinated' by Agiulfus. Agiulfus may have been one of the Gothic envoys and the act may have been a dramatic signal that the treaties with the Romans were now considered to be over.[40]

Probably in an associated move, and 'to show his outstanding daring', an individual named Basilius 'gathered together *bacaudae* and killed federates in the church of Tyriasso (Tarazona)'.[41] Situated close to the area of Rechiarius' attack, it is likely that the two 'uprisings' were co-ordinated.

That these attacks were co-ordinated is proved by the fact that in July Rechiarius visited his new father-in-law in Gaul, but on the return journey he joined with Basilius and they pillaged the territory around Caesaraugusta, capturing the city of Ilerda with 'trickery' (see Map 13).[42] Since Theoderic now had a marriage alliance with Rechiarius, Aetius, who had previously relied on Gothic reinforcements for the campaigns in Spain, would be forced to rely solely on Roman troops.[43] Yet with Spain in a renewed upheaval, Aetius was faced with a trickier situation at court in Ravenna.

Attila and Chrysapius

In the east, Chrysapius, eunuch and *spatharius* (bodyguard) to Theodosius, instigated a plot to murder Attila.[44] Chrysapius had slowly risen to power over the preceding years and by 449 was the leading figure in the East. Unfortunately for him, Attila discovered the plot and attempted to extradite Chrysapius for punishment. Due to Chrysapius' superior position at court the attempt failed, and an embassy sent to Attila comprising Anatolius and Nomus, the latter being a loyal supporter of Chrysapius, managed to smooth things over. However, the incident hardened opposition to Chrysapius, and his enemies, especially Pulcheria, looked to weaken his position.

Yet that was not Attila's only infuriating problem. As part of the earlier treaty with Attila, Aetius had sent a Gaul named Constantius to act as Attila's secretary.

This Constantius had allegedly taken some golden bowls from Attila and sent them to a Roman banker named Silvanus. Attila now demanded that Silvanus be handed over to him.[45]

450

In hindsight the story of these continuous wars and the information that the West was bankrupt can lead to the assumption that what was needed at this time was imperial unity and the joining together of all imperial peoples to use whatever means was necessary to claw back the lost ground and restore the empire to its previous glory. Yet despite the fact that the West was in disarray, life for the moneyed classes continued as normal. Two laws passed in May 450 demonstrate that personal interests dominated over imperial ones: due to the focus on the wars by the government, unscrupulous tax collectors were being allowed to defraud the taxpayer, and there were problems collecting the taxes from Sardinia.[46] The situation was made worse by the fact that in 450 there was a famine in Italy, although the precise causes are unknown.[47]

However, these were not the worst events for Aetius. Either in 449 or in 450 Honoria, sister of Valentinian, was:

> caught in a clandestine affair with a certain Eugenius ... He was executed for the crime, and she was betrothed to Herculanus, a man of consular rank and of ... good character. [In response, she] ... sent the eunuch Hyacinthus to Attila offering him money to avenge her marriage. She also sent her ring as her pledge to the barbarian.
>
> *Prisc. fr. 17 = Joh. Ant. fr. 199,2 = Exc. De Ins. 84*[48]

Although this claim has been doubted, it is almost certain that the event happened.[49] Several interpretations are possible, but probably the correct interpretation of the passage is that Honoria was disgraced and betrothed to Herculanus, a man deemed to be safe from imperial pretensions, but a man in whom she had no interest. As a result, she petitioned members of the court for help. When this was not forthcoming, since the courtiers were either supporters of Valentinian or Aetius, both of whom appear to have agreed upon her marriage, she sought elsewhere for aid. The only other individual of any political or military standing who could possibly help her was Attila, who since the treaty of 443 was an 'honorary' *magister militum*. As a result, she offered him gold to take her side in the disagreement at court.

The act of attempting to enlist the aid of a barbarian is usually interpreted as a betrayal, since in hindsight the effects of her request were to be calamitous. This is a mistake. In the first place, Attila was an imperial officer and her last resort. Secondly, this was not the first time that a member of the court had appealed to the Huns for help against their opponents at court: Aetius owed his career to that ability. Finally, Honoria's mother had actually been married to a 'barbarian': Alaric's brother-in-law and successor Athaulf.[50] There was a family tradition of dealing with 'barbarian' individuals only indirectly connected with the court.

As proof of her identity, Honoria also sent her ring with the messenger. This gesture mirrored a common act of giving a specific personal item to the messenger as proof that the bearer was acting on the sender's behalf. In return, Honoria will have expected Attila simply to make a threat for the engagement to be annulled.

Furious, Valentinian now had to decide what to do with his sister Honoria. Messengers arrived from Theodosius advising that she be sent to Attila. However, the prolonged pleas for clemency from Placidia, the mother of Valentinian and Honoria, finally bore fruit. Honoria was banished from court and surrendered to the custody of Placidia.

Before any other action could be taken, events in the East again intervened. The emperor Theodosius injured his spine after falling from his horse.[51] Despite the best efforts of his physicians, on 28 July he died in Constantinople at the age of forty-nine.[52] The only surviving male member of the House of Theodosius was Valentinian in the West.

Claim to the Throne

According to Priscus, Valentinian now decided that he wanted to be the emperor of both East and West: the first emperor of a united empire since Theodosius I in 395.[53] Although unsubstantiated elsewhere, the claim may be true. As the last male heir to the throne, Valentinian almost certainly saw himself as the only valid claimant to the Eastern Empire. The East was in a far stronger financial position than the West and a large infusion of money may have helped the West to reconquer some lost areas and so stave off the West's terminal bankruptcy. Yet if it is true, the claim was not transmitted to the East. Without an obvious heir, Pulcheria, the sister of Theodosius II, would soon lose her position of political independence. As a result, she decided to raise her own emperor and so ensure her continuation in power. Her choice fell on Marcian, the man who had been captured by Gaiseric in Africa in 432. He was immediately summoned and on 26 August 450 was crowned the forty-second emperor at Constantinople with the consent and approval of the Senate and the army. Marcian immediately married Pulcheria, so ensuring that he was seen as part of the Theodosian dynasty.[54] With the death of Theodosius, Chrysapius had lost his only means of support and shortly afterwards he was beheaded by the order of Pulcheria, so one bone of contention with Attila was removed.[55]

Again according to Priscus, at this point Valentinian wanted to lead an army to Constantinople 'to remove Marcian from his throne'.[56] Aetius disagreed, and Priscus claims that this disagreement was a major cause of Valentinian's unhappiness with Aetius' domination.

Yet the claim that Valentinian wanted to invade the East is unlikely. The East was much stronger both militarily and financially than the West and would have easily been able to defeat any 'invasion' by Valentinian. Furthermore, by 450 the court and bureaucracy of the East had a long tradition of separation from that of the West. A unified empire would, theoretically at least, result in a united court. Many powerful officials would have lost power, or at least had their influence reduced by the arrival of the Western Emperor. Although in hindsight the possibilities are tantalising, in reality the Eastern court would not accept the imposition of Valentinian as emperor in Constantinople.[57]

Marcian

With the elevation of Marcian there was an immediate change in policy in the East. Unlike his imperial predecessors, who had been forced to rely from a young age upon ministers and generals, Marcian was a mature individual who had spent his career rising through the ranks of the army. His confidence in his military abilities was high and he had no fear that a strong *magister militum* would force him to relinquish the reigns of power, as had happened in the West. As a result, one of his first decisions was to put a halt to the paying of subsidies to the Huns, and messengers were sent to Attila informing him of the new regime.

Only a few months later Placidia, Valentinian's mother, also died and was buried in the monastery of St Nazarius at Ravenna.[58] She had supported Valentinian throughout his rule and had been the power behind the throne for the last quarter of a century, whenever possible guarding her son from outside political interference. Although she appears to have been an opponent of Aetius at the beginning, the lack of opposition to his dominance implies that she was later reconciled to him, especially after she became convinced that he was not aiming to either take the throne himself or to remove Valentinian and replace him with his own nominee. As a result, it is possible that in her later years she actually supported him. It should be acknowledged, though, that she may never have reconciled with Aetius, but was unable to muster enough support to oust him.[59] With her death Valentinian now became susceptible to political machinations at court.

Consequently, Attila received two pieces of news in quick succession. The first was that Theodosius had died and that Marcian, the new, more militant emperor of the East, was not going to pay the subsidies Attila expected. The second was Honoria's request for help.[60]

Chapter 13

Crisis*

450

The request from Honoria wasn't the only diplomatic activity in the west in which Attila was embroiled. The king of the Franks had died. At an unknown date his younger son had been sent on an embassy to Rome. He had been befriended by Aetius, who had adopted him as his son, promised to support him in his claim to the throne and then sent him home laden with gifts.[1] This was a shrewd move by Aetius. An alliance with the Franks would eliminate the need to station troops in the north east of Gaul and allow him to use them in other theatres of war. Further, the alliance would result in the Franks themselves protecting the northern frontiers against tribes from further inside *Germania*. When the Frankish king died, the younger son seized the throne. The support of Aetius had proved to be decisive, so the elder son of the Frankish king decided to appeal to the only power that could oppose Aetius. He went to Attila and asked for the Hun's support in his claim to the throne.[2] Any attempt to support the elder son would break Attila's agreement with the West and precipitate war.

However, when Honoria's request arrived, followed by the news that Theodosius had died, Attila saw a way forward. In response to the two envoys, Attila decided to reply in an aggressive fashion. Realizing that Christian ambassadors would have a better chance of achieving his aims than pagans, Attila sent two embassies, both composed of Goths, to Constantinople and to Italy.[3]

The embassy to Constantinople was straightforward. Attila demanded the payment of the tribute, plus the missed payments. The *Chronicon Paschale* also claims that he included the message 'My master and your master Attila commands you through me to make ready a palace for him.'[4] It is unlikely that this is correct, and the concept that Attila believed that he could overthrow the Roman empire is mistaken, especially as the *Chronicon Paschale* only claims that Attila wanted 'a' (singular) palace, not the throne. It is probably better to assume that this is a device used by the author to highlight Attila's arrogance and pride, and so use it as a counterpoint to his later fall, a popular theme amongst Christian writers.

Attila's grasp of political opportunities is nowhere more apparent than with his use of Honoria's offer. The likelihood is that Honoria was expecting him to use

---

* The events in this reconstruction, especially those relating to 450, are based upon the primary sources. However, readers should be aware that the majority of these sources are undated, and so open to different interpretations. Furthermore, the accuracy of some of the sources, especially Jordanes, is open to question. For more details, see the Introduction.

his influence to stop her marriage, much as his predecessors had used theirs to manoeuvre Aetius back into power. Attila appeared to be following her request when he sent envoys to the West demanding that unless Honoria was given 'the sceptre of sovereignty, he would avenge her'. Unfortunately, Attila also demanded her hand in marriage.[5] He had picked on one item and used it to change Honoria's request into something far more alarming for the west: Attila chose to interpret Honoria's inclusion of her ring as a proposal of marriage.[6]

He was to be disappointed: both of his envoys received a negative reply.[7] In the case of the East it was a straight refusal to pay, but with the additional response that if he kept the peace they would give him gifts. From the West came a denial that Honoria could be married to Attila, since she was already engaged to another. Furthermore, the envoy reported that the West had refused Honoria any regal rights to the throne, 'since the rule of the Roman state belonged not to females but to males'.[8]

Calmly accepting the denial of both emperors could have encouraged his rivals to see him as weak and so have precipitated a civil war amongst the Huns and their subjects. Attila was the leader of a 'vast military machine which demanded action and an influx of rewards, otherwise it could easily turn on him'.[9] He had to declare a war. He now had to decide which option to take. Attacking the East was a possibility, but there were three major problems. One was that the provinces that were within reach had been plundered on several occasions in previous years. The likelihood is that the amount of booty he would obtain would be minimal. Furthermore, ravaging already ravaged areas was unlikely to put enough pressure on Marcian to force him to agree to Attila's terms. Secondly, and more importantly, Marcian was not Theodosius II. Theodosius from a very young age had been at the mercy of warring political groups within the government. Marcian was a mature, strong-willed individual who would not yield to pressure from his courtiers. The political contacts Attila had fostered in Constantinople, and which had almost certainly helped to hinder policy making, had been rendered powerless. Finally, Marcian was a military man. If Attila invaded – unlike his predecessors, who had used the army sparingly to avoid having a 'military dictatorship' such as existed in the West – Marcian could gather as many troops as he needed and personally lead them against Attila.

On the other hand, Attila believed that if he attacked Gaul he was on stronger ground. He could guarantee support from those Franks who supported the older brother of the deceased king. Furthermore, if his political strategy was correct, he could easily divide the nations of the west, especially if he could convince the Goths of Theoderic to abandon their treaty with Rome. This would mean that Aetius' allies would be limited to only 'half' of the Franks and possibly the settled Alans.

The later historian Jordanes, along with the 'Chronicle of Fredegar', claims that at least part of the reason why Attila contemplated the attack on Gaul was because he was bribed by Gaiseric to attack the Goths.[10] Allegedly, this is because Gaiseric was afraid that Theoderic would try to avenge his daughter's earlier mutilation. Obviously, if Theoderic was already at war with the Huns, Gaiseric would be safe. In addition, Priscus claims that Attila attacked Gaul and the Goths partly because he was 'laying up a store of favour with Gaiseric'.[11]

If these claims are true, it would mean that Gaiseric was encouraging the Huns to wage war against the Romans. As a result, the statements are usually dismissed by historians. However, there is one additional piece of information that may hint that at least some of this story is true. In 450 Eudocia reached the age of twelve and according to Roman custom was now allowed to marry. In theory, she should have gone to Carthage to marry Huneric. The fact that she did not may hint at strained relations between Gaiseric and Valentinian – possibly caused by the knowledge that Gaiseric had suggested to Attila that he invade Gaul.[12]

In conclusion, although the two claims concerning a Vandal–Hun 'alliance' remain a possibility, they must be classed as of doubtful reliability, largely because Gaiseric had no influence over events and, despite his control of the sea, would be unable to help Attila in central Gaul. Further, the reasons for Attila wishing to retain Gaiseric's friendship and alliance are not made clear by Priscus. It is perhaps best to assume that in the confusing times of late 450 and early 451 envoys were travelling throughout the Western Empire and to Attila in the east, including those from the Vandals. What was really said at these meetings was unknown, even at the time, but gossip within the empire may have suggested that the Vandals wanted Attila to invade the West and that Attila agreed with the Vandal envoys who suggested that the softest target for Attila was Gaul. The truth will never be known. Yet whether influenced by Gaiseric or not, Attila now began to send envoys to Italy to talk with Aetius and to Gaul to talk with the Franks, the Alans and with Theoderic, the king of the Goths. Attila's policy was clearly one of divide and conquer.

After weighing his options, Attila had decided that war with the west was the better of the two. The East had always been stronger than the West and was now led by a military emperor who was prepared to marshal the forces of the whole East to defeat Attila. Attila knew when to cut his losses. His envoys in Constantinople agreed a treaty with the new emperor, which was 'surprisingly favourable to Rome': the concept that this was due to the 'wisdom of his East Roman interlocutors' is mistaken.[13] Attila simply wanted a peaceful border in the East when he invaded the West. It is possibly during the negotiations for this treaty that Attila complained about the Roman cultivation of those lands five days' march deep along the Danube between Pannonia and Novae in Thrace, which were supposed to have been left deserted.[14]

It was only Aetius' relationship with Attila's predecessors that had saved the West from Hunnic attack. Attila knew that attacking Italy would be problematic, since Aetius would be ready to defend the Alps against any attempt to enter Italy, and theoretically Aetius had enough forces to enable him to block the passes. It is possible that before he decided to attack Gaul Attila had attempted to have Aetius removed. However, the accuracy of this claim is uncertain.[15]

There is yet another possible reason for Attila's decision to invade Gaul. At an unknown time he had received 'divine' evidence of his destiny:

And though his temper was such that he always had great self-confidence, yet his assurance was increased by finding the sword of Mars, always esteemed sacred among the kings of the Scythians. The historian Priscus says it was discovered under the following circumstances: 'When a certain shepherd beheld one heifer of his flock limping and could find no cause for this wound, he anxiously followed the trail of blood and at length came to a sword it had unwittingly trampled while nibbling the grass. He dug it up and took it straight to Attila. He rejoiced at this gift and, being ambitious, thought he had been appointed ruler of the whole world, and that through the sword of Mars supremacy in all wars was assured to him.'

Jordanes Getica 35.183 = Priscus, fragment 11.2

There is one other factor that may have affected Attila's decision to attack Gaul rather than either the East or Italy. Although usually ignored, in 448 a leader of the *bacaudae* in Gaul named Eudoxius had fled to Attila.[16] Although his fate is nowhere mentioned, there is a strong possibility that part of Attila's reason for attacking Gaul was out of the belief, fed by Eudoxius, that the *bacaudae* in the north would rise up to support him against the empire.

Attila was now determined to fulfil his destiny and the weaker half of the Roman Empire would be his target. Accordingly, he sent envoys to Italy. The message to Aetius had two parts. The first demanded that Honoria be handed over to Attila, claiming that she had been betrothed to him, and as proof Attila sent the ring she had sent to him. More alarmingly, he also demanded that 'Valentinian should resign to him half of his empire, since Honoria had received the sovereignty of it from her father and had been deprived of it by her brother's greed'.[17] No doubt also included in the message was a further demand that Silvanus the banker be handed over (see Chapter 14). In the meantime, Attila prepared for war.

451

As he gathered his armies ready to travel west, Attila's diplomatic tactics struck a new note. He now declared that in his new role as co-emperor and 'guardian of Roman friendship, he would wage (war) only against the Goths'.[18] No doubt he claimed that this was only his duty, both as the prospective husband of and co-ruler with Honoria and as honorary *magister militum*. This would not have been the first time that an army of Huns had destroyed Germanic intruders in the West: in 437 under Rua they had annihilated the Burgundians.

This was a plausible claim and was doubtless intended to create division and turmoil in the Western court. However, Attila had underestimated Aetius. The court in Italy stood firm and rejected the claim. In part, this was thanks to the fact that Aetius was aware of the other envoys that Attila had sent, and of their missions – probably thanks to a spy network both within Gaul and within the Hunnic court. Aetius may have been receiving information from several sources in Attila's court, including Orestes, who later had a major role in the West. Furthermore, Aetius may have provided several officials to the Huns, some or all of whom reported to him, and it is possible that his son Carpilio was still a hostage with the Huns at this time and able to inform Aetius of events at the Hunnic court.[19]

It is also possible that many of the older Huns, who were contemporaries of Aetius and knew him from his days as a hostage, did not support Attila in his attack on the West. This allowed Aetius to inform the emperor and the Senate that Attila was also attempting to form a 'barbarian coalition' of Huns, Franks, Alans and Goths in Gaul.

Attila's message to the Franks was quite simple. It was a call to arms for supporters of the older brother of the dead king and an attempt to gain support against the younger brother, the adopted son of Aetius. Since Aetius was already supporting the younger son, there was little Aetius could do except reply in kind, attempting to rally support for his foster-son.

Attila sent envoys to the Alans under Sambida, leader of those Alans who had been settled in the area of Valence (see Map 14). According to Jordanes, Sambida now considered the possibility of joining Attila, although if so this was no doubt out of fear rather than disloyalty to Aetius.[20]

Amid all this frantic political activity it was the Hunnic envoys to the Goths that were the cause of gravest concern to the Romans. In a direct contradiction to the message to Rome, Attila sent a message to Theoderic urging him to break his treaty with the Romans, and remember instead the recent defeats he had suffered at the hands of Aetius.[21] Aetius was able to use Attila's duplicity for his own purposes, sending embassies to Theoderic to request an alliance and informing him of Attila's claim that he was going to attack the Goths. Unsure of whom to trust and of what Attila's intentions actually were, Theoderic decided to remain neutral and follow his own policies.[22]

The Western Alliance[23]

For his part, Aetius began an attempt to build a 'western alliance' against the Huns. Apart from the attempts to gain the Goths' support, Aetius also sent envoys to other peoples in the west, including all of those who had signed treaties to serve as *foederati* when called upon. Obviously, he could rely on at least a large percentage of the Franks, the supporters of the deceased king's younger son who was his own adopted son.[24] At the same time, he sent messengers to the Sarmatians – an alternative and poetic name for any of the nomadic tribes from the east, but which in this case denotes the Alans of Sambida and Goa. Although under pressure from Attila to join with the forces from the east, Sambida now bowed to Roman pressure and agreed to fight against the Huns.[25]

In his bid to join together the military powers of the whole of the west, Aetius also sent messengers to several distinct political western entities.[26] One of these was the *Armoriciani*, the semi-independent natives of Armorica, by this date possibly under 'British' leadership.[27] Another was the '*Liticiani*' or 'Liticians', of unknown origin but perhaps the remnants of old units of *laeti* now living on the extreme edges of the empire but still willing to serve the Romans.[28] Also included were the '*Ripari*' (Riparians), Franks from northern Gaul, and the '*Olibriones*', 'once Roman soldiers and now the flower of the Allied forces'.[29] It has been suggested that the *Olibriones* were old Roman units of *riparienses* from northern Gaul, now serving the Franks.

By this time these units were probably largely manned by Franks, although the new recruits may have been trained in traditional Roman fighting techniques by the Roman officers and their descendants in command of the units.[30] An unexpected addition to the list is the Saxons, which would appear strange given their isolation from events, unless they had established otherwise-unknown enclaves in north Gaul, possibly around the regions of Bologna (Boulogne) and Bessin.[31] Jordanes also notes the inclusion of several tribes of 'Celts' and 'Germans', although these are not individually named. Finally, Aetius managed to convince the Burgundians he had settled in Gaul also to join the alliance.

However, despite the agreements of all of these people, the main concern for Aetius remained enlisting the aid of the most powerful force in Gaul, the Goths of Theoderic.

The Invasion of Gaul

Whilst the diplomatic activity was still ongoing, in early 451 Attila arrived on the Rhine. However, he had not neglected his homeland. At the same time as his main force moved west another group of Huns attacked the Balkans, probably in an attempt to pin down the Eastern forces and prevent co-operation between the two empires.[32] This demonstrates that Attila did not trust Marcian to keep to the terms of the treaty. On the Rhine he set his men to building boats using wood from the German forests, before crossing the Rhine and entering Gaul 'as if he had the right to ask for a wife that was owed to him'.[33]

Despite being called a 'Hun' army, Attila's army was actually composed of many different tribes. Sidonius provides a list of those tribes allegedly joining with Attila's attack, yet it should be remembered that in some cases the poem may be following traditional literary motifs rather than accurately enumerating the tribes involved.[34]

The tribes listed include the Geloni from the region of the Volga, the Neuri and Bastarnae from the Ukraine, the Sciri from the region of modern Odessa, the Rugi from Pomerania, the Bructeri from the Weser and the Thuringi from Bavaria.[35] Also included is a contingent from those members of the Burgundians who had remained in their original homeland around the Vistula rather than taking up Aetius' offer of land in Gaul. Finally, those Franks who supported the claim of the deceased king's elder son appear to have joined Attila en route.

However, the main allied contingents were provided by the Ostrogoths under their leaders, the brothers Valamir, Thiudimer and Vidimer, and the Gepids under their king, Ardaric. In fact, Valamir and Ardaric were even recognized by Attila himself as being of far higher value than the other kings.[36]

The course of the Hunnic attack on Gaul is sparsely attested and open to different interpretations. The main problem is the fact that medieval ecclesiastical chronicles exaggerated the effects of Attila's attacks. The medieval chronicles include a list of towns that claimed to have been attacked by Attila, yet many of them are now known to have escaped unscathed.[37] What follows is a list of the towns noted as being attacked, taken largely from the *Acta Sanctorum* (Acts of the Saints), a collection of minor *hagiographies* (biographies of saints), which include in the text stories concerning the behaviour of religious leaders as their towns were attacked by the Huns, plus an analysis of the accuracy of the claims.[38] Along with the accounts of Gregory of Tours, Sidonius Apollinaris and Jordanes, amongst others, these help to expand on the course of the war.

The War

Attila marched through *Germania* towards Gaul. The fact that the Alamanni are not mentioned in any of the sources concerning the invasion suggests that they either simply bowed to the inevitable and let him pass unhindered or that the Huns passed to the north of the Alamannic territory.[39] The first city that Attila is known to have attacked was Metz, on 7 April – Easter Eve.[40] It was quickly taken and sacked.[41] Following this early success, Attila 'ravaged a great number of other cities'.[42] The meaning of the term ravaged is open to question. Most authorities assume that the towns were stormed and sacked, but this would have taken time, and the speed of the Hunnic advance suggests that this was not the case. In the context of the war and of the late Roman empire it is more likely that in reality a large proportion of the towns 'ravaged' were not themselves attacked: rather, their supporting territories would have been scoured by the Huns for provisions for their large army whilst the inhabitants cowered behind the city walls.[43] After this, the areas ravaged would have needed a large amount of time to bring them back to full productivity. However, some of the more strategically important towns, and any towns that were inadequately defended, were no doubt attacked and sacked in the traditional manner.

Several towns are described in the *Acta* as being attacked. Reims was captured and sacked, with its bishop (Saint) Nicasius being killed, and Tongres (Tongeren) was also sacked, although its bishop, (Saint) Servatius, escaped to die shortly thereafter.[44] According to the *Gesta Treverorum* (Deeds of the Treveri) Trier was attacked too, an event possibly supported by excavations in the twentieth century.[45] Other towns alleged to have been attacked during Attila's invasion are Strasbourg, Worms, Mainz, Cologne, Cambrai, Arras, Tournai, Therouanne, Cologne, Amiens and Beauvais.

It is possible that either Strasbourg or Worms were attacked and sacked, as they were on the route towards the centre of Gaul. Yet the claims that Cologne, Tournai, Cambrai, Therouanne and Arras were also sacked would appear to be unlikely. Instead, it is probable that a small picked force was separated from the main army and sent north in an attempt to force the Franks to submit to Attila's nominee for the Frankish throne. The Frankish king would in return be expected to establish a firm base and recruit troops for the upcoming campaign (see Map 14). As Attila was expecting a military reaction from the Romans, the 'Frankish' detachment will have been given orders to move quickly, so it is likely that these towns had their territories 'ravaged' by the invading Huns as they marched to rejoin the main force, and in their search for supplies for their large army, rather than being captured and sacked.

Yet there is another possible explanation for the widespread devastation of northern Gaul. Attila may have moved his army in separate columns, which would

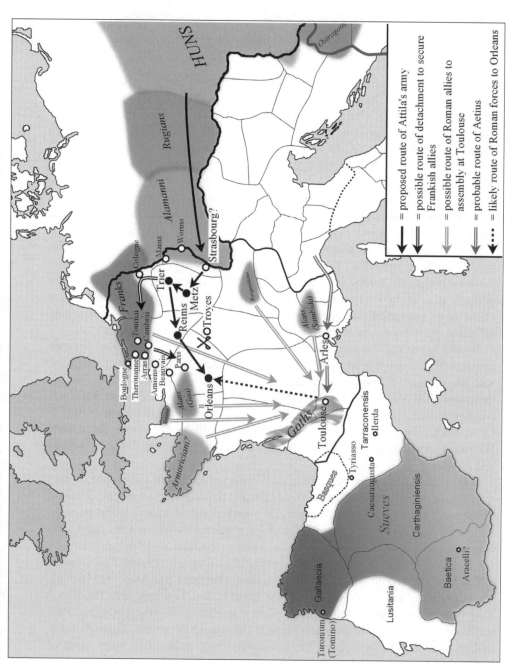

Map 14. *Atilla's Invasion of Gaul*

= proposed route of Attila's army

= possible route of detachment to secure Frankish allies

= possible route of Roman allies to assembly at Toulouse

= probable route of Aetius

= likely route of Roman forces to Orleans

also explain how the Huns were able to sack so many towns. The main force may have moved from Metz to Orleans with two or more contingents operating on its flanks. This would have been difficult for the Romans to oppose because there were many threats and Aegidius may not have been strong enough or mobile enough to do more than withdraw ahead of Attila.[46]

This is unlikely. Attila would not have known how the different groups within Gaul were going to respond to his invasion. Nor did he know of their likely deployment. The chances are that, apart from the 'Frankish' detachment, he would have wanted to keep his troops concentrated to meet any threat from the Romans. The majority of damage not caused by the main force is probably attributable to either the troops sent to the Franks or to the activities of the Hunnic scouts as they scoured the countryside for supplies and information.

In addition, thankfully for the future capital of France, Paris was bypassed. Although normally attributed to the intervention of (Saint) Genevieve, in reality at this period the city was small and insignificant. What is more likely is that the city itself was ignored by the Huns – who were intent upon rejoining Attila – rather than being saved by divine intervention: only the surrounding territories were scoured in the search for supplies.[47]

One factor emerges from the Huns' attacks on the cities of Gaul: all of the 'sacked' cities were taken quickly before the Huns pressed on to new targets. This can be contrasted to the siege of Aquileia in the following year.[48] It is obvious that the towns and cities of Gaul did not have large garrisons, and that the men who had once been expected to defend them had been removed and were now part of the Gallic field army. This may have been according to Aetius' orders: no doubt he wanted to concentrate as many troops as possible to face the Huns. Conversely, that he needed to withdraw garrisons from the cities implies that Aetius was fast running out of recruits.

The Roman Response

There is no evidence for the activities of the Gallic army when Attila invaded Gaul. Although it is possible that some of the troops were ordered to act as garrisons for the threatened cities, the fact that these cities were taken very quickly implies that this is unlikely. Instead, it is probable that the Gallic army was ordered by Aetius to retreat in front of the advancing Huns, heading for either Toulouse to join the Goths or to Arles to join with Aetius when he crossed the Alps into Gaul.

Whilst the Huns were ravaging the north east of Gaul Aetius crossed the Alps from Italy with 'a thin, meagre force of auxiliaries without legionaries' (*tenue et rarum sine milite ducens robur in auxiliis*).[49] It would appear that he had been anticipating a Hunnic attack on Italy after their diplomacy had neutralized the Goths.[50] Once across the Alps, Aetius would have been expecting to meet the Gallic field army before joining the Goths and advancing to face the Huns.[51] The remainder of his forces were left in Italy, partly to guard the emperor from attack across the Alps, but possibly also to deal with any unrest in Italy: at this moment of crisis the crops in Italy had failed and the region was threatened with the prospect of famine.[52]

Unexpectedly, he now found that the Goths were waiting on events in their own territory and refusing to join with him against the Huns. He travelled to Arles and pondered his next move.

In desperation, Aetius made a final attempt to win the support of Theoderic against Attila. Despite the gravity of the situation, and contrary to expectation, he did not travel to Toulouse in person. Instead, Aetius, intent on using the best man for the job, sent Avitus. Avitus was a favourite of king Theoderic I, having first visited the Gothic court in either 425 or 426. After this he had been involved with the education of Theoderic's son Theoderic. Avitus had also had a military career, serving under Aetius in the campaigns of 430, 431 and 436. Following his successful career under Aetius, Avitus was promoted to be *magister militum per Gallias* in 437, and had helped raise the siege of Narbo by Theoderic. In 439 he had become *praefectus praetorio Galliarum*, during which tenure in 439 he negotiated the peace treaty with Theoderic. After this, he had retired to his estates.[53] With his prolonged activity in Gaul and his personal contacts with Theoderic, Avitus was the ideal man for the task at hand.

After a brief but intense bout of diplomatic manoeuvring, Avitus succeeded where Aetius had failed. He convinced the Goths that their interests would be best served by an alliance with Rome against the Huns, although it must be acknowledged that the fact that the Huns had instantly begun to ravage Gaul probably had at least some influence on the negotiations.[54] Furthermore, it is possible that rumours concerning the possible attempts by Gaiseric to influence Attila to attack had some weight in Theoderic's judgement: Theoderic would never forgive Gaiseric for what had happened to his daughter.

Abandoning his policy of self-reliance, Theoderic prepared for war, taking with him his two eldest sons, Theoderic and Thorismund.[55] His other sons were left in Toulouse. In the meantime, it is likely that Aetius called for reinforcements from Italy prior to advancing further into Gaul, as it was now clear that the Goths would not attempt to invade Italy. It is probably at this point that news reached Pelagia that Aetius was in great difficulty in Gaul. She now began praying for his safety and the success of the war.[56]

It may also have been at about this time that news arrived in Orleans that the Huns had invaded. Anianus, the bishop of the city, realized that Orleans would be a target for the Huns, since it was the last major city denying them access to the Goths in Aquitania. Anianus therefore travelled to Arles to meet Aetius and request aid for the city.[57] With Aetius' assurances that he was now advancing to join with the Goths and face Attila in battle, Anianus left Arles and returned home.

Although Attila was roaming Gaul unhindered, there was one major factor that was to prove to be his undoing. Aetius had the advantage of interior lines of supply, as well as the logistical support of the Western Empire. Early in the year Aetius had ordered Ferreolus, the *praefectus praetorio Galliarum* (Praetorian Prefect of Gaul), to organize the collection of supplies and equipment at pre-designated locations.[58] With supplies assured, the allies (with the exception of the Goths) joined forces, almost certainly at Arles. This is the most logical place for them to collect, since the

Huns were threatening locations in the north or east of Gaul, and it is almost certain that Aetius had ordered that supplies be collected at the city ready for the upcoming campaign. The move would also allow the Goths and Burgundians to be supplied by the imperial government: as they gathered and began the march to confront the Huns, Ferreolus' logistical abilities kept the Romans and their allies supplied with the necessities needed for the campaign.[59]

In direct contrast, Attila's coalition was forced to rely on plundering the local areas for supplies. Although a viable means of support, they did not have large reserves of supplies and so could not afford to either be blockaded or to have their lines of retreat cut off. Any such occurrence would result in the army quickly being reduced to starvation and of having to surrender to Aetius. Attila could not afford to be surrounded.

The Siege of Orleans

Eventually, Anianus' fears came to be realized. Even as Aetius travelled to Toulouse to join with Theoderic, Attila's forces arrived at Orleans and began to lay siege to the city.[60] Deploying battering rams and doubtless other siege-engines, Attila's men began their assault.[61] There are two different accounts of the siege, and by combining them it is possible to gain a clearer view of the event. The city was under heavy siege and the Huns were preparing their forces when 'four days' storm of rain' hampered their attempts to take the city.[62] However, after the rain had cleared, on 14 June they launched an attack that breached the walls and they prepared to take the city.[63] At this moment, the armies of the West arrived.[64] With his forces dispersed and doubtless concerned about his supplies and line of retreat, Attila immediately called off the attack and retreated from the city.[65]

Although the story has undoubtedly been embellished by the ancient chroniclers, and the end of the siege dramatically embellished to enhance the story, it is clear that the siege of Orleans was a close-run thing. It is only thanks to the speedy arrival of the allies that the Huns were stopped from entering and plundering the city. Moreover, Hunnic success would have left the route into the Gothic heartlands open. With the Huns at large in his own territories it is uncertain whether Theoderic would have remained loyal to Aetius or changed sides and joined Attila in order to spare his people from attack. Whatever the case, the siege of Orleans proved to be the high point of Attila's attack on the West. Unwilling to chance being cut off from his way home and blockaded, Attila retreated towards the Rhine with the allies in hot pursuit.

The Pursuit

Having been forced to raise the siege, Attila retired in front of the Romans and their allies. The direction his forces took implies that he was aiming to retreat from Gaul, or at least outdistance the pursuit in order to reform and prepare a fresh plan for the campaign. Unfortunately for Attila, this was not to be. Five days after the end of the siege Attila arrived at Troyes. The city was unprotected and could be easily taken and sacked by the Huns. It is claimed in the *Acta Sanctorum* that it was only the saintly actions of Lupus, the Bishop of Troyes, who pleaded with Attila to spare the city that it was saved from destruction. However, although Lupus probably met Attila outside the city, it was not the bishop's pleas that saved Troyes. Attila would have been more intent on the actions of the pursuing allies than on Troyes' plight. Although Troyes was undefended and easy to attack, the allies were in close pursuit, and Attila could not spare the time for sacking the city, which would have resulted in large numbers of his men losing discipline and no doubt getting drunk. The loss of time in reordering his forces after the sack might have been a worry, but even more was the prospect of his disorganized and dispersed forces being attacked by the Romans and their allies as the Huns sacked the town.[66]

Yet there was one other factor. Troyes was on the River Seine. As Attila's forces gathered on the nearby plains known as the Campus Mauriacus and awaited the daybreak, Attila himself was no doubt aware that there was little chance of him escaping with his troops unhindered across the river.[67] Furthermore, he needed to safeguard the plunder he had already taken. Leaving the spoils behind would have demoralised his men and damaged his prestige. He could afford neither.

Crossing the river by bridge would take a very long time, and there was a good chance of his forces being attacked by the pursuing allies. Attila decided that this was the place where he was going to stand and face them. Possibly the allied force outnumbered the Huns slightly, as Attila, who had shown himself perfectly happy to take aggressive action in the past, acted very defensively as soon as the combined Roman–Visigoth army came close.

Chapter 14

The Battle of the Catalaunian Plains

In the afternoon of 19 June 451 Aetius' forces finally caught sight of the Hunnic army. For an unknown reason his Frankish allies clashed with the Gepids before darkness fell. In a brief but savage engagement neither side could gain the advantage and the onset of night brought the fighting to a halt. Although Jordanes claims that 15,000 men died in this encounter, it is certain that these figures are vastly inflated.[1] However, the clash was proof to Attila that on the following day Aetius would not balk from fighting a set-piece battle.

On the morning of 20 June 451 the two armies prepared for battle.[2] Its location is unknown, although many suggestions have been proposed. The difficulty lies in the vague terms used by the sources. Jordanes, Hydatius and the *Chronica Caesaraugusta* note that the battle was fought on the 'Catalaunian Plains'.[3] However, the Gallic Chronicler of 511 locates it on the Mauriac Plain, which is echoed by the *Consularia Italica*, Gregory of Tours and the *Lex Burgundionum*.[4] Theophanes writes simply that Attila was defeated at the River Lygis (Loire).[5] On the other hand, the claim by Malalas that Attila was defeated on the River Danube is certainly mistaken.[6] Nothing has yet been proved decisively.[7]

Soothsayers

According to Jordanes, Attila was in doubt as to the outcome of the battle, so decided to 'inquire into the future through soothsayers. These men examined the entrails and bones of cattle and foretold disaster for the Huns.'[8] However, they also announced that the leader of the enemy would fall, and Attila took this to mean that Aetius would be killed. Although it is likely that Attila sought the advice of soothsayers, as this was a common feature of non-Christian societies because forecasting the future could often influence the morale of the army, the detail given is of doubtful accuracy. Instead, its inclusion in the text may be Jordanes' method of emphasising Attila's barbarity, since he took part in a pagan ritual that was no longer relevant to the Christian Romans. Unfortunately, without corroborating evidence, it is unlikely whether the truth will ever be known.

The Deployment

The only detailed description we have of the battle is that given by Jordanes.[9] Although in most cases Jordanes needs to be used with care, the fact that this is the only description of the battle forces reliance on his account, yet the end result can be confusing.

For example, the traditional account followed by most modern historians has the Visigoths attacking a hill on the right flank and dominating the battle from there.[10] This is mirrored in other writers and has become accepted. Its origins are unclear, but the following extract may give a clue as to its source. It is a translation of Jordanes:

> Now this was the configuration of the field of battle. It rose [on one side] [sic] into a decided undulation which might be called a hill.
>
> *Hodgkin, 1892, Vol. 2, 127*

The fact that the phrase 'on one side' has been added leads to the conclusion that all of the modern interpretations of the battlefield are based upon this addendum, although the author does not state his source and so it cannot be traced further back. However, both the original Latin and the translation of Jordanes' account do not support this reconstruction, so is worth quoting:

> *Convenere partes, ut diximus, in campos Catalaunicos. Erat autem positio loci declivi tumore in editum collis excrescens. Quem uterque cupiens exercitus obtinere, quia loci oportunitas non parvum benificium confert, dextram partem Hunni cum suis, sinistram Romani et Vesegothae cum auxiliariis occuparunt, relictoque de cacumine eius iugo certamen ineunt.*
>
> *Jordanes, Getica, 39 (196–197)*

> The armies met, as we have said, in the Catalaunian Plains. The battle field was a plain rising by a sharp slope to a ridge, which both armies sought to gain; for advantage of position is a great help. The Huns with their forces seized the right side, the Romans, the Visigoths and their allies the left, and then began a struggle for the yet untaken crest.
>
> *Translation CC Mierow*

Therefore, discounting the earlier interpretations, the battlefield appears to have been a plain dominated by a ridge across its centre, not by a hill, although the ridge was higher in some places than others (see Plate 30). Having reached this conclusion, the rest of the passage from Jordanes is easier to interpret, although there are still one or two points that are uncertain.

As already noted, Jordanes claims that the Huns 'seized the right side, the Romans, the Visigoths and their allies the left'. If Jordanes' use of 'right' and 'left' refers to 'east' and 'west' respectively, which is a simple conclusion from both his phrasing and from the allies' line of advance, the Huns were on the east of the plain and the allies on the west, with the ridge crossing the battlefield near the centre. Yet this sentence gives us evidence that Jordanes' account needs to be treated with caution. The Huns are the enemy, and the appearance of other tribes as their allies – especially the Ostrogoths – is unwelcome to Jordanes. In direct contrast, Jordanes focuses on the Visigoths almost to the exclusion of the Romans. This demonstrates Jordanes' bias: the work is a history of the Goths, both branches, and so the

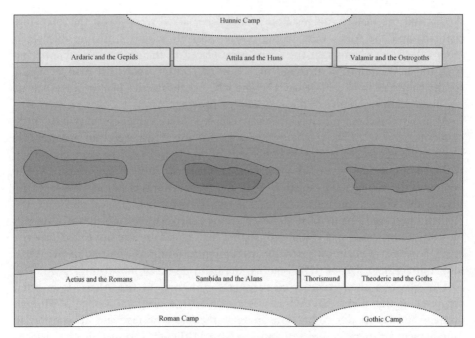

Hunnic Camp

| Ardaric and the Gepids | Attila and the Huns | Valamir and the Ostrogoths |

| Aetius and the Romans | Sambida and the Alans | Thorismund | Theoderic and the Goths |

Roman Camp

Gothic Camp

Catalaunian Plain 1 Deployment

appearance of the Ostrogoths on the side of Attila is downplayed and that of the Visigoths overplayed in order to boost their status. This needs to be borne in mind throughout the analysis of the battle.

Attila arrayed his forces with himself and his Huns in the centre. The Ostrogoths, and possibly some of the minor allies, were placed on Attila's left wing specifically to face the Visigoths, as Attila had faith in their king Valamir and his brothers Thiudimer and Vidimer. The Gepids, and possibly some other allied troops, appear to have been on the right wing under the Gepid king Ardaric.

The tactics of Attila appear to have been remarkably simple and based on the assumption that Aetius would adopt the traditional Roman deployment of cavalry on the flanks and infantry in the centre. In this scenario, Attila's whole army was to advance to the top of the hill, and then the two flanks, under his most trusted subordinates, would charge at the enemy cavalry whilst the Huns used their traditional tactics to pin the enemy infantry in the centre and cause as much confusion as possible with a hail of missiles. At the point where one or both flanks of the alliance broke, the Huns would then be in a position to put pressure on the remaining enemy, and possibly be able to follow the retreating Romans and so turn the flanks of the centre. The enemy would then collapse, leaving the Huns to pursue, a tactic at which they excelled.

Unfortunately for Attila, Aetius was not a typical Roman general. The western allies deployed with the Visigoths taking the right wing, with Theoderic in charge of the extreme right and Thorismund in charge of the troops next to the centre.

Aetius and the majority of his Roman and other allied troops took the left wing. Sambida and the Alans were in the centre, possibly with a stiffening of Roman troops. Jordanes claims that the Alans were placed in the centre, 'thus contriving with military caution to surround by a host of faithful troops the man in whose loyalty they had little confidence. For one who has difficulties placed in the way of his flight readily submits to the necessity of fighting.'[11]

Although this interpretation is usually accepted at face value, in reality it has little to recommend it.[12] The major difficulty is that the Alans were not surrounded. Once battle began, the troops on either side of the Alans would be more concerned with the opposition, as would any troops stationed to support the Alans. On the contrary, the deployment suggests that Aetius was unworried, as otherwise by placing the Alans in the centre Aetius was taking a great risk. Should they rout, the Roman lines would be divided and each sector easily dealt with piecemeal. As will be seen, Aetius' trust was vindicated. Rather than a realistic attempt to evaluate the truth, Jordanes was almost certainly attempting to minimize the role of the Alans and contrast it to that of the Visigoths, the main object of his writing.

The question then remains concerning Aetius' use of the Alans. It is often forgotten at this point that Aetius was a man with a deep knowledge of Hunnic strategy and tactics due to his time amongst them as a hostage and his continuing employment of them as *foederati* and *bucellarii*. Although speculation, the chances are that he foresaw that the Huns would deploy using a standard formation, especially since they were being assisted by large numbers of subject troops and this would help to avoid confusion. If this is the case, then Aetius must have predicted the deployment and placed the Alans in the centre for a purpose.

It is likely that Aetius was using his knowledge of the Huns against them. Knowing that they would deploy their own forces, comprised mainly of horse archers, in the centre, Aetius deployed the Alans – whose troops used roughly the same tactics – to face them. Rather than being faced by a solid block of relatively immobile infantry in the centre, Attila found himself faced by the mobile and highly skilled Alans. Furthermore, these men had been fighting alongside the Romans for many years and knew how to fight effectively as their allies. Unable to use the Huns' standard hit-and-run tactics in the centre, Aetius will have hoped that Attila would be confused about which course to take. This would give him time to destroy Attila's flanks.

With this in mind, Aetius' deployment makes complete sense. He hoped that the Alans would be able to at least hold the Huns in the centre, if not beat them to the crest of the hill. However, the two strongest divisions were on the flanks, and there can be little doubt that he was intending for these troops to deliver the fatal blow to the Huns and their allies.

There is one other, highly debatable, possibility to be borne in mind. Aetius, like all educated Romans of his day, would have been taught by use of the classics. Amongst these were the works of Polybius and Livy. It is not impossible that Aetius, aware of the Huns' probable deployment, had decided to emulate two of the great generals of the past: Hannibal, one of the great enemies of Rome, and Scipio

Africanus, Hannibal's opponent. In 216 BC at the Battle of Cannae Hannibal had turned the flanks of the Roman army and surrounded them.[13] At the Battle of Ilipa in 206 BC Scipio Africanus had outmanoeuvred a Carthaginian army before attacking its flanks and routing its centre.[14] By destroying Attila's flanks and surrounding his centre, the Visigoths on the right and the Romans on the left could possibly advance to the vicinity of the Hunnic camp, so copying the earlier strategies. Additionally, the tactic would trap the Huns and so negate their greatest advantage: their mobility. This is speculation of the highest order, but it is often forgotten that the classic works that still survive were copied because they were popular and people read them. This is as true of late antiquity as it is today. Although the concept that the Romans of the late empire would utilize the tactics of a bygone era remains conjecture, and is not usually considered by modern historians, it must remain a possibility.

With a ridge between them, both Aetius and Attila would have known the tactical advantage of possession of the crest. With this in mind, it is surprising that the battle began 'about the ninth hour of the day' (early to mid afternoon). The late start is allegedly due to the fact that Attila was scared by the omens and decided to wait: if the battle should prove to be a disaster, in this way darkness would cover the retreat of the Huns and allow many of them to escape.[15]

This does not, however, explain why Aetius did not make the first move. The likelihood is that both generals realized that a pre-emptive attempt to attack without a proper deployment could lead to disaster. Both sides had troops capable of making fast attacks on isolated and unsupported formations. Therefore, a combined assault would be necessary to win the battle.

Furthermore, any aggressive move by small groups could easily lead to confusion amongst their own armies. Both armies were comprised of large numbers of troops with little experience of working together and without a common language. Deployment would take a long time. In addition, there were troops on opposite sides who spoke the same language, so care and accuracy of deployment would avoid the risk of troops attacking their own allies. As a result, both generals chose to slowly deploy their troops ready for battle. The deployment was crucial: thanks to language difficulties and the lack of joint training, both sides would find changes difficult to make.

The Battle[16]

The armies now set in motion, both attempting to seize the crest and so dominate the battlefield. Again, Jordanes' account is open to debate: 'The Huns with their forces seized the right side, the Romans, the Visigoths and their allies the left, and then began a struggle for the yet untaken crest.'[17] All depends upon the interpretation of right and left. In the majority of modern accounts the Huns seize the hill to their right, opposing Aetius himself, while the Visigoths beat the Ostrogoths to the crest and so dominate the battlefield on their flank. Yet this analysis is almost certainly mistaken. The real course of events can be seen by arranging Jordanes' account into a chronological course of events.

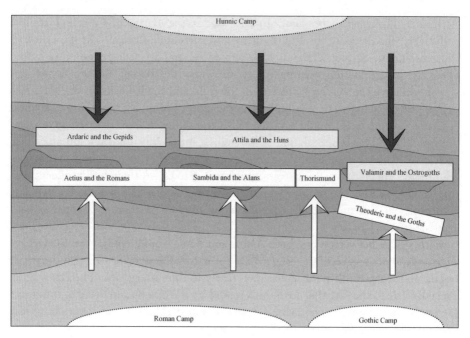

Catalaunian Plain 2 Stage 1

As already stated:

> The Huns with their forces seized the right side, the Romans, the Visigoths and their allies the left, and then began a struggle for the yet untaken crest.
>
> *Jord. Get. 38 (197)*

This is followed by a description of the deployment of the Romans and their allies, following which:

> So then the struggle began for the advantage of position we have mentioned. Attila sent his men to take the summit of the mountain, but was outstripped by Thorismud and Aetius, who in their effort to gain the top of the hill reached higher ground and through this advantage of position easily routed the Huns as they came up.
>
> *Jord. Get. 38 (201)*

What has happened is clear – Jordanes is describing the battle from the Roman lines. Attila's forces had occupied the crest on the right of the Romans, facing the Visigoths. At least part of Attila's plan to defeat the Romans' wings, as hypothesized above, looked to be succeeding. In contrast, Aetius had seized the left side of the crest facing the Gepids, who were no doubt weakened by their skirmish of the night before. In a joint operation, Aetius' troops – including the Alans – had then taken the centre of the ridge, helped by the Visigothic forces under Thorismund.

Attempting to dislodge the allies from this strong position, the Huns were easily beaten back as they climbed the slope.

The Huns now became demoralized by their failure and Attila was forced to make a speech:

> Now when Attila saw his army was thrown into confusion by this event, he thought it best to encourage them by an extemporaneous address ...

Jord. Get. 39 (202)

The text of the speech need not be analyzed in detail, since it is extremely unlikely that Jordanes would have been able to write, word for word, a speech made by Attila. In fact, it is unlikely that Attila made any speech at all, since in the din and confusion of the battle his words would have been lost to all but a few.[18] The wording is a rhetorical piece invented by Jordanes, but one small part of the speech is useful, as he gives clues as to the nature of the battlefield:

> They seek the heights, they seize the hills and, repenting too late, clamour for protection against battle in the open fields.

Jord. Get. 39 (204)

The use of the plurals 'heights' and 'hills' reinforces the concept suggested earlier that there was not just a single hill on the right hand side of the Romans' deployment area, but rather a long crest, with some parts being higher than others, especially in the centre.

Encouraged, the Huns and their allies renewed their assault on the crest:

> And although the situation was itself fearful, yet the presence of their king dispelled anxiety and hesitation. Hand to hand they clashed in battle, and the fight grew fierce, confused, monstrous, unrelenting – a fight whose like no ancient time has ever recorded. There such deeds were done that a brave man who missed this marvellous spectacle could not hope to see anything so wonderful all his life long.

Jord. Get. 40 (207)

However, the Visigoths on the extreme right of the Roman line appear to have been unable to take the ridge in front of them. At this point there was a potential disaster for the Roman allies:

> Here King Theoderic, while riding by to encourage his army, was thrown from his horse and trampled under foot by his own men, thus ending his days at a ripe old age. But others say he was slain by the spear of Andag of the host of the Ostrogoths, who were then under the sway of Attila. This was what the soothsayers had told to Attila in prophecy, though he understood it of Aetius.

Jord. Get. 40 (209)

By way of contrast, both Malalas and the *Chronicon Paschale* claim that Theoderic was killed by an arrow.[19] Since this is very late evidence it is probably less likely than the accounts given by Jordanes: however, there remains the remote possibility that it is accurate.

It is interesting to note that Jordanes, writing the history of the Goths, does not mention the Ostrogoths during the course of the battle anywhere but at this point. The reason is almost certainly that he wanted to minimize the fact that the Ostrogoths fought against the Romans alongside Attila, later reviled as the 'Scourge of God'. However, Jordanes had access to the descendents of Andag, and so may have recorded a family tradition that may in fact have contained the true course of events. Theoderic had been killed by Andag as he led his men uphill against the Ostrogoths. Yet the news did not immediately spread.

Unaware of his father's death and as darkness was beginning to descend, Thorismund saw from the top of the ridge that the Huns to his front were beginning to lose heart and that they were trapped between their wings and their camp. He also located Attila's position in the battle. Thorismund seized the opportunity and led his forces in a downhill charge at the Huns opposing them, trying to reach Attila. Unable to use their traditional hit-and-run tactics, the Huns disintegrated and began to rout, in the process exposing Attila to danger:

> Then the Visigoths, separating from the Alans, fell upon the horde of the
> Huns and nearly slew Attila. But he prudently took flight and straightway

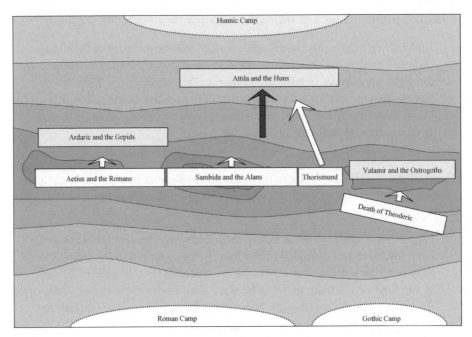

Catalaunian Plain 3 Stage 2

shut himself and his companions within the barriers of the camp, which he had fortified with wagons. A frail defence indeed; yet there they sought refuge for their lives, whom but a little while before no walls of earth could withstand.

Jord. Get. 40 (210)

When Attila fled the field his army, including his allies, also seem to have lost heart. As the sun set what was left of the Huns and their allies attempted to retire to their camp and await the dawn. Others wandered lost in the darkness. Many of these men were killed, and no doubt large numbers of them forgot their alliance to Attila and fled the field and attempted to make their way back to their homes – especially the Franks. Yet Attila's decision to postpone the battle now paid dividends. In the darkness, confusion quickly spread:

> But Thorismud, the son of King Theoderic, who with Aetius had seized the hill and repulsed the enemy from the higher ground, came unwittingly to the wagons of the enemy in the darkness of night, thinking he had reached his own lines. As he was fighting bravely, someone wounded him in the head and dragged him from his horse. Then he was rescued by the watchful care of his followers and withdrew from the fierce conflict. Aetius also became separated from his men in the confusion of night and wandered about in the midst of the enemy. Fearing disaster had happened, he went about in search of the Goths. At last he reached the

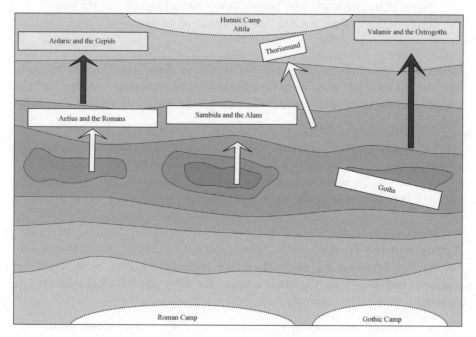

Catalaunian Plain 4 Stage 3

camp of his allies and passed the remainder of the night in the protection
of their shields.

Jord. Get. 40 (211–212)

With a high level of confusion, and expecting the worst, the allies awaited the dawn,
with Thorismund receiving treatment for his head wound. Much to their surprise:

> At dawn on the following day, when the Romans saw the fields were piled
> high with bodies and that the Huns did not venture forth, they thought
> the victory was theirs, but knew that Attila would not flee from the battle
> unless overwhelmed by a great disaster. Yet he did nothing cowardly, like
> one that is overcome, but with clash of arms sounded the trumpets and
> threatened an attack. He was like a lion pierced by hunting spears, who
> paces to and fro before the mouth of his den and dares not spring, but
> ceases not to terrify the neighbourhood by his roaring. Even so this
> warlike king at bay terrified his conquerors. (213) Therefore the Goths
> and Romans assembled and considered what to do with the vanquished
> Attila. They determined to wear him out by a siege, because he had no
> supply of provisions and was hindered from approaching by a shower of
> arrows from the bowmen placed within the confines of the Roman camp.
> But it was said that the king remained supremely brave even in this
> extremity and had heaped up a funeral pyre of horse trappings, so that if
> the enemy should attack him, he was determined to cast himself into the
> flames, that none might have the joy of wounding him and that the lord of
> so many races might not fall into the hands of his foes.

Jord. Get. 40 (212–213)

Determined to capture or kill Attila, the victorious allies now deployed troops to
contain the Huns, but at the same time began the task of dealing with the dead and
wounded on the battlefield. Foremost in their minds was the absence of Theoderic:

> Now during these delays in the siege, the Visigoths sought their king and
> the king's sons their father, wondering at his absence when success had
> been attained. When, after a long search, they found him where the dead
> lay thickest, as happens with brave men, they honoured him with songs
> and bore him away in the sight of the enemy.

Jord. Get. 40 (214)

Aetius and the Goths

On the day following the battle the Huns remained in their camp. Once the
Visigoths had recovered Theoderic's body, the allies needed to decide what to
do next:

> Thorismund was eager to take vengeance for his father's death on the
> remaining Huns, being moved to this both by the pain of bereavement and

the impulse of that valour for which he was noted. Yet he consulted with the Patrician Aetius (for he was an older man and of more mature wisdom) with regard to what he ought to do next. But Aetius feared that if the Huns were totally destroyed by the Goths, the Roman Empire would be overwhelmed, and urgently advised him to return to his own dominions to take up the rule which his father had left. Otherwise his brothers might seize their father's possessions and obtain the power over the Visigoths. In this case Thorismund would have to fight fiercely and, what is worse, disastrously with his own countrymen. Thorismud accepted the advice without perceiving its double meaning, but followed it with an eye toward his own advantage. So he left the Huns and returned to Gaul. Thus while human frailty rushes into suspicion, it often loses an opportunity of doing great things.

Jord. Get. 41 (215–217)

This passage is echoed by Gregory of Tours, who similarly claims that Aetius told Thorismund that he should return home as otherwise he 'would be cheated out of his father's kingdom'. Interestingly, Gregory also notes that Aetius gave the same advice to his foster-son, the young son of the deceased Frankish king, who had also fought at the battle.[20] Gregory then goes on to say that the reason for the advice was to enable Aetius to collect the booty from the battlefield before returning to Italy.[21]

Modern historians have tended to question Aetius' motives in allowing the Huns to escape. However, this overlooks the military realities of the time. The Franks had been, in effect, fighting a civil war at the battle. It was no doubt possible for the victor, Aetius' foster-son, to delay and help in the assault on Attila's camp. Yet the outcome was still in doubt. The Huns were clearly prepared to defend themselves to the last and in their defence there was a distinct possibility that the Frankish leader would be killed, as had already happened to Theoderic. This would lose Aetius a valuable ally.

The same can be said of Thorismund. Thorismund had five brothers: (another) Theoderic, Euric, Frederic, Retemer and Himnerith.[22] Aetius' chief negotiator with the Goths, Avitus, would have told him that Thorismund was probably the weakest and the most inclined to work alongside the Romans rather than against them. Furthermore, Aetius and Thorismund had just fought together and defeated one of the greatest enemies of the Romans, Attila. Relying on his new-forged friendship and support, Aetius chose to advise the new king to return home and ensure that his brothers did not claim the throne in his absence. Four of them had remained in Toulouse and so were in a position to depose him quickly once news of their father's death arrived, unless he took affirmative action.

Aetius no doubt concluded that the defeat had seriously weakened Attila's position. The Huns relied on fear and their reputation as invincible warriors to cow their subjects into submission. The defeat to Aetius was a major blow to Attila's prestige. It was reasonable to expect that any subsequent invasion of Gaul by Attila would be met by a renewed alliance of the Romans, Visigoths and Franks.

Furthermore, Attila's losses meant that his own army would be weaker, especially as many of his allies had doubtless retired in the night and were now separated from the Huns, and even possibly on their way home. Aetius might also have expected that at least some of Attila's subjects would be unwilling to support a second invasion of Gaul.

A further factor in the equation is that Attila was the nephew of Aetius' friends Rua and Ochtar. Although they were now dead, Aetius may have been hoping that the defeat would spur Attila into accepting a similar role as 'friend' of Aetius, rather than as an enemy, and so allow Rome and the Huns to resume their former partnership. To defeat heavily Attila and the Huns now could result in Attila being unwilling to allow Huns under his control to serve the Romans as *foederati* or *bucellarii* in the future. Although this would have been a distant hope, Aetius may have still harboured it. Furthermore, his own armies had suffered heavy losses, and the West's desperation for manpower resulted in an unwillingness to take risks and heavy losses when the same result – the retreat of Attila – could be obtained by peaceful means.

On the other hand, all of this would be lost if either Attila was able to repulse an attack on his camp or if either or both of Aetius' allies were to die in the attempt: after all, Theodoric had already died and Thorismund had only just avoided a similar fate. Assessing his options in the cold light of day, Aetius came to the conclusion that keeping his new-found allies alive and well in Gaul would help most by ensuring continuing peace in the area, as well as deterring Attila from further attacks by the threat of a renewal of the alliance. After his deliberations, Aetius chose to disband the army and send them all home. The Visigoths under their new king returned to Toulouse, where 'although the throng of his brothers and brave companions were still rejoicing over the victory he yet began to rule so mildly that no one strove with him for the succession to the kingdom'.[23] In a like manner, the Franks and the other allies journeyed north to their own homelands.

When the allies withdrew and dispersed, Attila was at first fearful of a trick and thought that they would attack as he left his camp. As a result, he waited in his camp for a long time.[24] When he was certain that he was safe, he gathered the remnants of his forces and began the long march home. His thoughts would have been busy with plans both to negate the negative political ramifications of his loss and to have his revenge on Aetius, the only man who had ever defeated him in battle.

Aftermath

The Romans accepted that they had only won the battle with the help of the Goths, a fact acknowledged by the Roman chroniclers.[25] The value of the Gothic alliance is also stressed by Sidonius in his poem in praise of Avitus, the man who made the alliance possible, although this may also have been an attempt by Sidonius to ingratiate himself with his new overlords, the Goths.[26]

The writings of the chroniclers and Sidonius clearly emphasize that the battle was seen as important shortly after it had occurred, but it is possible that at the time the battle was seen as just yet another barbarian raid. For example, Prosper, who was hostile to Aetius, ignores the battle, but even he could not have overlooked it if it had been instantly recognized as one of the most important events of the fifth century.[27]

Yet in retrospect many historians have seen this battle as one of the pivotal incidents that shaped modern Europe. It has been suggested that had Attila won a new, non-Christian empire would have come into existence between the Atlantic and the Black Sea.[28] Yet early in the twentieth century doubts began to be raised about this concept. The main objection must remain that Attila's empire only existed while he was alive. Upon his death it fragmented. Even had he conquered Gaul, upon his death his sons would still have been unable to maintain the empire and it would have quickly fallen apart.[29] Gaul might have been damaged and the specific history of France changed, but Christianity would have been maintained and the impact of the Huns been only fleeting.

Gaul

When Attila withdrew from Gaul he left behind a group of provinces that had been devastated by his invasion. The inhabitants were left in a perilous condition, but, in spite of expectations, in this difficult time the officials appear to have rallied to the support of the provincials, rather than attempting to take advantage of the situation. Ferreolus, the *praefectus praetorio Galliarum*, immediately petitioned the emperor for tax remissions, whilst Avitus also supplied aid to the inhabitants.[30] The shock of the attack would take time to pass. At around the same time as the officials arrived from Ferreolus asking for tax remissions in Gaul, Valentinian was continuing to help those Africans who were still suffering from their extended exile.[31]

Furthermore, it is possible that the invasion of Gaul, despite disrupting production and damaging property, may not have been as harmful as usually accepted. Although towns were originally the centre of productive and economic forces, these functions had gradually passed to more rural areas. Moreover, in time of war it has been suggested that the population of the towns, knowing that they were likely to be the focus of an attack, would leave and take refuge in the surrounding countryside.[32] As a result, although the capture of a town was obviously a dreadful occurrence, a large proportion of the population would have survived unharmed, and the main locations for economic re-growth may have been at least relatively untouched. This may help to explain the relatively fast rebirth of towns that in theory should have been devastated and beyond recovery if the sources are followed literally.

Chapter 15

Attila's Invasion of Italy

In late summer or early autumn Attila returned home to find that contrary to expectations the East had been fighting 'vigorously against the Huns in the Balkans'.[1] However, his grievances against the East were small compared with his need to restore his aura of invincibility. Over the winter months between 451 and 452 Attila spent his time consolidating his position at home and preparing for a return to the fray. He will have been heartened by the news that the western allies had gone their separate ways and may have known that there was – or appears to have been – little contact between the victors. He began to look at the options for the new year.

In Gaul, Thorismund began the process of cementing his rule. However, in one respect at least he appears to have been dissatisfied. His father had been killed fighting as an ally of the Romans and he himself had been close to death. Yet there is no record of any agreements between Aetius and Thorismund, either extending Thorismund's dominions in Gaul or rewarding him with an imperial position. It is likely, though improbable, that Thorismund was offended by the apparent lack of gratitude of the emperor. Like Attila, he began to make his plans for the new year, his aim being to establish himself as his father's heir despite having several brothers as rivals. He may also have started to look at ways to put pressure on Aetius for the rewards he felt he deserved. In the north, the new Frankish king settled down to rule, and the survivors of the contingent from Armorica no doubt returned home confident that their part in the victory would be acknowledged by the empire.

Back in Italy it was finally accepted that most of the landowners dispossessed by the Vandals' conquest of Africa were not going to be allowed by Gaiseric to return and regain all of their lands. As a result, Valentinian arranged for them to be leased lands in Sitifensis and Caesariensis (see Map 12) as compensation, with full inheritance rights.[2]

Whilst these measures were being implemented Aetius would have been focusing on the recruitment and training of recruits to replace the losses in the battle. This may not have been as difficult as in previous years: the Battle of the Catalaunian Plains was the first recorded major defeat of the Huns and it is certain that Aetius' reputation as a general and a leader of men now reached new heights. The glory of winning such an unexpected victory, coupled with the large amount of booty taken from the field of battle, probably resulted in there being a small increase in the number of volunteers for the army. With the Goths and the Franks as allies and with Attila running home defeated, Aetius will have felt a certain sense of security when looking forward to the new year. He may even have begun making plans for limited reconquests of 'lost' areas, hoping in this way to begin the process of restoring the empire's financial ability to survive.

452

Militarily, all seemed well as the campaign season of 452 began. There was no sign of a Hunnic backlash against the defeat and affairs in Gaul appeared to have settled. The Vandals in Africa remained peaceful and were adhering to the treaty of 442. Overall, Aetius will have been pleased with his position. However, domestically there remained the problem of famine in Italy. No doubt Aetius used alternative resources for grain, such as Gaul, Sicily and the merchants of the East, much as he had done following the fall of Africa in 439, which may have helped to alleviate the problem. However it is unlikely that these temporary measures were a solution, especially since conditions in Gaul and Sicily may not have been ideal either. His priority at the time was the provisioning of Rome, since if the inhabitants of Rome rebelled due to famine he and Valentinian would be put under extreme pressure by the population.[3]

The Invasion of Italy

Unfortunately for Aetius, Attila was determined to avenge his defeat and regain his aura of invincibility.[4] The fact that he had been defeated could easily lead to internal unrest in the Hunnic empire. Furthermore, there was also the possibility that the victorious Aetius in the West and the new regime of Marcian in the East would co-operate militarily to oppose him. Yet in one respect, Attila had a great advantage: he realized that the alliance between Aetius and Thorismund had been forged only thanks to his own invasion of Gaul. Intelligence from the West, possibly from Franks unhappy with their new young king, may have informed Attila of how close the Goths had been to remaining neutral during his invasion of Gaul. Attila correctly assumed that if he attacked Italy the Goths would not join in the defence and so he would only have to face the forces of Aetius.[5] Yet it took Attila a long time to gather his troops together ready for another invasion of the West. This was doubtless in part due to the losses he had suffered in Gaul, a hypothesis reinforced by the fact that, for this second invasion, he did not leave troops behind to pin down the forces of the East.[6]

In the early summer of 452 Attila invaded Italy.[7] His course took him through Illyricum and across the Julian Alps into the north-east corner.[8] In the previous year Aetius had been expecting Attila to invade Italy, yet Prosper claims that this invasion was a 'complete surprise'.[9] This has usually been accepted, but analysis has disputed the claim.[10] The main reason why the claim has been accepted is the statement that Aetius 'failed to make use of the barriers of the Alps'.[11] In some ways this makes sense militarily – a determined defence of the passes at the mountains would have caused Attila serious losses and may have caused him to turn back. Yet the impression is actually false. Although applicable to high mountain ranges, the theory does not apply to the Julian Alps, which are lower and easier to traverse than their northern counterparts.[12] In the past, attempts to defend these passes had ended in

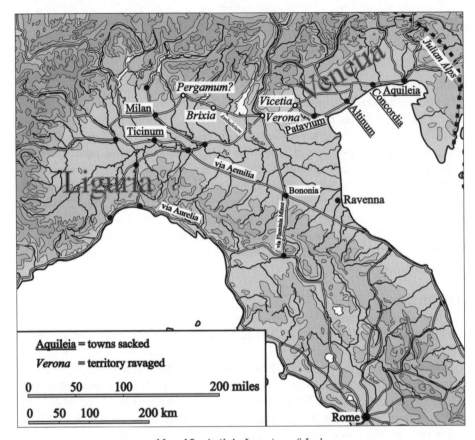

Map 15. Attila's Invasion of Italy

defeat, especially as the defences that were in place, the *Claustra Alpium Juliarum* (Fortifications of the Julian Alps), were lightly held and mainly intended to halt barbarian raids that had penetrated into Illyricum from the east.[13] Knowing that in the height of summer the mounted and fast-moving Huns would easily outflank his positions, Aetius probably decided not to attempt a forward defence, but rather to retreat and call on reinforcements from the west. In the meantime he probably reinforced the garrison of Aquileia, which would be the first city reached by the Huns.

Towards the end of June Attila did indeed reach Aquileia. Over fifty years earlier, in 401, the Gothic leader Alaric had invaded Italy and, having no knowledge of siege warfare and believing that Aquileia was too strong to attack, had simply bypassed the city.[14] In contrast, Attila had the ability to capture cities and he appears to have thought it unwise to bypass Aquileia, possibly since the garrison would be in a position to threaten his lines of communication, his rear and to block his return home. In contrast, Alaric had had no desire to return to Illyricum. Attila immediately began a siege using a variety of siege engines.[15] Attila will have hoped for a quick siege, much as had happened to many cities in Gaul the previous year.[16] If so, he was to be disappointed: 'He pressed the siege there long and hard ... from within the bravest of Roman soldiers withstood him.'[17] Attila's need for a very fast campaign was thwarted by the defenders of Aquileia. Instead, in the middle of a famine in Italy he found himself besieging the city for three months.[18] Eventually, his army began to lose heart and think of home, but Attila noticed that the storks that nested in the city were carrying their young away.[19] Seeing this as an omen, he ordered his troops to renew the assault, and either in late August or early September the city fell to the Huns. In anger at its resistance, Attila and his troops savagely plundered it, although Jordanes' claims that no trace of the city was left are false.[20]

Despite the fact that Attila was in the north east of Italy, Aetius continued to address the problems of famine, issuing an edict to ensure the arrival of animals in Rome to feed the population.[21] However once the scale of Attila's invasion became known, Prosper claims that Aetius 'believed his only hope lay in a full retreat from Italy', but that a 'sense of shame' stopped this proposal.[22] Prosper does not state where Aetius would have retreated to, and, indeed, there were very few places left in the West where the Roman emperor would be safe. The only possibility is that Aetius was intending to take Valentinian to Constantinople and there to seek the support of the Eastern Emperor Marcian to provide an expedition to retake Italy.

Although Prosper's claim is usually dismissed or ignored, given later events, it is clear that Aetius was in contact with Marcian, and the episode would make sense if Aetius was convinced that he would be unable to face Attila in battle without external help. Consequently, it is possible to suggest that Aetius did in fact send messengers to Marcian asking for help and mooting the possibility of exile for himself and Valentinian should Attila overrun Italy. Fortunately for Aetius, Marcian agreed to send help as soon as he could.[23] Even more fortunately, the defenders of Aquileia gave Aetius the breathing space he needed to organize his forces.

Whilst Aetius was negotiating with the East, which given the distances involved probably took up to at least two months, Attila successfully stormed Aquileia and then led his forces deeper into Italy. Advancing further into Venetia and Liguria, he besieged and sacked Mediolanum (Milan) and Ticinum (Pavia).[24] According to Paul the Deacon, at the same time – the actual chronology is unknown – Attila also sacked Concordia, Altinum (Altino) and Patavium (Padua). Paul goes on to say that the Huns in addition attacked Vicetia (Vicenza), Verona, Brixia (Brescia) and Pergamum (Bergamo?).[25] It is unclear whether these cities were actually sacked, since Paul's phrasing is somewhat ambivalent. However, it is possible to conclude from the wording that Concordia, Altinum and Patavium were sacked, and that the territories of Vicetia, Verona, Brixia and Pergamum were ravaged, although the cities themselves remained untouched.

In Milan it is claimed by Priscus that Attila saw a painting of the Roman emperors on golden thrones with 'Scythians lying dead before their feet', over which he ordered a painter to paint 'Attila upon a throne and the Roman emperors heaving sacks upon their shoulders and pouring out gold before his feet'.[26] Although the origin of the story is unknown, it is possibly true, as it would accord with what we assume of the temperament of Attila from the sources.

It is unknown at this time what Aetius was doing or where he had positioned the Roman forces. As he was awaiting reinforcements from the East, it is possible that he was in one of the ports on the eastern coast of Italy. If this is the case, it was almost certainly Ravenna.

The other options were that Aetius, recognizing that he could not defend the valley of the River Po against the mobile Huns, resolved to defend Rome, especially as the ongoing famine would have made supplying a large army difficult. He may also have hoped that the Huns would be demoralized by a long siege of Aquileia and withdraw.[27] As a final note, it was traditional Roman tactics to attack large enemy forces within the empire when the barbarians were on the way home laden with loot and so more likely to fight.

If any of these scenarios are applicable, then it is possible that Aetius positioned his forces in Bononia (Bologna). This not only covered the major routes to the south of Italy – it also covered the crossing of the Apennines, via the *Via Flaminia Minor* leading directly to Rome. If Attila decided to attack Ravenna, Aetius would also be in a position to fall on his unprotected rear. In this way, Aetius could ensure that Attila's activities were confined to the north of Italy. Furthermore, if the Huns began to retreat, he was in a good position to harass them as they left Italy.

However, Attila and his men were not having everything their own way: 'The Huns ... were victims of divine punishment, being visited with heaven-sent disasters: famine and some kind of disease.'[28] Attila had made the mistake of invading Italy when the region was suffering from a failure of the harvest. Outside the walls of Aquileia his men had been suffering the effects of the siege, mainly hunger due to a shortage of provisions and probable a disease, such as dysentery, which affected armies that were stationary for too long a time.[29] Attila's strategy had no doubt been aimed at a very quick campaign, as had happened in Gaul: he had not organized the 'substantial logistic support' needed to supply the army during what, in the event, turned out to be a series of sieges.[30]

Passing into the valley of the River Po did not help in any significant way. Although provisions for the horses would have been easier to secure, with the inhabitants having little food of their own the Huns were unable to secure provisions without sacking cities and looting the imperial granaries. After they had penetrated as far as Ticinum, Attila faced a dilemma. At this point the lack of supplies was probably being very keenly felt. The only options were to either return home or attempt to cross the northern Apennines and so march down the *Via Aurelia* to Rome. According to Priscus, Attila's followers pointed to the fate of Alaric after he had sacked the 'Eternal City' in 410, fearing that Attila, like Alaric, would die if he sacked Rome.[31] Although Attila was probably superstitious, if he had wanted to he could easily have ignored this advice. However, things were not that simple. The Huns were suffering from hunger and sickness. Furthermore, it is probably at around this time when news arrived that Marcian had sent forces out of Illyricum to attack the practically defenceless homes of the Huns.[32]

Aetius and Aetius

At about the same time Aetius himself had received reinforcements from the East. Unfortunately, there is confusion around the source of this information. Hydatius writes that:

> The Huns ... were victims of divine punishment, being visited with heaven-sent disasters: famine and some kind of disease. In addition, they were slaughtered by auxiliaries sent by the emperor Marcian and led by Aetius, and at the same time they were crushed in their settlements by both heaven-sent disasters and the army of Marcian.

Hyd. s.a. 452–453

The wording of this statement could have been clearer. What makes it harder to interpret is the fact that by 452 there was a second Flavius Aetius, this time a general in the East. Some historians have conflated the two Aetiuses, seeing them as a single individual.[33] However, it is clear that there were two men: the Eastern Aetius was Praetorian Prefect of the east in 425 when the Western Aetius was in Gaul.[34] Furthermore, the Eastern Aetius was present at the sixth session of the Council of Chalcedon on 25 October 451 when the Western Aetius was still dealing with the fallout of Attila's invasion of Gaul.[35] The Eastern Aetius was clearly the East's nominee for Consul in 454, possibly as a reward for his campaigns against the Huns in the previous two years. Finally, there are two inscriptions referring to Aetius in Syria, one dating to after the death of the Western Aetius.[36]

The reason for the confusion, other than the identical name of the two generals, is Hydatius' account. Hydatius lived in Spain and his information coming from the East would have been late and confusing to him. He knew that Aetius, the western *patricius*, had received reinforcements from the East. He was also told that Aetius had led troops into the Hunnic homelands. Due to the mixed-up nature of the tale, and uncertain that the two men were separate individuals, it is likely that Hydatius' wording was ambiguous in order to cover his own confusion.

As a result of these deliberations, it is possible to propose that Marcian sent two armies out of the East. The first was a smaller force that was sent to reinforce Aetius in Italy. With these Aetius put pressure on the Huns as they retired across northern Italy. The second force was led by the Eastern general Aetius and invaded the homeland of the Huns in an attempt to weaken them and also to force them to leave Italy to defend their homes.[37] If this interpretation is accepted, it allows for an easier reading of the passage and also a clearer interpretation of events, especially with regard to Attila's decision to leave Italy without fighting Aetius.

With the news that Aetius had been reinforced from the East, Attila was certain that his chances of negotiating with the emperor were over. He began the withdrawal from Italy, which was very slow due to the number of wagons carrying the booty and the large number of captives being forced to march away from their homes. In the meantime, once the reinforcements arrived, Aetius was in a position to put further pressure on the Huns to leave. As they re-crossed northern Italy towards the east Aetius and his men were able to harass their rear, destroy any stragglers that were lagging behind and attack any foraging parties sent out from the main host.

Pope Leo

When Attila and his men reached the territory of Ambuleium in Venetia and were crossing the River Mincius, a tributary of the River Po, envoys arrived from Valentinian.[38] The nature and result of this embassy has been the subject of controversy ever since.

The story begins with Prosper, who is supported by Victor Tonnensis, the Chronicle of Cassiodorus and Priscus.[39] Accompanied by Trygetius, *Vir Praefectorius* – the same man who had negotiated the treaty with the Vandals in 435 – and Avienus, who had been consul in 450, Leo met Attila:

> The king received the whole delegation courteously, and he was so flattered by the presence of the highest priest that he ordered his men to stop the hostilities and, promising peace, retired beyond the Danube.

> *Prosper, s.a. 452, tr. Maenchen-Helfen*

During the course of the Middle Ages this story was magnified until now it is almost totally altered. For example:

> When Attila marched on Rome, Leo went out to meet him and pleaded for him to leave. As Leo spoke, Attila saw the vision of a man in priestly robes, carrying a bare sword, and threatening to kill the invader if he did not obey Leo; Attila left. As Leo had a great devotion to Saint Peter the Apostle, it is generally believed the first pope was the visionary opponent to the Huns. When Genseric [sic] invaded Rome, Leo's sanctity and eloquence saved the city again.

> *http://saints.sqpn.com/pope-saint-leo-the-great/August 2010*

Interestingly, Hydatius, who as Bishop of Aqua Flaviae would be expected to make the most of this opportunity to promote Catholicism, makes no mention of the Pope.

The main objection to this version of events is that, far from marching on Rome, Attila was in the north-east of Italy and marching away from the city. However, if Leo was not attempting to save Rome, as is usually portrayed, the question remains as to the actual reasons for him being present.

This was simply due to the fact that Valentinian, the emperor, requested him to lead the delegation. As a major religious figure he was of immense political stature and his presence added sincerity and grace to the meeting: it will have been expected that this would influence Attila's decisions concerning the embassy.

The origin of the story of Saint Peter and the flaming sword probably lies with Paulus Diaconus, who claims that one of Leo's attendants 'threatened the king with a drawn sword', a story later embellished by Isidore of Seville, amongst others.[40] However, Leo's main purpose was not to 'order' Attila to withdraw. Fortunately, a letter from Eastern bishops to Pope Symmachus dated to 512 or 513 shows that Leo's task was to negotiate the release of captives, not only of the Christians, but 'if that can be believed, Jews and Pagans'.[41] In return for a large sum of gold he had brought with him, Leo was able to obtain the release of many – but not all – of the captives.

Attila also agreed to continue his retreat from Italy. However, he repeated his demand that Honoria be surrendered to him, threatening to invade again unless she was sent to him 'with her due share of the royal wealth'.[42] Realistically, he was not in a position to make good on his demands. Attila's invasion had gone some way towards repairing the damage to his reputation of the previous year, but it was still far from a complete success. Furthermore, the attack on the homes of the Huns demonstrated that his boasts about controlling the Eastern Roman Empire was no longer true. Attila retired to his homeland, this time determined on vengeance against the East, whose actions had helped to thwart his plans.

Conclusion

The major difference between the invasions of Gaul and Italy was the defence of Aquileia. In 451 Attila had taken a number of cities in quick succession, a fact that had allowed him to penetrate deep into Gaul. Aetius will have quickly realized that a long defence of any of the Gallic cities would have given him more time to organize the defence of Gaul and may even have halted the invasion. Accordingly, Aetius may have stationed a strong garrison in Aquileia as soon as he heard of Attila's approach. The three-month siege of Aquileia caused Attila to lose a great part of the campaign season, and coupled with the heavy losses and the beginnings of disease ultimately brought the campaign to an abrupt end.

Aetius' strategy is usually seen as poor, mainly due to the fact that he allowed Attila to enter Italy without attempting to defend the Julian Alps. However, as noted above, this is unrealistic. Having realized that he could not defend the Alps, Aetius had resorted to delaying tactics, reinforcing Aquileia in the hope that the city would hold out and give time for the East to organize a relief force for Italy. Although Aetius would have been hoping simply for help in Italy, Marcian's decision to send the other Aetius on campaign against the Huns' homeland was a major bonus. Furthermore, Aetius had understood that as long as he guarded the Apennines Attila would not be able to threaten Rome, and Ravenna was still impregnable behind its marshes. With famine throughout Italy meaning that Attila's forces would struggle to feed themselves, time was on Aetius' side.

Once the troops arrived from the east there can be little doubt that Aetius used his forces to harass the Huns as they retreated across northern Italy. This, together with the envoys sent by Valentinian, determined Attila that the West, although fragmented, was simply too strong whilst led by Aetius. Attila took the only course open to him. Having saved at least a little face by ransoming some of the prisoners in negotiations with Pope Leo, the Huns returned home to begin the rebuilding of their shattered homesteads and Attila's palaces.

Chapter 16

The End

453

Following his 'victory' in Italy, Attila turned his mind to the East. Since Marcian had ascended the throne the East had been troublesome for Attila. With the West nominally chastised, he returned to his usual stance with the East. Early in 453 he not only demanded the payment of tribute but also the arrears that had not been paid to him since before the death of Theodosius.[1] In response, Marcian sent emissaries to meet with Attila to negotiate, but he refused to treat with them and the mission was a failure.[2]

Yet this attitude benefited the east more than Attila. Marcian had concluded peace treaties with both the Persians in the east and the Blemmyes and Nobades south of Egypt. With peace on his other frontiers, Marcian, although wary of the threat still posed, was no longer fearful of the Huns and was prepared, if necessary, to fight.[3] Marcian's dogged refusal to pay was no doubt also reinforced by the fact that Attila had now been 'beaten' twice and there was in all likelihood increased tensions within Attila's empire as the subject nations considered the possibility of a rebellion against Hunnic rule. It is possible, although impossible to prove, that Marcian had sent agents into Hunnic territory with the specific intention of stirring up discontent and encouraging a rebellion.

Prior to leading his men against the East, Attila:

> took in marriage according to the custom of his race a very beautiful girl named Ildico. At his wedding he gave himself up to excessive celebration and he lay down on his back sodden with wine and sleep. He suffered a haemorrhage, and the blood, which would ordinarily have drained through his nose, was unable to pass through the usual passages and flowed in its deadly course down his throat, killing him.
>
> *Prisc. fr. 24.1*[4]

There is a claim in Malalas that Attila did not die of natural causes but that Aetius bribed his *spatharius* (bodyguard) to kill him.[5] This is extremely unlikely as it is not mentioned elsewhere, and Malalas, writing so long after events, does not explain where he obtained the information. So passed the ruler of the empire of the Huns and the greatest external threat to Roman imperial security.

When the news arrived in Constantinople and Rome no doubt there was great relief: the individual who had welded the disparate tribes of the Huns into a major military force had died. Yet at the same time there would have been great concern over what would happen to Attila's empire: after all, one of his sons could easily emulate – if not better – the acts of the 'Scourge of God'.

This was not to be. Rather than closing ranks and ensuring that the Hunnic Empire remained one whole body, Attila's sons immediately began a civil war to determine who would inherit it.[6] Attila had numerous wives, and although it is not known if all of them bore him children, there is a good chance that he left his empire to be divided amongst many sons, who 'themselves almost amounted to a people'.[7]

The East
The relief with which the news of the Huns' implosion was received was tempered by some unhappy news, especially for Marcian. In July 453 his wife, his link with the Theodosian dynasty, died, leaving her property for 'charitable purposes'.[8] Marcian now had to survive without her political support, so he was extremely fortunate that the death of Attila and the outbreak of a civil war amongst the Huns gave him and the East a breathing space in which to cement his position as sole ruler.

The West
In the West the death of Attila and the eruption of civil war amongst the Huns will also have been greeted with relief: indeed, Aetius may have hoped that at least one of Attila's sons would appeal to him for aid, so allowing a return to the former situation where he and at least one section of the Huns were close allies.

However, it was events in Gaul that dominated his attention. Probably after hearing of Attila's death, and so knowing that Gaul was secure from Hunnic attack, Thorismund attacked and defeated the Alans north of the Loire.[9]

The event may have caused some confusion in the sources. Jordanes writes that in 453 the Goths and the Alans united to defeat a second invasion of Gaul by the Huns, this time without Roman aid.[10] There is no other evidence for this campaign and, given the timescale, it is very unlikely that it happened. The reasons for Jordanes' odd account are unknown. Jordanes may have known of the Goths and the Alans fighting and may have been simply confused, assuming that the two must have been fighting the Huns rather than each other. If so, the account should probably be seen as an attempt to boost further the reputation of the Goths, this time by having them beat the Huns with the help of the Alans but without Roman aid. On the other hand, it may simply have been an attempt to disguise the fact that in 453 the Goths were again on the warpath and fighting against the empire.

The reasons for the Gothic attack on the Alans are unclear. In part at least Thorismund may have been annoyed at the lack of any reward for the Battle of the Catalaunian Plains. It can be assumed that Aetius believed that the Goths had been fighting as part of their *foedus* with Rome. Thorismund may have expected more. Despite the death of his father and his own narrow escape there does not appear to have been any recompense to the Goths from Aetius, neither in land nor in appointments within the Roman military hierarchy. It is also likely that Thorismund, like his father before him, wanted to extend his power both politically at Rome and territorially in Gaul. Furthermore, internal politics may have played a part, since a failure to extract any rewards would result in his brothers, who remained watching in the wings, being ready to remove him if his reign was not satisfactory.

In this context the attack makes sense. The Alans, originally led by Goa, who by this time may well have died with the event not being recorded, were staunch allies of Aetius and could be expected to join him in any war with the Goths. By defeating them in a pre-emptive strike, Thorismund would weaken Aetius' alliance and ensured that his own northern border was safe from attack.

Understandably, Aetius appears to have been completely taken by surprise by the attack on his ally. According to Sidonius, he led his army north out of Italy to help the Alans and stop the Goths from extending their frontier northwards, although the nature of the forces he commanded and their employment remain obscure.[11]

In response Thorismund now turned his attention to the south and laid siege to Arles, the 'capital' of Gaul.[12] According to Sidonius, although he tried Aetius could not break the siege of Arles.[13] However, at this point events took a strange turn. Resident in the city was Ferreolus, the *praefectus praetorio Galliarum*. In an unexpected twist Ferreolus invited Thorismund into the besieged city and entertained him at a banquet. His methods were decidedly odd, but effective. During the banquet somehow Ferreolus convinced Thorismund to lift the siege.[14] The Goths returned to Aquitaine.

It is possible that even at this late stage Thorismund was willing to accept a nominal reward for the help the Goths had given against Attila and for the death of his father. Although the attribution is uncertain, it is possible that as part of the agreement reached between Thorismund and Ferreolus and later ratified by Aetius, Frederic, Thorismund's brother, was given the post of *magister militum* in the West, since he was shortly afterwards attested as fighting in Spain on behalf of the Romans.[15]

Unfortunately for Thorismund, his brothers were dissatisfied with this course of events. Prosper notes that they were unhappy with the fact that Thorismund had gone to war with Aetius.[16] Further, the description of Theoderic (Thorismund's younger brother and the next in line to the throne) given by Sidonius portrays an individual with pro-Roman leanings.[17] Perhaps his brothers were unhappy with the fact that Thorismund had so quickly broken the peace with Aetius.

To compound his error Thorismund did not have the will to grasp his opportunities, since although his siege of Arles was too strong to be broken by force he agreed to withdraw. In the ensuing negotiations Thorismund's brothers could have expected more than a single Roman military post and may have felt that Thorismund was too indecisive to rule properly.[18] He was clearly not the type of forceful, dynamic leader that was needed by the Goths.

Whatever the cause, later that year the brothers quarrelled and Theoderic and Frederic conspired to remove Thorismund.[19] In the end, Thorismund was defeated by his brothers and garrotted.[20] With his death Theoderic succeeded to the throne and is now known as Theoderic II.[21] Interestingly, given Theoderic's alleged pro-Roman bias, the peace treaty agreed between Ferreolus and Thorismund remained active and Theoderic made no attempt to declare war on Rome. In fact, it is likely that he was more politically astute than his brother and had recognized that the Goths had more to gain by joining the Romans than by opposing them. Frederick had just been appointed as *magister militum* and such military positions in the Western army would gain the Gothic leaders legitimacy in the eyes of the Gallic population and so ease the transferral of Gallic loyalty within the Gothic kingdom. It would also help later, when the Goths could be seen as inheritors of the Roman political body rather than as barbarian settlers.

Spain

At around the same time as the Goths attempted to expand their influence in Gaul, Mansuetus, the *comes Hispaniarum*, and Fronto, also a *comes*, were sent as envoys to the Sueves. Whilst Aetius and the allies had been preoccupied with events in Gaul and engaged in battle with Attila the Sueves had again broken the peace and launched raids against their neighbours. As was the normal case by now, the threat of war from Aetius, probably combined with the news of the defeat of Attila in Gaul and his subsequent death, convinced the Sueves to accept yet another treaty, re-establishing 'the terms which had (previously) been imposed', though doubtless without the need for the Sueves to return the acquired booty.[22]

454

If not before the new year then almost certainly at the start of it Aetius received the news that the Hunnic empire, already in the grip of civil war, now faced internal revolt.[23] With the death of Attila his treaties with other peoples became void, and the hostages given by Aetius – probably including his son Carpilio – returned home. At the same time the bureaucrats sent by Aetius to serve Attila when he was made honorary *magister militum*, including Orestes, also returned. They will have brought the news that a revolt had begun against Hunnic rule. Ardaric, the king of the Gepids, had been one of Attila's most trusted allies.[24] He didn't give the same respect to Attila's sons as he had to their father, probably angered that the sons were squabbling over Attila's empire and had 'allotted war-like kings and peoples like household servants'.[25] In response he raised the standard of revolt. Other tribes emulated his actions and within a short time an alliance was formed against the Huns.

The Battle of the Nedao[26]

At an unknown date, but most likely in 454, in a great battle the two opponents met at the River Nedao (Nedava). The forces of the Huns were led by Ellac, the eldest of Attila's sons and his personal favourite. Due to the nature of the rebellion it would appear that most, if not all, of Attila's other sons joined Ellac's forces in an attempt to defeat the rebels.

Ardaric and his Gepids had enlisted the help of the Ostrogoths, the Rugians, the Sueves, the Alans and the Heruls, amongst others. Although it may appear surprising that many of the tribes listed are to be found within the boundaries of the

Roman Empire – for example, the Sueves in Spain – it should be remembered that the troops represent those tribes who did not join in the invasion of the Roman Empire, either preferring or being compelled to remain in their original homelands under the dominion of the Huns.

In a fierce battle the Huns, unexpectedly, were heavily defeated and Ellac himself 'died fighting so bravely that, had his father been alive, he would have wished for an end so glorious'.[27] After his death the Hunnic empire disintegrated with the survivors fragmenting and separately following those sons of Attila who were still alive. The Huns ended near the coasts of the Black Sea, disunited and unable to reconstruct the empire of Attila. Although they were to play a minor part in events for the next century, they lost their ability to influence happenings and slowly passed into history.

Spain

With the attention of the imperial government focused on Gaul, yet again the *bacaudae* in Spain became active. As part of the treaty with Thorismund before his death, or possibly as part of a new, unattested treaty with the new king Theoderic, Frederic, the brother of Theoderic, was sent to Spain with an army. Whether this army was composed solely of Gothic troops or of Romans or was an allied force is unknown. Once in Spain Frederic attacked the *bacaudae* of Tarraconensis, slaughtering large numbers 'under orders from the Roman government'.[28]

Aetius

In Italy Aetius would have been in high spirits: Gaul was at peace, the Vandals were quiet, Spain was being chastised for its presumption and now the empire of the Huns was being dismantled. His position was now such that he could browbeat Valentinian into agreeing to his demands. At some point prior to 454 Eudoxia, the wife of Valentinian, had decided that the best man to become emperor after the death of Valentinian was Majorian, the member of Aetius' staff who had fought alongside him at the Battle of Vicus Helena.[29] His military ability was promising and he appealed to Eudoxia as being well suited to continue the Theodosian dynasty. Accordingly, she proposed that he be married to Valentinian's daughter Placidia, the heir to the throne since Eudocia was betrothed to Huneric, Gaiseric's son, and so ineligible to rule.

Unfortunately for Majorian, Aetius was now in such a strong position that Valentinian could deny him nothing. Instead of a betrothal, Majorian retired from active service and went to live on his private property in the country.[30] The retirement is said by Sidonius to have been due to the political manipulations of Aetius' wife Pelagia.[31] With Majorian removed from the scene, Valentinian agreed to the betrothal of Placidia and Aetius' son Gaudentius in place of Majorian.[32]

Although Sidonius' claims are suspect, since they are part of a panegyric delivered to Majorian, the story is probably near to the truth. Valentinian may have long harboured resentment of the general who had supported his rival in 424 and have wanted Majorian as his successor on the throne rather than agreeing to Aetius' plans. By betrothing Majorian to Placidia Valentinian would ensure that Aetius' control of the West was weakened. The chances are that Valentinian was opposed to Aetius' proposal but had little option but to accede to the betrothal of Gaudentius and Placidia.

Although the betrothal doubtless annoyed Valentinian, for other members of the court the idea was anathema. The army was already totally dominated by Aetius, who used his military position to control Valentinian. If Gaudentius was betrothed and married to Placidia then Aetius' domination would continue long into the future. Opposition to Aetius began to grow.

Doubtless Eudoxia and Valentinian encouraged such opposition to neutralize Aetius. He had by now been in command of the army for twenty years and as a result his supporters had received the lion's share of the important political and military commands. Furthermore, his health still seemed to be good and there appeared to be no end to his domination. Opposition grew.

Paradoxically, the collapse of the Hunnic empire also weakened Aetius politically. Earlier, he had been supported by the Huns. From the late 440s his skills as a general and his knowledge of the 'barbarian' way of thought had helped to maintain his dominant position in the face of the barbarian threat. Now, with the Huns removed, Aetius was seen as no longer critical to Valentinian's survival.[33]

As a result, two major political figures at court began to intrigue against Aetius. The first of these was Petronius Maximus, a major political leader in the West. He had been consul in 433 and 443 and was created *patricius* at some time before 445.[34] Yet despite having been Aetius' supporter, it was clear that he would never become as powerful as Aetius.[35] It may be that he hoped that when Valentinian died he would be a viable candidate for the throne. However, Gaudentius' betrothal meant that Maximus would never accede to any greater power than he already wielded. Unhappy with this state of affairs, he began to cast his net for other like-minded individuals who were unhappy with Aetius' dominance.

He quickly found an accomplice. Heraclius, a eunuch and the *primicerius sacri cubiculi* (officer of the imperial bedchamber), was also unhappy with Aetius' power, and so the two men began a conspiracy to overthrow him.[36] Slowly, Heraclius was able to convince Valentinian that Aetius was using the betrothal as a means of overthrowing Valentinian himself.[37]

The Death of Aetius

Knowing that the army was supportive of Aetius, the conspirators decided that the only way for Valentinian to eliminate him was when he was unprotected by the troops. Accordingly, Valentinian and Heraclius decided that the best time would be when Aetius was in the palace to hold a planning meeting with Valentinian, since he was not allowed bodyguards in the presence of the emperor. On either 21 or 22 September 454 Aetius duly arrived at court and was in a planning meeting with Valentinian to discuss proposals to raise money when 'with a shout Valentinian suddenly leaped up from his throne and cried out that he would no longer endure to be abused by such treacheries'[38] before stabbing Aetius with his sword. Heraclius, who was nearby, withdrew a concealed cleaver and the two men, raining blows upon Aetius' head, killed him.[39] Shortly afterwards they also killed Boethius, the *praefectus praetorio*, an ally and friend of Aetius.[40] A further number of Aetius' supporters were also killed.[41]

The bodies of the two men were displayed in the Forum whilst Valentinian called a meeting of the Senate and gave a speech denouncing Aetius and his close supporters. Valentinian was afraid that Aetius' supporters in the Senate would support a revolt against him.[42] It was probably at this time that he enquired of an unknown Roman whether he had done well in executing Aetius. The oft-quoted reply to Valentinian was that the Roman 'was not able to know whether he had done well or perhaps otherwise, but one thing he understood exceedingly well, that he had cut off his own right hand with the other'.[43]

Militarily, Valentinian knew that he had to maintain the good will of the army and especially of those troops – particularly Aetius' *bucellarii* – who had been loyal to Aetius and might now support a usurper. By the time of Aetius' death the *praesental* army of the West had shrunk. Aetius' personal following of *bucellarii*, mainly composed of Huns, comprised a large proportion of the Western 'field army'.[44]

As a result, and probably following the plan he had wanted all along, Valentinian recalled Majorian from his 'retirement' and made him *comes domesticorum* (count of the household), allocating Aetius' *bucellarii* to him in the hope that their loyalty would be transferred to Majorian, alongside whom many will have served, and that he would prevent a coup.[45] Believing that Valentinian would now allow him to marry Placidia, Majorian would have been happy to oblige the emperor.

Knowing that Aetius' death would also precipitate actions in the wider world, at the same time Valentinian sent envoys to the barbarians, the one to the Sueves being called Justinianus.[46] What actions the Goths, the Sueves, the Alans and especially the Vandals would have taken are unknown. Events in Rome quickly changed the political circumstances of the West forever.

The Death of Valentinian

Maximus now attempted to dominate Valentinian in a manner similar to Aetius. When he endeavoured to have Valentinian nominate him for the consulship he was opposed by Heraclius, who may have been a supporter of Majorian.[47] Angry at his ambition being thwarted, Maximus summoned Optila and Thraustila, two of Valentinian's guards. These two men had served in Aetius' *bucellarii* before being promoted to the imperial guard. Additionally, Thraustila is claimed to have been Aetius' son-in-law, married to an un-named daughter.[48] Unfortunately, this is attested nowhere else, and it is unlikely that Valentinian would have continued to employ a relative of Aetius in his personal guard after murdering him. However, given Valentinian's naïve policy towards Aetius, this should not be taken for granted and so the concept remains an interesting possibility. In their meeting Maximus blamed the death of Aetius squarely on Valentinian and strongly suggested that the two men take revenge on Valentinian for Aetius' 'execution'.[49] He also claimed that

Valentinian had brought shame on his house by raping Maximus' wife, although this is unlikely.[50]

In the meantime it would appear that Valentinian, recognizing that to continue to rule in safety he would need the support of the army, began to pay more attention to the troops, taking part in military exercises with them and hoping by his presence to boost their support for him.[51] As part of these routines he regularly attended the training sessions on the Campus Martius. A few days after Maximus' meeting with Optila and Thraustila, on 16 March 455, Valentinian, accompanied by Heraclius, was exercising on the Campus Martius with a few guards. After he had dismounted from his horse, Optila, Thraustila and their followers drew their swords and killed both Valentinian and Heraclius.[52] Despite his attempts to win their loyalty, not one of his guards or the troops in the area attempted to intervene: their loyalty was apparently still given to Aetius. With Valentinian's death the House of Theodosius, or at least the male heirs, came to an inglorious end.

Chapter 17

Aftermath

The assassination of Valentinian caused 'disorder and confusion' in Rome.[1] According to Priscus, the army was divided between supporting Maximus and a certain 'Maximian', the son of Domninus and attendant of Aetius.[2] It is possible, though uncertain, that Priscus' text at this point is corrupt and that 'Maximian' is to be identified as the later emperor Majorian: the two words are very similar in ancient Greek and so it is possible that a later copyist made a mistake.[3] What is certain is that, in effect, the army could not decide whether to follow the policies of Aetius (Maximian/Majorian) or to adopt a new set of policies (Maximus).

The matter was decided very quickly. Maximus began to distribute money to influential people and at the same time forced Eudoxia, Valentinian's widow, to marry him by threatening her with death if she refused.[4] Theophanes also claims that Eudoxia was raped by Maximus, but he may have been confused as to the actual course of events and so took the worst possible interpretation.[5] Maximus further ordered that Eudoxia's daughter Eudocia marry his son, the newly proclaimed *Caesar* Palladius, despite the fact that she was betrothed to Huneric, son of Gaiseric.[6] In an attempt to reinforce his position, Maximus may also have arranged the betrothal of Placidia to Olybrius, a leading senator in Rome, who probably threw in his lot with Maximus as a result. On 17 March, the day after Valentinian's death, Maximus was proclaimed emperor in Rome.[7]

Eudoxia was, understandably, furious at her treatment. She had always wanted Majorian as the new emperor and Maximus' actions alienated any hope of her agreement to his schemes.[8] She pondered her options. Her next move could be interpreted as a betrayal of Rome, and in fact it is now ignored by many historians, probably being seen as mere rumour and scandal rather than fact.[9]

Eudoxia could not appeal to the East for help since her aunt Pulcheria had died and the emperor Marcian would most likely not be willing to intervene on her behalf.[10] The Western court was either unable or unwilling to take her part against the new emperor. Her only hope lay with the barbarians. The Goths were one possibility, but the more obvious course of action – and the one she took – was to appeal to Gaiseric, her daughter's potential father-in-law, for help.[11]

Although at first surprising, when the move is analyzed it is clear that Eudoxia was not betraying Rome but rather following the example set by Aetius, who had more than once appealed to barbarians for aid, although in his case it was the Huns. Furthermore, Gaiseric was settled in Africa as *socius et amicus cum foedere*.[12] As an ally of her former husband, Gaiseric was the obvious person for her to appeal to.

Moreover, Maximus' decision to force Eudocia to marry Palladius was an added incentive to Gaiseric to evict Maximus from the throne. Eudoxia may have been hoping that Gaiseric, as her ally, would enter Italy, remove Maximus, and then join with her to elevate Majorian.

Unfortunately, Eudoxia made one grave error in her assumptions. She assumed that Gaiseric, as her former husband's ally, would agree to help her. However, the barbarian invaders of the Roman Empire, or at least Gaiseric, appear to have had a different interpretation of alliances. To Eudoxia and to modern eyes an alliance is an agreement on behalf of political institutions to support each other. Gaiseric and other Germanic tribesmen did not interpret things in this way. Gaiseric's alliance and treaty was with Aetius and Valentinian, the individuals who had concluded the negotiations with him.[13] As a result, with their deaths the treaty was perceived by Gaiseric as being void. Furthermore, without the threat of Aetius, Italy was now open to raids. The message from Eudoxia also demonstrated to Gaiseric that there was confusion in Rome.[14] No doubt hoping to create further disorder, Gaiseric instantly cut the supply of grain to Rome and, deciding that a swift attack would meet little resistance, collected his army and set sail, not just for Italy, but directly for Rome.

THE WEST

Hearing of the assassination of Aetius, early in the campaign season of 455 the barbarians along the Rhine had begun to take advantage of the loss of Rome's most outstanding soldier. The Saxons began to spread their raids along the coast, the Franks began to encroach on the two 'Belgian' provinces, and the Alamanni crossed the Rhine into Roman territory and began to expand their holdings.[15] These attacks were only to be expected. In the previous twenty years any attempts to expand had been met by the Roman army under Aetius, usually supported by Huns, and the attackers forced to retire to their previous borders. Now, with the Hunnic empire in cataclysmic decline and Aetius dead, all of the barbarian tribes saw their chance and took it.

The Goths

Since the settlement of the Goths in 418/419 the policies of the West, including those of Constantius III, John, and, of course, Aetius, had been to minimize the impact of the settlement on political affairs. The fact that the Gothic kings wanted to play a more central role in the affairs of the West, or at least expand their territories, is emphasised by the number of wars that they fought with Rome between 419 and 454. Seeking to cement his position as emperor Maximus promoted Avitus, the man who had been Aetius' negotiator with the Goths, as *magister utriusque militiae praesentalis*.[16]

The timing was good as the Goths, aware of the death of Aetius, had decided once again to attempt to expand their political power and dominions.[17] Preparing their armies, the Goths were ready to march when Avitus arrived. The events that follow are taken from Sidonius' panegyric to Avitus, so may not be strictly accurate.[18]

Avitus clearly had a military and political reputation in the West.[19] According to Sidonius, when the news arrived that Avitus had been made *magister militum*, the Franks and the Alamanni quickly retreated to their previous frontiers and the Saxons stopped their raids through fear. Although the extent of their capitulation is no doubt exaggerated, Avitus' reputation appears to have at least given them pause for thought and slowed down their rate of advance.

Once he had received messages from these tribes asking for peace, Avitus, leaving the army behind, went to Toulouse simply as an envoy. Due to Theoderic's relationship with Avitus, and to the esteem in which he was held, the Goths agreed to forego any attacks upon the empire.

The concept that Theoderic accepted a new treaty simply due to Avitus' influence is probably exaggerated. Sidonius was Avitus' son-in-law and the story is part of Sidonius' panegyric to him. Yet if the new treaty was not arranged simply because of Theoderic's admiration for Avitus, there must be another reason for the Goths' alliance with Rome.

The chances are that the alliance was agreed on condition that Maximus accepted Theoderic as an ally and an equal, a policy that undid the guiding principle of all of the previous rulers who had fought to keep the Goths in a subordinate position.[20] Despite the reversal of policy, the agreement was good news for Maximus. However, bad news was soon to follow.

The Sack of Rome

Landing near Rome, Gaiseric advanced to 'Azestus'.[21] Maximus heard the news on 31 May.[22] Maximus, who had little military experience and was aware that not all of the army was happy with his elevation, immediately panicked and fled.[23] Sickened by his cowardice, his bodyguard left him to run. As he was leaving the city a by-stander threw a rock that hit him on the temple and killed him. The crowd then tore his body to pieces.[24]

Leaderless, and with any available troops apparently refusing to fight, the city of Rome bowed to the inevitable. Gaiseric entered the city. Contrary to the expectations of Eudoxia, he did not come as a liberator. As he was about to release his troops on the defenceless city Pope Leo convinced Gaiseric not to let his troops burn, kill or torture the citizens, but nevertheless the city was put to the sack for fourteen days and 'emptied of all its wealth, and many thousands of captives, all that were satisfactory as to age or occupation, along with the Queen and her children, were taken away to Carthage'.[25] Also taken was Gaudentius, Aetius' son.[26]

Once back in Africa Eudocia was kept in safety prior to her marriage to Huneric, following the earlier betrothal and the agreement of 442. As Placidia was betrothed to Olybrius she was not married to anybody by Gaiseric. Instead, both she and her mother Eudoxia were simply held by Gaiseric in Carthage.[27] Although the Eastern Emperor Marcian sent envoys on two occasions to Gaiseric demanding a halt to hostilities and the return of Eudoxia, Eudocia and Placidia, these were ignored.[28]

With the West in disarray, Gaiseric rapidly extended his holdings, taking the whole of Roman Africa west of Cyrenaica, the Balearic Islands, Sardinia and Corsica.

He then went on to have a long career interfering in imperial politics to further his own ends before dying of old age in 477.

Italy

In the meantime, the imperial throne passed to Avitus. In a complete break with the policies of the past he accepted the support of the Goths, being nominated as emperor by Theoderic. For the first time a barbarian group within the boundaries of the empire was involved in politics at the highest level, even to the point of appointing an emperor.

Avitus appointed a man named Remistus as *magister militum et patricius* and Ricimer, an individual of mixed barbarian descent, as *comes*. Ricimer was sent to face the Vandals, who were attacking Sicily, defeating them in a land battle at Agrigentum and again at sea near Corsica in 456.[29] Gaiseric's hopes of annexing Sicily were thwarted, and as a result of his victories Ricimer was made *magister militum* by a grateful Avitus.[30]

The Goths

Prior to these developments the Sueves in Spain attempted to enlarge their kingdom by annexing Roman territory. Although both the emperor in Italy and Theoderic, King of the Goths, ordered them to stop, the Sueves refused to bow to diplomatic pressure. Finally, in 456, Theoderic invaded Spain with a large army and defeated them.[31] By this action Theoderic laid the foundations for the Visigothic Kingdom of Spain.

Unfortunately for Avitus, Gaiseric still dominated the seas and Avitus remained unpopular in Italy due to the famine caused in Italy by the complete loss of grain from Africa.[32] As a result he was forced to dismiss his Gothic bodyguard, but in order to pay them he stripped 'bronze fittings' and other metals from public buildings, selling the resultant goods to merchants for the funds.[33]

The people of Rome rebelled against Avitus and, correctly judging the prevailing mood, Ricimer betrayed his patron and joined with Majorian in rebellion. Remistus was killed and one month later, on 17 October 456, Avitus was defeated at the Battle of Placentia and killed.[34] Thus was set in motion Ricimer's domination, which resulted in a series of short-lived emperors being crowned and executed. The West now began its short decline into obscurity.

This was not helped by the fact that the Goths, upon hearing of Avitus' death, instantly rebelled, along with the Burgundians. With the West in turmoil, from December 456 to April 457 the Roman Empire was nominally reunited under the sole rule of the Eastern Emperor. Unfortunately, at this critical juncture Marcian died (26 January 457), and it was not until the appointment of Leo (7 February 457) as the new emperor that new political plans could be instigated in the East. One of Leo's first moves was to appoint Majorian as *magister militum* alongside Ricimer.[35] Yet the invasion of a group of Alamanni proved that a new emperor of the West was needed.[36] On 6 April 457 the army acclaimed Majorian.[37] After settling into his new rule in 458 and 459 Majorian led the troops on a campaign to restore order in Gaul.

As part of the build up to the campaign, Majorian sent envoys to the Huns in the hope of enlisting their help in his armies. The embassy was a success, but succeeded in more than Majorian may have hoped: a letter from Nicetas, Bishop of Aquileia, to Pope Leo survives asking what should be done concerning the 'returning captives'. It would appear that a large number of the captives taken during Attila's invasions of the West were returned in 458 as part of the agreement between Majorian and the Huns. Released in Dacia and Moesia, these people's first port of call on their journey home was Aquileia, and the bishop had been swamped by the refugees.[38]

LATER EVENTS

Placidia, Eudoxia and Eudocia

Around the year 462 Gaiseric finally saw his son Huneric marry an imperial princess when he was wed to Eudocia after their long engagement.[39] Gaiseric was doubtless happy with the marriage on all levels, especially politically: theoretically, any sons of Huneric and Eudocia would have a claim to the throne of the West, although the chances of the Senate in Rome acquiescing to the rule of a '*semi-barbarus*' would be slim. After the marriage Eudoxia and Placidia were finally allowed to return home, possibly in 464, after being ransomed by the Eastern emperor Leo.[40]

Once home, Placidia was married to Olybrius, to whom she was already betrothed. Olybrius had fled from Rome during the sack of 455 and was destined to be emperor of the West for a short time in 472.[41] In the early 460s there is evidence that Gaudentius, Aetius' son, was still alive in Carthage.[42] Unfortunately, after this date there is no source that tells of his ultimate fate.

THE END OF EMPIRE

In the West in the years after 456 a bewildering series of short-lived emperors ruled until in 476 the last of these, titled Romulus Augustulus, was forced to abdicate by the *magister militum* Odoacer. After negotiations with Zeno, by this time emperor of the East, Odoacer agreed to rule the West – now little more than Italy – in the name of the empire. The Eastern nominee for the Western throne, Julius Nepos, lived for four more years in Illyricum before his death in 480. Nominally, he was the last Roman Emperor of the West. Without an orderly succession and a strong military leader, the West would survive for only one more generation after the death of Aetius.

Conclusion

It is difficult to reach any firm conclusions about Aetius. The greatest difficulty lies with the paucity of the sources. In addition to their rarity, their lack of detail makes it difficult to appreciate his achievements and failures, let alone establish what he was like as a person. A significant factor that adds to the difficulty is Aetius' long career, for some of which he was not the main policy maker. As a result, his career needs to be broken into three distinct parts: his youth and time as a hostage, his time as an 'associate' general and his time as sole *magister militum*. The evidence for his time as *magister militum* is poor but for the other two periods is almost non-existent.

AS A HOSTAGE
Aetius' youth is largely unknown and little understood. Although it is believed that he was earmarked for a military career from an early age, there was no guarantee that he would fulfil any latent potential. The turning point in his life was when he was sent as a hostage to the Goths and then the Huns. This separated him from his contemporaries who remained within the empire and gave him experience that they lacked. Further, his time amongst the Goths and the Huns influenced both his behaviour and his career, as his behaviour amongst the Goths and Huns no doubt differed from what would have been expected within the Roman military hierarchy. The fact that he was sent whilst still young, when he will have been less set in his ways and so have absorbed more than a fully grown adult, resulted in him knowing how the barbarians' minds worked and allowed him to use their more aggressive tactics and strategies.[1] His time as a hostage also allowed him to make close friends of the leading Goths and Huns of his own age and the extensive time he spent with the Huns resulted in these friendships remaining close when his friends rose to positions of power. These factors would be of vital importance in his future career.

AS AN 'ASSOCIATE' GENERAL
Aetius first came to prominence in 423. At this time the Franks were occupying large areas of Gaul on the imperial side of the Rhine, the Goths were occupying large areas of Aquitania and the Vandals had merged with the Alans to form a new 'superpower' in Spain. Also in Spain, the Sueves continued to act as an independent kingdom.

There is no clear indication of the status of the barbarian leaders in the West. Although some may have had official posts within the imperial government, others did not. However, whether they did or didn't, it would appear that they considered themselves to be independent of imperial control and free to engage in diplomatic activity on their own behalf, regardless of whether this conflicted with imperial aims.

In the years between 423 and 433 Aetius was one of the three (later two) most influential men in the Western Empire. The civil conflicts between 424 and 433 were of much shorter duration than those following the rebellion of Constantine I in the early-fourth century.[2] Unlike the earlier civil wars, in 423–424 and again in 432–433, there was paralysis at the political centre in Ravenna that allowed 'untamed alien forces' to 'pursue their own agendas, largely unhindered'.[3] Local troops facing the barbarians remained static, awaiting the outcome of the civil wars and relying on the victors to defeat the barbarians.

Once appointed *magister militum per Gallias* Aetius spent his time reversing the local effects of the civil war. During the civil war the Franks had attempted to expand into vacant agricultural areas along the frontier, but were pushed back by Aetius, the Goths had attempted to extend their power in Gaul, but were defeated and forced to retreat by him, and the Burgundians attempted the same expansion but suffered the same fate.

Away from Aetius' command, in Spain the Sueves maintained their independence and also attempted to expand their sphere of influence. Yet the greatest danger was in Africa. In 429 the Vandals and their allies crossed from Spain to Mauretania before advancing along the coast to threaten Carthage and the province of Africa itself.

SOLE RULE

When Aetius took sole control of Western affairs in 433 he had many pressures to deal with. The Franks, the Goths, the Sueves and the Vandals all needed to be faced with the full might of the *praesental* army. Obviously, this was impossible. Fortunately for Aetius, in 435 his envoy managed to secure a treaty with the Vandals that gave them the less-productive areas of the African coast whilst reserving the most productive provinces for Rome. With peace in Africa Aetius was finally able to bring the Goths and Franks to heel, while at the same time, and with the help of his allies the Huns, the Burgundians were decimated and brought under the close control of the empire.

The factors that helped Aetius and the West to recover from an almost impossible position are varied and interconnected. The main point to note is the generalship of Aetius. He had 'learned warfare from the Scythians [Huns]' and so did not conform to the stereotypical image of a late Roman general.[4] The army commanded by Aetius was expected to take the initiative and assault enemy positions, which is very different from the standard late Roman tactic of ambush and siege – although Aetius was not averse to using these tactics when the situation required them.

Furthermore, the army was constantly on the move. It was efficient and well supplied thanks to a successful logistic operation. Between 425 and 439 Aetius and his generals fought at least eleven campaigns, no doubt with losses in both men and material. The fact that the army continued to fight successfully can be attributed to a good replacement system, especially of trained troops.[5] However, it is possible that the majority of the replacements were now mercenaries from outside the empire. The continuing success also demonstrates that Aetius appears to have trained and instilled a high level of discipline in his men, whatever their origin. It is possible, though not attested, that his successes may have partially eased the burden of recruitment, since an army that is winning will attract volunteers whereas a losing army will not.

Yet the recruits his success attracted were not sufficient to maintain constant military campaigns on more than one front and the constant campaigning resulted in a steady attrition that slowly reduced the strength of the *praesental* army. To replace the losses Aetius needed the wholehearted support of the aristocracy, both to supply recruits and to pay the taxes needed for the upkeep of the army. It was not forthcoming. At this vital juncture:

> the two main groups in the [West] – the senatorial aristocracy and the Catholic Church – disassociated themselves from the fate of the Roman army that defended them. Both groups unwittingly sapped the strength of the army and of the imperial administration; and, having hamstrung their protectors, they found, somewhat to their surprise, that they could do without them.[6]

The only way that Aetius could keep the army at the strength needed to campaign was to enlist foreign mercenaries. This was a feasible proposition when the empire was rich, but in the mid 430s the financial resources of the empire were becoming stretched.

It appeared that by the end of the 430s Aetius was regaining control of the west. One event in 439 dashed his hopes. When the richest province of Africa was lost to the Vandals it sounded the death knell for the West. The imperial coffers, already low, could not stand the loss of the African income and with the failure of the African campaign of 441 the end was nigh. In 444 Valentinian was forced to admit that the West was bankrupt. Furthermore, the loss of Africa sent a signal to the other barbarians on Roman soil that the West was too weak to resist and internal conflict with the barbarians grew.

War with the Huns
Unfortunately for Aetius, this loss of political and military control occurred just as the Huns began to reach the height of their power under Attila. Attila now displaced Aetius as the main political focus in the West, largely due to the power of the Huns but also due to the apparent weakness of the West and Aetius' inability to interfere in the workings of *Germania*. Attila was thus able to use his policy of divide and rule to ensure confused loyalties in the West prior to the invasion of Gaul.[7] Fortunately for Aetius, Attila's policy failed when confronted with the undivided and politically more mature Goths. Without the Goths, Gaul would almost certainly have been lost to the empire: although the Hunnic empire collapsed after Attila's death, the West would not have had the strength to reconquer Gaul. Instead, the Goths, the Franks

and the 'Armoriciani' would have moved into the vacuum left by the collapse of the Huns.

Attila's invasion of Italy almost reversed the result of Aetius' victory in Gaul. Aetius' decision to reinforce the garrison of Aquileia and await reinforcements from the East is an indication of the reduced strength of the *praesental* army in Italy. The decision could easily have resulted in a catastrophic defeat. Fortunately, Aetius had correctly judged that Attila would be forced to capture Aquileia and that with additional troops the garrison could hold out for a long time. Although the eventual sack was a catastrophe for the inhabitants, the length of the siege gave Marcian the time needed to collect his forces and launch an attack into the Hunnic homelands, as well as sending troops to help Aetius in Italy.

Further, Aetius knew that time was on his side. He knew that the Huns did not have a large baggage train, instead relying to a large part on finding supplies as they campaigned. With the famine in Italy Aetius doubtless expected the Huns to suffer losses from hunger as well as the inevitable disease that accompanied famines. The Italian campaign demonstrates that Aetius was a realist with a strong grasp of strategy and tactics, both his own and those of his enemies.

Up to 450, when Attila began to consider invading the West, Aetius had relied on a policy of 'government through punitive expedition', which enjoyed mixed success. Gaul was brought back under imperial control, but the situation in Spain was changed with the marriage of Rechiarius, king of the Sueves, and the daughter of Theoderic, king of the Goths. Aetius had relied on supplements of Gothic manpower to maintain the Roman position in Spain. With this lost, the Sueves were allowed to again extend their sphere of influence – much to the detriment of the empire's prestige and coffers.[8]

By 452 the empire in the West was in dire straits. By this date Britain, most of Spain, the richest provinces of Africa, and large parts of Gaul had either been lost to barbarian kingdoms that only accepted the nominal rule of Rome or had established virtual independence from Roman rule.[9] Financially, the empire was in the last stages of bankruptcy. Despite this, to the people living at the time there were signs of recovery. Although only nominally subject to Rome, the Vandals and the Goths remained at peace and Aetius was able to gain their cooperation in both Gaul and Spain. Furthermore, the barbarians' acceptance of Roman rule – however nominal – meant that politically Aetius could claim that Rome still 'ruled' all the West, with the possible exception of Britain.

AETIUS AND STILICHO

Modern historians have tended to view Stilicho as a Vandal who helped to bring about the fall of the West, largely due to the perception that he was willing to do deals with his fellow-barbarian Alaric and was preparing to start a civil war against the East in 406 rather than defending the West against invasion. The fact that the Vandals, Alans and Sueves crossed the Rhine frontier and stopped the projected invasion of Illyricum is perceived as highlighting Stilicho's failure as a military commander, bent on causing an unnecessary civil war instead of monitoring the borders and anticipating the barbarian attack.[10]

Conversely, Aetius has tended to be viewed in a more sympathetic light than Stilicho. No doubt this is mainly due to both his long tenure in control of the West and the fact that throughout that time he continuously fought to maintain the West's integrity, on several occasions – and in contrast to Stilicho – even gaining military support from the East.

Yet there are several parallels between the two commanders. Both had contacts with powerful barbarians – Stilicho with Alaric and Aetius with Rua – and at times were forced to rely on these contacts to support their position. Both also had to deal with weak emperors who had come to the throne at a young age and never displayed the necessary ability to rule independently of the *magister militum*.

Furthermore, both had tried to arrange marriages to ensure that their grandchildren were heirs to the throne. Stilicho had managed to arrange two marriages with Honorius, first with his elder daughter and then, after her early death, with his younger daughter. The first of these had been accepted, but the second had caused opposition to grow in the Senate. Neither had resulted in the hoped-for offspring. Aetius (or possibly his wife) had forced Valentinian to accept the betrothal of his daughter with Aetius' son. Again this had provoked a growth of opposition at court, but in this case the resistance had coalesced and Aetius had been killed before the marriage had taken place.

Finally, shortly after their deaths Rome – the symbolic capital of the empire – was sacked, in 410 by Alaric and in 455 by Gaiseric. Historians have blamed the sack of 410 on Stilicho, accusing him of failing to eliminate Alaric when he had the chance in 402. On the other hand, Aetius' success in repeatedly defeating barbarians and the good fortune he experienced when Attila died before him has resulted in blame for the sack of 455 by Gaiseric being laid elsewhere: principally with Valentinian for killing his vastly experienced and capable *magister militum*, and with Eudoxia for inviting Gaiseric to intervene in Italy after Maximus had been crowned emperor.

In spite of these assumptions, a close analysis of events has shown that Stilicho was not really to blame for the events of 408, but rather the Italian troops, as they played into Alaric's hands when they massacred the families of Stilicho's *foederati*, forcing thousands of the *foederati* to change their allegiance and join Alaric.[11] Moreover, Eudoxia cannot realistically be blamed for Gaiseric's sack of Rome in 455: there can be little doubt that he would have attacked the city whether invited by her or not.

Although neither general was perfect, the majority of the blame must be laid at the feet of the two emperors who removed their capable generals without having either the ability to lead the troops themselves nor the strength of purpose to promote a capable warrior from within the court to take control of the army and defeat the invaders.

Stilicho and Aetius, who certainly knew each other, although they were from different generations, were responding to the specific, and vastly different, problems with which they were faced. Neither could find all of the answers.

THE BARBARIAN SETTLEMENTS

In recent years there has been a revolution concerning interpretations of the effects of the barbarian invasions that took place mainly during the period of Aetius' lifetime. Historians have tended to highlight the continuity between the Roman and the 'barbarian successor' kingdoms, especially with regard to the Goths and the Vandals. The apparent continuity of imperial institutions has allowed historians to downplay the dislocation and bloodshed caused by both the invasions and the almost-continuous civil wars.

This has been overplayed. Having no administrative structures of their own, when the barbarian kingdoms came into existence they naturally adopted and adapted the imperial structures that were in place, with the 'king' taking the place of the emperor and the nobles the place of the absentee aristocracy. As a result, the administrative structure continued, and is now being interpreted as a sign that the takeover was (relatively) peaceful, which has concealed both the level of warfare that continued to take place and the fact that in many places in the West imperial power had actually collapsed and the burden been assumed by local 'warlords', whether of barbarian or Roman origin, prior to the foundation of the barbarian kingdoms.[12]

A further difficulty lies in interpretations of the origins of the barbarian settlements. There is a tendency, especially in histories describing the long periods from Constantine's death to the 'Fall of the West', to perceive all barbarian settlements as being forced on the West by hostile foreign invaders.[13] This is not the case. There were five types of settlement by barbarians on Roman territory.[14]

The first of these was where barbarians attempted to impose their settlement without imperial sanction, for example, the Salian Franks in 358 and other Frankish tribes in 428. These were quickly counter-attacked and forced to leave the territory they had just occupied. That this infiltration continued and that it eventually succeeded after Aetius' death is a sure sign of imperial weakness.

The second type of settlement was where terms were imposed by Rome and were simply to the benefit of the Romans without interest in the effects on the barbarians. These were the types imposed on barbarians throughout most of imperial history. Unfortunately, by the time of Aetius the Romans had effectively lost the ability to force such settlements on the barbarian invaders, although the settlement of the Burgundians in Gaul in 443 and 456 might fit this category. Following their decimation by the Huns, the Burgundians were settled as 'citizens' in a similar manner to equivalent situations in the earlier empire. It is only the fact that the Burgundians maintained a separate identity for the short period until the fall of the West, after which they managed to establish a small independent kingdom for themselves, that makes it appear as if they were yet another barbarian invader whose invasion helped dismantle the empire.

The third type was where usurpers allowed barbarians to settle on condition of their military support. Examples include the Sueves, Vandals and Alans who were allowed by the usurper Maximus to settle in Spain in 409.[15] In this case the tribes-men were always liable to be attacked by 'legitimate' imperial forces intent on either destroying them, moving them to a separate settlement area or of forcing them to accept new treaties that were more beneficial to Rome.

The fourth type was where, with Roman agreement, the barbarians were settled on roughly equal terms to Rome. These agreements include the settlement of the Goths in Aquitaine in 418–419 and the Vandals in Africa in 442. The Goths were settled in 418–419 partly in recognition of what they had achieved in Spain, but mainly because an attempt to destroy them was too risky. Therefore, they were granted land specifically in return for their alliance. The Vandals were allowed to retain Africa when it became apparent that the Eastern army was needed to face the Huns and that the Western army could not face the Vandals alone, since a defeat in Africa would certainly have resulted in the total loss of Gaul to the Goths and probably to the complete collapse of the West. The main difference between the Vandals and the other Germanic invaders is that the Vandals asserted and maintained their independence from an early date thanks both to their geographical location and to the military and political ability of Gaiseric. From his secure base in Africa Gaiseric established an independent kingdom that was to last until the reconquest under Belisarius in 533–534.

The final type of settlement is one where barbarian troops were rewarded for their loyal service to Rome and can be seen as the equivalent of earlier land grants of 'colonies' to troops after their retirement from service. The two settlements of Alans in Gaul in 440 and 442 should be interpreted as the settling of veterans on their own land after long and faithful service, although in both cases Aetius had ulterior motives for the settlements. For example, that of the Alans under Goa in 442 was partly to inhibit the rebellions of the *bacaudae* in Armorica. Yet it is better to see their settlement as a traditional reward of land for Roman veterans, rather than a barbarian invader annexing large parts of Gaul in the face of imperial impotence.

Whatever the nature, the method of settling barbarians in Gaul and Spain, which was begun before Aetius came to power, was very effective in the short term and helped to maintain the empire. However, in the long term the net result was a loss of revenue without a similar reduction in costs. This is mirrored in the hiring of mercenaries. Although effective in the short term, in the long term the mercenaries retired to their own territories and the money that they had earned left the empire.[16]

Overall, however, it should be remembered that despite appearances the empire did not admit that the lands in Gaul, Spain and Britain had been permanently lost.[17] Aetius' recovery of control in Gaul in the mid 440s was certainly seen as a sign of imperial recovery, as evidenced by the appeal to him from Britain for help. Whilst Aetius was alive contemporaries probably believed that the worst was over and that imperial recovery would allow life to return to what it had been in previous centuries. This was no more so than after the repulse of Attila from Gaul and Italy, followed by his death and the collapse of the Hunnic empire.

One further aspect deserves attention – the treatment of the barbarian leaders in the West as compared to the East. It has been observed that in the East the barbarian aristocracy were offered military posts and were integrated into the empire, whereas in the West no such employment was offered and so the barbarian kings remained separate and eventually overthrew the West.[18] This is not strictly accurate. In the West the barbarian leaders had large numbers of followers, usually equivalent to one of the Roman field armies. To allow such leaders a military post would necessitate allowing their followers to join the army in similar fashion. This would result in the new commanders suddenly becoming equivalent in power to the established Roman military leaders. This obviously was not allowed until after Aetius' death, after which it can be interpreted as one of the major reasons for the collapse of imperial authority in the West.

In the East, on the other hand, the barbarian leaders had a smaller troop of followers. In normal circumstances, the barbarian followers were separated from their leader and deployed away from Constantinople. The leader was then entrusted with the command of Roman troops loyal to the empire. In this way the barbarian general was not allowed to become a threat to the empire. The only time when this rule was not followed allowed the Goth Gainas, in the year 400, to take command of a joint army of his own troops and the followers of his barbarian colleague Tribigild. Although his time in power was short, it ensured that the East did not allow a repetition of these circumstances. When the Gothic general Theoderic later threatened the stability of the East, he was sent to Italy, saving the East from further disruption.

AETIUS: 'TERROR OF THE BARBARIANS AND THE SUPPORT OF THE REPUBLIC'?

Despite the difficulties, it is possible from the few remaining sources to glean a hint of what Aetius was like as a person. The fact that Boniface was willing to allow him to live after defeating him at the Battle of Rimini suggests that he was a man who was trusted by his contemporaries. This is emphasized by the fact that Boniface, as a political and military mover at Court, may have known of Aetius from an early age. It is even more the case when the long-standing support of the Huns is taken into account. It is unlikely that they would have continued to support a man who continually failed to honour his personal agreements.

He appears to have been a man of compassion and humanity, as well as a realist, as evidenced by his treatment of the African refugees. At a time when the empire was bankrupt Aetius and Valentinian passed laws to relieve the refugees of their tax burden, even though Aetius was no doubt desperate for income to strengthen the army.

Yet this should not blind us to the fact that Aetius was a political and military commander who had a sense of his own superiority that made him prepared to risk all in civil war. His actions cost many lives, first in support of John and then on his own against Boniface. It would appear that as long as he was recognized as being needed, if not pre-eminent, he was trustworthy, yet when this was removed he could be self-centred enough to force others to do things his way.

On the other hand, when he was defeated by Boniface he appears to have accepted that Boniface was the better man and to have stepped aside, retiring to his estates and being content to allow Boniface his chance of running the empire as military guardian to Valentinian. It should not be forgotten, however, that he would have had friends and supporters in the Senate and the court who would have kept him aware of political developments and he was almost certainly simply waiting for an opportunity to step forward and resume the burden of political and military life.

His chance came with the death of Boniface. It is clear that Aetius did not hold Sebastian in the same esteem as he had held Boniface and was willing to plunge the empire into civil war to regain his position and oust Sebastian – although to a large part the attempts on his life certainly made Aetius more willing to risk all.

In combination, these qualities appear to have endeared him to both contemporaries and later historians. It is noticeable that it was only after 'ruling' the West unopposed for twenty years that effective opposition to his control materialized. Even then, after his execution the troops remained loyal to his memory, standing aside as Valentinian was killed and then failing to arrest and punish the murderers.

LAST OF THE ROMANS
Yet the real test of Aetius' ability is when his time in power is compared to the events immediately after his fall. The rapid fragmentation and collapse of the West attests to his determination and ability to hold the disintegrating empire together despite the odds.

One of the most important facets of his personality appears to have been that he was able to command undivided loyalty in his subordinates. In turn, he was able to use their military ability for the benefit of the empire, sending several independent armies to different theatres in Gaul and Spain, confident that the generals he appointed would not raise the standard of revolt.[19] Later commanders in the West did not have this luxury.

Aetius was a superb military commander and politician, but even had he lived longer he could not have saved the West. He was fighting against the tides of history. The financial decay of the West coupled with the moral decay of the aristocracy removed any chance he had of defeating the barbarians and re-establishing a viable empire.

Aetius established a reputation as an excellent general and a fierce defender of Roman power. As long as he was alive, despite numerous attempts to promote their influence, the kings of the barbarian kingdoms remained subordinate to the emperor. After his death the situation changed dramatically. The Goths became emperor-makers, promoting Avitus to the throne. The heart of the empire was now subordinate to the wills of a king whose main interest was the expansion of his own power, not the good of Rome. Simultaneously, the Vandals, released from the treaty and no longer afraid of military interference, launched a series of attacks that annexed large areas to their kingdom, whilst at the same time drastically reducing the area still loyal to Rome. Although the sack of Rome by Gaiseric in 455 is still seen as important, in reality it was the loss of territory that was most damaging to the empire. Neither of these events would have happened during Aetius' lifetime. The moral effect of having an able military leader in control subdued the barbarians and concealed the weakness of the empire from its inhabitants.

It is true to say that 'If all the barbarian conquerors had been annihilated in the same hour, their total destruction would not have restored the empire of the West: and if Rome still survived, she survived the loss of freedom, of virtue, and of honour.'[20] Aetius' rearguard action was valiant and full of valorous deeds, but in the end it was doomed to failure simply because there was no one of his quality to replace him. Without a dynamic military leader at least his equal in ability the West could not survive

Outline Chronology

Massacre of the families of the federates in Italy. Federate troops join Alaric. Formation of the Visigoths. Alaric lays siege to Rome in an attempt to secure military post for himself. Honorius refuses Alaric's request for a military post. Alaric raises siege

409   Revolt of Gerontius in Spain and installation of Maximus as Emperor. Vandals, Sueves and Alans enter Spain. Alaric lays siege to Rome for a second time. Alaric promotes Priscus Attalus as Emperor. Pestilence in Spain

410   Alaric deposes Attalus and lays siege to Rome for third time. Rome sacked by Goths. Traditional date for the formal secession of Britain from the empire with the 'Rescript of Honorius'

411   Flavius Constantius becomes *magister militum* and begins to restore the fortunes of the west

413   Constantius campaigns against Athaulf and the Goths. Settlement of Goths in Aquitaine begins

416–419   Combined Gothic–Roman campaigns in Spain destroy power of Alans and Siling Vandals. The survivors join the Asding Vandals

417   Constantius marries Galla Placidia, sister of Honorius

419   Birth of Valentinian, son of Constantius and Galla Placidia

c.420   Death of Charaton, release of Aetius

421   Constantius III made joint-Augustus. Death of Constantius III

422   Castinus and Boniface sent against Vandals in Spain. They quarrel and Boniface flees to Africa. Castinus defeated by Vandals. Galla Placidia breaks with Honorius and moves to Constantinople, taking her son Valentinian with her

423   Death of Honorius. Theodosius II in Constantinople delays declaration of new emperor. The *patricius* Castinus names John as Emperor. Aetius made *cura palatii*. Possible date of Aetius' marriage to Carpilio's daughter

424   Late in the year John sends Aetius to the Huns to ask for support in John's claim to the West. October, Theodosius declares his cousin Valentinian III emperor of the West and betroths Valentinian to his daughter Licinia Eudoxia

425   Eastern army invades West. John takes refuge in Ravenna but is betrayed by the garrison and executed. Three days after execution Aetius arrives with a Hunnic army: battle with Eastern forces under Aspar. Aetius and Placidia (mother of Valentinian III) reach agreement: Huns paid off, Aetius made *comes et magister militum per Gallias*, Felix made *magister militum praesentalis* and *patricius*. Valentinian crowned 23 October, aged six. Vandals capture Cartagena and sack Seville

426   Aetius defeats Goths besieging Arles. Vandals occupy Seville

427   Felix contrives disgrace of Boniface: civil war in Africa

428   Aetius defeats Franks on the Rhine. Vandals occupy Seville

429	Aetius made *magister militum praesentalis* (*magister equitum*), remaining subordinate to Felix. Truth concerning contrived disgrace of Boniface emerges. May 429 Vandals cross Straits of Gibraltar to Africa. August 429 inscription at Altava in North Africa attests to movement of Vandals towards Carthage. Darius brokers truce with Vandals. Sueves plunder Lusitania
430	Aetius destroys a Gothic group near Arles led by Anaolsus. Returning to Italy, Aetius accuses Felix of plotting against him. The troops kill Felix and his wife. Aetius defeats Iuthungi (Alamanni) in Raetia. Sueves pillage central Gallaecia. In Africa, Vandals break truce and defeat Boniface in battle. Siege of Hippo begins. Saint Augustine dies 28 August in the third month of the siege
431	Aetius defeats Nori in Noricum. Aetius accepted as Consul for 432. Sueves pillage Gallaecia. Vandals raise siege of Hippo. Franks capture Tournai and Cambrai
432	Aetius Consul for the first time. Aetius defeats Franks on the Rhine. Boniface and Aspar, an Eastern *magister militum*, defeated by Vandals. Sack of Hippo. Boniface returns to Italy: Aetius attacks him at the Battle of Rimini but is defeated and returns to his estates. Boniface dies of wounds received in the battle and his son-in-law Sebastian takes control in Rome. Alleged attack on Aetius, who flees to the Huns
433	Aetius returns and is installed as *magister militum*. Sebastian flees. Aetius marries Pelagia, widow of Boniface
435	Treaty with the Vandals, giving them parts of North Africa. Aetius defeats the Burgundians and signs a treaty. Tibatto leads a *bacaudic* rebellion in 'Farther Gaul'. Aetius made *patricius* 5 September
436	Aetius sends army into Armorica under Litorius to fight the *bacaudae*. Goths declare war and begin siege of Narbonne. Burgundians break treaty
437	Litorius defeats Tibatto and raises Gothic siege of Narbonne. Aetius receives help from the Huns, who attack and decimate the Burgundians. Sueves pillage Gallaecia. Franks capture Cologne and Trier. Vandals begin persecution of Catholic priests and begin tentative raids in the Mediterranean. 21 October marriage of Valentinian III and Licinia Eudoxia in Constantinople. Aetius attends wedding. Aetius Consul for the second time
437/438	Unknown commander sent to Spain and defeats Sueves
438	Peace treaty with Sueves. Publication of *Codex Theodosianus* in Constantinople. Vandal raids increase, focusing on Sicily
439	*Codex Theodosianus* accepted in West. Death of Litorius, treaty with Goths. Sueves under their new king Rechila capture Emerita. Probable death of Rua and accession of Bleda and Attila. Treaty of Margus between Huns and the East. 19 October Vandals capture Carthage

440	Sueves capture Mertola. Aetius settles the Alans of Sambida near Valence. Vandals lay siege to Panormus in Sicily and raid Bruttium
440/441	Birth of Gaudentius, son of Aetius
441	*Bacaudic* rebellion in Tarraconensis. Astyrius sent with an army and 'slaughters' the rebels. Sueves capture Seville and take control of Baetica and Carthaginiensis. The East sends an army to retake Africa: it stops in Sicily. Persians and Huns declare war on the East
442	The Eastern army is recalled from Sicily after a peace treaty is signed with the Vandals giving them the province of Africa and other territories in the area. Pestilence in the empire. Settlement of the Alans in 'Farther Gaul'
443	Remnant of the Burgundians settled in Savoy. Astyrius recalled from Spain and his son-in-law Merobaudes sent to replace him. Merobaudes 'smashes the *bacaudae* of Aracelli'. Treaty between Aetius and Attila: parts of Pannonia ceded to the Huns, Attila made honorary *magister militum*, Constantius sent to act as Attila's secretary and Aetius' son Carpilio sent as one of the hostages. Clodio, king of the Franks, captures Arras and besieges Tours
444	Valentinian III acknowledges the bankruptcy of the West. Siege of Tours by Franks ends. With his borders secure against the Empire, Attila has his brother Bleda assassinated and assumes sole control of the Huns
444/445	A new tax, the *siliquatum*, levied in the West
445	Aetius ambushes the Franks at Vicus Helena. Peace treaty agreed between the West and the Franks. Vandals attack Turonium in Gallaecia. Statue of Aetius erected in the Atrium Libertatis
446	Aetius Consul for the third time. On 1 January Merobaudes reads panegyric. Aetius leads a victory procession through the streets of Rome. Plea from the Britons for aid. Vitus sent to Spain but defeated by Rechila and the Sueves
447	27 January major earthquake in Constantinople: part of the walls collapse. Huns' envoys rejected and Attila devastates Thrace and Illyricum. Huns withdraw after contracting 'sickness of the bowels'
448	East signs a peace treaty with the Huns. New annual tribute set at 2,100 pounds of gold and land along the Danube from Pannonia to Thrace vacated by Rome. Rechila attacks the 'farthest reaches' of Gallaecia then dies: Rechiarius the new king. *Bacaudic* revolt in northern Gaul under Eudoxius. Sigisvult made *patricius*
449	Astyrius made consul. Firminus, a Gaul, made Praetorian Prefect of Gaul. Theoderic, King of the Goths, gives his daughter in marriage to Rechiarius, King of the Sueves. In February, Rechiarius attacks the Basques in northern Spain. Basilius leads *bacaudic* uprising in Spain. Rechiarius and Basilius join forces and capture Ilerda
449/450	Honoria, sister of Valentinian, caught having affair with Eugenius

450   Eugenius executed; Honoria appeals to Attila for support. 28 July death of Theodosius. Theodosius' sister Pulcheria chooses Marcian as new emperor; crowned on 26 August 450. He immediately rejects all treaties with the Huns. Attila chooses to invade the West in 'support' of Honoria rather than attempt to defeat Marcian. Aetius recognizes the danger and begins attempts to establish an alliance to face Attila. Aetius holds his troops in Italy, expecting Attila to invade

451   Attila invades Gaul, razing and ravaging many cities. Eastern forces fight the Huns in the Balkans. Attila lays siege to Orleans. After much debate the Goths under Theoderic join with Aetius. The combined force raises the siege of Orleans and pursues the Huns eastward. Battle of the Catalaunian Plains: defeat of Attila and death of Theoderic. Beginning of famine in Italy. Sueves ravage large areas of Spain

452   Attila invades Italy, sacking Aquileia and capturing many cities. Aetius guards the Apennine passes. Attila's forces, suffering from hunger and disease, begin to retreat from Italy. Reinforced from the East, Aetius harasses their rear. Forces from the East under the Eastern general Aetius invade the Hunnic homelands. Attila meets Pope Leo and ransoms some of his captives before leaving Italy

453   Attila prepares a campaign against the East. Death of Attila: civil war in the Hunnic empire. Thorismund, the new King of the Goths, attacks the Alans in northern Gaul. He then lays siege to Arles. Thorismund persuaded to raise the siege by Ferreolus. Frederic, brother of Thorismund, made *magister militum*. New peace treaty made with Sueves. Death of Thorismund

454   *Bacaudic* revolt in Tarraconensis: Frederic, brother of Thorismund, sent with an army and slaughters large numbers of rebels. Betrothal of Aetius' son Gaudentius with Valentinian's daughter Placidia. Opposition to Aetius coalesces on Petronius Maximus. Battle of the Nedao and collapse of Hunnic empire of Attila. Assassination of Aetius

455   Beginnings of expansion of Goths, Saxons, Franks and Alamanni. Assassination of Valentinian III. Maximus proclaimed emperor. Avitus sent as envoy to the Goths. Eudoxia, Valentinian's widow, appeals to Gaiseric for help. Vandals land in Italy. Maximus panics and is killed by the Roman mob. Sack of Rome by the Vandals and capture of Eudoxia, Pelagia, Eudocia and Gaudentius. Gaiseric then conquers the whole of Roman Africa west of Cyrenaica, the Balearic Islands, Sardinia and Corsica. Goths proclaim Avitus as Emperor. Sueves ravage Roman Spain

456   Theoderic II invades Spain and defeats the Sueves. Avitus appoints Ricimer as *magister militum*, who defeats Vandals on land near Agrigentum and at sea near Corsica. Rebellion of Majorian; defeat and death of Avitus

461   Death of Majorian: Ricimer rules the West, elevating and destroying a series of short-lived emperors

472	Death of Ricimer. Gundobad becomes *magister militum*
473	On the death of his father, the king of the Burgundians, Gundobad abdicates his post and leaves Italy to fight for his inheritance
474	The Eastern emperor Leo appoints his nephew Julius Nepos as Western Emperor
475	Orestes appointed *magister militum* by Nepos. Orestes rebels and evicts Nepos from Italy: Nepos takes refuge in Illyricum. Orestes elevates his son Romulus Augustulus to emperor. Orestes refuses to bow down to the demands of the imperial mercenaries. They rebel under Odoacer. Death of Orestes. Romulus Augustulus deposed
480	Death of Julius Nepos. End of Western Empire

Imperial Family Tree

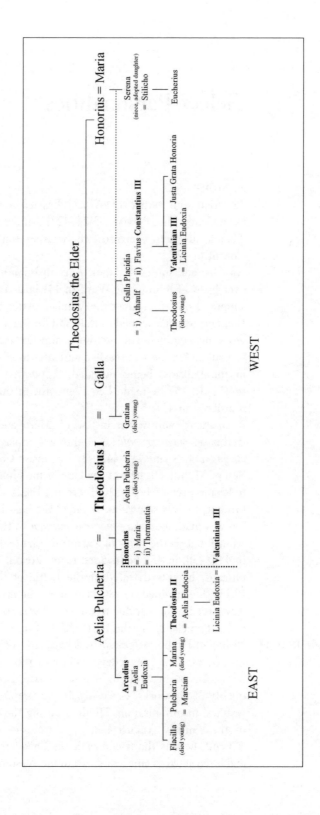

Select Personalities

Aetius	c.390–454.
Ardabur	An Alan and father of Aspar. Eastern *magister militum*, he defeated the Persians (421–422) before being sent by Theodosius II to overthrow the usurper John in the West. Consul in 427.
Aspar	An Alan and son of Ardabur. Accompanied his father in the overthrow of John in the West. In 431 he arrived in Africa to support Boniface against the Vandals. After being defeated, Boniface was summoned to Italy and for the next two to three years he conducted a holding campaign against Gaiseric. Consul in 434, he was recalled and later fought against Attila in the Balkans, being defeated. Appointed *patricius* prior to 451. In 457 he made Leo I emperor in the East. He was murdered in 471.
Astyrius	A Spaniard and father-in-law of Merobaudes, he served Aetius as *magister militum*, fighting campaigns against the *bacaudae* in Spain 441–443. He was made Consul in 449.
Attila	Son of Mundiuch, he was the king of the Huns in succession to Rua in partnership with his brother Bleda. After killing his brother, he was sole ruler. Invaded the East in 441 and 447. He was made honorary *magister militum* in the West in 449. After Honoria the sister of Valentinian III had asked for help in 449/450, in 451 he invaded Gaul. Forced to retreat from Orleans, he was defeated at the Battle of the Catalaunian Plains. Determined on revenge, in 452 he invaded Italy, but was forced to retreat due to hunger, disease and the ravaging of his homelands by the East. He died in 453.
Augustine (Saint)	Bishop of Hippo, Augustine was baptised by (Saint) Ambrose in 387. He is acknowledged as one of the founding fathers of the Christian Church. A prolific writer, the volume and quality of his works, especially *De civitate Dei* (*City of God*) resulted in canonisation. He died during the siege of Hippo by the Vandals, August 438.
Avitus	A Gaul, he was the friend of King Theoderic of the Goths and often acted as ambassador from the Western court. Served

under Aetius against the Iuthungi in 430 and the Nori in 431. Master of the Troops in Gaul in 437 and Praetorian Prefect of Gaul in 439. He acted as Aetius' envoy to the Goths in 451 and persuaded them to join the alliance against Attila. After the death of Aetius he was made *magister militum* in 455 and in the same year was made emperor. Defeated by Ricimer in a civil war, he was made Bishop of Placentia shortly before his death.

Boniface   A native of Thrace, Boniface rose to become Count of Africa in 422. In this year he was assigned to accompany Castinus against the Vandals, but argued with Castinus and fled to Africa. Remained loyal to Placidia after the death of Honorius. Accused of treachery by Felix in 427, Boniface was forced to defend himself against imperial attacks until the truth was discovered and he was restored to imperial favour in 430. In the same year he was defeated by the Vandals in Africa and besieged in Hippo. The Vandals raised the siege in 431 and in 432 Boniface, accompanied by Aspar, again fought the Vandals and lost. Shortly after he was summoned to Italy and made *patricius* by Placidia. He defeated Aetius at the Battle of Rimini but died shortly after. One of his last acts was to allegedly tell his wife Pelagia to marry Aetius.

Carpilio   Son of Aetius, he was sent to Attila as ambassador and in 443 he was one of the hostages exchanged with Attila.

Castinus   Made *magister militum* by Honorius in 422, he was sent to Spain to fight the Vandals. He quarrelled with Boniface and was then defeated by the Vandals. On Honorius' death he promoted John to be emperor. After John's defeat and execution, Castinus was exiled in 425.

Charaton   Overlord of the Huns from c.412, it is likely that Aetius spent a lot of time as a hostage with the Huns under Charaton.

Clodio/Chlogio   King of the Franks, in 431 he captured Tournai and Cambrai, and in 437 Cologne and Trier. In 443 he captured Arras and besieged Tours. In 444 the siege was raised and in 445 the Franks were defeated by Aetius at Vicus Helena. The cities of Cologne and Trier were returned to the Romans.

Darius   *vir inlustris* (illustrious individual), he negotiated a (temporary) truce with the Vandals in 429.

Ellac   Eldest son of Attila, he was killed fighting the Huns' rebellious subjects at the Battle of the Nedao in 454.

Eudoxia   Full name Licinia Eudoxia, she was the daughter of Theodosius II and was married to Valentinian III in 437. They had two children, Eudocia and Placidia. After the assassination of Valentinian in 455 she was forced to marry the new emperor Maximus. She appealed to Gaiseric, who then sacked Rome, captured Eudoxia and her two daughters and took them back to Carthage. Around the year 462 Eudoxia's daughter Eudocia finally married Huneric, son of Gaiseric, and Eudoxia and Pelagia were sent to Constantinople.

Felix
When the Eastern campaign against the Western usurper John succeeded, Valentinian (Placidia) appointed Felix as the new *magister militum* and *patricius* of the West. In 427 he led a successful expedition against the Huns living in Pannonia. In 430 he was accused of plotting against Aetius and killed by the troops in Ravenna.

Gaiseric
King of the Vandals (428–477), Gaiseric led them out of Spain into Africa. In 435 he agreed terms with the West which gave the Vandals large areas of Africa to live in before, in 439, he successfully captured Carthage. The failure of the campaign to oust Gaiseric in 441–442 resulted in the Treaty of 442, in which Gaiseric was given large areas of fertile land in North Africa, including the city of Carthage. After the death of Valentinian in 455 Gaiseric believed that his treaty obligations were over and he sacked Rome before expanding his empire to include all of Africa west of Cyrenaica, plus the Balearic islands, Sardinia and Corsica. After defeating two further attempts by the empire to defeat him in 460 and 468, Gaiseric finally concluded a treaty with the East in 476 before his death in 477.

Gaudentius
Second son of Aetius, born c.440. In 454 Aetius arranged for a betrothal between Gaudentius and Placidia, daughter of Valentinian III. After Aetius' death, Gaudentius was captured by the Vandals in the sack of Rome in 455 and taken to Carthage. He was still alive in the early 460s.

Gundichar
King of the Burgundians in the early 430s, he was defeated by Aetius after attempting to extend his dominions in 435. His rebellion in 436–437 resulted in Aetius calling upon the Huns for help. The Burgundians were decimated and Gundichar was killed. This may have been the origin of the Nibelungen cycle.

Honorius
Roman Emperor 395–423. His death without an heir in 423 prompted the succession crisis that resulted in the elevation of John and the start of Aetius' dramatic rise to pre-eminence.

Huneric
Son and heir of Gaiseric, he was married to a daughter of Theoderic, king of the Goths. In 442 he was sent as a hostage to Valentinian III. He appears to have made a favourable impression and was betrothed to Valentinian's daughter Eudocia. His first wife was mutilated and sent home. After

the sack of Carthage in 455 Eudocia was captured and kept at Carthage until she was finally married to Huneric c.462. He ruled the Vandals 477–484.

John

A *primicerius notariorum* in 423, after the death of Honorius he was made *Augustus* by Castinus. John sent Aetius to the Huns to gain their support, but they arrived too late to save John. In 425 he was captured by the Eastern forces supporting the claim of Valentinian (III) and executed.

Litorius

Appointed as *comes rei militaris* in Gaul in 436 to defeat the *bacaudae* led by Tibatto in Armorica, he then marched to relieve the siege of Narbonne by the Goths in 437. In 439 he was made *magister militum per Gallias* and forced the Goths to retreat towards Toulouse. He was killed attempting to defeat the Goths.

Majorian

A military commander under Aetius, he fought against the Franks and was besieged in Tours in 443–444. In 445, along with Aetius, he defeated the Franks at Vicus Helena. By 454 he had withdrawn from public life, probably under pressure from Aetius and Pelagia: Eudoxia may have wanted Majorian to marry her daughter Placidia and so be the next heir to the throne. Pelagia was against this, and with Majorian's withdrawal from public life she arranged that her son Gaudentius was betrothed to Placidia instead. After the death of Aetius, Valentinian recalled Majorian. He remained a powerful figure during the short reign of Valentinian's successor Maximus. Shortly after Avitus was made emperor Majorian rebelled. In 457 he was crowned emperor and in 460 led an unsuccessful campaign against the Vandals in Africa. In 461 he was deposed by Ricimer and five days later he was executed.

Maximus

After a long and distinguished career, including being the Praetorian Prefect, Consul and *patricius*, in 454 he was intimately involved, along with the eunuch Heraclius, in the death of Aetius. Realising that Heraclius would block any attempts he made to take Aetius' place, Maximus is alleged to have urged Optila and Thraustila to murder Valentinian. On Valentinian's death, Maximus assumed the throne, marrying Valentinian's widow Eudoxia. When he learned that the Vandals had landed near Rome Maximus panicked and fled. As he attempted to leave Rome he was struck by a missile and the mob then turned on him and tore him to pieces.

Merobaudes

A native of Spain, possibly of Germanic ancestry, he was acclaimed as both a poet and a general. Panegyrist to Aetius, he also served in a military capacity under Aetius in 430 and 431 against the Alamanni and the Nori. In 435 he was honoured by a statue in Trajan's Forum and was probably declared *patricius* on the marriage of Valentinian and Eudoxia in 437. In 443 he was made *magister militum* and sent to Spain to relieve his father-in-law Astyrius in the campaign against the *bacaudae*.

Mundiuch   Brother of Rua and Octar, joint kings of the Huns. His sons were Bleda and Attila.

Octar   Brother of Rua and Mundiuch, he was joint king of the Huns until his death in 530.

Optila   Either a Hun or a Goth, he served in Aetius' bodyguard before being transferred to the bodyguard of Valentinian III. After Aetius' death Optila assassinated Valentinian, and Thraustila the eunuch Heraclius, on the Campus Martius in 455.

Pelagia   Wife of Boniface and Aetius. Of Gothic origin, and so starting as an Arian, she converted to Catholic Christianity upon marrying Boniface, although it is claimed that she had their daughter baptized as an Arian. On Boniface's death he is reported to have told her to marry Aetius, which she did, bearing him a son named Gaudentius. In 454 she is said to have been strongly against the betrothal of Majorian and Eudocia, managing to block this and arrange for Eudocia's betrothal to Gaudentius instead.

Placidia   Full name Aelia Galla Placidia. Daughter of Theodosius I, in 414 she was married to Athaulf, the 'king' of the Goths. Their son Theodosius died soon after his birth and Athaulf was assassinated in 415. Returning to the empire, in 417 she married Constantius, the *patricius* of her brother Honorius, giving birth to Honoria and Valentinian, the future Valentinian III. Constantius was made Emperor in 421 and Placidia was declared *Augusta* at the same time. Unfortunately, Constantius died later the same year. After the death of her brother Honorius in 423 she campaigned in Constantinople for her son Valentinian to be accepted as Emperor of the West. After the East's successful campaign to oust the usurper John, in 425 Placidia regained her place as *Augusta* in the West and acted as regent to her son Valentinian III. She undoubtedly took part in the political manoeuvres of Felix, Boniface and Aetius and in 432 recalled Boniface in an attempt to oust Aetius from his pre-eminent position in the West. This succeeded, but Boniface died shortly afterwards and Aetius returned to power. Any evidence for later opposition to Aetius is implied rather than explicit and it may be that she accepted Aetius as her son's protector, recognising that Aetius would

	not attempt to remove Valentinian and replace him with Aetius' own nominee. She died in 450.
Pope Leo I	Bishop of Rome (Pope) from 440, in 452 Leo was sent on an embassy to Attila, apparently to organize the release of Attila's captives. The story has changed over time into the well-known version where he saved Rome from sack with the aid of divine intervention. In 455 he attempted to intercede with Gaiseric during the sack of Rome, and may have been responsible for Gaiseric limiting the course of the sack to looting.
Rechiarius	Son of the Suevic king Rechila, after Rechila's death in 448 he plundered widely in Spain. He also married the daughter of Theoderic I. He made a peace treaty with Rome in 452 and renewed it in 454. After Aetius' death he again began expanding Suevic territories in Spain, despite threats from Theoderic II. Shortly afterwards Theoderic II invaded Spain and Rechiarius was defeated and killed.
Rechila	A pagan king of the Sueves he succeeded to the throne in 438. He oversaw Suevic expansion in Spain when Aetius was concentrating his energies on Gaul and Africa. Prior to his death in 448 he had conquered the majority of Gallaecia, Baetica and Carthaginiensis.
Rua	Brother of Mundiuch and Octar, he was joint king of the Huns between his accession c.420 and death in 439. A staunch ally of Aetius, during his reign he supported Aetius' successful attempt to regain his position in 433. His death ended the alliance between Aetius and the Huns and resulted in the accession of Attila and Bleda.
Sebastian	Son-in-law of Boniface, between Boniface's death in 432 and Aetius' return in 433 he was *magister militum* in the West. Fleeing the capital, he took refuge in the East, where he earned a poor reputation for allowing his followers to act as pirates. In 444 he fled to Toulouse and from there to Spain. He finally attempted to take refuge with the Vandals in Africa, but Gaiseric distrusted him and had him killed.
Sigisvult	One of Aetius' most gifted subordinates, he was a Germanic Arian, although his origin is unknown. In 427 he was sent to Africa to continue the civil war against Boniface. He was in command in Africa until Boniface's reinstatement at court in 429. As part of the wedding celebrations of Valentinian III and Eudoxia he was made Consul alongside Aetius in 437. Made *magister militum*, in 440 he organized Italian defences against the Vandals after they had conquered Africa. In 448 he was made *patricius*, but his career after this is unknown.

Theoderic I   King of the Visigoths (418–451), he succeeded Wallia in 418 and oversaw the foundation of the Gothic kingdom in the West. Unhappy with both the limits set on his kingdom and with his exclusion from Roman politics, he made several attempts to correct these grievances by attacking the empire, most notably in 425 and 436–439. In 451 he agreed to join Aetius against Attila. He was killed at the Battle of the Catalaunian Plains.

Theoderic II   Son of Theoderic I, in his youth he was taught by the Roman Avitus. He accompanied his father to the Battle of the Catalaunian Plains in 451. Unhappy with the rule of his brother Thorismund, Theoderic and his brother Frederic had Thorismund murdered and Theoderic became king. In 455 he supported Avitus' claim to the imperial throne. In the same year his envoys to his brother-in-law Rechiarius of the Sueves was rebuffed and Theoderic invaded Spain, capturing and killing Rechiarius. He oversaw the first expansion of the Goths and the establishment of an enlarged realm.

Theodosius II   Eastern Emperor (402–450). Married to Aelia Eudocia, in 437 his daughter Licinia Eudoxia married the Western Emperor Valentinian III, so re-uniting the dynastic lines of the two halves of the empire. Not a military man, he presided over the period when the East was forced to pay ever-larger 'subsidies' to the Huns under Attila and was also under pressure from the Persians in the east.

Thorismund   King of the Visigoths (451–453). Eldest son of Theoderic I, Thorismund accompanied his father to the Battle of the Catalaunian Plains in 451. Although Theoderic was killed, Thorismund's actions in driving through the centre of the Hunnic lines in an attempt to kill Attila resulted in the Huns' flight and the victory going to the Romans and their allies. Assuming the throne, Thorismund attacked the Alans north of the Loire in 453 and also laid siege to Arles, possibly in anger at the lack of rewards he believed he was owed by Aetius for the death of his father at the Catalaunian Plains. Shortly afterwards he was murdered by his brothers Theoderic II and Frederic.

Thraustila   Possibly Aetius' son-in-law. Either a Hun or a Goth, he served in Aetius' bodyguard before being transferred to the bodyguard of Valentinian III. After Aetius' death Optila assassinated Valentinian, and Thraustila the eunuch Heraclius, on the Campus Martius in 455.

Trygetius   In 435 he was Aetius' envoy who negotiated the treaty with the Vandals in Africa. In 452 he accompanied Pope Leo in his embassy to the Huns to secure the release of their prisoners as they retreated from Italy.

Uldin

King of the Huns (400–408). He was allied to the Romans prior to 406 but invaded Thrace in 408. Possibly succeeded by Rua.

Valentinian III

Emperor of the West (425–455). Coming to the throne aged only six, Valentinian's early years were dominated by his mother Placidia and his later years by Aetius. He married Eudoxia in 437. Allegedly a weak ruler, in 454 he was induced by Maximus and Heraclius the eunuch to kill Aetius, possibly in the hope that he would then be allowed to rule in person. The following year he was killed on the Campus Martius by Optila and Thraustila.

Notes

Introduction

1. Gibbon, *History of the Decline and Fall of the Rome and the Barbarians Roman Empire*, Vol. 2, p. 380.
2. Heather, *Goths and Romans*, p. 5ff.
3. Mathisen and Shanzer, *Society and Culture in Late Antique Gaul*, p. 273.
4. For the Chronicles of Prosper and Hydatius and the Gallic Chronicles of 452 and 511 Muhlberger, *The Fifth-Century Chroniclers*, is an invaluable introduction and commentary, from which much of this section is derived.
5. Muhlberger, *The Fifth-Century Chroniclers*, p. 2.
6. Ibid., p. 147.
7. Whitby and Whitby, *Chronicon Paschale 284–628 AD*, p. ix.
8. Muhlberger, *Fifth-Century Chroniclers*, pp. 147, 213.
9. Ibid., p. 213.
10. Ibid., p. 73ff.
11. Ibid., p. 98. For more on Prosper's 'unhappiness' with Aetius, see p. 99ff. Muhlberger comments: 'one wonders what Prosper might have said if Aetius had not been ruling when he wrote'. However, Prosper wrote in editions, and in the last edition of 455 Aetius was dead, so we might be seeing Prosper's 'official' opinion.
12. Halsall, *Barbarian Migrations and the Roman West*, p. 237, n. 78.
13. Oost, 'Aetius and Majorian', p. 23.
14. This section is based largely upon Clover, *Flavius Merobaudes: A Translation and Historical Commentary*, p. 7ff.
15. PLRE Vol. 1, *Merobaudes* 2.
16. Clover, *Flavius Merobaudes*, p. 8ff, esp. p. 8, n. 6 and n. 11.
17. See especially Chapters 7, 8 and 10.
18. On the similarities between the existing fragments of Merobaudes and the works of Claudian, Clover, *Flavius Merobaudes*, pp. 32–33: citing Vollmer, *MGH: AA* 14, pp. 3-6, 12-13, 16-20.
19. See Chapter 8.
20. For a detailed analysis of these poems, along with a bibliography, see Clover, *Flavius Merobaudes*, pp. 16–28.
21. The dating of this piece is extremely difficult and several possibilities exist. The dating of 443–446 is that given by Clover, *Flavius Merobaudes*, pp. 32–41, where he also discusses the other hypotheses.
22. Wood, in CAH, pp. 519–520.
23. *Cod. Th.* 1.1.5 (26 March 429).
24. Freeman, 'Aetius and Boniface', p. 423.

25. Gaiseric being spelt 'Zinzirich', *Chron. Pasch.* s.a. 439.
26. Kulikowski, 'Nation versus Army: A Necessary Contrast?', p. 69, n. 2.
27. Collins, *Visigothic Spain 409–711*, p. 19.

Chapter 1

1. Birth 391, Clover, *Flavius Merobaudes*, p. 30.
2. Kulikowski, *Rome's Gothic Wars*, pp. 144–145.
3. Merob. *Carm.* 4.42–43.
4. Jord. *Get.* 34 (176).
5. PLRE Vol. 2, *Gaudentius 5*, 493–494, translating Greg. Tur. 2.8. (citing Renatus Profuturus Frigeridus). See also Zos. 5.36.1; Jord. *Get.* 34 (176). The claim that Gaudentius was a Goth, based upon the late-Roman use of the term 'Skythian' for the Goths, appears to be mistaken.
6. Heather, *The Fall of the Roman Empire*, p. 281.
7. Greg. Tur. 2.8; (*Anonyma* 6).
8. I would like to thank Perry Gray for his thought-provoking input on Gaudentius' political influence in Italy.
9. *Cod. Th.* 9.17.3.
10. On Stilicho, O'Flynn, *Generalissimos of the Western Roman Empire*, p. 15.
11. For a summary of current thinking, ibid., p. 15. On Stilicho, see Greg. Tur. 2.8 (*a puero praetorianus*): cf. PLRE vols 1 and 2I, *Stilicho*.
12. *Cod. Just.* 12.23; description of the post, *Codex Justinianus*, 12.23 (p. 9). See also, Jones, *The Later Roman Empire, 284–602*, PLRE 2, p. 174, n. 67.
13. Jones, *The Decline of the Ancient World*, p. 200.
14. Ibid., p. 139.
15. Ibid., p. 140 ff.
16. A similar system was adopted by Adolf Hitler in Germany between 1933 and 1945. The main purpose appears to have been to encourage friction between individuals, resulting in there being less chance of these same men allying with each other to overthrow Hitler. Although unattested, it is possible that the emperors followed this tradition as a matter of policy, rather than of mere chance.
17. For a more detailed discussion of the *Notitia*, see the Introduction.
18. Jones, *Decline of the Ancient World*, p. 173.
19. A good example of this followed Stilicho's war against Gildo in 398. When Stilicho seized Gildo's lands for the empire following his victory, they were so great that a new official, the *comes Gildoniaci patrimonii* (Count of the Patrimony of Gildo), had to be appointed to administer them. Hughes, *Stilicho*, p. 112; Zos. 5.13.4.
20. Rouche, 'Autopsy of the West', pp. 29–31.
21. Ibid., p. 31.
22. Ibid., pp. 34–35.
23. Thompson, 'Peasant Revolts in Late Roman Gaul and Spain', p. 1506.
24. These laws appear to have been introduced by Diocletian in the hope of solving internal problems of recruitment, training and social mobility. cf. Fossier, *The Cambridge Illustrated History of the Middle Ages 350–950*, p. 8.

25. For a more detailed examination of the cause and effect of these changes, see Hughes, *Stilicho*, pp. 151–152.
26. Fossier, *Cambridge Illustrated History*, p. 8.
27. Cf. Halsall, *Barbarian Migrations and the Roman West*, p. 249, where he notes that the Bacaudae in Spain were 'local landlords who had established their own authority'.

Chapter 2

1. It is possible that Stilicho 'revived or manufactured a claim' that Theodosius had ordered that the prefecture of Illyricum be attached to the West: CAH, p. 121.
2. For both hostages, Zos. 5.36.1.
3. '400,000 Gauls and Germans': Zos. 5.26.3. On a more believable estimation of numbers, see the discussion in Hughes, *Stilicho*, p. 164.
4. Zos. 5.26.4.
5. Williams and Friell, *Theodosius*, p. 155.
6. Soz. 8.25.
7. Soz. 8.25: Zos. 5.27.2.
8. Zos. 5.27.2.
9. For a more detailed analysis of these events, see Hughes, *Stilicho*, p. 177 ff.
10. *Chron. Gall. 452* s.a. 442.
11. Olymp. *fr.* 12, perhaps giving the date as late 406, cf. PLRE Vol. 2, *Marcus 2*, 719: Zos. 6.2.1, giving the date as 407; cf. Soz. 9.11.2.
12. '*municeps eiusdem insulae*', Oros. 7.40.4.
13. Paschoud on Zos. 5.27.1–2 suggests a date in February (referenced in Kulikowski, 'Barbarians in Gaul', p. 333, n. 48): Burns, *Barbarians Within the Gates of Rome*, p. 210 suggests the date of 1 March.
14. Dating, Burns, *Barbarians Within the Gates of Rome*, p. 210; reason for overthrow, Kulikowski, 'Barbarians in Gaul', p. 332.
15. For a full itinerary of the cities attacked, see Hughes, *Stilicho*, pp. 183–184.
16. We are not informed directly that Constantine attempted to ally himself with the Vandals, Sueves and Alans. However, Oros. 7.40.4 and 7. 28. describes 'unreliable alliances' with barbarians and how these treaties were 'not strictly kept'. This can only relate to treaties with the invaders.
17. Oros. 7.28.
18. Oros. 7.40.5.
19. Zos. 5.27.2.
20. As a reward for his service, Heraclianus was made *comes Africae*: Zos. 5.37.6; PLRE Vol. 2, *Heraclianus 3*, p. 539. He remained loyal to Honorius and was granted the consulship in 413. In that same year he rebelled, aiming to become emperor, before being murdered.
21. Zos. 5.34.4. For the date of the execution, *Addit. Ad Prosp. Haun.* s.a. 408.
22. Zos. 5.34.5.
23. Zos. 5.37.6.
24. Zos. 5.36.1.
25. Greg. Tur. 2.8; Merobaudes, *Pan*, 2.1–4; Zos, 5.36.1
26. Zos. 5.37.1.

27. Jovius retained close ties with Alaric, Soz. 9.4.4.
28. Zos. 48.3.
29. Zos. 48.4.
30. Zos. 5.45–52; Soz. 9.7.
31. Zos. 6.12.3.
32. Zos. 6.8.
33. Zos. 6.6–12; Soz. 9.7.
34. Zos. 6.13; Soz. 9.9.
35. Zos. 6.5.2.
36. For a greater analysis of this interpretation, see Hughes, *Stilicho*, 213–214.
37. Probably following the rules of *hospitalitas*: cf. Burns, *Rome and the Barbarians*, p. 59; Hydatius 49; 'Gerontius made peace with the barbarians', Olymp. *fr.* 17.1.
38. Hyd. s.a. 411.
39. Hyd. s.a. 411.
40. Matthews, *Western Aristocracies and Imperial Court*, pp. 354–356, 382.
41. Attacks from 'beyond the Rhine', Zos. 6.5–6; attack by Saxons, *Chron. Gall. 452*, no. 62.
42. Zos. 6.5–6: 'Now the defection of Britain and the Celtic peoples took place during Constantine's tyranny.'
43. Goldsworthy, *The Fall of the West*, p. 303.
44. Oros. 7.43.
45. Matthews, *Western Aristocracies*, p. 331. Oros. 7. 43. A complex and debatable passage in Orosius also implies that a peace treaty had been concluded, although no date is given, Oros. 7.43.
46. Kulikowski, The Visigothic Settlement in Aquitania', p. 28; Hydatius, *passim*, but cf. Oros. 7.41.7.
47. Collins, *Visigothic Spain 409–711*, p. 15.
48. For the alternative date of 419, see Schwarcz in Mathisen and Shanzer, *Society and Culture in Late Antique Gaul*, pp. 15–25. Although a compelling argument, for the sake of simplicity the date of 418 will continue to be used.
49. PLRE Vol. 2, *Theodericus 2*, 1070. cf. Sid. Ap. *Carm.* 7.505.
50. Sid. Ap. *Carm.* 7.505. Theoderic is nowhere mentioned as Alaric's son, and since Sidonius attests that Theoderic's son, also called Theoderic, was the grandson of Alaric, Theoderic must have married Alaric's daughter.
51. For a more detailed discussion, see TS Burns, 'The Settlement of 418' in Drinkwater and Elton, *Fifth Century Gaul*, p. 62ff, and bibliography.
52. Philost. 12.4.
53. CEV Nixon, 'Relations between Visigoths and Romans in Fifth-Century Gaul' in Drinkwater and Elton, *Fifth Century Gaul*, pp. 64–74.
54. Olymp. *fr.* 8; PLRE Vol. 2, *Constantius 17*, p. 322.
55. Nixon in Drinkwater and Elton, *Fifth Century Gaul*, p. 72.
56. cf. Burns in ibid., p. 57.
57. Ward-Perkins, *The Fall of Rome and the End of Civilization*, p. 56, referencing A. Loyen, 'Les Débuts du royaume wisigoth de Toulouse', *Revue des études latines* 12 (1934), pp. 406–415.

58. Ward-Perkins, *Fall of Rome*, p. 67.
59. Jones, *The Decline of the Ancient World*, p. 68.
60. Ibid., p. 81 ff: cf. Bury, *History of the Later Roman Empire*, Vol. 1, p. 207.
61. As described in the Visigothic Code of Euric, Bury, *History of the Later Roman Empire*, p. 206, n. 89.
62. Jones, *Decline of the Ancient World*, p. 81.
63. Ward-Perkins, *Fall of Rome*, p. 66.
64. Rouche in Fossier, *Cambridge Illustrated History*, p. 53.
65. Ward-Perkins, *Fall of Rome*, p. 70.
66. Rouche, 'Break up and Metamorphosis', p. 53.
67. Hyd. s.a. 418.
68. Collins, *Visigothic Spain 409–711*, p. 25, referencing C. Courtois, *Les Vandales* (Paris, 1955), p. 229.
69. Poss. 28.
70. Heather, *Fall of the Roman Empire*, pp. 264–265.
71. Hyd. s.a. 419, Burgess, tr., p. 87.
72. Heather, *Fall of the Roman Empire*, p. 265.
73. Hyd. s.a. 420, referenced in PLRE Vol. II, *Asterius 4*, 171.
74. Hyd. s.a. 420.
75. Greg. Tur. 2.8; Merob. *Pan.* 2.1–4. Unfortunately, neither reference gives a date for Aetius' time as a hostage to the Huns.
76. For an in-depth analysis of the history of the Huns, see Maenchen-Helfen, *The World of the Huns*: for the period in question, esp. p. 70ff.
77. Soc. 7.43.3.
78. Invasion if Thrace, e.g. Soz. 8.25.1; help against Radagaisus, e.g. Oros. 7.37.12.
79. PLRE Vol. 2, *Uldin* 1180; Soz. 11.5.1.
80. Examples of Huns serving others are plentiful: the *bucellarii* serving Aetius himself; the claim by Ammianus that the Gothic king Vithimer, fighting against the first inroads of the Huns in the fourth century, used Hunnic mercenaries (31.3.3); Huns being used by Castinus later in 424 against Boniface (Pseudo-Aug. *Ep.* 4, PL33, 1095); see Chapter 7.
81. MacGeorge, *Late Roman Warlords*, p. 12.
82. Olymp. *fr* 18.
83. Jord. *Get.* 180.
84. For a full discussion of the problems surrounding Rua and Octar, see Maenchen-Helfen, *World of the Huns*, p. 80ff.
85. Olymp. *fr.* 34.
86. Marc. com. s.a. 419.
87. *Parens principum*; PLRE Vol. 2, *Constantius 17*, 323, *Insc*r. 1–2; Emperor, PLRE Vol. 2, *Constantius 17*, 324; Theoph. AM 5913; Placidia *Augusta*, Olymp. fr. 31, Prosp. s.a. 423, 425; Valentinian *nobilissimus*, Olymp. *fr.* 34; Philost. 12.12.
88. Olymp. *fr.* 34
89. Olymp. *fr.* 34; Philost. 12.12.
90. Philost. 12.12.

91. Olymp. *fr.* 40; Philost. 12.12.
92. Date, Soc. 7.22.20; cause, Philost. 12.13.

Chapter 3

1. Greg. Tur. 2.9.
2. Ibid.
3. O'Flynn, *Generalissimos of the Western Roman Empire*, pp. 74–75.
4. The dating is slightly problematic, but unimportant. Prosper has him as *Dux* in 422 (s.a. 422), but he is then acknowledged as *magister* in 423 (s.a. 423). However, Hydatius states that he is magister in 422 (s.a. 422). The confusion in the sources is most likely caused by a similar political confusion following the unexpected death of Constantius III in 421. Cf. Cass. *Chron.* s.a. 422.
5. Olymp. *fr.* 22.2; PLRE Vol. 2, *Boniface 3*, p. 238.
6. Aug. *Ep.* 189.
7. Prosp. s.a. 422.
8. Ibid.
9. Prosp. s.a. 422; Hyd. s.a. 422; *Chron. Gall.* 511 no. 571.
10. Aug. *Ep.* 220.
11. Hyd. s.a. 422: Salv. *De gub. Dei*, 7.11. The claim in CAH that he was killed appears to be a mistake: CAH, Wood, *The Fall of the Western Empire and the End of Roman Britain*, p. 519.
12. Heather, *The Fall of the Roman Empire*, p. 265.
13. O'Flynn, *Generalissimos*, p. 75.
14. Prosp. s.a. 423.
15. Olymp. *fr.* 38.
16. *Ann. Rav.* s.a. 423.
17. Date, *Ann. Rav.* Col. 2.10–12; Castinus' involvement, Prosp. s.a. 423; Hyd. s.a. 424. Matthews, *Western Aristocracies*, p. 379; cf. Soc. 7.23.
18. *Ann. Rav.* Col. 2.10–12.
19. PLRE Vol. 2, *Castinus 2*, p. 270. On the theory that Theodosius accepted Castinus' own proposal of himself as candidate for consul, see O'Flynn, *Generalissimos*, p. 75. On the failure of the embassy, see for example, Greg. Tur. 2.8; Soc. 7.23.3 ff.; Philost. 12.13.
20. Philost. 12.13.
21. *Cod. Th.* 2, 17.3; Aug., *Civ. Dei*, 18.54.
22. Merob. *Pan.* 2.110–114.
23. Greg. Tur. 2.8.
24. Greg. Tur. 2.8; cf. Philost. 12.14.
25. Greg. Tur. 2.8.
26. Prisc. *Rom.* 3; Cass. *Var.* 1.4.11.
27. 'Aetius ... while still a youth, spent three years in the hands of Alaric as a hostage, and then was passed on to the Huns. Later in life he became the son in law of Carpilio, one-time head of the imperial household and then governor of the palace.' Greg. Tur. 2.8.
28. Prosp. s.a. 424.

29. Ibid.
30. Hughes, *Stilicho*, p. 101ff.
31. Pseudo-Aug., *Ep.* 4, PL33, 1095, cited in Maenchen-Helfen, *World of the Huns*, pp. 76–77.
32. Prosp. a.424: 'John's defences were weaker because he tried to recapture Africa, over which Boniface was maintaining his control.'
33. Matthews, *Western Aristocracies*, p. 379; *Sirm.* 5 (9 July 425); Arian tendencies, Freeman, 'Aetius and Boniface', p. 430.
34. Prosp. 424.
35. cf. Heather, *Fall of the Roman Empire*, p. 281.
36. *Chron. Min.* 1.470.
37. Prosp. s.a. 424.
38. Olymp. *fr.* 43. The appointment as *Caesar* was normal, with the appointment as *Augustus* certain to follow at the appropriate time, yet the manner of the appointment was also doubtless to ensure that Theodosius maintained seniority, rather than Valentinian being seen as an equal.
39. Greg. Tur. 2.8; Olymp. Fr. 46; Marcel. com. s.a. 424.
40. Philost. 12.13.
41. PLRE Vol. 2, *Candidianus 3*, 257.
42. Soc. 7.18, 20 and 23; Joh. Ant. *fr.* 195; Theoph. AM 5918
43. 'with gold': Greg. Tur. 2.8.
44. For a more detailed account of the Huns, see esp. Chapter 12.
45. Philost. 12.13. Socrates (7.23) claims that Theodosius had taken Salona as soon as Honorius had died. This would seem an odd manner in which to begin the new rule of the west.
46. Philost. 12.13.
47. Ibid.
48. Olymp. *fr.* 46.
49. CAH. 136.
50. Olymp. *fr.* 43.2; Blockley, 209 and 220, n. 84.
51. Philost. 12.13.
52. Matthews, *Western Aristocracies*, p. 380.
53. Soc. 7.23 suggests that the passage was assisted by angels, but a rather more prosaic manner of entry seems preferable. Philostorgius suggests that there was a battle outside the city, but his imprecise claim that 'there was some sort of battle' (12.13) may be a way of describing the confusion surrounding Aspar's unexpected entry into the city.
54. Proc. 3.3.9; Philost 12.13.
55. Philostorgius following Olympiodorus claims 'as many as 60,000'; Olymp. *fr.* 43.2; Philostorgius 12.14. Also, Cass. *Chron.* s.a. 425.
56. Greg. Tur. 2.8.
57. 'Heavy slaughter on both sides': Olymp. *fr.* 43.2.
58. Philost, 12.14; Greg. Tur. 2.8; Prosp. s.a. 425.
59. Philost. 12.14 (Olymp. *fr.* 43.2). On ceding of Pannonia, see Maenchen-Helfen, *World of the Huns*, p. 89.

60. O'Flynn, *Generalissimos*, p. 74.
61. Soc. 24.
62. Hyd. s.a. 425; PLRE Vol. 2, *Fl. Constantius Felix 14*, 461. O'Flynn follows Prosper in dating the patricianship to 429 (Prosp. s.a. 429).
63. *Chron. Min.* 1. 471.
64. It is possible that either luck or his political and marital contacts helped Castinus to survive at this time, although without evidence it has been decided that the main reason was his decision to maintain a low profile.
65. *Cod. Th.* 6.2.25 (26 April 426).
66. It is possible that Aetius simply retained the title of *comes*, but the level and the duration of his activity suggest the more senior post of *magister militum*, although there is no record elsewhere of the name of any *magister militum per Gallias* between 411 and 429: O'Flynn, *Generalissimos*, pp. 78 and 82 and 176, n. 35.
67. *Chron. Gall 452.* s.a. 425.
68. PLRE Vol. 2, *Boniface 3*, pp. 238–239.

Chapter 4

1. For a more detailed examination of many aspects of the late Roman army, see Sabin, van Wees and Whitby (eds), *The Cambridge History of Greek and Roman Warfare*.
2. For a more detailed examination of the *Notitia*, and of the changes in the army from the reign of Diocletian, see e.g. Elton in Sabin, van Wees and Whitby, *The Cambridge History of Greek and Roman Warfare, Vol 2*, p. 271ff.'
3. Hoffmann, D, 'Der Oberbefehl des spätrömischen Heeres im 4. Jahrhundert n. Chr.' in DM Pippidi (ed.), *Actes des IXe Congrès International d'études sur les frontières romains* (Cologne, 1974), pp. 381–397, as referenced in Liebeschuetz, *Barbarians and Bishops*, p. 54, n. 8.
4. For examples, see Appendix.
5. Southern and Dixon, *The Late Roman Army*, p. 57.
6. Elton in Sabin, van Wees and Whitby, *The Cambridge History*, p. 270.
7. For a more detailed discussion of the Roman army hierarchy, see Elton, *Warfare in Roman Europe AD 350–425*, pp. 89–107.
8. Ibid., p. 99.
9. Ibid., p. 95.
10. *Not. Dig. Oc* VII.
11. Jones, *The Later Roman Empire, 284–602*, Appendix III.
12. For the earlier losses, see Hughes, *Stilicho, passim*.
13. Jones, *Later Roman Empire*, Appendix III; Jones, *The Decline of the Ancient World*, p. 81; Heather, *Fall of the Roman Empire*, p. 175.
14. Jones, *The Later Roman Empire*, p. 1434.
15. Elton, *Warfare in Roman Europe*, pp. 91–92.
16. Rouche, 'Autopsy of the West', p. 26. The 'Ripuarian' Franks, possibly derived from *ripa* ('river bank'), were from the west bank of the Rhine; the 'Salian' Franks, possibly from *sal* ('salt', 'sea-side', although other derivations are possible) were from Toxandria (north Belgium).
17. Elton in Sabin, van Wees and Whitby, *Cambridge History*, p. 281.

18. Hughes, *Stilicho*.
19. *Cod Th.* 7.13.16 (406).
20. For a full discussion on the size of units and the problems of dating any changes, see for example Coello, *Unit Sizes in the Late Roman Army*, *passim*; Nicasie, *Twilight of Empire*, p. 23ff.; Southern and Dixon, *The Late Roman Army*, pp. 29–33; Elton, *Warfare in Roman Europe*, p. 89ff; Elton in Sabin, van Wees and Whitby, *Cambridge History*, p. 278ff.
21. By the fifth century these were sometimes known as the *obsequium*: Elton in Sabin, van Wees and Whitby, *Cambridge History*, p. 278.
22. On *milliary* units, Elton, *Warfare in Roman Europe*, p. 89ff.
23. Elton in Sabin, van Wees and Whitby, *Cambridge History*, 271.
24. Elton, *Warfare in Roman Europe*, p. 90. As an earlier example, in Alexandria Caesar's Legio VI had fewer than 1,000 men left of its original 'paper' strength of approximately 5,000 men (Caesar, *Alexandrian War*, 69), and in the Civil Wars his legions average fewer than 3,000 men (Caesar, *Civil Wars*, 3.6 and 3.89).
25. Elton, *Warfare in Roman Europe*, p. 129.
26. Liebeschuetz, *Barbarians and Bishops*, p. 20.
27. See Southern and Dixon, *Late Roman Army*, p. 69.
28. Elton, *Warfare in Roman Europe*, p. 129.
29. Jones, *Decline of the Ancient World*, p. 82.
30. *Cod. Th.* 15.1.13.
31. Zos. 4.23.2-4.
32. For example, the troops that were led by Scipio Africanus in the third century BC were first trained to meet his demanding standards before being led on campaign.
33. For examples, see Amm. Marc. 27.2.2–8, 22.7.7
34. Gildas, *De Excidio et Conquestu Britanniae*, 2.18.
35. For a full discussion, Coulston, 'Later Roman Armour, 3rd–6th Centuries AD'.
36. Milner (tr.), *Vegetius*, p. 19, n. 6.
37. Bishop and Coulston, *Roman Military Equipment from the Punic Wars to the Fall of Rome*, p. 208; Amm. Marc. 16.10.8, 19.8.8, 24.6.9, 25.1.16 etc.
38. MacMullen, *Corruption and the Decline of Rome*, pp. 185 and 274, n. 15.
39. Veg. 2.15 and 4.21.
40. Veg. 4.22.
41. No examples of the *plumbatae tribolatae* have been found, so the weapon must still remain a possibility rather than a certainty.
42. Elton, *Warfare in Roman Europe*, p. 108.
43. Veg. 2.15.
44. Bishop and Coulston, *Roman Military Equipment*, p. 205.
45. Veg. 2.15.
46. Elton, *Warfare in Roman Europe*, p. 108.
47. Ibid.
48. Amm. Marc. 19.6.7; Proc. 2.21.7.
49. Theoph. *Hist.* 8.4.13.
50. Lasso, Elton, *Warfare in Roman Europe*, p. 108.
51. Bishop and Coulston, *Roman Military Equipment*, pp. 213–214.

52. Ibid., p. 213.
53. Attaching of crests, ibid., p. 214.
54. Earlier claims, e.g. James, 1986, cited in ibid., p. 230, n. 43.
55. I would like to thank the members of www.romanarmytalk.com for their in-depth discussions on these topics: for example at www.romanarmytalk.com/rat/view topic.php?f=17&t=25150&p=224574&hilit=spangenhelm#p224574 (December 2008–July 2009).
56. Elton, *Warfare in Roman Europe*, p. 110ff.
57. Bishop and Coulston, *Roman Military Equipment*, p. 216.
58. For more detailed analysis of mail manufacture, see ibid., pp. 241–242 and associated bibliography.
59. Coulston, 'Later Roman Armour, 3rd–6th Centuries AD', p. 143.
60. For example, Bishop and Coulston, *Roman Military Equipment*, p. 208.
61. Germanic influence, ibid., p. 217; guardsmen using round shields, Elton, *Warfare in Roman Europe*, p. 115.
62. Amm. Marc., 16.12.6
63. Elton, *Warfare in Roman Europe*, p. 97.
64. Elton in Sabin, van Wees and Whitby, *Cambridge History*, p. 278ff.; *Cod. Th.* 7.17.1.
65. Elton, *Warfare in Roman Europe*, p. 100.
66. Rance, 'Battle', p. 343.
67. For example, the Battle of the Frigidus (394) and the invasion of Italy by the east in order to place Valentinian I upon the throne in 425.
68. Vegetius, *Epitome of Military Science*, 1.20.
69. For example, in 393–394 Stilicho conducted a campaign against Alaric in the Balkans, finally blockading him into surrender. Alaric was forced to serve in the army that Theodosius led at the Battle of the Frigidus in 394. On the other hand, when the Gothic king Radagaisus led his troops into Italy in 405–406 he was blockaded and defeated in the hills near to Faesulae, after which he was executed and Stilicho enrolled 12,000 of Radagaisus' men into the Roman army.

Chapter 5

1. This includes the armies of the (Visi)Goths, the Franks, the Alamanni, the Burgundians and the Vandals, amongst others.
2. For example, the Goths: Wolfram, *History of the Goths*, p. 145.
3. Elton, *Warfare in Roman Europe*, p. 22.
4. Ibid., p. 72.
5. Ibid.
6. Proc. 3.5.18.
7. Pohl, 'Ethnicity, Theory and Tradition'.
8. Elton, *Warfare in Roman Europe*, p. 41.
9. Ibid., p. 43.
10. From the third century on, the deposition of swords becomes slightly more common in burials, although the finds at Ejsbøl North in Jutland has spearmen outnumbering swordsmen by a factor of three-to-one: Todd, *The Early Germans*, pp. 41–42.

11. Elton, *Warfare in Roman Europe*, p. 58.
12. Veg. 1.20.
13. Elton, *Warfare in Roman Europe*, p. 58.
14. Todd, *Early Germans*, p. 35.
15. Aur. Vic. *Caes.* 21.2.
16. Todd, *Early Germans*, p. 39.
17. Although usually dismissed as poor in comparison to the composite bow, it should be noted that the English longbow of the Middle Ages was made from a single piece of wood, utilizing the differences in compression and flexibility between the heartwood and the outer layers.
18. Agathias, *Hist.*, 2.5.4.
19. Elton, *Warfare in Roman Europe*, p. 68.
20. For example, Proc. Vandals 3.8.15–28; Goths 5.27.1ff.
21. Isidore, *Etymologiae*, 18.6.9: http://penelope.uchicago.edu/Thayer/L/Roman/Texts/Isidore/18*.html#6 (June 2009).
22. Greg. Tur. *securis* e.g. 2.27, 8.30: *bipennis* e.g. 8.19, 10.27.
23. Elton, *Warfare in Roman Europe*, p. 65.
24. Ibid., p. 108.
25. Bishop and Coulston, *Roman Military Equipment*, p. 200.
26. Elton, *Warfare in Roman Europe*, p. 65.
27. Ibid., p. 67.
28. Defined by the Bosworth-Toller dictionary as a short-sword or dagger: http://beowulf.engl.uky.edu/~kiernan/BT/bosworth.htm, p.853 (June 2009).
29. Elton, *Warfare in Roman Europe*, p. 65.
30. Ibid., p. 67.
31. Amm. Marc. 16.12.24. Unfortunately, the claim does not seem to be attested by the reference.
32. Elton, *Warfare in Roman Europe*, p. 70.
33. Ibid., p. 69.
34. Ibid., p. 45.
35. Ibid., p. 74.
36. Amm. Marc. 16.12.21–2 and 37–42.
37. Elton, *Warfare in Roman Europe*, p. 81.
38. I would like once again to thank Chris Constantine of spitfirehorsebows.com for the illuminating discussions on the difference between the symmetrical and asymmetrical bow.
39. Ammianus, translated by Maenchen-Helfen, *World of the Huns*, pp. 201–202.
40. For example, Zos. 5.20: Agathias 1.22.
41. See Chapter 15.
42. Heather, *The Goths*, p. 98.

Chapter 6

1. For comparison, Jones, *Later Roman Empire*, p. 1434 estimates the strength of the Gallic army at 34,000.
2. Matthews, *Western Aristocracies*, p. 333.

3. Ibid., p. 345ff.
4. Heinzelmann, in Drinkwater and Elton, *Fifth Century Gaul*, p. 245.
5. The most obvious example of this is Hydatius, who made appeals in person to Aetius concerning conditions regarding the Sueves.
6. Matthews, *Western Aristocracies*, p. 336 and n.1.
7. Ausonius, *Ordo Urbium Nobilium* 10.
8. MacMullen, *Corruption and the Decline of Rome*, p. 171; Mitchell, *A History of the Later Roman Empire: AD 284–641*, pp. 351–354.
9. Mitchell, *History of the Later Roman Empire*, p. 355.
10. *Chron. Gall. 452*, s.a 425; Prosp. s.a. 424.
11. For example, Elton, *Warfare in Roman Europe*, p. 42 notes that the Goths 'quickly established a kingdom': cf. Mitchell, S, *A History of the Later Roman Empire*, p. 110; Kulikowski, *Rome's Gothic Wars*, p. 183.
12. See Hughes, *Stilicho*, p. 135ff. for a discussion of Alaric's use of this title. For alternate uses of the title '*rex*', see for example Gillett, *On Barbarian Identity*, p. 116ff.
13. Hughes, *Stilicho*, p. 135.
14. O'Flynn, *Generalissimos*, p. 73
15. Burns, *Rome and the Barbarians*, p. 53.
16. cf. Nixon in Drinkwater and Elton, *Fifth Century Gaul*, pp. 68–69.
17. Paul. Pella, 377f: Heather, 2002, 87-8.
18. Elton, 2004, 42-3.
19. Nixon in Drinkwater and Elton, *Fifth Century Gaul*, p. 72.
20. Prosp. s.a. 425.
21. For example, Matthews, *Western Aristocracies*, p. 329; Heather in Drinkwater and Elton, *Fifth Century Gaul*, p. 85.
22. Matthews, *Western Aristocracies*, 335.
23. For an alternative view, see for example ibid., p. 329, who claims that the attack was due to the fact that the Goths were isolated, both with regards to communications and trade from the Mediterranean.
24. This course of events is based upon Sid. Ap. *Carm.* 7. 215–226, 481–483, 495–499. The Eparchius Avitus under consideration was Sidonius' father-in-law and is attested as visiting his relative Theodorus, a hostage at the court of Theoderic. The most likely date for this is shortly after the conclusion of the war of 426.
25. PLRE Vol. 2 gives a date of either 425 or 426 (*Aetius 7*, 22). See also the discussion of the chronology of the chronicles in the introduction.
26. cf. *Gall. Chron. 452*, s.a. 425.
27. For further analysis of the chronicles, see the Introduction.
28. Prosp. s.a. 426.
29. Freeman, 'Aetius and Boniface', p. 436ff. claims that the problem, as illustrated by the letters of St Augustine, was that Boniface was no longer interested in fulfilling his duties and had lost control of large parts of Africa. Although a possibility, the details are outside the scope of a book on Aetius.
30. Proc. 3.3.14–22; John Ant. *fr.* 196; Theoph, AM 5931.
31. Prosp. s.a. 427. Oost, 'Some Problems in the History of Galla Placidia'.

32. A view also supported by O'Flynn, *Generalissimos*, pp. 78–79.

33. The main part of this version of events is taken from Procopius, 3.3.14–22. Although in this version it is Aetius who makes the accusation, it has been assumed that although Procopius has named the wrong individual, the germ of the story is correct.

34. Prosp. s.a. 427; O'Flynn, *Generalissimos*, p. 79.

35. Prosp. s.a. 427; Mavortius, PLRE Vol. 2, *Mavortius 1*, 736; Gallio, PLRE Vol. 2, *Gallio*, 492; Sanoeces, PLRE Vol. 2, *Sanoeces*, 976; Maenchen-Helfen, *World of the Huns*, pp. 77, 419–420.

36. Prosp. s.a. 427; *Chron Gall. 452*, s.a. 424; *Comes*, Aug. *Coll. Cum Maximino 1*, *Sermo* 140, PLRE Vol. 2, *Fl. Sigisvultus*, 1010.

37. Halsall, *Barbarian Migrations and the Roman West*, p. 240; Goths in Africa, Aug. *Coll. Cum Maximino 1*, *Sermo* 140.

38. Aug., *Coll. Cum Maximino 1*, *Sermo* 140; PLRE Vol. 2, *F. Sigisvultus*, 1010.

39. Marc. com. s.a. 427.

40. Jord. *Get.* 166.

41. This campaign is dated to 428 by Prosper and Cassiodorus, but possibly to 432 by Hydatius. On the confusion prevalent in the chronicles, see the Introduction.

42. Elton in Drinkwater and Elton, *Fifth Century Gaul*, p. 167.

43. Prosp. s.a. 425 and 428; Cassiodorus, *Chron.* s.a. 428

44. Heinzelmann, in Drinkwater and Elton, *Fifth Century Gaul*, p. 243.

45. Halsall, *Barbarian Migrations*, p. 238.

46. Const., *Vit. Germ.* 12.

47. Prosp. s.a. 429. Wood, 'Fall of the Western Empire', pp. 251–252, claims that Prosper associated the mission with a Roman imperative, although a close reading of the two suggests that they are in fact complementary.

48. Hyd. a. 425, 426 and 428.

49. Hyd. s.a. 425: the reference is to Mauretania Tingitania.

50. Hyd. s.a. 428.

51. It is possible that the Vandals at this stage were actually *foederati* called up by Felix to supplement the forces of Sigisvult. Blaming Boniface for inviting the Vandals to Africa may be later propaganda aimed at discrediting an enemy of Aetius. Rather than capturing Cartagena, the Vandals may have mustered in southern Spain in accordance with their *foedus* with the imperial court. This could explain why there was no opposition to their move to Mauretania. However the fact that they had recently been subjected to an unprovoked attack by the Roman government weakens this proposal.

52. PLRE Vol. 2, *Andevotus*, 86, cf. Hyd. s.a. 438.

53. PLRE Vol. 2, *Andevotus*, 86, cf. Cassiodorus, *Variae*, 5.29 for a similar-named individual who was an Ostrogoth.

54. Hyd. s.a. 429.

55. Ibid.

56. Dating: Prosp. s.a. 427; *Chron. Pasch.* s.a. 428; Hyd. s.a. 429; *Gall. Chron. 452*, s.a. 430. Boniface responsible for the crossing to Africa: Proc. 3.3.22–6; Jord. *Get.* 33.167.

57. Hyd. s.a. 429, 'Gaiseric, king of the Vandals, abandoned the Spanish provinces in the month of May, crossing along with all the Vandals and their families from the coast of the province of Baetica to Mauretania and Africa.' For a more detailed critical analysis of the accuracy of the 'chronicles', see 'Introduction'. But cf., for example, Cass. *Chron.* s.a. 427.
58. See 'Chronology'.
59. cf. Heather, *Fall of the Roman Empire*, p. 268.
60. Schwarcz, "The Settlement of the Vandals in North Africa', p. 51.
61. Proc. 3.3.22–6; Jord. *Get.* 33.167. Jordanes was describing one of the traditional enemies of the Goths and Procopius was discussing the campaigns of his patron, who defeated heretics and barbarians, so their biases are evident.
62. Mathisen, 'Sigisvult the Patrician, Maximinus the Arian, and Political Stratagems in the Western Roman Empire c. 425–40', pp. 189–191.
63. Heather, *Fall of the Roman Empire*, p. 267.
64. Vict. Vit. 1.2.
65. Proc. 3.5.18–19.
66. Vict. Vit. 1.2.
67. Numbers, Heather, *Fall of the Roman Empire*, p. 269. It should be noted that the province of Mauretania Tingitana was classed as part of Hispania, rather than of Africa by the Romans.

Chapter 7

1. It may be useful to read this with reference to the Outline Chronology to aid understanding.
2. Hughes, *Stilicho*, esp. p. 38.
3. MacGeorge, *Late Roman Warlords*, p. 5.
4. Hyd. s.a. 425; PLRE, *Fl. Constantius Felix 14*, 461. O'Flynn follows Prosper in dating the patricianship to 429 (Prosp. s.a. 429). See also Chapter 5.
5. Although it is certain that Felix, Aetius and Boniface all had a close company of political supporters, their relative strengths are unknown.
6. Proc. 3.3.27–30.
7. The senator Darius the chief peace negotiator: Aug. *Ep.* 229–231 (www.ccel.org/ccel/schaff/npnf101.vii.1.CCXXIX.html): (October 2010).
8. O'Flynn, *Generalissimos*, p. 79.
9. *Cod. Th.* 11.30.68.
10. The fact that messengers were sent to Constantinople asking for help is not explicitly stated in the sources. However, reinforcements arrived in Africa in 431, an event which must have been precipitated by an embassy from the West. See later in the chapter, and Proc. 3.3.35; Theoph. AM 5931.
11. Aug. *Ep.* 229.
12. *Cod. Th.* 12.6.3; PLRE Vol. 2, *Theodosius 8*, 1101.
13. For a further analysis of this appointment, see Chapter X.
14. Dating: Prosp s.a. 429; Hyd. s.a. 430. On the use of these military titles and their meanings, see Chapter 6 and Hughes, *Stilicho*, pp. 48–49.
15. Hughes, *Stilicho*, pp. 48–49.

16. For the opposite view, see O'Flynn, *Generalissimos*, pp. 175–176, n. 25.
17. Compare with Prosp. s.a. 432, where Boniface is later made *comes et magister utriusque militiae* to counter Aetius. O'Flynn, *Generalissimos*, p. 79.
18. Hyd. s.a. 430. Anaolsus' fate is unknown.
19. *Chron. Gall. 452* s.a. 430; Hyd. s.a. 430; Sid App. *Carm.* 7.233.
20. See chapters 7 and 8.
21. PLRE Vol. 2, *Octar*, 789–790.
22. Soc. 7.30: 'Uptaros' = 'Octar'.
23. Prosp. s.a. 430. See also Joh. Ant. *fr.* 201.3 (referenced in O'Flynn, *Generalissimos*, p. 79).
24. Hyd. s.a. 430.
25. It is possible that Felix was a Western general who had remained loyal to Placidia. However, the fact that he was killed by the troops implies that this was not the case.
26. Vict. Vit. 1.8. Some of the buildings Victor claims were destroyed by the Vandals had already been 'overthrown' by the Catholics in Africa, whilst others may simply have already been in decline before the advent of the Vandals: cf. Moorhead, *Victor of Vita*, p. 5, n. 8.
27. Marcillet-Jaubert, *Les Inscriptions D'Altava*, no. 147.
28. Heather, 2005, 269.
29. Aug. *Ep.* 230 (AD 429), where Darius, in a reply to Augustine, hopes that the peace with the Vandals will last.
30. Vict. Vit. 1.1.
31. Heather, *Fall of the Roman Empire*, p. 268.
32. *Not. Dig. Oc.* 25; c.15,000 *comitatenses* and 15,000 *limitanei*: Heather, *Fall of the Roman Empire*, p. 268.
33. This is shown by the fact that after he had been reinforced by Eastern troops Boniface lost another battle against Gaiseric: see below.
34. Poss. 28.
35. Merob. *Carm.* 4, 'an offspring of heroes, and a descendant of kings'; Sid. Ap. *Carm* 5, 203ff.
36. Schwarcz, 'Settlement of the Vandals', p. 51.
37. Proc. 3.3.30–31; 3.3.34.
38. Possidius (29) states that Augustine died in the 'third month of the siege'. As Augustine is known to have died on 28 August, this means that the siege began in May or June, depending upon the exact meaning of Possidius' words.
39. Poss. 28. It is probable that the Vandals maintained the ships used in the crossing to Africa and that these followed the main body along the North African coast.
40. Poss. 28.
41. Prosp. s.a. 430.
42. Hyd. s.a. 430.
43. Ibid.
44. Ibid., s.a. 431.
45. Greg.Tur. 2.9; Clover, *Flavius Merobaudes*, p. 43.
46. Hyd. s.a. 432. Although it has been posited that Hydatius was conflating the campaigns of 428 and 432, this is unlikely since he took a personal part in the

embassy to Aetius to request aid against the Sueves, and the campaign of 428 is attested separately by Prosper (s.a. 428), who is usually accurate in these matters.

47. Hyd. s.a. 431. Aquae Flaviae is almost certainly now Chaves, Portugal: www. portugal-info.net/transmontana/chaves.htm (May 2010).
48. Hyd. s.a. 431.
49. Prosp. s.a. 431.
50. Fourteen-month siege, Vict. Vita, 3.10.
51. Proc. 3. 3. 35: dating the siege, Possidius notes that Augustine died in the third month of the siege. According to Prosper (s.a. 430) the date of his death was 28 August 430, the third month of the siege. The siege lasted for fourteen months, Vict. Vita, 3.10: therefore, the siege was from May–June 430 to July–August 431.
52. Dating the arrival to 431, PLRE Vol. 2, *Fl. Ardabur Aspar*, 166, noting a letter written during the Council of Ephesus in 431; ACOec. 1.4, p. 76. Reinforcements from 'both Rome and Byzantium', Proc. 3.3.35.
53. Aetius responsible for arrangements, Heather, *Fall of the Roman Empire*, p. 285.
54. Proc. 3.3.35–36; Evagr. 2.1; Theoph. AM 5931, 5943; Zon. 13.24.12.
55. Evagr. 2.37–38.
56. Theoph. AM 5931; Evagr. 2.1; Proc. 3.4.2ff.
57. Poss. 28.
58. *Addit. Ad Prosp. Haun.* s.a. 432, *Chron. Min. I*, 301; Merob., *Pan I, fr.* IIA.
59. Hyd. s.a. 432.
60. Hyd. s.a. 431.
61. Hyd. s.a. 432.
62. The order may date to late 431, just after Aetius had left for the campaign in Gaul.
63. Aspar remained in Africa until at least 434; PLRE Vol. 2, *Fl. Ardabur Aspar*, 166.
64. Prosp. s.a. 432; cf. *Chron. Gall. 452*, s.a. 432; Marcell. com, s.a. 432; Proc. 3.1.3; cf. John Ant. *fr.* 201.3
65. Marcell. com. s.a. 432, 435.
66. cf. Stilicho, Constantius (III).
67. Hyd. s.a. 432.
68. *Addit. ad Prosp. Haun.* s.a. 432: '*Pugna facta inter Aetium et Bonifatium in V do Arimino.*'
69. Prosp. s.a. 432; *Gall. Chron. 452*, s.a. 432; *Addit. ad Prosp. Haun.* s.a. 432; Marcell. com. s.a. 432; John. Ant. *fr.* 201.3 (who claims that Aetius defeated Boniface); PLRE Vol. 2, *Aetius 7*, 23.
70. Marcell. com. s.a. 432. The claim that Aetius was *patricius* in this entry is probably Marcellinus simply using the title by which he could be definitely identified and anachronistically applying it to the past.
71. Prosp. s.a. 432.
72. Illness, Prosp. s.a. 432: 'Although he fought a battle with Aetius, who was opposing him, and defeated him, he died a few days later of illness.' Wounds, *Gall. Chron. 452*, s.a. 432: 'Boniface was wounded in a battle against Aetius but retired from it to die'; 'three months later', Marcell. com. s.a. 432.
73. Olymp. *fr.* 40.
74. cf. Castinus.

75. Hyd. s.a. 432; cf. Vict. Vit. 1.19
76. Prosp. s.a. 432.
77. Prosp. s.a. 432
78. *Chron. Gall. 452*, s.a. 432; Maenchen-Helfen, *World of the Huns*, p. 86.
79. For a detailed analysis and bibliography of these discussions, see Maenchen-Helfen, *World of the Huns*, p. 90ff.
80. Prosp. s.a. 432.
81. Ibid.: '[Aetius] used their [the Huns'] friendship and assistance to obtain the peace of the emperors and get his power restored.' Chron. Gall. 452, '[Aetius] returned to Roman territory with the help he had asked for.' cf., for example, Heather, *Fall of the Roman Empire*, p. 262: Aetius returned 'with enough reinforcements to make Sebastian's position untenable'.
82. 'The Goths were summoned by the Romans to bring help', *Chron. Gall. 452*, s.a. 433. Although there is no mention of a battle in the sources, there is a small chance that a battle occurred but that the sources that have survived simply fail to mention it.
83. 'An able advisor and an active soldier', Vict. Vit. 1.19, but Victor may have idolized Sebastian as the son of the 'African' Boniface. 'Piratical' activities, Suid. Θ 145; Prisc. *fr.* 4. Although his later actions do not necessarily mean that he was prey to this activity earlier in his career, it is notable that he was later declared a public enemy by the Romans and fled, finally residing with the Vandals in Africa until Gaiseric had him killed: see PLRE Vol. 2, *Sebastianus III*, 983–984 for a more detailed account of his life.
84. Hyd. s.a. 434.
85. Ibid., 433.
86. Ibid.
87. Heather, *Fall of the Roman Empire*, p. 369.

Chapter 8

1. Marc. com. s.a. 432; John Ant. *fr.* 201.
2. Visigoth, cf. Sid. App. *Carm.* 5.128, 203–204; Merob. *Carm.* 4.17. Arian and daughter baptized as an Arian, Aug. *Ep.* 220.4 (a.427 or 429); PLRE Vol. 2, *Pelagia 1*, 856.
3. Greg. Tur. HF. 2.7; PLRE Vol. 2, *Pelagia 1*, 857
4. Clover, *Flavius Merobaudes*, p. 31.
5. Merob. *Carm.* 4.17; Clover, *Flavius Merobaudes*, p. 31.
6. John. Ant. *fr.* 201.3.
7. Although this is nowhere specifically stated, this is the most likely reason for the lack of campaigning represented in the sources. For a similar process undertaken by Stilicho, see Hughes, *Stilicho*, pp. 30–33.
8. *Comes rei privatae, Cod. Th.* 11, 20.4^a (19 May 423).
9. Heather, *Fall of the Roman Empire*, pp. 285–286.
10. Prosp. s.a. 435; cf. *Laterc. Reg. Vand. et Al. (Hispani 1)*.
11. The consul for the east was Areobindus.
12. Proc. 3.4.13–15.

13. Schwarcz, 'Settlement of the Vandals', p. 52.

14. Prosp. s.a. 435. Isidore in his 'History of the Vandals' notes only that the Vandals arrived in Mauretania and Africa: *H. Vand.* 74: *Chron. Min. II*, 297.

15. Halsall, *Barbarian Migrations and the Roman West*, p. 243.

16. Bury, *A History of the Later Roman Empire From Arcadius to Irene*, vol I, p. 170.

17. PLRE Vol. 2, *Geisericus*, 497.

18. Heather, *Fall of the Roman Empire*, p. 269, map 10, p. 286.

19. Prosp, s.a. 437.

20. *Nov. Val.* 13 and 34.

21. C. Courtois, *Les Vandales en Afrique* (Algeria, 1955), p. 170 and n. 2, cited in Schwarcz, 'Settlement of the Vandals', p. 53.

22. cf. Courtois, *Les Vandales*, pp. 172–175, cited in Schwarcz, 'Settlement of the Vandals', p. 54, n.35.

23. Schwarcz, 'Settlement of the Vandals', p. 53.

24. In his translation and commentary Moorhead notes that the title *dux* is 'surprising' as Geiseric had 'become king the previous year': Moorhead, *Victor of Vita*, p. 3, n. 2.

25. Schwarcz, 'Settlement of the Vandals', p. 57.

26. Ibid., pp. 56–57.

27. Sid. Ap. *Carm.* 7.234.

28. *Gall. Chron. 452.* s.a. 435.

29. Date, *Chron. Gall. 452*, s.a. 435.

30. *Comes*, Prosp. s.a. 436; O'Flynn, *Generalissimos*, pp. 83–84.

31. Sid. Ap. *Carm.* 7. 246–247.

32. Jones, *The Later Roman Empire, 284–602*, p. 1434.

33. Prosp a. 435; cf. Cass. *Chron.* s.a. 435.

34. Hyd. s.a. 443.

35. Const. *Vit. Germ.* 25–27.

36. Wood, 'The Fall of the Western Empire and the End of Roman Britain', pp. 252–253.

37. Date, *Ann. Rav.* s.a. 435.

38. On Stilicho's wars, see Hughes, *Stilicho, passim.*

39. MacGeorge, *Late Roman Warlords*, p. 6, n. 3.

40. Prosp. s.a. 436.

41. Ibid.

42. For a more in-depth discussion, see the Introduction.

43. Hyd. s.a. 436.

44. There remains the possibility that the two wars were against two different groups of 'Burgundians'. Although possible, the lack of evidence means that certainty is impossible.

45. *Vetto*, Hyd. s.a. 431. See Chapter 9.

46. Jord. *Get.* 36.

47. In 431 the Vandals were still at war with the Romans in Africa, so a Gothic alliance with the Vandals would have been interpreted by Aetius as an extremely hostile move, necessitating action. Since no action was taken at this time, the later date is preferred. Clover, 'Geiseric and Attila', p. 106 dates the alliance to between 440 and 442. However Jordanes (36.184) claims that Huneric had children, and there is no

mention of any other wife. As a result, time needs to be allowed for their children to be born, so the earlier date is preferred.

48. Prosp. s.a. 439. It is possible that *Vetericus* is identical with *Vitericus*, as attested in PLRE Vol. 2, *Vetericus*, 1157. For more information on Vetericus see below.

49. Elton in Drinkwater and Elton, *Fifth Century Gaul*, p. 169.

50. Prosp. s.a 436; Hyd. s.a. 436.

51. Prisc. *fr.* 11.1.

52. O'Flynn, *Generalissimos*, p. 176 n. 30: 'around 435 parts of Pannonia officially ceded to the Huns'. The terminology used by Priscus may indicate that by the time of the agreement, Rua was dead and that the treaty was actually agreed with his successor: Prisc. *fr.* 11.1; Maenchen-Helfen, *World of the Huns*, p. 87ff. Rua dead in 434, *Gall. Chron.* s.a. 434.

53. Sid. Ap. Carm. 7. 246–247. Dates, *Chron. Gall. 452*, s.a. 435 and 437.

54. *Chron. Gall 452*, s.a. 437.

55. Sid, Ap. *Carm.* 7.246–248; Prosp. s.a.. 436; Hyd. s.a. 436, s.a. 437.

56. Prosp. s.a. 436.

57. Ibid.

58. Sid. Ap. *Carm.* 7.244–271, 278–294.

59. PLRE Vol. 2, *Eparchius Avitus*, 196–198.

60. Sid. Ap. *Carm.* 7.255; PLRE Vol. 2, *Eparchius Avitus*, 197.

61. Sid. Ap. *Carm.* 7.244–294.

62. Hyd. a. 437.

63. *Chron. Gall. 452*, a. 436

64. Halsall, *Barbarian Migrations and the Roman West*, p. 244; referencing e.g. Barnish in Drinkwater and Elton, *Fifth Century Gaul* .

65. Hyd. s.a. 437.

66. Jord. *Get.* 34 (176).

67. Merob. *Pan I, fr.* IIA 22–23.

68. Salvian, *de Gub. Dei.* 6.8; cf. Salvian, *Ep.* I.

69. Valentinian travelling to Constantinople, Prosp. s.a. 437.

70. *Chron. Pasch.* s.a. 437.

71. O'Flynn, *Generalissimos*, p. 83.

72. *Chron. Pasch.* s.a. 437; *Ann. Rav.* s.a. 437. cf. Soc. 7.44.

73. Rossi, I 698; inscription, Xystus, *Ep.* 9–10, CIG, 9427; PLRE Vol. 2, *Aetius 7*, 25.

74. For references, PLRE Vol. 2, *Sigisvultus*, 1010.

75. This theory may be compared to O'Flynn, 'For some reason the Eastern government agreed to having two Western consuls'. *Generalissimos*, p. 81.

76. Soc. 7.44.

77. This interpretation of Merobaudes, *Panegyric I*, fragment *IIA* is not conclusive: for further analysis, see O'Flynn, *Generalissimos*, p. 177, n. 45; Clover, *Merobaudes*, pp. 36–37.

78. Prosp. s.a. 437 gives a relatively detailed account of Gaiseric's attempts to convert the Catholic clergy in Africa to Arianism.

79. Africa, *Cod. Th.* 16.5.63 (4 August 425); empire-wide, *Cod. Th.* 16.5.64 (6 August 425), both issued in Aquileia.

80. Prosp. s.a. 437.

81. Ibid., s.a. 438.

82. PLRE Vol. 2, *Eparchius Avitus*, 197.

83. Ibid., *Litorius*, 684-685.

84. Hyd. s.a. 438.

85. Merob. *Pan. I*, fr. IIB. This can be compared to the phrase 'Measures against the Goths in Gaul went well' used by Prosper, s.a. 438.

86. Hyd. s.a. 438.

87. Ibid.

88. *Chron. Gall. 452*, s.a. 438.

89. Long, G in Smith, W, *A Dictionary of Greek and Roman Antiquities* (London, 1875), pp. 302–303: http://penelope.uchicago.edu/Thayer/E/Roman/Texts/secondary/SMIGRA*/Codex_Theodosianus.html (June 2010).

90. *Min. Sen.* 5.

91. Pharr, *The Theodosian Code and Novels and the Sirmondian Constitutions*, p. 6, n. 55.

92. *Nov. Val.* 1.1 (8 July 438).

93. Merob. *Pan. 1*, usually dated to 439, but more likely dating to c.446: see Clover, *Flavius Merobaudes*, pp. 36–38. The first, lost panegyric was given in 432.

94. PLRE Vol. 2, *Aetius 7*, 25–26.

95. Prosp. s.a. 439.

96. PLRE Vol. 2, *Litorius*, 685. For a discussion of the other possibilities, including *magister militum* of Spain, O'Flynn, 84.

97. For a full discussion of this matter, including a bibliography, see O'Flynn, *Generalissimos*, p. 84ff. plus footnotes.

98. O'Flynn, *Generalissimos*, p. 85.

99. Hyd. s.a. 439.

100. For example, Prosp. s.a. 439; Hyd. a. 439. Rather than him being executed, Salvian claims that he simply 'wasted away in a barbarian prison': Salv. *De Gub. Dei*, 7. 39–43. Cassiodorus (s.a. 439) simply notes Litorius' death.

101. Prosp. s.a. 439: see above.

102. *Chron. Gall. 452*, s.a. 440 notes that in that year Aetius returned to Italy 'having pacified disturbances in Gaul'.

103. Salvian, *De Gub. Dei*, 7.9–10.

104. Merob. *Pan 2*, 153–186: commentary, analysis and bibliography, Clover, *Flavius Merobaudes*, pp. 58–59.

105. Prosp. s.a. 439; Hyd. s.a. 439; Sid. Ap. *Carm.* 7, 308–312.

106. Prosp. s.a. 439; Hyd. s.a. 439.

107. Halsall, *Barbarian Migrations and the Roman West*, pp. 246–247.

108. O'Flynn, *Generalissimos*, p. 178, n. 52.

109. *Chron. Gall. 452*, s.a. 440: see note 99.

110. Hyd. a. 439.

111. For an analysis of the chronology and of the various sources and interpretations, Maenchen-Helfen, *World of the Huns*, p. 90ff.

112. Prisc. *fr.* 2.

113. 'Scythian kings', Ibid.

114. Ibid.; 'Treaty of Margus', Maenchen-Helfen, *World of the Huns*, p. 90.
115. Olymp. *fr.* 41.2.
116. *Cod. Th.* 14.16.3 (26 November 434).
117. Plinthas wanting to profit from the treaty, Prisc. *fr.* 2; Maenchen-Helfen, *World of the Huns*, p. 91. cf. PLRE Vol. II, *Fl. Plinta*, 892.
118. Soc. 7.43.
119. *Chron. Gall. 452*, s. a. 434.
120. e.g. Prosp. s.a. 437; the decimations of the Burgundians in 437; the presence of the Huns alongside Litorius in 439.
121. Priscus, *fr.* 2: cf. *Chron. Gall. 452*, s.a. 434. On the dating, see Maenchen-Helfen, *World of the Huns*, pp. 90–93. There is a claim that Mundiuch himself may have been a joint ruler: Jord. *Get.* 180, 257; cf. Priscus. *fr.* 12. However, the meaning is slightly obscure and it is more likely that he died before his brothers.
122. Maenchen-Helfen, *World of the Huns*, p. 85ff.
123. Priscus, *fr. 2.*
124. Soc. 7.43.

Chapter 9

1. Mitchell, *A History of the Later Roman Empire: AD 284–641*, p. 345.
2. For a more detailed examination of these developments, including a more extensive bibliography, see ibid., p. 346 and associated references; Heather, *Fall of the Roman Empire*, p. 276ff. and associated references.
3. Aug. *Ep.* 93. 1.2.
4. Hays, '*Romuleis Libicisque Litteris*', p. 103.
5. cf. the description of these events by Gibbon, *History of the Decline and Fall*, Vol. 2, pp. 334–335.
6. Mitchell, *History of the Later Roman Empire*, p. 312.
7. Heather, *Fall of the Roman Empire*, p. 279ff.
8. Ibid., p. 281.
9. Vict. Vit. 1.7; Prosp. s.a. 437.
10. Arian bishops placed in 'deserted' basilicas: Vict. Vit. 1.9.
11. Prosp. s.a. 439; Marc. com. *Chron.* s.a. 439; Cass. *Chron.* s.a. 439.
12. Hyd. s.a. 439; *Laterc. Regum Vand. et al.* 2 (439); Marc. com. s.a. 439; Cass. *Chron.* s.a. 439. Although the precise date is sometimes disputed, it was seen as accurate by the Vandals, as it was used by Geiseric for the dating of at least some of his coins: Steinacher, The So-called Laterculus Regum Vandalorum et Alanorum', p. 175.
13. Hyd. s.a. 439.
14. cf. Vict. Vit. 1.14.
15. Schwarcz, 'Settlement of the Vandals', p. 55.
16. Vict. Vit. 1.12.
17. Hyd. s.a. 439.
18. Vict. Vit. 1.12.
19. Ibid., 1.14.
20. Heather, *Fall of the Roman Empire*, p. 294.
21. Shanzer, 'Intentions and Audiences', p. 286 citing Courtois, *Les Vandales*, p. 292.

22. On the dissemination of news, see Hughes, *Stilicho*, pp. 102–103; the law, *Nov. Val.* 4 (24 January 440), dealing with attempts of *decurions* to evade their duties by entering the church.

23. Hughes, *Stilicho*, ch. 8; supplies from Gaul and Spain, e.g. Claudian, *de Cons. Stil. I*, 314ff.; *de Cons. Stil. II*, 393ff.

24. *Nov. Val.* 6.1 (2 March 440).

25. Ibid., 6.2.1. (14 July 444).

26. Ibid., 5 (3 March 440).

27. Ibid., 7 (4 June 440); on later re-issue of the law, ibid. 1.3 (5 March 450). See Chapter 13.

28. Ibid., 5 (3 March 440).

29. D(ominus) n(oster) Placidus Valentin[ianus providen] / tissimus omnium retr[o principum] / salvo adque concordi [d(omino) n(ostro) Fl(avio) Theo] / dosio Invictissimo Au[g(usto) ad decus no] / minis sui Neapolitana[m civitatem] / ad omnes terra mari[que incursus] / expositam et nulla [securitate] / gaudentem ingenti [labore atque] / sumptu muris turrib[usq(ue) munivit]: CIL X 1485 = ILS 804 = Fiebiger – Schmidt 33.

30. *Cod. Th.* 15.15.1 (5 October 364).

31. This is the first dated information that Sigisvult had been promoted to the post of *magister militum*: cf. O'Flynn, *Generalissimos*, p. 83.

32. *Chron. Gall. 452*, s.a. 440. For an analysis of the settlements of the Alans in Gaul, see Chapters 10 and 11.

33. PLRE Vol. 2, *Albinus 10*, 53.

34. Prosp. s.a. 440; PLRE Vol. 2, *Aetius 7*, 26.

35. *Chron. Gall. 452*, a. 440

36. *Nov. Val.* 4 (24 January 440).

37. Twyman, 'Aetius and the Aristocracy', p. 488ff.; *Nov. Val.* 7.1.

38. Twyman, 'Aetius and the Aristocracy', p. 489.

39. Ibid.

40. On the theory of a protracted struggle between Aetius and opposing factions, see ibid., *passim*.

41. Ibid., pp. 488–489; *Nov. Val.* 7.2.

42. *Chron. Pasch.* s.a. 439.

43. On the controversy concerning the walls, Whitby and Whitby, *Chronicon Paschale 284–628 AD*, p. 72, esp. n. 243.

44. Gathering of fleet, *Nov. Val.* 9.1 (24 June 440); invasion of Sicily, *Chron. Pasch.* s.a. 439; Cass. *Chron.* 440; Panormus, *Continuatio Chronicorum Hieronymianorum*, 120 (AD 440); Hyd. s.a. 440.

45. Cass. *Var.* 1.14, although the dating is insecure: see *Cassiodorus*, Barnish (tr.), p. 11, n. 7.

46. Suid. 145.

47. Hyd. s.a. 444.

48. Ibid., 445, 449.

49. *Nov. Val.* 9.1 (24 June 440).

50. Pope Leo, *Ep.* 54, 606, 1271–1271, as cited by Maenchen-Helfen, *World of the Huns*, p. 108, n. 495.

51. Prosp. s.a. 440.
52. Hyd. s.a. 449.
53. *Nov. Val.* 1.2 (after 24 June 440, but the exact date is unknown).
54. An edict addressed to Areobindus shows that he was still in Constantinople in March 441: *Nov. Theod.* 7.4 (6 March 441).
55. On the date, Clover, *Flavius Merobaudes*, pp. 29–30.
56. *Addit. Ad Prosper Haun* s.a. 455 = *Chron. Min. I*, 303; Clover, *Flavius Merobaudes*, p. 29, n. 5.

Chapter 10

1. Hyd. s.a. 440.
2. PLRE Vol. 2, *Censorius*, 280: cf. *Agiulfus*, 34.
3. *Nov. Val.* 10.1, 2, 3, and 4 (all dated 14 March 441).
4. Date of appointment, Hyd. s.a. 441; relationship, Hyd. s.a. 443.
5. Ibid., 441.
6. Reference to the 'attenuated resources of Our loyal taxpayers'; *Nov Val* 10 (14 March 441).
7. Hyd. s.a. 441.
8. Ibid.
9. As with the later expedition of Belisarius, Sicily was the main staging point prior to the planned invasion of Africa itself. Hughes, *Belisarius*, pp. 78–79; Proc. 3.13.24ff. See also Nic. Call. *HE* 14.57; Cass. *Chron.* s.a. 441.
10. Evag. 1.19.
11. *Cod. Just.* 12.8.2.4.
12. Maenchen-Helfen, *World of the Huns*, pp. 110–111.
13. PLRE Vol. 2, *Ariobindus 2*, 145.
14. *Cod. Just.* 12.8.2 (440–441); PLRE Vol. 2, *Germanus 3*, 505.
15. PLRE Vol. 2, *Ansila 1*, 92–93. Prosper allocates the title *ducibus* to all three commanders: Prosp. s.a. 441.
16. PLRE Vol. 2, *Inobindus*, 592; PLRE Vol. 2, *Arintheus*, 142–143, where it is suggested that he is the same individual as '*Agintheus*', although this is open to doubt.
17. Prosp. s.a. 441.
18. Hughes, *Stilicho*, p. 78ff.
19. Marc. com. s.a. 441.
20. Ibid.: attack on Theodosiopolis and Satala, and ending by late June, cf. *Nov. Theod.* 5.1 (26 June 441).
21. The war is dated to 442 by Prosper, who conflates the war and the treaty into a single entry dated to the year of the treaty. Prosp. s.a. 442; Marc. com. s.a. 441.
22. Main story Prisc. *fr.* 6.1; Attila and Bleda, Marcell. com,. 2.81.
23. Viminacium and Naissus, Priscus, *fr.* 6.2; Singidunum, Marcell. com. s.a. 441.
24. Maenchen-Helfen, *World of the Huns*, p. 116, referencing Alfoldi, *Der Untergang der Römerherrschaft in Pannonien*, 2 vols (Budapest 1924–1926), Vol. 2, p. 96. See also Chapter 10.
25. Prisc. *fr.* 6.1.
26. *Chron. Pasch.* s.a. 442; Cass. *Chron.* s.a. 442.

27. *Chron. Pasch.* s.a. 441; Marcell. com. 2.80.
28. PLRE Vol. 2, *John the Vandal*, 13, 597.
29. Marc. com. s.a. 441. The text is ambiguous and implies that Aspar and Anatolius fought against both the Persians and the Huns, which although possible would have entailed long periods of very fast travel.
30. Marcell. com. 441.
31. Schwarcz, 'Settlement of the Vandals', p. 50.
32. Merob. *Carm. 1*, 17–18; *Carm. 2*, 13–14.
33. For a more detailed discussion and bibliography concerning the significance of Huneric's betrothal, see Clover, *Flavius Merobaudes*, p. 54.
34. *Cod. Th.* 3.14.1. This law appears to have only been followed selectively. For example, Stilicho's father was a Vandal who married a Roman. However, it may be that by accepting service in the army (Stilicho's father) or by being part of a treaty (Huneric) the non-Romans automatically became classed as citizens, and so the law only applies to Romans marrying 'invading and unaccepted' barbarians.
35. Jord. *Get.* 36 (184)
36. Heather, *Fall of the Roman Empire*, p. 371.
37. Clover, *Flavius Merobaudes*, p. 54, esp. n. 115.
38. *Nov. Val.* 13 (21 June 445). The delay was no doubt due to the time taken for requests for remission from the conquered territories to be agreed.
39. Proc. 3.5.11–17, Byrsa, Mitchell, *A History of the Later Roman Empire: AD 284–641*, p. 347.
40. For a more detailed analysis and bibliography, see e.g. Schwarcz, Settlement of the Vandals, p. 54ff.
41. Schwarcz, 'Settlement of the Vandals', p. 55.
42. *Nobles*, Mitchell, *History of the Later Roman Empire*, pp. 347–348; on the *warriors*, Salvian, *De gub. Dei* 7.89, states that the Vandals were 'city dwellers', suggesting that they remained centred upon the main cities such as Carthage. This would not have been the case if the Vandals had been scattered as farmers throughout Africa.
43. This has been confirmed by the discovery of 45 written 'tablets' dating to the end of the fifth century: Ward-Perkins, *Fall of Rome*, p. 201, n.11, referencing, C. Courtois et al., *Tablettees Albertini: Actes privés de l'époque vandale* (Paris, 1952).
44. Fulgentius of Ruspe, Ferrandus, *V. F.* 1.4. Eno, RB (tr.), *Fathers of the Church* 95 (Washington, 1997), referenced in Schwarcz, 'Settlement of the Vandals', p. 55.
45. Schwarcz, 'Settlement of the Vandals', p. 55, citing Duval, N, 'Discussions des communications publiées dans le numero 10', *Antiquité Tardive*, 10 (2002), p. 38.
46. Shanzer, 'Intentions and Audiences, pp. 286–287.
47. Examples of laws (all from Victor of Vita): Vandals barred from entering Nicene Churches, 2.9; Nicenes forbidden to work at court, 1.43; commensality between Vandals and Nicenes forbidden, 2.46; two Vandal 'confessors' (near-martyrs), 3.38.
48. Hitchner in Drinkwater and Elton, *Fifth Century Gaul*, p. 128: Mitchell, *History of the Later Roman Empire*, p. 348.
49. Mitchell, *History of the Later Roman Empire*, p. 348.
50. On the Vandals being settled under Roman rule, Merob. *Pan II*, 24ff.
51. cf. Wood, CAH, p. 537.

52. Halsall, *Barbarian Migrations and the Roman West*, p. 247.
53. Mitchell, *History of the Later Roman Empire*, pp. 356–357.
54. Prosp. s.a. 442.
55. Theoph. AM 5942; Marc. com. 442; *Chron. Pasch.* s.a. 442.
56. Theoph. AM 5942.
57. Maenchen-Helfen, *World of the Huns*, p. 110ff., esp. p. 117; war ended by August 442, *Cod. Just.* 2.7.9; increased payments, Theoph. AM 5942.
58. Hyd. s.a. 442.
59. On the reordering of the defences, *Nov. Theod.* 24 (12 Sept 443).
60. Maenchen-Helfen, *World of the Huns*, p. 117.
61. *Chron. Gall. 452*, s.a. 451–452.
62. Const. *Vita Germ.* 28.
63. *Gall. Chron.* s.a. 441–442.
64. *Chron. Gall. 452*, s.a. 441–442.
65. Wood's claim that Aetius may have made concessions to the Saxons by giving them land in Britain appears unlikely: CAH, p. 519.

Chapter 11

1. Hyd. s.a. 442: see also Chapter 11.
2. Sidonius, *Carm.* 5.206ff.; Clover, *Flavius Merobaudes*, p. 44ff. Majorian on Aetius' personal staff, PLRE Vol. 2, *Maiorianus*, 702.
3. Sid. Ap. *Carm.* 5.266–268; PLRE Vol. 2, *Maiorianus*, 702.
4. Sid. Ap. *Carm.* 5.266–268; PLRE Vol. 2, *Ricimer 2*, 942–943.
5. *Nov. Val.* 2.3.1 (17 August 443).
6. 'Africans' not having to repay loans, *Nov. Val.* 12.1.; levying of interest forbidden, *Nov. Val.* 12.3 (both 19 October 443).
7. Fulgentius of Ruspe, Ferrandus, *V. F.* 1.4. RB Eno (tr.), *Fathers of the Church* 95 (Washington, 1997) referenced in Schwarcz, 'Settlement of the Vandals', p. 55.
8. *Nov. Val.* 6.1.3 (25 March 443).
9. *Nov. Th.* 24.1.4 (12 Sept 443) = *Cod. Just.* 11.60.3.
10. *Chron. Gall. 452*, s.a. 443.
11. CAH, 519–520.
12. Hyd. s.a. 443.
13. *Nov. Val.* 11 (13 March 443).
14. For example, O'Flynn, *Generalissimos*, p. 177, n. 43.
15. Sirago, *Galla Placidia*, p. 349, n. 2, referenced and discussed in Clover, *Flavius Merobaudes*, p. 10. n. 32.
16. Sid. Ap. *Carm.* 5. 206ff.; dating, Clover, *Flavius Merobaudes*, p. 44ff.
17. Clover, *Flavius Merobaudes*, p. 44ff.
18. Cass. *Var.* 1.4.11; expecting an attack, Merob. *Pan.* 2. 55: cf. Heather, *Fall of the Roman Empire*, p. 338.
19. Maenchen-Helfen, *World of the Huns*, pp. 89–90; Priscus 21–23. This would explain the passage in Priscus (fr. 11.1) which notes that Orestes, Attila's *notarius* (secretary), was by origin a Roman who 'lived in Pannonia close to the river Save which became subject to the barbarian [Attila] by the treaty made with Aetius'.

20. *Nov. Val.* 6.2.3.1. See also earlier in the Chapter, '444'.
21. Prisc. *fr.* 8.
22. Conversation with Perry Gray, March 2011.
23. Prisc. *fr.* 8.
24. Ibid., 11.3; Cass. *Var.* 1.4.11.
25. Heather, *Fall of the Roman Empire*, p. 296.
26. *Nov. Val.* 15.1 (between 11 September 444 and 18 January 445).
27. Ibid. 24 (25 April 447).
28. Ibid. 16 (18 January 445).
29. Ibid. 26.1 (29 Nov 444).
30. *Chron. Gall. 452*, s.a. 446
31. Prosp. s.a. 444; Cass. *Chron.* s.a. 444; Marcel. com. s.a. 445; *Chron. Gall. 452*, s.a. 446. Both Jordanes (*Get.* 181) and Theophanes (AM 5942) fail to provide a date for the event.
32. Prisc. *fr.* 13.3.
33. Clover, *Flavius Merobaudes*, pp. 45 and 43, n. 17.
34. Hyd. s.a. 445.
35. Halsall, *Barbarian Migrations and the Roman West*, pp. 249–250 where he suggests that it may be associated with Eudocia's engagement to Huneric.
36. See also, e.g., Bartoli, *Rendiconti della pontificia accademia romana di archeologia*, ser. 3, XXII (1946–1947), pp. 267–273; Mazzarino, *Renania romana*, p. 298 ff., and tavola 1 facing p. 316; referenced in O'Flynn, *Generalissimos*, pp. 81, 176, n. 32.
37. *Nov. Val.* 17 (8 July 445). For a list of the other titles used by Aetius, Ensslin, KLIO XXIV (1931), p. 481ff.
38. Clover, 54–55.
39. The actual date for the panegyric is unknown, but from internal and other evidence it should date to somewhere between 443 and 446. for a more detailed analysis, see Clover, 1971, 32f, and esp. 36-8.
40. Clover, *Flavius Merobaudes*, pp. 33–34.
41. Gallic bishops, *Nov. Val.* 17 (8 July 445); children sold into slavery, *Nov. Val.* 33 (31 Jan 451); pigs, *Nov. Val.* 36 (29 June 452); for more information, O'Flynn, *Generalissimos*, p. 86.
42. Merob. *Pan 2*; Clover, *Flavius Merobaudes*, p. 41ff.
43. Clover, *Flavius Merobaudes*, pp. 41–42.
44. The analysis that follows is based mainly on ibid., p. 42ff.
45. O'Flynn, *Generalissimos*, pp. 81–82.
46. This can be compared to the richer East, which was not only able to meet the 'subsidies' of Attila, but also able to allow remissions of taxes throughout the period (e.g. *Cod. Th.* 5.12.3; 11.28.15 and 16 and 17).
47. On the dating, Wood, 'The Fall of the Western Empire', p. 256.

Chapter 12

1. Hyd. s.a. 446: main army in Italy to face Huns, Heather, *Fall of the Roman Empire*, p. 345. Vitus may have been one of the temporary *magistri* sent to Spain to deal with the Sueves and *bacaudae* (conversation with Perry Gray).

2. Halsall, *Barbarian Migrations*, p. 250.
3. Hyd. s.a. 446.
4. Ibid.
5. Halsall, *Barbarian Migrations*, p. 250.
6. Implied by statement of the Gallic Chronicler, s.a. 447. For full analysis see below.
7. Date and extent of collapse, Joh. Mal. 14. 22 (363); see also Prisc. *fr.* 5; Marcell. com. s.a. 447.
8. On the date, Maenchen-Helfen, *World of the Huns*, p. 117ff. Prisc. *fr.* 9.3; Marcell. com. s.a. 447; Jordanes *Rom.* 331; Theoph. AM 5942.
9. Prisc. *fr.* 9.1
10. Maenchen-Helfen, *World of the Huns*, pp. 118–19: Prisc. *fr.* 9.1.
11. Prisc. *fr.* 9.1.
12. *Chron Gall. 452*. s.a. 447.
13. Call. 104.
14. Ratiaria, Maenchen-Helfen, *World of the Huns*, p. 118; Athyras, Prisc. *fr.* 5.; Marcianopolis, Marcell. com. s.a. 447; *Chron. Pasch.* s.a. 447.
15. Details of rebuild, Joh. Mal. 14. 22 (363); 'Rebuilt in three months'; Marcell. com. s.a. 447.
16. Flight of the Huns, Nestorius, 363–368; due to 'sickness of the bowels', Isaac of Antioch, *Homily on the Royal City*, referenced and translated in Maenchen-Helfen, *World of the Huns*, 121–123.
17. Prisc. *fr.* 9.3. Unfortunately, no details are given by Marcellinus (s.a. 448).
18. Prisc. *fr.* 11.1; 'dangerous for the future', Maenchen-Helfen, *World of the Huns*, p. 124.
19. Whitby in Sabin, van Wees and Whitby, *Cambridge History*, p. 326.
20. Hyd. s.a. 448.
21. Halsall, *Barbarian Migrations*, p. 250.
22. *Chron. Gall. 452*, s.a. 448.
23. Jord. *Get.* 36 (191).
24. Gild. 2. 20.
25. Heather, *The Fall of the Roman Empire*, pp. 347–8.
26. Geoffrey of Monmouth, *British History*, Chapter 12, suggesting that Conan Meriadoc was the founder of the Kingdom of Brittany. However, it should be noted that this is a very late document written in the twelfth century, so its accuracy is extremely doubtful. http://books.google.com/books?id=FUoMAAAAIAAJ& printsec=frontcover&dq=geoffrey+of+monmouth&as_brr=3#v=onepage &q&f=false (January, 2011)
27. Const. *Vita Germ.* 5. 38, which notes that he had a *cancellarius* (secretary) named Volusianus: cf. Mansi, V 1163, 1167, 'which although a forgery contains genuine historical matter' (PLRE Vol. 2, Sigisvultus, 1010).
28. Opponents to Sigisvult's 'patriciate' include Ensslin and Demandt, acceptance includes Sundwall and Stein. For a more detailed analysis, including references and bibliography, see O'Flynn, *Generalissimos*, pp. 86–86 and 178, n.47.
29. *Fasti*, Rossi I. 745, 747; SB 9515 (PLRE 2, 1243); Leo, *Ep.* 23–4, 27–40, 42, 44–5, 47–51, 54.

30. Twyman, 'Aetius and the Aristocracy', p. 482ff.
31. The debate centres around Stein's claim that Aetius, in league with the Italian aristocracy, thwarted Valentinian's attempts to raise taxes and supplement the armed forces. For further discussion, see ibid, passim.
32. PLRE Vol. 2, Theodosius 8, 1101: *Cod. Th.* 12.6.3.
33. Twyman, 'Aetius and the Aristocracy', p. 480, n.1.
34. Ibid., p. 488ff.
35. Ibid., p. 488.
36. *Nov. Val.* 1.3 (14 March 450); see also Chapter 10.
37. Conversation with Perry Gray.
38. *Chron. Gall. 452*, s.a. 449.
39. Ibid.
40. Hyd. s.a. 449 (Burgess). PLRE Vol. 2, *Censorius*, 280, dates the event to 448.
41. Hyd. s.a. 449.
42. Ibid.
43. Halsall, *Barbarian Migrations*, p. 250.
44. For the full story, Prisc. *fr.* 7, 8, 12–13; Joh. Ant. *fr.* 198.
45. Prisc. *fr.* 11.2.314ff.
46. Tax collectors, *Nov. Val.* 1.3; Sardinia, *Nov. Val.* 1.3.6 (5 March 450).
47. Famine, *Nov. Val.* 33 (no precise date).
48. cf. Marc. com. s.a. 434, who claims that Honoria was pregnant and sent to Constantinople.
49. On the doubts, see Maenchen-Helfen, *World of the Huns*, p. 130.
50. Heather, *Fall of the Roman Empire*, p. 335.
51. *Chron. Pasch.* s.a. 450.
52. The accident happened near the River Lycus not far from the city: *Chron. Pasch.* s.a. 450: Joh. Mal. 14.10 (358), 14. 27 (367); Cass. *Chron.* s.a. 450. Vict. Tonn. s.a. 450.1.
53. Prisc. *fr.* 30. 1. = Joh. Ant. *fr.* 201. Although Theodosius II had theoretically been sole emperor in 424, he had made no attempt to impose his rule on the West.
54. Date, *Chron. Pasch.* s.a. 450; Hyd. s.a. 450; *Chron. Gall. 452*, s.a. 450; Cass. *Chron.* s.a. 450; Vict. Tonn. s.a. 450.3; Pulcheria as the main instigator, Theoph. AM 5942.
55. Prosp. s.a. 450; Theod. Lect. *Epit.* 353; *Addit ad Prosp. Haun.* s.a. 450; *Coll Avell.* 99.11; *Chron. Pasch.* s.a. 450; beheaded, Joh. Mal. 14.31 (368) etc.
56. Prisc. *fr.* 30. 1. = Joh. Ant. *fr.* 201. I have accepted Blockley's translation for this difficult passage.
57. cf. Heather, *Fall of the Roman Empire*, p. 371.
58. Agnellus, *Liber Pontificalis Ecclesiae* Ravennatis, 42; *Chron. Gall. 452*, s.a. 450; Proc. 3.4.15.; burial Agnellus, *Liber Pontificalis Ecclesiae Ravennatis*, 42.
59. Conversation with Perry Gray.
60. Prisc. *fr.* 20.1.

Chapter 13

1. Prisc. *fr.* 16, cf. Greg. Tur. 2.7.
2. The chronology is based on the description given by Priscus, *fr.* 20.3, where Attila's support of the elder son followed the death of the king. But cf. PLRE Vol. 2,

Aetius 7, 27, where the assumption is that the king of the Franks died during the Battle of the Catalaunian Plain.

3. Gothic embassies, *Chron Pasch.* s.a. 450; cf. Prisc. *fr.* 17.
4. *Chron. Pasch.* s.a. 450. The message is echoed by Malalas, 14.10 (358).
5. Prisc. *fr.* 20.1.
6. Ibid., 17.
7. Ibid.
8. Ibid., 20.1.
9. Heather, *Fall of the Roman Empire*, p. 366.
10. Jord. *Get.* 184-5.
11. Prisc. *fr.* 15.
12. On the strained relations between Gaiseric and Valentinian in 450, Clover, 'Geiseric and Attila', p. 108.
13. PLRE Vol. 2, *Attila*, 182: 'East Roman interlocutors' mistakenly praised, Heather, *Fall of the Roman Empire*, p. 334.
14. Prisc. *fr.* 11.
15. Joh. Ant. *fr.* 199.2.
16. Prosp. s.a. 448.
17. Prisc. *fr.* 20.3.
18. Hyd. s.a. 451.
19. Conversation with Perry Gray. The date of Carpilio's return from being a hostage – or even if he was ever sent home – are unrecorded.
20. Jord. *Get.* 194 (37). The reality of this claim is insecure, as will be discussed in the next chapter.
21. Ibid., 186 (36).
22. The fact that the Romans sent more than one messenger is a possible conclusion from the passage in ibid. (188–189: 36) where 'several arguments' were needed by the ambassadors to convince Theoderic to fight, possibly from more than one embassy.
23. The list is based on ibid. 36 (191). It may be confused due to the fact that Jordanes was writing approximately 100 years after the events being described, and so has confused the peoples fighting alongside Aetius. Additional information and some of the analysis, Hodgkin, *Italy and Her Invaders*, p. 109ff.
24. Prisc. *fr.* 16; cf. Greg. Tur. 2.7.
25. Jord *Get.* 37 (194).
26. The list is derived from ibid., 36 (191).
27. See Chapter 12.
28. Hodgkin, *Italy and Her Invader*, p. 109.
29. Jord, *Get*, 36 (191).
30. Hodgkin, *Italy and Her Invaders*, p. 109.
31. Hodgkin is followed by Bury, *History of the Later Roman Empire*, p. 292, n.55: Boulogne and Bessin, Rouche, in Fossier, *Cambridge Illustrated History of the Middle Ages 350–950*, p. 55.
32. Maenchen-Helfen, *World of the Huns*, p. 131, esp. nn. 614—616.
33. *Chron. Gall. 452*, s.a. 451.

34. Sid. Ap. Carm. 7.319–325. Sidonius (and Jordanes) may have embellished their lists to reflect that the two armies were formed from many peoples.
35. Locations, Hodgkin, *Italy and Her Invaders*, p. 106ff.
36. Jord. *Get.* 38 (199–200).
37. Hodgkin, *Italy and Her Invaders*, pp. 117–118.
38. The relevant lives in the *Acta* are summarized in ibid., p. 114ff.
39. Maenchen-Helfen, *World of the Huns*, p. 129, n. 604.
40. Greg. Tur. 2.6.
41. Sid. Ap. *Ep.* 2.5; Greg. Tur. 2.6: Hyd. s.a. 451.
42. Greg. Tur. 2.7.
43. This hypothesis is supported by Gordon, *Age of Attila*, p. 107.
44. Hodgkin, *Italy and Her Invaders*, p. 115ff.
45. Maenchen-Helfen, *World of the Huns*, p. 131 and n.618.
46. Conversation with Perry Gray.
47. Hodgkin, *Italy and Her Invaders*, p. 116ff.
48. See Chapter 17.
49. Sid. Ap. *Carm.* 7, 329–330.
50. Maenchen-Helfen, *World of the Huns*, p. 129, referencing letters of Pope Leo I: see esp. n. 605 and 606: Leo, Ep. 41.
51. Sid. Ap. *Carm.* 7. 329–330.
52. As implied by *Nov. Val;.* 29 (24 April 450) and *Nov. Val.* 33 (31 January 451): Clover, 'Geiseric and Attila', p. 116 and see Thompson, *The Huns*, p. 161.
53. Sid. Ap. *Carm.* 7.215–317: see Chapter 7.
54. Ibid., 7.339ff. The agreement was reached when the Huns were already in Gaul; Aetius persuaded Theoderic via Avitus to join with him against Attila, 'who had attacked many Roman cities': Joh. Mal. 14.10 (358). cf. Sidonius, who claims that Theoderic waited until the last minute, Sid. Ap. *Carm.* 7. 328–331. See also Bury, *History of the Later Roman Empire*, p. 292.
55. Thorismund, Greg Tur. 2.7; Theoderic, Jord. *Get.* 190.
56. Greg Tur 2.7.
57. Ibid.
58. Sid. Ap. *Carm.* 7.12.3.
59. Conversation with Perry Gray.
60. Theoph. AM 5943.
61. Greg Tur. 2.7. Modern sources, for example Bury, *History of the Later Roman Empire*, p. 292, n.58 suggest that there was no siege, but that Aetius and Theoderic arrived at the city first. The versions given by Gregory of Tours and in the *Acta Sanctorum*, supported by the testimony of Sidonius (Ep. 8.15. 1) have been preferred.
62. Hodgkin, *Italy and Her Invaders*, p. 121, n.1: 'The Life of Saint Anianus' from the *Acta Sanctorum*.
63. For the date, *Vita Aniani*, ch. 7, p. 113: '*octavodecimo kal. Iulias*', referenced in Bury, *History of the Later Roman Empire*, p. 292, n. 59.
64. Greg. Tur. 2.7.
65. cf. Sid. Ap. *Ep.* 8.15.1, where the city was 'invaded but never plundered'.

66. Hodgkin, *Italy and Her Invaders*, p. 122.
67. Greg Tur. 2.7.

Chapter 14

1. Jord. *Get.* 41 (217).
2. Date following Bury, *History of the Later Roman Empire*, pp. 292–293, n. 59.
3. Jord. *Get.* 36 (191–192) and 38 (196–197): Hyd. s.a. 451: *Chron. Caes.* s.a. 450.
4. *Chron. Gall. 511*, s.a. 451, 'Tricassis pugnat loco Mauriacos'; *Consul. Ital.* (*Prosp. Havn.*), 'quinto miliario de Trecas loco nuncupato Maurica in eo Campania'; Greg. Tur. 2.7, 'Mauriacum campum'; *Lex Burg.* 17.1, 'pugna Mauriacensis'.
5. Theoph. AM 5943.
6. Joh. Mal. 14.10 (358).
7. For further analysis, Bury, *History of the Later Roman Empire*, p. 293, esp. n.60.
8. Jord. *Get.* 37 (196).
9. Ibid. 38 (197ff).
10. This is the story given by Gibbon, who notes that: 'This spacious plain was distinguished, however, by some inequalities of ground; and the importance of an height which commanded the camp of Attila was understood and disputed by the two generals': *History of the Decline and Fall*, Vol. 2, pp. 370–371.
11. Jord. *Get.* 38 (197–8).
12. e.g. Hodgkin, *Italy and her Invaders* Vol. 2, p. 126.
13. For a modern appraisal of this battle, and a more detailed bibliography, Goldsworthy, A K, *Cannae*, Weidenfeld & Nicolson, 2001.
14. For a modern appraisal and references, see A. Goldsworthy, *In the Name of Rome: The Men Who Won the Roman Empire* (Phoenix, 2003).
15. Jord. *Get.* 37 (197).
16. Again, the detail given here is obtained from ibid., 38–40 (197–212). It is probable that he derived his material from Priscus: Mitchell, *History of the Later Roman Empire*, pp. 28–29.
17. Jord. *Get.* 38 (197).
18. The use of pre-battle speeches is an old tradition and is usually included in histories even if the words are pure fiction. The authors followed a format. Jordanes was writing well after the period so much of his account may be based on oral history rather than written accounts and he wanted to please his Gothic audience: conversation with Perry Gray.
19. Joh. Mal. 358. *Chron. Pasch.* s.a. 450.
20. Greg Tur. 2.7; see also *Addit. Ad Prosp. Haun.* s.a 451.
21. Greg Tur. 2.7; *Addit. Ad Prosp. Haun.* s.a 451.
22. PLRE 2, *Theodericus 2*, 1070.
23. Jord. *Get.* 41 (218).
24. Ibid.
25. Prosp. s.a. 451; Hyd. s.a. 451; *Chron. Pasch.* s.a. 451 (who confuses Theoderic with the earlier Gothic 'king' Alaric); Greg. Tur. 2.7; Cass. *Chron.* s.a. 451. cf. Cass. *Variae* 3.3.
26. Sid. Ap. *Carmina* 7, esp. 330ff.

27. Maenchen-Helfen, *World of the Huns*, p. 126.

28. Possibly following Creasey, *The Fifteen Decisive Battles of the World*, ch. 7.

29. Bury, *History of the Later Roman Empire*, p. 294.

30. Ferreolus, Sid. Ap. *Carm.* 7.12.3; Avitus, Sid. Ap. *Carm.* 7.338ff.

31. *Nov. Val.* 34 (13 July 451).

32. Rouche, 'Autopsy of the West, pp. 44–45.

Chapter 15

1. Clover, 'Geiseric and Attila', p. 109, esp. n.20.

2. Heather, *Fall of the Roman Empire*, p. 294: *Nov. Val.* 34 (13 July 451).

3. *Nov. Val.* 36 (29 June 452); see below.

4. He was 'enraged' by the 'unexpected defeat in Gaul'; *Chron. Gall. 511*, s.a. 452.

5. Prisc. *fr.* 22.1 = Jord. *Get.* 42. 219–24.

6. Maenchen-Helfen, 1973, 132.

7. Date, Maenchen-Helfen, *World of the Huns*, pp. 132–135: probably before Aetius issued *Nov. Val.* 36 (29 June 452), as this talks of warfare – possibly in Italy.

8. Attila travelled through 'Pannonia'; Prosp. s.a. 452.

9. Ibid.

10. Disputed, Maenchen-Helfen, *World of the Huns*, p. 134.

11. Prosp. s.a. 452, who notes that the invasion was unexpected and so Aetius had accordingly taken no actions to defend the passes across the Julian Alps.

12. See Paul. Diac. 2.9: Maenchen-Helfen, *World of the Huns*, p. 135.

13. For example, Theodosius defeating Magnus Maximus at the Battles of Siscia and Poetovio.

14. Hughes, *Stilicho*, p. 138.

15. Prisc. *fr.* 22: Marc. com. s.a. 452: Cass. *Chron.* s.a. 452: Greg. Tur. 2.7. Siege engines, Jord. *Get.* 42 (221).

16. See Chapter 13.

17. Prisc. *fr.* 22.

18. Paul Diac. 14.9. Paul gives 'three years', but this is obviously an error: cf. Maenchen-Helfen, *World of the Huns*, p. 133, n. 628.

19. Prisc. *fr.* 22; Paul Diac. 14.9.

20. Burning of Aquileia Theoph. AM 5945; Jord. *Get.* 42 (221): analysis, Maenchen-Helfen, *World of the Huns*, pp. 136–137.

21. *Nov. Val.* 36 (29 June 452).

22. Prosp. s.a. 452.

23. This is proved by later events: see below.

24. Prisc. *fr.* 22.1 = Jord. *Get.* 42. 219–24.: 'Taken some cities by storm' Hyd. s.a. 452–3.

25. Paul Diac. 14.11.

26. Prisc. *fr.* 22.3.

27. Conversation with Perry Gray.

28. Hyd. s.a. 452–3.

29. Compare this to the invasion by the Franks during the Wars of Belisarius, when the Franks lost a third of their army to disease: Hughes, *Belisarius*, p. 172.

30. Heather, *Fall of the Roman Empire*, p. 340.

31. Prisc. *fr.* 22.1 = Jord. *Get.* 42. 219-24. Alaric had died shortly after the sack of Rome.
32. Hyd. s.a. 452–3.
33. Freeman, 'Aetius and Boniface' claims that 'we first hear of Aetius in his own peninsula as prefect of Constantinople in the consulship of Maximus and Plintha (p. 428). He also notes that 'Aetius' was made consul in 454 and that therefore 'Aetius was killed during his fourth consulship' (p. 418). In this he is combining the careers of the two Aetius's. Muhlberger also denies that there was a second Aetius (*Fifth-Century Chroniclers*, p. 231. n. 86).
34. PLRE Vol. 2, *Aetius 1*, 19–20.
35. Ibid.
36. Ibid. *8*, 29–30.
37. Although earlier attested as a civilian administrator, Hydatius calls Aetius '*Aetio duce*', implying that he commanded the army: Hyd. s.a. 452: PLRE 2, *Aetius 8*, 29.
38. Prisc. *fr.* 22.1 = Jord. *Get.* 42. 219–24.
39. Prosp. s.a. 452: Vict. Tonn. s.a. 449: Cass. *Chron.* s.a 452: Prisc. *fr.* 22.1.
40. Paul Diac. 14.12: Maenchen-Helfen, *World of the Huns*, pp. 140–141.
41. Maenchen-Helfen, *World of the Huns*, p. 141 referencing *Patrologiae Latina* 52, 59–60.
42. Prisc. *fr.* 22.1 = Jord. *Get.* 42. 219–24.

Chapter 16

1. Prisc. *fr.* 23.1, 2: Jord. *Get.* 225.
2. Prisc. *fr.* 23.3.
3. Maenchen-Helfen, *World of the Huns*, p. 143: Jord. *Get.* 255.
4. See also Prisc. *fr.* 24.2; Marc. com. s.a. 454; Cass. *Chron.* s.a. 453; Vict. Tonn. s.a. 453.2; Theoph. AM 5946.
5. Joh. Mal. 14.10 (359).
6. Theoph. AM 5946: Prisc. *fr.* 25 = Jord. *Get.* 50 (259–263).
7. Prisc. *fr.* 25 = Jord. Get. 50 (259–63).
8. Date, Hyd. s.a. 453. PLRE Vol. 2, *Pulcheria*, 930; *Chron. Pasch.* s.a. 453; Theoph. AM 5945.
9. *Addit. Ad Prosp. Haun.* s.a. 453.
10. Jord. *Get.* 43 (225-229).
11. Sid Ap. *Ep.* 7.12.3.
12. *Chron. Gall. 511*, no. 621.
13. Sid Ap. *Ep.* 7.12.3
14. Sid. Ap. *Ep.* 7. 12. 3; *Chron. Gall. 511*, no. 621.
15. PLRE Vol. 2, *Fredericus 1*, 484; Hyd. s.a. 453–454. See below.
16. Prosper (s.a. 453) claims that it was his willingness to wage war against Rome that was his downfall.
17. Sid. Ap. *Carmina*, 7.424ff.
18. cf. Jordanes (*Get.* 41 [218]), who describes his rule as 'mild'.
19. Quarrel, Hyd. s.a. 452; Prosp. s.a 453; *Addit. ad Prosp. Haun.* s.a. 453; *Chron. Gall. 511*, no. 621; Jord. *Get.* 228; Greg. Tur. 2.7.
20. Greg. Tur. 2.7.

21. *Addit. ad Prosp. Haun.* s.a. 453; Jord. *Get.* 229.
22. Hyd. s.a. 452–453.
23. Prosp. s.a. 453.
24. Jord. *Get.* 38 (199–200).
25. Prisc. *fr.* 30. 1. = Joh. Ant. *fr.* 201.
26. The information on this battle is drawn from Priscus (*fr.* 30. 1. = Joh. Ant. *fr.* 201) unless otherwise stated.
27. Prisc. *fr.* 30. 1. = Joh. Ant. *fr.* 201.
28. Hyd. s.a. 453–4.
29. Joh. Ant. *fr.* 201.6: on Vicus Helena see Chapter X.
30. Sid. Ap. *Carmina*, 5.290–300.
31. Ibid. 5. *passim.*
32. Prosp. s.a. 454.
33. Heather, *The World of the Huns*, p. 372.
34. PLRE 2, *Maximus 22*, 749–751.
35. On his support, see Chapter 11.
36. Prisc. *fr.* 30 =Joh. Ant. *fr.* 201. cf. Prosp. s.a. 454.
37. Prosp. s.a. 454. cf. Evag. 2.7 (54).
38. 21 Sept = *Addit. ad Prosp. Haun.* s.a. 454: 22 Sept = *Ann. Rav.* s.a. 454.
39. Prisc. *fr.* 30. 1. = Joh. Ant. *fr.* 201.
40. Prisc. *fr.* 30. 1. = Joh. Ant. *fr.* 201; Cass. *Chron.* s.a. 454; Marc. com. s.a. 454; Vict. Tonn. s.a. 454; Prosp. s.a. 454; Theoph. AM 5946: Evag. 2.7 (54).
41. Aetius killed along with a number of *honorati* (distinguished citizens), Hyd. s.a. 454.
42. Prisc. *fr.* 30 =Joh. Ant. *fr.* 201.
43. Proc. 3.4.28.
44. Oost, 'Aetius and Majorian', p. 25.
45. Sid. Ap. *Carmina*, 5.306–308: Joh. Ant. *fr.* 201, 4–5.
46. Hyd. s.a. 453–4.
47. Prisc. *fr.* 30 =Joh. Ant. *fr.* 201. Priscus claims that Maximus also wanted to be *patricius*, but other evidence suggests that he was already *patricius* in 454: PLRE Vol. 2, *Maximus 22*, 750–751.
48. *Addit. Ad Prosp. Haun.* s.a. 455.
49. Prisc. *fr.* 30.1.
50. Evag. 2.7: analysis, Whitby, *The Ecclesiastical History of Evagrius Scholasticus*, 82, n. 87.
51. Oost, 'Aetius and Majorian', p. 25.
52. Joh. Mal. 360; *Addit. Ad Prosp. Haun.* s.a. 455; Marc. com. s.a. 455; Jord. *Rom.* 334; John Ant. *fr.* 201.5; Greg. Tur. 2.8; PLRE Vol. 2, *Placidus Valentinianus 4*, 1139; plot by Maximus and Heraclius, Vict. Tonn. s.a. 455.

Chapter 17

1. Prisc. *fr.* 30.1 = Joh. Ant. *fr.* 201.
2. Prisc. *fr.* 30.1 = Joh. Ant. *fr.* 201.
3. Prisc. *fr.* 30.1 = Joh. Ant. *fr.* 201. cf. PLRE 2, Maximianus 5, and Blockley, *The Fragmentary Classicising Historians of the Later Roman Empire*, p. 393, n.134.

4. Prisc. *fr*. 30.1 = Joh. Ant. *fr*. 201.
5. Theoph. AM 5947.
6. Joh. Ant. *fr*. 201.6. Hyd. s.a. 455.
7. Prisc. *fr*. 30.1 = Joh. Ant. *fr*. 201; *Addit. ad Prosp. Haun*. s.a. 455; Vict. Tonn. s.a. 455; Joh. Mal. 360, 365; Evag. 2.7 etc.
8. Joh. Ant. *fr*. 201.6.
9. For example, Halsall, 2, *Barbarian Migrations*, Heather, *Fall of the Roman Empire* and Mitchell, *History of the Later Roman Empire* ignore Eudoxia's alleged part in Gaiseric's actions, simply noting that Gaiseric was attempting to avenge the insult to his son by Eudocia's betrothal to Palladius.
10. Theoph. AM 5947.
11. Prisc. *fr*. 30.1 = Joh. Ant. *fr*. 201; Evag. 2.7 (54).
12. Clover, *Flavius Merobaudes*, p. 54, esp. n.115. See Chapter 11.
13. cf. Halsall, *Barbarian Migrations*, p. 255.
14. Dissolution of the peace treaty, Eudoxia's message, and the weakness of the new regime, Prisc. *fr*. 30.1 = Joh. Ant. *fr*. 201.
15. Sid. Ap. *Carmina*, 7.369–375.
16. Ibid., esp. 7.377–378, 432 and 464–8. See Sidonius Apollinaris, *Poems and Letters*, Anderson (tr.), pp. 148–149, n. 6.
17. Sid. Ap. *Carmina*, 7.360ff.
18. Ibid., 7.388ff.
19. See Chapter 14.
20. Heather, *Fall of the Roman Empire*, p. 378.
21. Prisc. *fr*. 30.1 = Joh. Ant. *fr*. 201.
22. Date, Theoph. AM 5947; cf. Prosp. s.a. 455. The *Fasti Vindobonenses Priori* date the event to 12 June, but see Bury, *History of the Later Roman Empire*, p. 205 and n. 2: note that the *Anonymus Cuspiniani* are now referred to as the *Fasti Vindobonenses Priori*.
23. Prisc. *fr*. 30.1 = Joh. Ant. *fr*. 201.
24. Prisc. *fr*. 30.1 = Joh. Ant. *fr*. 201; Prosp. s.a. 455.
25. Prosp. s.a. 455. Vict. Tonn. s.a. 455; Joh. Mal. 14.26 (365–6); Theoph AM 5947, etc.
26. Hyd. s.a. 455.
27. Theoph. AM 5947.
28. Prisc. *fr*. 24.
29. Hyd. s.a. 456; Prisc. *fr*. 24; Sid. Ap. *Carmina* 2.367.
30. *Auct. Prosp. Haun*. s.a. 456.
31. Isidore of Seville, *Chron*. 110.
32. Joh. Ant. *fr*. 201.6; 202.
33. Joh. Ant. *fr*. 202.
34. *Auct. Prosp. Haun*. s.a. 456; Vict. Tonn. s.a. 456; Joh. Ant. *fr*. 202; Theoph. AM 5948.
35. *Fast. Vind. Prior*. s.a. 457 (582).
36. Sid. Ap. *Carmina* 5.373–385.
37. *Fast. Vind. Prior*. s.a. 457 (583).

38. Maenchen-Helfen, *World of the Huns*, pp. 142, 162.
39. Theoph. AM 5949.
40. *Chron. Pasch.* s.a. 455; *Chron. Pasch.* s.a. 464. cf. Joh. Mal. 14.31 (368) and Evagrius (2.7 [54]), who claims that Eudoxia and Placidia were returned 'to placate Marcian in the East'. See also Theoph. AM 5949.
41. Evag. 2.7 (54–5).
42. Sid. Ap. *Carmina* 5. 203–206; Hyd. s.a. 455; Joh. Ant. *fr.* 88.

Conclusion

1. Sid. Ap. *Carmina* 7. 230.
2. Heather, *Fall of the Roman Empire*, p. 262.
3. Ibid., pp. 262–3.
4. Sid. Ap. *Carmina* 7. 230.
5. Elton, 'Defence in Fifth-Century Gaul', p. 170.
6. Brown, *World of Late Antiquity*, p. 119
7. Halsall, *Barbarian Migrations*, p. 252.
8. cf. ibid. p. 250f.
9. Heather, *Fall of the Roman Empire*, p. 348.
10. Hughes, *Stilicho*, p. 177ff.
11. Ibid., p. 210ff.
12. cf. CAH, 537.
13. See, for example, Ward-Perkins, *Fall of Rome*, p. 54.
14. Based on Elton, *Warfare in Roman Europe*, p. 55.
15. Hughes, *Stilicho*, pp. 213–214.
16. Elton, 'Defence in Fifth-Century Gaul', p. 171.
17. cf. Halsall, *Barbarian Migrations*, p. 248.
18. Brown, *World of Late Antiquity*, p. 124.
19. This can be compared with Stilicho, who had earlier sent a man named Mascezel to Africa to reconquer the province, but after the success of the campaign had had Mascezel killed.
20. Gibbon, *History of the Decline and Fall*, Vol. 2, p. 382.

Select Bibliography

PRIMARY SOURCES

Additamenta Ad Chronicon Prosperi Hauniensis   *Chronica Minora, Vol. 1*

Agnellus *Liber Pontificalis Ecclesiae Ravennatis*   online at www.documentacatholica omnia.eu/30_10_0805-0846-_Agnellus_%28Andreas%29_Ravennatensis.html

Annals of Ravenna   Bischoff, B and Koehler, W, 'Eine Illustrierte Ausgabe Der Spätantiken Ravennater Annalen' in WRW Koehler, *Medieval Studies in Memory of A. Kingsley Porter*, Vol. 1 (New York, 1969), pp. 125–138

Anonymus Cuspiniani   see *Fasti Vindobonenses Priori*

Augustine *Collatio cum Maximino*   online at www.augustinus.it/latino/conferenza_ massimino/conferenza_massimino.htm

——, *Epistles* (*Letters*)   online at www.ccel.org/ccel/schaff/npnf101

Blockley, RC *The Fragmentary Classicising Historians of the Later Roman Empire: Eunapius, Olympiodorus, Priscus and Malchus: Vol. 2* (Liverpool, 1983)

Carmen de Providentia Divina   online at www.documentacatholicaomnia.eu/02m/ 0390-0463,_Prosperus_Aquitanus,_Carmen_De_Provvidentia_Divina_%5BIncer-tus%5D,_MLT.pdf

Cassiodorus *Chronica*   online at http://ia311003.us.archive.org/0/items/chronicamino rasa11momm/chronicaminorasa11momm.pdf

——, *Variae*, SJB Barnish, tr. (Liverpool, 1992)

Chronica Caesaraugusta   *Chronica Minora, Vol 2*

Chronica Gallica 452   Burgess, R in RW Mathisen and D Schanzer (eds), *Society and Culture in Late Antique Gaul: Revisiting the Source*, (Aldershot, 2001), pp. 52–84. See also Murray, AC

Chronica Gallica 511   Burgess, R in RW Mathisen and D Schanzer (eds), *Society and Culture in Late Antique Gaul: Revisiting the Source* (Aldershot, 2001), pp. 85–99. See also Murray, AC

Chronicon Paschale   *Chronicon Paschale 284–628 AD*, M Whitby and M Whitby, trs (Liverpool, 1989) The Civil Law See Scott, SP

Codex Justinianus   *The Code of Justinian*, FH Blume, tr., online at http://uwacadweb. uwyo.edu/blume&justinian/default.asp

Collectio Avellana   online at www.archive.org/stream/corpusscriptoru02wiengoog #page/n9/mode/2up

Constantius of Lyon '*Vita sancti Germani* (The Life of Saint Germanus)', FR Hoare (tr.). In T Noble and T Head, *Soldiers of Christ: Saints' Lives from Late Antiquity and the Early Middle Ages*, (Pennsylvania State University Press, 1994), pp. 75–106.

Consularia Italica   *Chronica Minora, Vol. 1.*

Corpus Inscriptionum Latinarum online at http://cil.bbaw.de/cil_en/dateien/datenbank_eng.php

Corpus Scriptorum Ecclesiasticorum Latinorum (CSEL) online at www.archive.org/ http:// books.logos.com/books/5553#content=/books/5553

Eunapius See Blockley, RC

Eutropius *Breviarium historiae Romanae (Abridgement of Roman History)*, JS Watson, tr., online at www.forumromanum.org/literature/eutropius/index.html (February 2010)

Evagrius Scholasticus *Ecclesiastical History*, E Walford, tr., online at www.tertullian. org/fathers/index.htm#Evagrius_Scholasticus

Evagrius Scholasticus *The Ecclesiastical History of Evagrius Scholasticus*, M Whitby, tr. (Liverpool, 2000)

Exempla scripturae epigraphicae latinae online at http://ia331410.us.archive.org/0/ items/exemplascriptura00hbuoft/exemplascriptura00hbuoft.pdf and www.archive. org/details/exemplascriptura00hbuoft

Excerpta Barbari online at www.attalus.org/translate/barbari.html

Fasti Vindobonenses Priori Chronica Minora, Vol. 1

Gesta Treverorum online at www.documentacatholicaomnia.eu/02m/10501150,_Auctor_Incertus,_Gesta_Treverorum,_MLT.pdf

Gildas *De Excidio et Conquestu Britanniae* (On the Ruin and Conquest of Britain), JA Giles, tr., online at www.gutenberg.org/etext/1949

Hydatius *The Chronicle of Hydatius and the Consularia Constantinopolitana*, RW Burgess, ed. and tr. (Oxford, 1993)

Hydatius See Murray, AC

Isidore of Seville *Chronicon*, KB Wolf, tr., online at www.ccel.org/ccel/pearse/ morefathers/files/isidore_chronicon_01_trans.htm

John of Antioch (excerpts) Gordon, CD., *The Age of Attila* (Michigan, 1960)

John Malalas *The Chronicle of John Malalas*, E Jeffreys, M Jeffreys and R Scott, trs (Melbourne, 1986)

Jordanes *Getica (The Origins and Deeds of the Goths)*, CC Mierow, tr., online at www. northvegr.org/lore/jgoth/index.php (February 2010) http://people.ucalgary.ca/ ~vandersp/Courses/texts/jordgeti.html (February 2010)

—— *Getica* and *Romana*, online at http://www.archive.org/stream/iordanisromanae 00mommgoog#page/n8/mode/2up

—— *De origine actibusque Getarum*, online at www.thelatinlibrary.com/iordanes.html www.thelatinlibrary.com/iordanes1.html#L

—— *De summa temporum vel origine actibusque gentis Romanorum*, online at www. thelatinlibrary.com/iordanes.html

Leo the Great *Letters*, online at www.ccel.org/ccel/schaff/npnf212.i.html www. documentacatholicaomnia.eu/01p/0440-0461,_SS_Leo_I._Magnus,_Epistolae_ %5BSchaff%5D,_EN.pdf

Lex Burgundiensis The Burgundian Code, Drew, KF (tr.) (Pennsylvania, 1996)

Mansi, JD *Sacrorum conciliorum nova et amplissima collectio (The New and Most Complete Collection of the Sacred Councils)* online at www.documentacatholicaomnia.eu/01_

50_16921769-_Mansi_JD.html www.patristique.org/Mansi-Sacrororum-conciliorum-nova-et-amplissima-collectio.html?lang=fr http://gallica.bnf.fr/ark: 12148/bpt6k515865

Marius Aventicensis   *Chronica Minora, Vol 2.*

Merobaudes   Clover, FM, *Flavius Merobaudes: A Translation and Historical Commentary* (Philadelphia, 1971)

Miscellaneous   Günther, O, *Epistulae imperatorum pontificum aliorum inde ab a. CCCLXVII usque ad a. DLIII datae Avellana* ... (1895), online at www.archive.org/details/epistulaeimpera01gngoog

Murray, AC *From Roman to Merovingian Gaul* (Toronto, 2000)

Notitia Dignitatum   O Seeck, *Notitia dignitatum: accedunt Notitia urbis Constantinopolitanae et Laterculi provinciarum* (Berlin, 1876) online at http://daten.digitale-sammlungen.de/~db/bsb00005863/images/index.html?seite=179&pdfseitex= Olympiodorus see Blockley

Paulinus of Pella   *Eucharisticon (Thanksgiving)*, HG Evelyn White, tr., online at http://penelope.uchicago.edu/Thayer/E/Roman/Texts/Paulinus_Pellaeus/home.html

Paulus Diaconus   *Historia Romana (Roman History)*, online at www.thelatinlibrary.com/pauldeacon.html

Pharr, C *The Theodosian Code and Novels and the Sirmondian Constitutions* (Princeton, 1952)

Philostorgius   *Church History*, PR Amidon, tr. (Society of Biblical Literature, 2007)
——   *Epitome of the Ecclesiastical History of Philostorgius*, E Walford, tr., online at www.tertullian.org/fathers/philostorgius.htm

Priscus   see Blockley, RC

Prosper   see Murray, AC

Prosper Tiro   *Chronicum*, online at www.documentacatholicaomnia.eu/02m/0390-0463,_Prosperus_Aquitanus,_Chronicum_Integrum_In_Dua_Partes_Distributum,_MLT.pdf

Quodvultdeus   *De Haeresibus Sancti Augustini Epistolae Quatuor*, online at www.documentacatholicaomnia.eu/04z/z_0350-0450__Quodvultdeus__De_Haeresibus_Sancti_Augustini_Epistolae_Quatuor__MLT.pdf.html

Rutilius Namatianus   *de Reditu suo (A Voyage Home to Gaul)*, J Wight Duff and AM Duff, trs, online at http://penelope.uchicago.edu/Thayer/E/Roman/Texts/Rutilius_Namatianus/home.html

Sacrorum Conciliorum nova et Amplissima Collectio   JD Mansi, online at www.documentacatholicaomnia.eu/01_50_1692-1769-_Mansi_JD.html

Salvian   *De Gubernatione Dei (On the Government of God)*, online at www.documentacatholicaomnia.eu/04z/z_04000470__Salvianus_Massiliensis_Episcopus__De_Gubernatione_Dei_Octo_Libri__MLT.pdf.html
——   *De Gubernatione Dei (On the Government of God)*, EM Sanford, tr., online at www.ccel.org/ccel/pearse/morefathers/files/index.htm#On_the_Government_of_ God
——   *Epistolae*, online at www.documentacatholicaomnia.eu/04z/z_0400-0470__Salvianus_Massiliensis_Episcopus__Epistolae__MLT.pdf.html

Scott, SP *The Civil Law: Including The Twelve Tables, The Institutes of Gaius, The Rules of Ulpian, The Opinions of Paulus, The Enactments of Justinian, and The Constitutions of Leo*, online at www.constitution.org/sps/sps.htm

Sidonius Apollinaris   *Carmina*, online at www.documentacatholicaomnia.eu/02m/
    0430-0489,_Sidonius_Apollinaris_Episcopus,_Carmina,_MLT.pdf
——   Letters and Poems, 2 vols, WB Anderson, tr. (Harvard 1997).
——   *Poems and Letters*, 2 vols, WB Anderson, tr. (Harvard, 1936/1965)
Suda (Suida)   online at www.stoa.org/sol/
Theodorus Lector   *Historia Tripartita*, online at http://books.google.com/books?id=
    QF02EF4y4_4C&pg=RA1-PA395&lpg=RA37-PA394&dq=%22patrol.
    +gr.+LXXX#v=onepage&q&f=false
Theodosian Code and Sirmondian Constitutions   online at http://webu2.upmf-grenoble.
    fr/Haiti/Cours/Ak/Constitutiones.html
Theophanes   *The Chronicle of Theophanes Confessor: Byzantine and Near Eastern
    History AD 284–813*, C Mango and R Scott, trs (Oxford, 1997)
——   *Chronographia*, BG Niebuhr, tr. (Bonn, 1849), online at www.veritatis-societas.
    org/203_CSHB/0700-0800,_Theophanes_Abbas_Confessor,_Chronographia_
    %28CSHB_Classeni_Recensio%29,_GR.pdf (April 2010)
Vegetius   *Epitome of Military Science*, NP Milner, tr. (Liverpool 1996)
Victor of Tonnensis   *Chronica Minora, Vol 2.*
Victor of Vita   *History of the Vandal Persecution*, J Moorhead, tr. (Liverpool, 1992)
Victor Vitensis   *Commentarius Historicus De Persecutione Vandalica*, online at www.
    documentacatholicaomnia.eu/04z/z_0430-0484__Victor_Vitensis__Commentarius_
    Historicus_De_Persecutione_Vandalica_%5BTh_Ruinarti%5D__MLT.pdf.html
Victor Vitensis   *Commentarius Historicus De Persecutione Africae Provinciae*, online at
    www.documentacatholicaomnia.eu/04z/z_0430-0484__Victor_Vitensis__Historia_
    Persecutionis_Africae_Provinciae__MLT.pdf.html
Visigothic Code   http://libro.uca.edu/vcode/visigoths.htm
Zosimus   *New History*, RT Ridley, tr. (Canberra, 1982)

SECONDARY SOURCES

Bishop, MC and Coulston, JCN, *Roman Military Equipment from the Punic Wars to the
    Fall of Rome* (Exeter, 2006)
Blockley, RC, *The Fragmentary Classicising Historians of the Later Roman Empire:
    Eunapius, Olympiodorus, Priscus and Malchus: Vol. 2* (Liverpool, 1983)
Brown, P, *The World of Late Antiquity* (London, 1971)
——, *The Making of Late Antiquity* (Harvard, 1993)
Burns, TS, *Barbarians Within the Gates of Rome* (Indiana, 1994)
——, *Rome and the Barbarians, 100 B.C.–A.D. 400* (Baltimore, 2003)
Bury, JB, *A History of the Later Roman Empire from Arcadius to Irene Vol. 1* (London,
    1889), online at www.archive.org/stream/historyoflaterro00bury#page/n1/mode/
    2up
——, *A History of the Later Roman Empire from Arcadius to Irene Vol. 1* (London, 1889),
    online at www.archive.org/stream/ahistorylaterro04burygoog#page/n9/mode/1up
——, *History of the Later Roman Empire* (London, 1923), online at http://penelope.
    uchicago.edu/Thayer/E/Roman/Texts/secondary/BURLAT/home.html
Cameron, A and Garnsey, P, *The Cambridge Ancient History, Vol. VIII* (Cambridge,
    2004)

Christie, N, 'From the Danube to the Po: The Defence of Pannonia and Italy in the Fourth and Fifth Centuries AD', *Proceedings of the British Academy* 141 (2007): 547–578

Clover, FM, 'Geiseric and Attila', *Historia: Zeitschrift für Alte Geschichte* vol. 22, no. 1 (1st Qtr, 1973): 104–117

——, *Flavius Merobaudes: A Translation and Historical Commentary* (Philadelphia, 1971)

Coello, T, *Unit Sizes in the Late Roman Army* (Oxford, 1996)

Collins, R, *Visigothic Spain 409–711* (Oxford, 2006)

Coulston, JCN, 'Later Roman Armour, 3rd–6th Centuries AD', *Journal of Roman Military Equipment Studies* I (1990): 139–160

Creasy, E, *The Fifteen Decisive Battles of the World* (1851), online at www.gutenberg. org/dirs/etext03/tfdbt10.txt

Croke, B, *Count Marcellinus and his Chronicle* (Oxford, 2001)

Drinkwater, J and Elton, H, *Fifth Century Gaul: A Crisis of Identity?* (Cambridge, 2002)

Elton, H, *Warfare in Roman Europe AD 350–425* (Oxford, 2004)

——, 'Defence in Fifth-Century Gaul' in Drinkwater, J and Elton, H, *Fifth Century Gaul: A Crisis of Identity?* (Cambridge, 2002), pp. 167–176

Ferrill, A, *The Fall of the Roman Empire: The Military Explanation* (New York, 1991)

Fossier, R (ed.), *The Cambridge Illustrated History of the Middle Ages 350–950* (Cambridge, 1989)

Freeman, EA, 'Aetius and Boniface', *The English Historical Review* vol. 2, no. 7 (July 1887), pp. 417–465

Gibbon, E, *History of the Decline and Fall of the Roman Empire* (Liverpool, 1861, 4 vols)

Gillett, A, *On Barbarian Identity: Critical Approaches to Ethnicity in the Early Middle Ages* (Turnhout, 2002.

Goldsworthy, A, *The Fall of the West: The Death of the Roman Superpower* (London, 2009)

Gordon, CD, *The Age of Attila* (Michigan, 1960)

Halsall, G, *Barbarian Migrations and the Roman West* (Cambridge, 2007)

Hays, G, '*Romuleis Libicisque Litteris*': Fulgentius and the Vandal Renaissance' in Merrills, A, *Vandals, Romans and Berbers: New Perspectives on Late Antique North Africa* (Surrey, 2004), pp. 101–132

Heather, P, *Goths and Romans* (Oxford, 1991)

——, *The Goths* (Oxford, 1998)

——, *The Fall of the Roman Empire: A New History* (London, 2005)

——, *Empires and Barbarians* (London, 2009)

Hitchner, RB, 'Meridional Gaul, Trade and the Mediterranean Economy in Late Antiquity' in Drinkwater, J and Elton, H, *Fifth Century Gaul: A Crisis of Identity?* (Cambridge, 2002), pp. 122–131

Hodgkin, T, *Italy and Her Invaders* (8 vols, Oxford, 1880–1899), online at www.archive.org/stream/italyandherinva04hodggoog#page/n11/mode/1up

Honoré, T, 'Scriptor Historiae Augustae', *The Journal of Roman Studies* vol. 77 (1987): 156–176

Hughes, I, *Belisarius: The Last Roman General* (Barnsley, 2009)

——, *Stilicho: The Vandal Who Saved Rome* (Barnsley, 2010)

Humphries, M, 'International Relations' in P. Sabin, H. van Wees and M. Whitby (eds), *The Cambridge History of Greek and Roman Warfare, vol. 2* (Cambridge, 2007), pp. 23–26

Jones, AHM, *The Later Roman Empire, 284–602: A Social, Economic and Administrative Survey* (Oklahoma, 1964)

——, *The Decline of the Ancient World* (Harlow, 1966)

Kulikowski, M, 'Barbarians in Gaul, Usurpers in Britain', *Britannia 31* (2000): 325–345

——, 'The Career of the *comes Hispaniarum Asterius*', *Phoenix* 54, no. 1, (2000): 123

——, 'The Visigothic Settlement in Aquitania: The Imperial Perspective' in RW Mathisen and D Shanzer, *Society and Culture in Late Antique Gaul: Revisiting the Sources* (Aldershot, 2001), pp. 26–38

——, 'Nation versus Army: A Necessary Contrast?' in Gillett, A., *On Barbarian Identity: Critical Approaches to Ethnicity in the Early Middle Ages* (Turnhout, 2002), pp. 69–84

——, *Rome's Gothic Wars* (Cambridge, 2007)

Liebeschuetz, JHWG, *Barbarians and Bishops: Army, Church, and State in the Age of Arcadius and Chrysostom* (Oxford, 2004)

MacGeorge, P, *Late Roman Warlords* (Oxford, 2002)

MacMullen, R, *Corruption and the Decline of Rome* (Yale, 1988)

Maenchen-Helfen, OJ, *The World of the Huns: Studies in their History and Culture* (California, 1973)

Marcillet-Jaubert, J, *Les Inscriptions D'Altava* (Editions Ophrys, 1968)

Mathisen, RW, 'Sigisvult the Patrician, Maximinus the Arian, and Political Stratagems in the Western Roman Empire c. 425–40', *Early Medieval Europe* 8, part 2 (1999): 173–196

—— and Shanzer, D, *Society and Culture in Late Antique Gaul* (Aldershot, 2001)

Matthews, J, *Western Aristocracies and Imperial Court* (Oxford, 1998)

Merrills, AH, *Vandals, Romans and Berbers: New Perspectives on Late Antique North Africa* (Aldershot, 2004

Mitchell, S, *A History of the Later Roman Empire: AD 284–641* (Oxford, 2007)

Moorhead, J, *Victor of Vita: History of the Vandal Persecution* (Liverpool, 1992)

Muhlberger, S, *The Fifth-Century Chroniclers* (Cambridge, 2006)

Nicasie, MJ, *Twilight of Empire: The Roman Army from the Reign of Diocletian to the Battle of Adrianople* (Amsterdam, 1998)

O'Flynn, JM, *Generalissimos of the Western Roman Empire* (Edmonton, 1983)

Oost, SI, 'Aetius and Majorian', *Classical Philology* vol. 59, no. 1 (January 1964): 23–29

——, 'Some Problems in the History of Galla Placidia', *Classical Philology* vol. 60, no. 1 (January 1965): 1–10

Pharr, C, *The Theodosian Code and Novels and the Sirmondian Constitutions* (Princeton, 1952)

Pohl, W, 'Ethnicity, Theory and Tradition' in Gillett, A, *On Barbarian Identity: Critical Approaches to Ethnicity in the Early Middle Ages* (Turnhout, 2002), pp. 221–239

Rance, P, 'Battle' in P Sabin, H van Wees and M Whitby (eds), *The Cambridge History of Greek and Roman Warfare, Vol. 2* (Cambridge, 2007), pp. 310–341

Reece, R, *The Later Roman Empire: An Archaeology AD 150–600* (Stroud, 2007)

Rouche, M, 'Autopsy of the West: The Early Fifth Century' in R Fossier (ed.), *The Cambridge Illustrated History of the Middle Ages 350–950* (Cambridge, 1989), pp. 17–51

——, 'Break-up and Metamorphosis of the West: Fifth to Seventh Centuries' in R Fossier, R (ed.), *The Cambridge Illustrated History of the Middle Ages 350–950* (Cambridge, 1989), pp. 52–103

Sabin, P, van Wees, H, and Whitby, M (eds), *The Cambridge History of Greek and Roman Warfare, Vol. 2* (Cambridge, 2007)

Schwarcz, A, 'The Visigothic Settlement in Aquitania: Chronology and Archaeology' in RW Mathisen and D Shanzer, *Society and Culture in Late Antique Gaul* (Aldershot, 2001), pp. 15–25

——, 'The Settlement of the Vandals in North Africa' in AH Merrills, *Vandals, Romans and Berbers: New Perspectives on Late Antique North Africa* (Aldershot, 2004), pp. 49–58

——, 'Intentions and Audiences: History, Hagiography, Martyrdom and Confession in Victor of Vita's *Historia Persecutionis*' in AH Merrills, *Vandals, Romans and Berbers: New Perspectives on Late Antique North Africa* (Aldershot, 2004), pp. 271–290

Shanzer, D, 'Intentions and Audiences: History, Hagiography, Martyrdom, and Confession in Victor of Vita's Historia Persecutionis', in A. Merrills, *Vandals, Romans and Berbers: New Perspectives on Late Antique Africa* (Ashgate, 2004), pp. 271–290

Sivan, H, 'On Foederati, Hospitalitas, and the Settlement of the Goths in A.D. 418', *American Journal of Philology* 108, no. 4 (1987), pp. 759–772

——, 'Sidonius Apollinaris, Theodoric II, and Gothic-Roman Politics from Avitus to Anthemius', *Hermes* vol. 117, no. 1 (1989), pp. 85–94

Southern, P and Dixon, KR, *The Late Roman Army* (London, 1996)

Steinacher, R, 'The So-called Laterculus Regum Vandalorum et Alanorum: A Sixth-Century African Addition to Prosper Tiro's Chronicle?' in AH Merrills, *Vandals, Romans and Berbers: New Perspectives on Late Antique North Africa* (Aldershot, 2004), pp. 163–180

Thompson, EA, *A History of Attila and the Huns* (Oxford, 1948)

——, *The Huns* (Oxford, 1996)

——, 'Peasant Revolts in Late Roman Gaul and Spain', *Past and Present* no. 2 (November 1952): 11–23

Todd, M, *The Early Germans* (Oxford, 2004)

Tomlin, RSO, 'Army of the Late Empire' in J Wacher, *The Roman World* (London, 1990), pp. 107–120

Twyman, BL, 'Aetius and the Aristocracy', *Historia: Zeitschrift für Alte Geschichte* vol. 19, no. 4 (November 1970): 480–503

Ward-Perkins, B, *The Fall of Rome and the End of Civilization* (Oxford, 2005)

Whitby, M, 'The Late Roman Army and the Defence of the Balkans', *Proceedings of the British Academy* 141 (2007): 135–161

——, 'War' in P Sabin, H van Wees and M Whitby (eds), *The Cambridge History of Greek and Roman Warfare, Vol. 2* (Cambridge, 2007), pp. 310–341

——, *The Ecclesiastical History of Evagrius Scholasticus* (Liverpool, 2000)

Whitby, M and Whitby, M, *Chronicon Paschale 284–628 AD* (Liverpool, 1989)

Williams, S and Friell, G, *Theodosius: The Empire at Bay* (Yale, 1994)

Wolfram, H, *History of the Goths* (Berkeley, 1990)

——, *The Roman Empire and its Germanic Peoples* (Berkeley, 1997)

Wood, I, 'The Fall of the Western Empire and the End of Roman Britain', *Britannia* vol. 18 (1987): 251–262

Index